KNOWLEDGE HORIZONS

Knowledge Horizons

THE PRESENT AND THE PROMISE OF KNOWLEDGE MANAGEMENT

Edited by
Charles Despres
Daniele Chauvel

BUTTERWORTH
HEINEMANN

Boston   Oxford   Auckland   Johannesburg   Melbourne   New Delhi

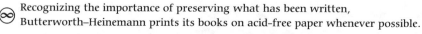
Recognizing the importance of preserving what has been written, Butterworth–Heinemann prints its books on acid-free paper whenever possible.

 Butterworth–Heinemann supports the efforts of American Forests and the Global ReLeaf program in its campaign for the betterment of trees, forests, and our environment.

Library of Congress Cataloging-in-Publication Data

Knowledge horizons : the present and the promise of knowledge management / edited by Charles Despres, Daniele Chauvel.
     p. cm.
  Includes bibliographical references and index.
  ISBN 0-7506-7247-1 (pbk. : alk. paper)
   1. Knowledge management. I. Despres, Charles. II. Chauvel, Daniele, 1947–

HD30.2 .K66 2000
658.4'038--dc21
                                              00-044418

British Library Cataloguing-in-Publication Data

A catalogue record for this book is available from the British Library.

The publisher offers special discounts on bulk orders of this book.
For information, please contact:

Manager of Special Sales
Butterworth–Heinemann
225 Wildwood Avenue
Woburn, MA 01801–2041
Tel: 781-904-2500
Fax: 781-904-2620

For information on all Butterworth–Heinemann publications available, contact our World Wide Web home page at: http://www.bh.com

10 9 8 7 6 5 4 3 2 1

Printed in the United States of America

Contents

v

Preface: Notes on the Horizons

> The folly of mistaking a paradox for a discovery, a metaphor
> for a proof, a torrent of verbiage for a spring of capital truths,
> and oneself for an oracle, is inborn in us.
>
> *Paul Valéry*

Valéry would recommend that we temper our enthusiasm, but it is difficult to do so. This book began with the ambition of assembling between two covers the best mainstream thinking on knowledge management, and in our estimation, it has largely succeeded. There are a few omissions among these chapters that we regret, authors whose contributions would have fulfilled completely our initial aim. Despite his help and encouragement, for example, Larry Prusak was eventually unable to participate in the book. But in spite of Larry's absence and that of one or two others, the outcome achieves a quality that exceeds the lofty expectations we had of those who are already recognized as thought leaders in their domain. In a word, we are thoroughly delighted to present this ensemble to the reader and appreciative that the authors allowed us to spark their efforts.

Valéry would appear to be correct in his observation that once they have appropriated, synthesized, or developed something of interest, people do tend toward oracular declarations. Our understanding is that this shortcoming impairs none of the authors in this volume. But it is the case that deep, serious study of a subject requires an immersion of one's self which inevitably erects intellectual frameworks that go on to condition the way we perceive and think about the world around us.[1] It is precisely for this reason that we sought to assemble leading thinkers on knowledge management, each charged with developing a chapter that anchored the state of the art in his or her specific area of expertise. The result is a book that sketches with broad strokes the mainstream—not the Critical,[2] nor the Postmodern—silhouette of this blooming, buzzing field.

Valéry was again correct when, in 1934, he wrote, "Just as water, gas, and electricity are brought into our houses from far off, so we shall be supplied with visual or auditory images, which will appear and disappear at a simple movement of the fingers, hardly more than a sign." We live in an "age of sand," as Robert Grant informs us in his chapter,[3] where the silicon thus obtained is transforming everyday life at a pace previously unknown. The semiotics of digitized representations, and their impact, is not to be underestimated whether in everyday life, work life, personal life, or community life. Information and communication technologies are in some ways responsible for the explosion of interest in knowledge management, but they are by no means the only roots of this field, nor are they the basis for its far-reaching implications. The reader will observe that with one tentative exception (Wensley and Verwijk-O'Sullivan, who hail from artificial intelligence), the chapters in this book hold with the wisdom that placing knowledge at the center of organizing is a social, and not a technological, challenge.

The reader will find that the pages that follow are organized in four simple sections which are designed to drill down to the core of knowledge management: (a) what it is and isn't, (b) what knowledge-intensive management might be, (c) what knowledge-intensive organizations might be, and (d) what the future may hold. In the first section, **Karl Wiig** provides a historical account of considerable and refreshing scope that goes beyond the typical banalities to embrace the evolution of knowledge in life as much as knowledge at work. **Robert Grant** masterfully outlines the new economics that is now implanting itself and charts the changes in management theory and practice that we can expect from serious future applications of "the knowledge perspective." **Charles Despres** and **Daniele Chauvel** summarize a research project that maps the major themes in applied knowledge management to suggest that, conceptually, the field is turning on a small handful of core dimensions (seven in all).

In the second part of the book, **Ikujiro Nonaka** and **Patrick Reinmoeller** argue that companies must move from static, context-free knowledge systems to ones that generate routines that produce and manage knowledge contexts-in-motion. **Anthony Wensley** and **Alison Verwijk-O'Sullivan** provide an extensive account of IT-based knowledge management tools—165 devices complete with references, links, and commentary. Beyond this, they discuss the nature, meaning, and function of the concept of "a tool." **David Teece** develops a very pointed, and a very expert, statement on the economics associated with knowledge and outlines a core set of organizational and managerial implications. **J.-C. Spender** supplies a typically authoritative text that examines the conceptual architecture one should associate with knowledge systems in organizations, beginning with where much of the field is now positioned and moving to where it might profitably evolve.

In the third section, **Peter Murray** draws on the well-known program of survey research he has conducted over the last few years (260 companies) to suggest how organizations that are serious about implementing a KM program may do so. **Michael Earl** and **Ian Scott** describe the characteristics of that new organizational genus, the Chief Knowledge Officer or CKO, who, they advise, has more to do with changing organizations than managing knowledge. **Etienne Wenger**, a pioneer of the concept, discusses what communities of practice are and are not, how they function, the sense in which they have always been with us, and the recorded benefits of seeing an organization through this optic. **Nicolas Rolland** and **Daniele Chauvel** outline the phenomenon of learning-based alliances, events where two companies dedicate themselves to transferring knowledge and competence for mutual benefit. **David Snowden** introduces the *Cynefin* (pronounced cun-ev-in) model of the social ecology that surrounds knowledge management—or should—and describes the dynamics that underlie knowledge based communities in an organization.

In the final section, **Bo Hedberg** draws on the farsighted research that he and his colleagues have been conducting in Stockholm (on "Imaginary Organizations") to once again describe the realities of organizing as we are now enacting them, or soon will be. **Stephan Haeckel** provides a visionary view of the sense-and-respond organization through which he develops a ". . . prescription for creating and leading large organizations that can systematically deal with unpredicted change." And if one cannot manage what one cannot measure, **David Skyrme** has laid a foundation for management in the new era with a chapter that discusses the measures and the metrics of the knowledge age.

And there you have it: an ensemble of expertise between two covers that should prove helpful and rewarding. We are grateful to the authors for investing themselves in this project and thank those two silent partners—the Theseus Institute and the Graduate School of Business, Marseille-Provence—for supporting the work. In the true spirit of knowledge management as we (Despres and Chauvel) embrace it, let us end this with a reflection and an offer. The reflection is that we take real satisfaction in making this knowledge available to you, the reader, and sincerely hope that this infinitely extensible public good (knowledge) allows you to expand horizons. The offer is that if we can help you do so in any way, please don't hesitate to contact us—or any of the authors, for that matter: all our coordinates are in the following pages.

Charles Despres
Daniele Chauvel
Sophia Antipolis
September 2000

NOTES

1. Will Rogers put it more simply: "There is nothing as stupid as an educated man if you get him off the thing he was educated in."
2. Here we are referring to Critical Theory.
3. As Grant remarks, the notion originates with Don Tapscott.

Contributing Authors

Daniele Chauvel (chauvel@theseus.fr)
Daniele is the Director of the Information Center at the Theseus Institute. She previously directed an IS-based center of continuing education for managers and, prior to that, introduced experimental computer-based systems in the French educational system. Her background is in structural linguistics, language, and communication, and she now centers her research and writing on the field of Information and Knowledge Management. Daniele has designed and conducted seminars on Knowledge Management for MBA students and senior executives. She is co-founder and co-director of the Theseus Knowledge Management Competence Center (KMC^2) with Charles Despres and has co-authored several articles on Knowledge Management.

Charles Despres (charles.despres@marseille-provence.cci.fr)
Charles obtained his Ph.D. by working on the organizing implications of large-scale information systems and has located his subsequent research at the intersection of "information," "organization," and "culture." Formerly a corporate executive and consultant in the USA, he joined Theseus after spending four years with IMD (Switzerland). Despres is currently Professor of Organization at the Graduate School of Business, Marseille-Provence (ESC-MP) and a Professor at Theseus, where he co-directs the Theseus Knowledge Management Competence Center (KMC^2) with Daniele Chauvel. Author of over 30 articles and chapters, he has concentrated his work on Knowledge Management since 1997.

Michael J. Earl (mearl@lbs.ac.uk)
Michael is Professor of Information Management at the London Business School and Director of the School Center for Research in Information Management. He works at the intersection of business strategy and information technology and has published widely in this domain. His articles have appeared in *MIS Quarterly*, *Harvard Business Review*, and *Sloan Management Review*. Recently, he completed studies on the role of the CIOs, CKOs, and CEOs and is involved with researching, teaching, and advising on matters related to e-business. He has collaborated with Ian Scott in his work on Knowledge Management, not only to study Chief Knowledge Officers but also to examine the contribution of networking to Knowledge Management.

Robert M. Grant (rgrant2208@aol.com)
Robert is Professor of Management at Georgetown University (Washington, DC) and City University (London). He studied economics at the London School of Economics and has held faculty positions at St. Andrews University (Scotland), London Business School, University of British Columbia, and California Polytechnic. His interests are in business strategy and firm performance, and his research has focused on corporate diversification, the role of resources and capabilities in conferring competitive advantage, knowledge management, organizational structure and design, and strategic change among oil and gas companies. His book, *Contemporary Strategy Analysis*, is the leading strategic management text among top-tier MBA programs in North America and Europe.

Stephan H. Haeckel (haeckel@us.ibm.com)
Stephan is Director of Strategic Studies at IBM's Advanced Business Institute and Chairman of the Marketing Science Institute. He has held responsibilities as IBM's corporate futurist during the 1980s, as a marketing specialist for Europe, and on the corporate staff. His 1999 book, *Adaptive Enterprise: Creating and Leading Sense-and-Respond Organizations*, has received wide acclaim from leading academics and practitioners of business strategy. Other publications on related topics have appeared in several books in the *Harvard Business Review*, *Planning Review*, *Annual Review of the Institute for Information Research*, and *The Journal of Interactive Marketing*. Stephan has engineering and MBA degrees from Washington University in St. Louis.

Bo Hedberg (boh@fek.su.se)
Bo is Professor of Management at the School of Business, Stockholm University. He heads a major research program on virtual corporations (Imaginary Organizations) and has advised both the current and the previous governments on IT developments. His academic foci are organizational learning, man–computer interaction, strategy formulation, and knowledge management. His career includes research chairs and appointments at WZB (Berlin), the University of Wisconsin, the London School of Economics, and the Swedish Center for Working Life, and responsibilities for electronic and retail banking as CIO of the Swedish Savings Banks. He has published widely on organizational learning, self-designing systems, systems design, man–computer interaction, and retail banking.

Peter Murray (p.n.murray@cranfield.ac.uk)
Peter is a Research Fellow in the Information Systems Research Centre at the Cranfield School of Management in Bedfordshire, England. Previously he was with Zeneca Pharmaceuticals in a variety of Information Systems executive roles including worldwide responsibility for Zeneca's R&D systems, and before that he held a number of management posts in an engineering conglomerate. His current areas of interest are Knowledge Management, Information Management as applied to intranets, Benefits Management, Resource Based Theory, and e-commerce. He has acted as a consultant to a number of major global organizations and has written widely on Knowledge Management.

Ikujiro Nonaka
Ikujiro holds the Xerox Distinguished Professorship in Knowledge at the Haas School of Business at the University of California, Berkeley. He is also the Founding Dean of the Graduate School of Knowledge Science at the Japan Advanced Institute of Science and Technology (JAIST). He has authored and co-authored several award-winning books, including *The Knowledge Creating Company* (with Hirotaka Takeuchi), and has written highly acclaimed articles in academic and managerial journals both in Japan and overseas. He edits several international journals and designs international seminars for managers.

Patrick Reinmoeller (reinmoe@aol.com)
Patrick is an Assistant Professor at the Graduate School of Knowledge Science at the Japan Advanced Institute of Science and Technology (JAIST). He is also a Visiting Professor at the University Carlo Cattaneo in Italy and a Lecturer in Keiei Soshikiron (Management and Organization Theory) at Kanazawa Gakuin University. His current research focuses on how organizations and their managers can foster innovation. He is the author of two books and several academic articles, and the co-author of academic and managerial articles in Japanese and international journals.

Nicolas Rolland (rolland@theseus.fr)
Nicolas is a Research Fellow with the Theseus Institute and a doctoral student at University Pierre Mendes in Grenoble. At Theseus he has conducted research projects focused on action learning, knowledge transfer in alliances, organizational learning, and the processes involved when banks go multinational. Rolland has authored a chapter on action learning in French multinationals and holds a masters degree in economics and management from University Pierre Mendes.

Ian A. Scott (iscott@lbs.ac.uk)
Ian is Visiting Research Fellow at the London Business School in the Center for Research on Information Management. He was formerly a Director at the World Bank, where he was responsible for information systems, administration, and organization. Previous to that, he was a Lecturer in Economic Geography at Durham University. Ian has worked with Professor Michael Earl on research studies in Knowledge Management. He lives and works both in the UK and USA and also consults for international business and public service organizations.

David J. Skyrme (david@skyrme.com)
David is a management consultant specializing in Knowledge Management. His career spans 25 years in the computer industry, in which he held senior management roles in DEC UK, including UK Strategic Planning Manager and creating and managing a knowledge center. He left DEC in March 1993 to establish his own management consultancy, now the UK business partner of ENTOVATION International. He speaks and writes regularly on the subject of Knowledge Management. Among his publications are the in-depth management reports *Creating the Knowledge-based Business* and *Measuring the Value of Knowledge and Knowledge Networking: Creating the Collaborative Enterprise*.

David Snowden (snowded@uk.ibm.com)
After holding a variety of roles in Data Sciences, David joined IBM in 1997 and now directs the Institute of Knowledge Management for Europe, the Middle East, and Africa. His involvement with Knowledge Management includes work on indirect disclosure techniques for knowledge mapping, knowledge representation, cultural sense making, and story construction as a repository of tacit knowledge. An author of many articles on the subject, he is currently a visiting Fellow in Knowledge Management at the European Business School of the University of Surrey. He is also a regular speaker at conferences in Europe, Africa, Asia, and the USA, particularly on the subject of tacit knowledge.

J.-C. Spender (spender@ibm.net)
After service in experimental submarines, Spender received an MA in Engineering from Oxford, then worked in nuclear engineering (Rolls Royce), computing (IBM), and banking before obtaining his PhD from Manchester Business School. He held faculty positions at City University Business School (London), York University (Toronto), and UCLA before returning to business with high-tech startups in Silicon Valley. He subsequently joined the University of Glasgow in Scotland, Rutgers, and the New York Institute of Technology, and has recently become Dean of the School of Business Management at SUNY's Fashion Institute of Technology in New York City. His current research relates to organizational knowledge and its management, especially technological knowledge, and he is extremely interested in new Internet-based modes of education.

David J. Teece (teece@haas.berkeley.edu)
David is the Mitsubishi Bank Professor of International Business and Finance and Director of the Institute of Management, Innovation, and Organization at the Haas School of Business at the University of California, Berkeley. He is the author of numerous books and articles on technological innovation, technology transfer, business organization, and public policy. He is co-editor and co-founder of the *Industrial and Corporate Change* journal and holds positions in associations and consortia such as the Consortium on Competitiveness and Cooperation and the Consortium for Research on Telecommunications Policy. Among his awards are the 1999 Andersen Consulting Award and the 1998 Clarendon Lectures in Management Studies from the University of Oxford.

Etienne Wenger (etienne@ewenger.com)
Etienne concentrates on the field of learning theory and its applications. After working as a teacher, he obtained a PhD in artificial intelligence from the University of California at Irvine and later joined the Institute for Research on Learning, where he developed the concept of "community of practice." He is the author of *Communities of Practice: Learning, Meaning, and Identity*, as well as two other books, and has published articles in *Fortune*, *Training*, and other journals. He is an independent consultant, researcher, writer, and speaker. Etienne works with people and organizations interested in developing new organizational, technological, and educational designs that focus on the synergy between learning and community.

Anthony K.P. Wensley (wensley@home.com)
Anthony is Associate Professor of Information Systems at the University of Toronto. His academic background includes degrees in engineering and philosophy from Cambridge University and the University of Surrey, an MBA from McMaster University, and a PhD from the University of Waterloo. He has held faculty positions at McMaster and the University of Waterloo. His research interests range from the study of process management to electronic commerce and knowledge management. He is particularly interested in the thoughtful and creative application of technology to solving business problems and creating new opportunities. He has published widely and is executive editor of *Knowledge and Process Management*.

Karl M. Wiig (kmwiig@krii.com)
Karl is Chairman and CEO of the Knowledge Research Institute, where he focuses on the management of knowledge at the organizational level. He has authored four books and over 40 articles on Knowledge Management, is co-founder of the International Knowledge Management Network, and has served as keynote speaker on six continents. He works extensively with client organizations in building internal knowledge management capabilities. Karl holds undergraduate and graduate degrees from Case Institute of Technology, was Director of Applied Artificial Intelligence and of Systems and Policy Analysis at Arthur D. Little, Inc., and served as a management consulting partner with Coopers & Lybrand.

PART I

Knowledge Management— What Is It?

CHAPTER 1

Knowledge Management: An Emerging Discipline Rooted in a Long History

Karl M. Wiig

INTRODUCTION Knowledge, what it is, what it means, and its roles for work and spiritual life, has a long history. The abstract considerations and speculations by philosophers and religious thinkers have been of particular significance. In addition, the emphasis on knowledge has always had a practical work-related and secular side. It is this aspect we pursue in this chapter.

Knowledge in the workplace—the ability of people and organizations to understand and act effectively—has regularly been managed by managers, coworkers, and proactive individuals. Those responsible for survival in competitive environments always have worked to build the best possible knowledge within their area of responsibility.

Knowledge, and other intellectual capital (IC) components, serve two vital functions within the enterprise.[1] They form the fundamental resources for effective functioning and provide valuable assets for sale or exchange. From business perspectives, explicit and systematic knowledge management has not been of general concern until recently, and as a result, availability of competitive expertise has been haphazard. This is now changing.

As we improve knowledge management (KM)—and as our competitors improve—we must continue to develop our KM practices. These efforts, which become increasingly sophisticated and demanding, must build upon the historic roots of knowledge-related considerations. In addition, we must pay attention to developments in technology and people-centric areas like cognitive sciences. In other words, we must rediscover the power of past thinking as well as understand opportunities that lie ahead.

HISTORY OF KNOWLEDGE MANAGEMENT

An historical perspective of today's KM indicates that this is an old quest. Knowledge, including knowing and reasons for knowing, was documented by Western philosophers for millennia, and with little doubt, long before that. Eastern philosophers have an equally long documented tradition of emphasizing knowledge and understanding for conducting spiritual and secular life. Many of these efforts were directed toward obtaining theoretical and abstract understandings of what knowledge is about.[2]

Practical needs to know—or particularly, needs for expertise and operational understanding—have been important since the battle for survival first started, perhaps before the first human. Managing practical knowledge was implicit and unsystematic at first, and often still is! However, the craft guilds and apprentice-journeyman-master systems of the thirteenth century were based on systematic and pragmatic KM considerations. Still, the practical concerns for knowledge and the theoretical and abstract epistemological and religious perspectives were not integrated then, and still are mostly kept separate.

Our present focus on knowledge, particularly for KM, is often explicitly oriented toward commercial effectiveness. However, there are emerging realizations that to achieve the level of effective behavior required for competitive excellence, the whole person must be considered. We must integrate cognition, motivation, personal satisfaction, feeling of security, and many other factors.[3]

The present KM focus is not driven by commercial pressures alone. A practical, often implicit, aspect of KM is that effective people behavior required for success rests on delegating intellectual tasks and authority to knowledgeable and empowered individuals. KM also represents an evolution of the move toward personal and intellectual freedom that started with the age of enlightenment and reason over 200 years ago. One notion was that through proper education, humanity itself could be altered, its nature changed for the better. As other social movements, this has taken a long time to penetrate, particularly into the conservative ranks and practices of management.[4]

The emergence of the explicit knowledge focus and the introduction of the term *knowledge management* in the 1980s was no accident.[5] Although it happened gradually and often was met with management uncertainty, it was a natural evolution brought about by the confluence of many factors. The developments that have led to our present perspectives on KM come from many areas. Some are intellectually based, while others are pragmatic and rooted in the need to innovate to secure real-life performance.

From our present-day perspective, in spite of increasing advances in thinking, there was little change in needs for practical KM until the industrial revolution changed the economic landscape in the seventeenth century. The introduction of factories and the related systematic specialization became more pronounced to support the ability to create and deliver goods in greater quantities and at lower costs. Still, KM was implicit and largely based on the apprentice-journeyman-master model. Schools and universities mostly fulfilled a tacit mission to provide education as required for a leading minority. To some extent, this tacit perspective survives to this day. Education, be it primary, secondary, or higher, is perceived to be "good" and of general value, often with less thought given to which knowledge must be developed for which specific purposes.

INTELLECTUAL ROOTS OF KNOWLEDGE MANAGEMENT

Intellectually, broad, present-day KM has many origins. One comes from abstract philosophical thinking. Another comes from concrete concerns for requirements of expertise in the workplace. Others come from perspectives of educators and business leaders. Recent perspectives come from efforts to explain economic driving forces in the "knowledge era" and the twentieth-century efforts to increase effectiveness.[6] Some of the intellectual roots include:

Historic Efforts
- Religion and philosophy (e.g., epistemology) to understand the role and nature of knowledge and the permission of individuals "to think for themselves."
- Psychology to understand the role of knowledge in human behavior.
- Economics and social sciences to understand the role of knowledge in society.
- Business theory to understand work, and its organization.

20th Century Efforts to Improve Effectiveness
- Rationalization of work (Taylorism), total quality management, and management sciences to improve effectiveness.
- Psychology, cognitive sciences, artificial intelligence (AI), and the learning organization to learn faster than the competition and provide a foundation for making people more effective.

These and other perspectives on the roots of KM are discussed by many authors.[7]

DIFFERENT KINDS OF KNOWLEDGE MANAGEMENT

We must specify what we mean by, and include within, broad KM. A few advanced enterprises pursue a central strategic thrust with four tactical foci as indicated in Figure 1.1. However, most tailor KM practices to their needs and environments and have narrower perspectives. Of these, some focus on knowledge sharing among individuals or on building elaborate educational and knowledge distribution capabilities. Some emphasize use of technology to capture, manipulate, and locate knowledge and initially, many focus on knowledge-related information management rather than on KM. Others focus on knowledge utilization to improve the enterprise's operational and overall effectiveness. Still others pursue building and exploiting IC to enhance the enterprise's economic value. Some exceptional enterprises have created "knowledge-vigilant" environments to focus constant, widespread attention on ensuring competitive IC to sustain long-term success and viability. The presumption is that competitive IC, properly utilized and exploited, is the central resource behind effective behavior.

Our definition of KM is broad and embraces related approaches and activities throughout the organization. From this view, KM is partly practical, basic, and directly aimed at supporting the enterprise's ultimate objectives. Other parts of KM are quite sophisticated and rely on an understanding of underlying processes to allow targeted KM focused on the organization's needs and capabilities. Many design systematic and explicit KM practices to create enterprise-wide, adaptive, contextual, comprehensive, and people-centric environments that promote continual personal focus on knowledge-related matters.

Broad KM is the systematic and explicit management of knowledge-related activities, practices, programs, and policies within the enterprise. Consequently, the enterprise's viability depends directly on:

- The *competitive quality* of its knowledge assets; and
- The *successful application* of these assets in all its business activities (i.e., realization of the knowledge assets' value).

From a slightly different perspective: "The goal of knowledge management is to build and exploit intellectual capital effectively and gainfully." This goal is valid for the entire enterprise, for all of the enterprise's activities, and has considerable complexity behind it.[8]

Some aspects of enterprise-wide intelligent-acting behavior are indicated in Figure 1.2. The model outlines elements that fall under the auspices of KM, such as learning, innovating, and the effective creation and application of knowledge assets (KAs). It also points to the need for permission, motivations, opportunities, and capabilities for individuals to act intelligently.

One important aspect for effective KM is the requirement to deal explicitly with the complexity of how people use their minds—that is, think—to con-

Figure 1.1 *Comprehensive Knowledge Management Strategy Focus Areas*

duct work. It concerns what they must understand and how they must possess specific areas of knowledge and have access to them to act effectively under different conditions. Similar considerations also hold on the organizational level.

Several aspects of effective, broad-based KM are of interest and should be emphasized. They dispel some myths often associated with KM and include:

- In the long run, KM initiatives and activities normally do not lead to more work. Instead, improved knowledge and its use, often far down in the organization, lead to less rework and hand-offs, quicker analysis, decision, and execution, particularly of nonroutine tasks and other desirable and work-reducing effects.
- KM activities and initiatives, instead of being additional functions, must to the largest extent possible be based on, and be part of, preexisting and ongoing efforts—often without making these more difficult, time consuming, or demanding.[9]
- People are often afraid to share their knowledge. They believe that they will lose the advantage that their expertise gives them among their peers and within the organization. However, under the best of circumstances, only a small fraction of an individual's applicable expertise can be elicited and shared. Frequently, only concrete, operational or routine knowledge can be communicated. Deep, broad insights are generally not available, and may not exist except as a capability to reason until the situation requires it. Importantly, when experts provide knowledge openly and widely, they tend to be considered important by their peers and gain status and recognition.
- Personal knowledge cannot be shared directly. Perspectives of, and information about knowledge can be communicated. Recipients make sense of

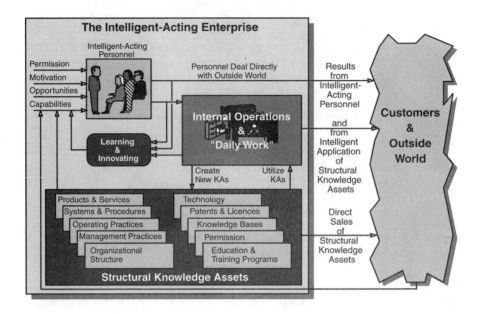

Figure 1.2   *Knowledge Assets, Learning and Innovation, and Internal Operations in the Effective Enterprise*

the received information and internalize their interpretation of the communication as new knowledge. Knowledge is built by complex learning processes and results in highly individual mental models and associations that, for some, may be quite different from the source knowledge.

To be competitive, proactive enterprises must increasingly manage knowledge systematically—although many KM activities and functions may be implicit in each employee's and department's daily work and practice. Enterprises will continue to be motivated by several end goals, to secure short-term success and long-term viability. A particular KM objective in support of whichever strategy the enterprise pursues, is to leverage the best available knowledge and other ICs to make people, and therefore the enterprise itself, act as effectively as possible to deal with operational, customer, supplier, and all other challenges to implement the enterprise strategy in practice.

KNOWLEDGE AND INFORMATION: THE NEED FOR CRISP DEFINITIONS

The intent with KM is to manage knowledge practically and effectively to reach broad operational and strategic objectives. That requires crystal-clear understanding of what is meant by knowledge. We must be specific about what knowledge is to manipulate, monitor, and judge how it affects—and is affected by—people, culture, KM activities, and other factors within the enterprise and its environment.

We must distinguish clearly between what we mean by "knowledge" and "information."[10] At first, it may appear that there is a continuum from signals to data to information to knowledge—and onwards, perhaps, to wisdom. However, when examining the nature of these conceptual constructs and the processes that create them, we find discontinuities that make information fundamentally different from knowledge.

Most people think of knowledge as a recipe—a defined procedure—to deal with a concrete, routine situation. However, few situations are repeated—most situations are novel, particularly in their details. Hence, knowledge must provide us with the capability—the understanding—that permits us to envision possible ways of handling different situations and to anticipate implications and judge their effects. It allows us to improvise and "jam."[11] Our knowledge—in the form of mental models, scripts, and schemata—provides us with the capability to work with novel situations by including not only concepts and predefined methods and judgments, but numerous connections with other detailed concepts, meta-concepts, and mental models.[12]

This discontinuity between information and knowledge is caused by how new knowledge is created from received information. The process is complex. To become knowledge, new insights are internalized by establishing links with already existing knowledge, and these links can range from firmly characterized relationships to vague associations. Prior knowledge is used to make sense of received information, and once accepted for inclusion, internalizes the new insights by linking with prior knowledge. Hence, the new knowledge is as much a function of prior knowledge as it is of received inputs. A discontinuity is thus created between the inputs and the resulting new knowledge. The resulting knowledge and understanding is formed by combinations of mental objects and links between them and allows us to sense, reason, plan, judge, and act.

A practical example portrays how information and knowledge differ. Consider the regular and supervisory control functions for an automated factory as illustrated in Figure 1.3. In this system, information is continually obtained on the operating state of the process. Knowledge from process experts is embedded in the process control programs to automate operations. The experts provide personal knowledge and deep understanding as general principles and specific cases on how to deal with routine and undesired operating situations. They may pool their process knowledge with that of other experts who have previously embedded knowledge on optimization and control principles in the generic computer software used to generate the control algorithms.

In addition, process operating history is analyzed (by conventional statistical methods or advanced knowledge discovery in databases [KDD]) to obtain selected process characteristics, including process dynamics. This information

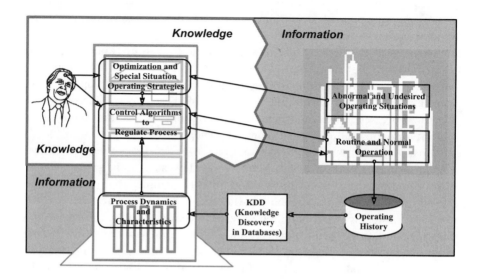

Figure 1.3 *Differences Between Knowledge and Information in Process Control*

also becomes part of the control algorithms embedded in the control computer after it has been interpreted and linked to the experts' personal knowledge.

DRIVING FORCES BEHIND KNOWLEDGE MANAGEMENT

The emergence of KM may be explained by the confluence and natural evolution of several factors. The needs to manage knowledge are strong. For those who now are engaged in KM, it is not an alternative or a luxury, but is a necessity driven by the forces of competition, marketplace demands, new operating and management practices, and the availability of KM approaches and information technology.

External Driving Forces

Most organizations operate in environments that they cannot control. Their viability and success are subject to external forces that they must live with and respond to as best they can to survive. Over the last decades, several external driving forces have emerged. Among these we find the following:

- *Globalization of business and international competition.* International commerce has increased. Products that were created within one company or country are now assembled from parts from multiple sources worldwide. Where before there were few product alternatives, now there are many. Production and service capabilities that were available from limited sources in advanced countries are now frequently found in countries that were formerly considered developing and incapable of sophisticated work. These developments have led to cutthroat competition, where only the most effective will survive by being effective in operations, marketing, and creation of products and services.

- *Sophisticated customers.* Customers have become more demanding. They increasingly desire customized products and services that support their success and in turn are needed to serve their own customers better. Everywhere there are requirements for new features, better fulfillment of individual needs, higher quality, and quicker response—all at an increasingly feverish pace. To survive in this environment, enterprises must perform on par with, or better than, their competition by improving their understanding of customer needs and capabilities.
- *Sophisticated competitors.* Competing organizations are constantly implementing innovations in products, services, and practices. They also implement "discontinuous breakthroughs" by adopting new technologies and practices. To keep up, these changes require constant learning to build competitive expertise.
- *Sophisticated suppliers.* Suppliers continue to improve their capabilities and can participate in creating and supporting innovations to deliver sophisticated products. To take advantage of these opportunities, enterprises must understand new supplier capabilities and how to integrate them with internal efforts, directions, and culture.

Internal Driving Forces

Within enterprises, developments of many types have created opportunities for managing knowledge better, and in some cases differently. Examples of important changes include:

- *Bottlenecks in enterprise effectiveness.* Typically, enterprise effectiveness is limited by restrictions in flows of work, information, and so on. Bottlenecks have been removed or relocated to other sites through many improvements: investments in technology and logistics, personnel working harder and longer, organized work tasks and work flows, improved information for decision making and other work (more accurate, complete, and timely), and increased intelligent automation of routine and simpler operational tasks. New requirements place demands on increased effectiveness and intelligent behavior. Bottlenecks have moved from visible and tangible sites to knowledge-intensive work areas that require better understanding and expertise.
- *Increased technological capabilities.* New KM approaches are made possible by advances in information management and technology and applied AI. Examples include groupware for collaborative work, knowledge encoding for knowledge bases, performance support systems, natural language understanding, and advanced search engines.

- *Understanding of human cognitive functions.* People and their work behavior are at the center of the effective enterprise. Therefore, it is important to incorporate better professional understanding of cognitive aspects of how knowledge—understanding, mental models, and associations—affect decision making and performing knowledge-intensive work when deciding how to conduct KM.

Ongoing Developments

Many developments are underway that will affect KM further. Some of these include:

- *Economics of ideas.* Innovations and new, path-breaking ideas have brought about knowledge-driven economic changes of societal significance.[13]
- *Information management and technology.* Information-related practices and capabilities are transforming the way business is conducted.
- *Cognitive science.* Our understanding of how people function has direct application to how we manage knowledge.
- *Shifts in bottlenecks.* Understanding best practices and others' experiences provides information about potential candidates for streamlining operations.
- *Customization requirements for sophisticated customers.* Great opportunities are available by satisfying unique customer demands on reasonable terms.
- *Sophisticated competitors.* Threats require agile behaviors and rapid learning to maintain viability.
- *Globalization.* International business changes provide business opportunities and threats that must be understood to be managed.

These and other driving forces encourage companies to focus attention and efforts on areas that provide the greatest payback. In general, it requires delivering "more with less." That, however, requires extensive understanding and ability to build and maintain competitive IC in many areas.

WHAT IS NEW?

KM practitioners recognize that KM has brought new elements into the enterprise. Entirely new perspectives and activities are introduced. Others are not new per se, but have taken on new roles. For example, there is little new in the concepts behind educating and training people to be able to deliver competent work. The same is true for many other KM-related activities. However, perspectives, priorities, and purposes are new.

Most knowledge-based organizations realize that the largest part of their market value is their IC, not the sum of their financial and tangible assets. They find that no one has specialized in understanding the mechanisms that govern the processes that result in valuable IC. They also realize that no one is responsible for maintaining and improving the value of these large assets.

What is new—certainly in the form of broadly accepted management thrusts—are the explicit, deliberate, and systematic approaches to orchestrate KM efforts and to rely on their results to achieve enterprise objectives. From management's point of view, the perspectives, coordination, facilitation, and monitoring activities necessary for active KM require new and different insights, emphases, and approaches. They also require new values, insights, and priorities. What is more, they require a new focus on the role that knowledge and understanding play in the enterprise's—and in individuals'—ability to deliver quality work.

Advanced KM now relies on new approaches that integrate theoretical and abstract perspectives of epistemology and cognitive sciences with the pragmatic considerations of expertise required to conduct business and the technical directions of information management and technology. Three additional conditions have also contributed to these developments. First among these are AI and management science's concern for how people reason and think when performing intellectual work, and the effect of knowledge and understanding to deliver quality work.[14] Second are learning theory, social sciences, and psychological concerns for approaches to effective learning, teamwork, and collaboration, and for cognitive styles.[15] Third are advances in information technology that allow extending KM practices into new areas by building on ontologies, natural language understanding (NLU), automated reasoning, and intelligent agents.

New understandings of how people make decisions have made it clear that previous principles for managing knowledge may be misguided. It now is realized that most decisions are made based on "intuition" (strong associations) rather than on deliberate and systematic reasoning.[16] This has considerable consequences for what knowledge people must possess and how they are supported to function effectively and deliver quality work under various conditions.

WHAT MAY LIE AHEAD FOR KNOWLEDGE MANAGEMENT?

KM promotes development and application of tacit, explicit, and embedded IC—that is, leveraging personal understanding, organizational action capabilities, and other intellectual assets to attain the enterprise's ultimate goals, such as ascertaining profitability, ensuring long-term viability, or delivering quality services. This perspective of KM, given its history, suggests that a number of developments will take place in coming years. They include:

- An area of increasing insight in the role that understanding—or meaning-connected knowledge—and abstract mental models play in intellectual work. The 1990's notion that "knowledge is actionable information" and similar early perspectives will be replaced by more detailed characterizations of both personal and inanimate knowledge. Insights from cognitive research and business experiences with deep knowledge will elucidate what, and how, people must understand to handle complex challenges competently.

- Caused by KM's importance, future practices and methods will be purposeful, systematic, explicit, and dependent on advanced technology for knowledge capture and codification, automated reasoning, natural language understanding, and so on. Overall, KM will become people-centric because it is the networking of competent and collaborating people that makes successful organizations.[17]

- Extensive experiences will spread from many organizations about how effective KM is organized, supported, and facilitated. Obvious changes will include placement and organization of the KM effort itself, be it a Chief Knowledge Officer (CKO) or a distributed effort. Changes that deal with reorganization of work and the abolishing of whole departments when their responsibilities are integrated into other operations will be prevalent but less apparent.

- Management practices will change to facilitate KM. Incentives will be introduced and disincentives eliminated to promote innovation, effective knowledge exchange ("sharing"), learning, and application of best knowledge for work. Cultural drivers such as management emphasis and personal behaviors will be changed to create environments of trust and efforts to find root causes of problems without assigning blame.

- KM perspectives and considerations will be embedded in regular activities throughout the enterprise. An example of how broadly KM may affect an organization is indicated in Figure 1.4. It highlights some separate and shared responsibilities for KM-related activities within research and development (R&D), human resources (HR), information management and technology (IM & IT), and a KM supervisory function.

- New practices will focus on combining understanding, knowledge, skills, and attitudes (KSAs) when assembling work teams or analyzing requirements for performing work.[18] The emphasis on complementary work teams will coincide with the movement toward virtual organizations where many in-house teams will include external workers who are brought in for limited periods to complement in-house competencies for specific tasks. The present use of consultants from large consulting houses is one manifestation but is expected to increasingly involve self-employed external knowledge workers.

- Most organizations will create effective approaches to transfer personal knowledge to structural IC to allow better utilization and leveraging. External subject-matter experts will leverage and sell their expertise to many enterprises for continued use.[19]

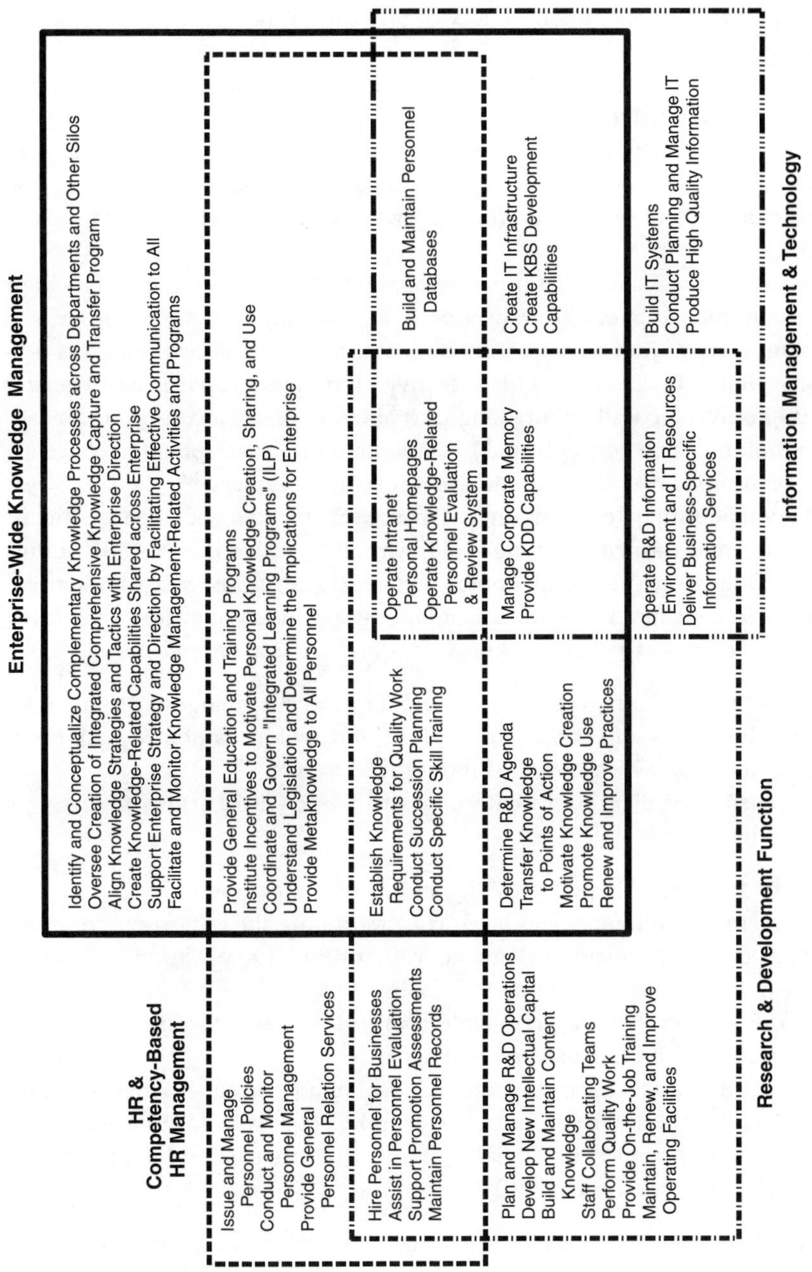

Enterprise-Wide Knowledge Management

Identify and Conceptualize Complementary Knowledge Processes across Departments and Other Silos
Oversee Creation of Integrated Comprehensive Knowledge Capture and Transfer Program
Align Knowledge Strategies and Tactics with Enterprise Direction
Create Knowledge-Related Capabilities Shared across Enterprise
Support Enterprise Strategy and Direction by Facilitating Effective Communication to All
Facilitate and Monitor Knowledge Management-Related Activities and Programs

Provide General Education and Training Programs
Institute Incentives to Motivate Personal Knowledge Creation, Sharing, and Use
Coordinate and Govern "Integrated Learning Programs" (ILP)
Understand Legislation and Determine the Implications for Enterprise
Provide Metaknowledge to All Personnel

Establish Knowledge
Requirements for Quality Work
Conduct Succession Planning
Conduct Specific Skill Training

Determine R&D Agenda
Transfer Knowledge
to Points of Action
Motivate Knowledge Creation
Promote Knowledge Use
Renew and Improve Practices

Operate Intranet
Personal Homepages
Operate Knowledge-Related
Personnel Evaluation
& Review System

Manage Corporate Memory
Provide KDD Capabilities

Build and Maintain Personnel
Databases

Create IT Infrastructure
Create KBS Development
Capabilities

Operate R&D Information
Environment and IT Resources
Deliver Business-Specific
Information Services

Build IT Systems
Conduct Planning and Manage IT
Produce High Quality Information

Information Management & Technology

Research & Development Function

HR & Competency-Based HR Management

Issue and Manage
Personnel Policies
Conduct and Monitor
Personnel Management
Provide General
Personnel Relation Services

Hire Personnel for Businesses
Assist in Personnel Evaluation
Support Promotion Assessments
Maintain Personnel Records

Plan and Manage R&D Operations
Develop New Intellectual Capital
Build and Maintain Content
Knowledge
Staff Collaborating Teams
Perform Quality Work
Provide On-the-Job Training
Maintain, Renew, and Improve
Operating Facilities

Figure 1.4 *Examples of Sole- and Shared-Responsibility KM Activities*

- Comprehensive approaches to create and conduct broad KM practices will become the norm. For example, designing, implementing, and operating comprehensive multimode knowledge transfer programs will be common.[20] Such programs include systematic approaches to integrate primary knowledge-related functions such as sourcing from internal and external knowledge experts; knowledge capture, codification, and organization into repositories; deployment (e.g., training and educational programs, expert networks, and knowledge-based systems [KBSs]); and functions where work is performed or knowledge assets are sold, leased, or licensed.

- Education and knowledge support capabilities such as expert networks or performance support systems (PSSs) will be matched to cognitive and learning styles and dominant intelligences.[21] That will help workers perform more effectively. Highly effective approaches to elicit and transfer deep knowledge will be introduced to allow experts to communicate understandings and concepts and facilitate building corresponding concepts, associations, and mental models by other practitioners.[22]

- KM will be supported by many AI developments. Some of these are intelligent agents, natural language understanding and processing functions, reasoning strategies, and knowledge representations and ontologies[23] that will continue to be developed and, by providing greater capabilities, will be relied on to organize knowledge and facilitate application.

To create broad and integrated capabilities, most of the changes introduced by these developments will not be stand-alone, but will be combined with other changes, many of which have foci different from KM.

Increased specialization in enterprises to work with various KM aspects will include:

- On the firm level: Expertise with emphasis on managing IC
- On the middle management level: Understanding the importance of managing local investments in, and coordination and application of, knowledge assets to meet operating objectives
- On the KM level: Enterprise-wide coordination and facilitation of KM-related functions, capabilities, and activities
- On the knowledge-operational level: Local hands-on capabilities to obtain and organize knowledge, automate knowledge, and build knowledge-based support and educational systems, and retrieve and communicate knowledge to end users

Realization that KM is the cornerstone of every knowledge organization's strategy will bring about:

- New ways of working, such as collaboration, and new ways of assembling expertise for special purposes

- New roles for people management
- New roles for training and education within the firm
- New roles and methods for knowledge capture, organization, automation, and deployment
- New focus for management science on organization of work with knowledge perspective, change management to facilitate growth and innovation, and on KM details
- New focus for strategy setting on developing knowledge, and IC-related opportunities and associated development of capabilities to realize and capitalize on the possibilities

As organizations develop their KM practice further, most enterprises after some time will pursue all four thrusts as part of their overall KM strategy.

The Changing Workplace

We do expect the enterprise to change. Advances in KM practices will continue to modify the workplace—sometimes drastically. Visible changes will be evident by increased application of, and reliance on, technology for cognitive support compared to the information focus of the 1980s and 1990s. Less visible changes may be more important since they will improve the way people work with their minds and thereby alleviate bottlenecks. The changes that people will experience in the workplace include:

- Emphasis on using interdisciplinary teams with a focus on the best mix of competencies and understanding to be applied to the work at hand. Figure 1.5 shows an example of the proficiency profile of such a team.
- Temporary nature of many employment situations. Emphasis will be placed on assembling short-lived teams with complementing knowledge profiles to address specific tasks. People will improve their personal expertise to maintain and enhance personal competitiveness.
- Good understanding of the importance of relying on strong mental associations and conceptual knowledge to guide direction of work.
- Better understanding by knowledge workers of how to implement enterprise strategy by the small decisions and acts that are part of their daily work.
- Greater willingness to collaborate with associates and coordinate with other activities.
- Increased personal understanding by employees of how they personally will benefit from delivering effective work.
- Greater job security and less hesitation to undertake complex tasks after employees build increased metaknowledge and professional or craft knowledge about work for which they are responsible.
- Increased reliance on automated intelligent reasoning to support work. For example, when they are confronted with complex situations, automa-

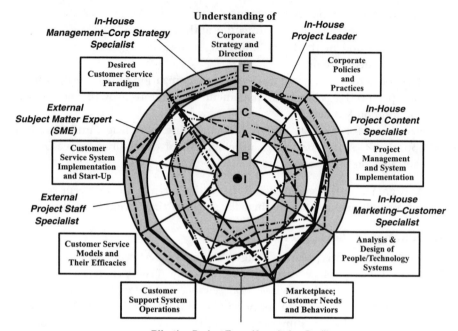

Effective Project Team Knowledge Profile

Figure 1.5 *Knowledge Profile Example of a Virtual Team with Six Members. I = Ignorant, B = Beginner, A = Advanced Beginner, C = Competent Performer, P = Proficient Performer, E = Expert.*

tion may assist knowledge workers by identifying and making available relevant support information and knowledge, making preliminary sense of the situation, and locating and presenting suggestions for how it should be handled.

• Intelligent agents deployed internally and externally will offload "data detective work" now required to locate and evaluate information required in many knowledge worker situations ranging from plant operators to ad hoc strategic task forces.

• New organization of the physical work environment will change the way people work together and allow greater richness and effectiveness of interaction. New work environments will be designed to foster knowledge exchange through networking and collaboration and facilitate innovations through serendipity.

• Improved understanding of different levels of work complexities and what that means for knowledge requirements. A useful categorization of work complexity consists of six levels:

1. Routine worktasks (simple, repetitive, and well understood)
2. Logical or less common variations (transformations) of routine situations
3. Complex, yet expected extensions of known routines integrated with external factors
4. Unexpected challenges (conditions), but with a mix of routines and external factors
5. Totally unexpected situations and nonroutine challenges, yet within the larger job scope
6. Unusual challenges outside job scope

In total, KM will lead to less effort to deliver present-day service paradigms. However, as Figure 1.6 indicates, work is changing to satisfy the ever-increasing market requirements for new features and capabilities in products and services. Successful organizations will provide better script and schema knowledge and work will expand to take advantage of the new capabilities. Even so, with increased responsibilities, knowledge workers are expected to feel more confident and have better understanding of the work to be done. They also will receive better knowledge support and more jobs will be done right the first time, adding to confidence and job satisfaction on the inside, and better market acceptance on the outside.

The nature of work is changing. Already, we have learned to prepare our workforce better, automate many routine functions, and organize work to deliver higher-quality products and services more effectively. There is a shift toward more complex work as outlined in Figure 1.6. There are many identifiable targets for intelligent automation in routine areas and potentials for application of greater understanding and expertise in more demanding work. Advanced technology and experiences by sophisticated organizations motivate continued refinement of work in general. Hence, to stay ahead of competitors, enterprises ask their personnel to engage in increasingly complex work to deliver better products and services. Service paradigms become more complex.

Toward a Knowledge Management Discipline

The changes to manage knowledge explicitly and in detail place great demands on supporting disciplines. They range from cognitive sciences and educational methods to management sciences and economics to AI and information management and technology. Enterprises pay new attention to maintaining and enhancing the competitive power of their IC. They realize that managing IC is complex and extensive and requires expertise and management attention. The new profession of KM specialists, from several academic fields, is becoming a reality. As indicated in Figure 1.7, the disciplines and other areas that KM relies on include:

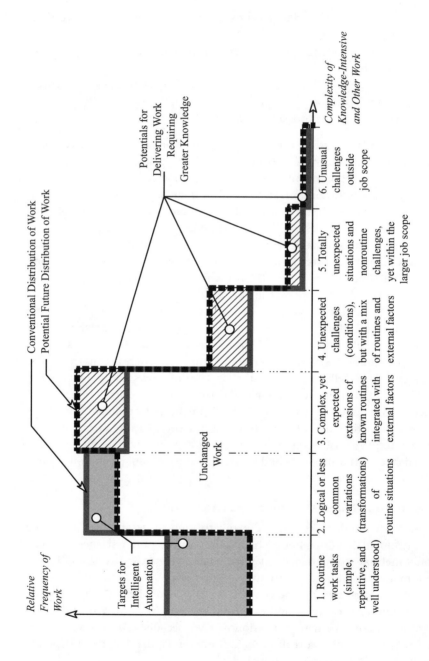

Figure 1.6 *Changes Will Make Work More Complex.*

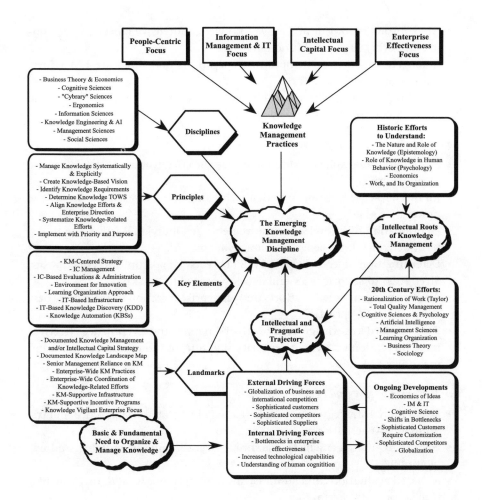

Figure 1.7 *A Perspective of the Emerging Knowledge Management Discipline*

Disciplines in Support of KM

- Business theory and economics to create strategies, determine priorities, and evaluate progress
- Cognitive sciences to understand how best to support knowledge workers' mental functioning required by their work settings
- "Cybrary" sciences to bring knowledge-related services to everyone[24]
- Ergonomics to create effective and acceptable work environments
- Information sciences to build supporting infrastructure and special knowledge-related capabilities
- Knowledge engineering to elicit and codify knowledge

- AI to automate routine and assist knowledge-intensive work with reasoning and other high-level functions
- Management sciences to optimize operations and integrate KM efforts with other enterprise efforts
- Social sciences to provide KM-related motivations, people processes, and cultural environments

General Principles for Effective KM

- Systematic and explicit KM to maximize the effectiveness of the enterprise business drivers
- Knowledge-based vision to provide the long-term basis for a broad KM practice
- Identification of knowledge requirements for individual functions to determine which knowledge to make available
- Determination of knowledge TOWS (Threats, Opportunities, Weaknesses, Strengths) to set priorities and develop needed KM tasks
- Alignment of knowledge efforts and enterprise direction to realize the best value of the KM practice
- Systematized knowledge-related efforts to make the KM practice effective
- Implementation of KM with priority and purpose to minimize waste and maximize KM value

Key Elements of KM Practices

- KM-centered strategy to achieve effective, integrated KM practice and coordinate KM activities
- Focused IC management to maximize overall value of building and exploiting IC
- IC-based evaluations and administration to optimize local IC investments, utilization, and caretaking
- Provision of environment for support of innovation to build competitive IC
- Learning organization approach to build competitive knowledge faster than competition
- IT-based infrastructure to provide effective support for KM
- IT-based knowledge discovery (KDD) to learn maximally from the past
- Knowledge automation (KBSs) to streamline operations

Landmarks for Developing KM Practices

- Documented KM and/or intellectual capital strategy indicating the extent and maturity of KM preparation
- Documented knowledge landscape map indicating understanding of knowledge TOWS

- Senior management reliance on KM indicating enterprise commitment
- Enterprise-wide KM practices indicating extent to which KM is pursued in practice
- Enterprise-wide coordination of knowledge-related efforts indicating sophistication of KM involvement
- KM-supportive infrastructure indicating potential efficiency of KM practice
- KM-supportive incentive programs indicating realization that KM is people-centric
- Knowledge vigilance indicating reliance on knowledge and IC for success and viability

Knowledge Management Must Justify Its Existence

Most organizations still pursue KM without ascertaining that hard business reasons require it. This is changing—and for good reasons. The premises are that competitive knowledge backed by deliberate KM is important for sustained success and viability and that the enterprise value largely comes from IC. It may therefore be irresponsible to pursue KM without having explicit understanding of how the efforts will be of value. There are several reasons for establishing the effects and benefits of potential KM actions. As the example in Figure 1.8 indicates, the immediate effects, followed by intermediate and final effects of the KM effort, should be explicated for five major purposes:

- To support KM planning, decision making, and priority setting, and to obtain estimates of magnitude and timeframe of potential benefits, costs, and risks
- To delineate the nature of expected and desired KM-related events and agree with stakeholders about suitable descriptions of expected events and their benefits or associated risks, and provide a graphical (visual) framework to support the collaborative KM planning process
- To enable the desired outcomes from KM efforts, delineate the various effects that are sought or expected with identification of ancillary activities that must be considered
- To promote understanding of desired effects to support implementation over the lifetime of the process by describing the events and associated characteristics
- To monitor the KM-influenced event process to manage it appropriately, and provide sufficient understanding of the anticipated events by outlining expectations over time in sufficient detail

The proposed KM efforts—and later, KM implementation—need to be outlined in some detail to support these purposes.

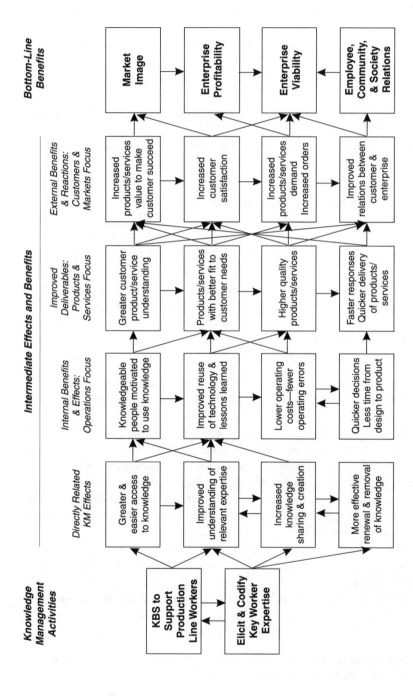

Figure 1.8 *Knowledge Management Activities Are Expected to Progress Through Internal and External Events to Deliver Bottom-Line Benefits*

CONCLUDING PERSPECTIVES

KM will continue to evolve and draw on support from many theoretical and methodological areas. For instance, cognitive sciences will increase understanding of decision making, cognitive support needed for work, effective learning, and skills transfer processes. Research on the nature of intellectual work will explicate how different kinds of knowledge are used, and should be possessed and accessed. Management sciences will provide methods for managing IC renewal, priorities, and investments. AI and advanced information technology will increase abilities to supplant and support complex work tasks. New directions such as the "economics of ideas," "economics of chance," and chaos theory will provide new perspectives and new guidelines for effective management in the knowledge society. New models for the theory of the firm will elucidate new tactical values, principles, and judgments.

However, much needs to be done. We do not understand much about knowledge. Our understanding of the cognitive aspects of human functioning (as related to decision making and knowledge-intensive work) is marginal. There is not an accepted economic "theory of knowledge" that is applicable to business or daily life. We do not have a general understanding of how to undertake comprehensive and systematic KM within an organization. We may need an entirely new theory of the firm to manage knowledge effectively—and to link it properly with enterprise strategy, tactics, and daily operations—while recognizing that in most organizations people and their behaviors contribute much more to the enterprise success than do the assets that conventionally are targets of management focus.

One key lesson to be learned is that we must adopt greater people-centric perspectives of knowledge. To be viable, we need constant learning, led by constant innovation. Technology goes only so far. It can provide us with only a rudimentary reasoning devoid of innovation and with concrete analyses of the past through approaches such as knowledge discovery in databases. People are the intelligent agents that create and act on new opportunities. It is those opportunities that will bring the world forward.

One doctrine of KM is the need to arrange our affairs to avoid rediscovering what earlier thinkers have created but maximize the reuse of valid knowledge and practices. We must adopt this tenet for our own work in KM.[25] General Colin Powell reminds us to "not invent what is already thriving!" Human history is not a history of cleverness and increasing acuity of vision. KM is not a result of people having become smarter, only more knowledgeable by building on powerful concepts inherited from prior generations.

NOTES

1. See, for example, Stewart (1997) and Sveiby (1997).
2. The epistemological considerations of the Greek philosophers Socrates, Plato, and Aristotle are well known. Perhaps less known in the West are the teachings of Lao

Tzu and Confucius in China, also from about 2,500 years ago. Indian philosophers also pursued similar topics.

3. See, for example, Boulding (1966), Cleveland (1985), Drucker (1988b), Stewart (1991), and Sveiby and Lloyd (1987).

4. Managers, by necessity, have been conservative. Management is not a science, and approaches to controlling the social, open systems of human and economic behavior in organizations and markets are fraught with problems and uncertainty (see Austin, 1996, and Hilmer and Donaldson, 1996). Successful management approaches, therefore, are built on traditions and long experience.

5. A perspective of the history of KM can be found in Wiig (1993).

6. See Romer (1989) and Kelly (1996).

7. See, for example, Cleveland (1985), Senge (1990), Simon (1976), and Wiig (1993).

8. Private communication from Fernando Simões, South African KM professional (1998). This definition was adopted by the Australian Parliament for their KM position paper.

9. Lucier and Torsilieri (1997).

10. From practical KM perspectives, operational definitions are: *Information* consists of facts and other data organized to characterize a particular situation, condition, challenge, or opportunity. *Knowledge* is possessed by humans or inanimate agents as truths and beliefs, perspectives and concepts, judgments and expectations, methodologies and know-how. Knowledge is used to receive information—to recognize and identify; analyze, interpret, and evaluate, synthesize, assess and decide; adapt, plan, implement, and monitor—to act. *Understanding* based on knowledge is used to determine what a specific situation means and how to handle it. Following this definition, information and rudimentary knowledge may be codifiable and may exist outside a person's mind. Understanding, however, may be difficult to codify and is primarily people based.

11. See Kao (1997).

12. See, for example, Gardner (1983), Gardner (1985), Lakoff (1987), Schank and Abelson (1977), and Wiig (1995).

13. Romer (1989) and Kelly (1996), op. cit.

14. See Suchman (1995).

15. Gardner (1983), op. cit.

16. See Bechara et al. (1997) and Klein (1998).

17. See Winograd (1988), Cannon-Bowers and Salas (1999) op. cit., and Wellman and Hampton (1999).

18. Cannon-Bowers and Salas (1999), op. cit.

19. See Edvinson and Malone (1997), Stewart (1991), Stewart (1997), and Sveiby (1997).

20. Wiig (1995) p. 358 discusses such programs.

21. See Kurtzman (1999).

22. Wiig and Wiig (1999) discuss some existing approaches and the reasoning behind them.

23. For an excellent discussion of ontologies and their role in KM, see Chandrasekaran et al. (1999).

24. "Cybrarians" combine expertise from library science and cyberspace to obtain and organize information and knowledge.

25. David Owens, a long-time KM practitioner and academic, reminds us emphatically about this point.

CHAPTER 2

Shifts in the World Economy: The Drivers of Knowledge Management

Robert M. Grant

INTRODUCTION Among the innovations that have swept through the world of management during the past two decades—total quality management, shareholder value creation, business process reengineering, and competence-based strategy—knowledge management has probably aroused the greatest interest and made the biggest impact. Measured by numbers of conferences and books, the attention attracted by knowledge management is remarkable. For consulting companies it has provided the basis for a whole new line of business. Among companies a new genus of knowledge officers has appeared. Unusual among major management innovations, knowledge management has captured the interest of both practicing managers and business school academics. One of the most encouraging features of the many conferences covering knowledge management is the participation and dialogue between academics and practitioners. The breadth of interest in knowledge management is also apparent across the range of business functions. Although early interest centered on strategy, IT, and new product development, knowledge management has extended into operations management, marketing, HR, and accounting and finance.

The purpose of this chapter is to explore two questions concerning the current knowledge revolution in management. First, why this recent explosion of interest in knowledge management? Second, what are the critically important contributions that the knowledge perspective offers to management theory and practice?

The first section of the chapter explores the reasons for the surge of inter-est and activity in knowledge management. I focus in particular on the changes that have occurred in the world economy. One of the key arguments of several leading exponents of knowledge management is that the new postindustrial, knowledge-based economy is fundamentally different from the economic structures of the past and that the "new rules" of competition and organization require new approaches to management. Certainly, the world economy at the end of the twentieth century does display unique char-acteristics such as the critical role of information and communication tech-nologies and the extent of globalization. At the same time, it is not apparent that the "knowledge-based economy" inhabited by "knowledge-intensive firms" and "knowledge workers" is fundamentally different from that which preceded it. Alternatively, it could be that the current enthusiasm for knowl-edge management is not so much the result of fundamental changes in our economic system, as the result of the discovery of new concepts and tools for dealing with the perennial issues of management. One of the themes that I shall develop is that all management is, in effect, about managing knowledge but, until recently, the principles of management have failed to take account of the critical role of knowledge and the implications of different types of management for coordinating organizations and generating profits from productive activity.

In moving on to the second major question—the central contributions of knowledge management—let me first address the issue of fad versus sub-stance. Like most social phenomena, management is subject to fashion, hype, bandwagon effects, misinformation, and the activities of unscrupulous entre-preneurs (in academe as well as consulting). Even if we exclude pure char-latanism, there will inevitably be a tendency for so broad a subject to attract "more needless obfuscation and woolly thinking by academics and consul-tants than any other" (*Financial Times*, 1999) and idiosyncrasies such as the interest of Saatchi & Saatchi's director of knowledge management, which in-volves "the totality of the consumer," including an innovative Japanese panty hose "embedded with millions of microcapsules of vitamin C and seaweed ex-tract that burst when worn to provide extra nourishment for the limbs" (*Wall Street Journal*, 1997a).[1]

My own view is that, despite its peculiar, superficial, and wrong-headed manifestations, knowledge management offers a set of ideas and insights that give it the potential to make the most important advance in manage-ment theory and practice of the past 50 years. Already, knowledge-based thinking is making important contributions to our thinking about informa-tion systems, strategy, innovation, and organizational design. Within firms and not-for-profit organizations, the introduction of knowledge manage-ment practices has shown some remarkable results in helping diffuse best practices, accelerate new product development, improve workplace design, and increase the effectiveness of strategic planning processes. Within the broad diversity of knowledge management concepts and practices, which offer the most promising avenues of development in terms of future management practices?

THE CURRENT BUSINESS ENVIRONMENT

The New Knowledge Economy

Closely associated with the surge of interest in knowledge management has been the advent of the new, knowledge-based, postindustrial economy. What is this New Economy? Among the characteristics identified in the flood of written commentary are the following:

- In contrast with previous periods of economic development, the primary factor of production in the new economy is knowledge, as opposed to capital in the industrial economy or land in the agrarian economy (Quinn, 1992; Drucker, 1993; Burton-Jones, 2000).
- It is concentrated on intangibles rather than tangibles (Stewart, 1997; Edvinsson and Malone, 1997). In terms of output this means a predominance of services over goods. In terms of inputs it means that the primary assets of firms are intangibles such as technology and brands rather than land, machines, inventories, and financial assets. The increasing irrelevance of tangible assets is indicated by the fact that by March 1999, the ratio of market value of the *Business Week* "nifty-fifty" had reached 12 times book value.
- It is networked—unprecedented interconnectivity is possible through the development of new communication media: cellular telephony, direct satellite communication, the Internet, and interactive TV. The digitalization of major aspects of almost all communication media has greatly expanded the potential for collaboration not just within organizations but also between organizations (Castells, 1999). Indeed, one consequence has been the declining role of formal organizations altogether as institutions for achieving coordinated action. The Internet itself has provided both a metaphor and a model for "virtual" organization—organization that lacks either formal structure or authority.
- It is digital. Don Tapscott (1995) has referred to the current era as the "age of sand" in that the central components of digital technology—the silicon chip and fiber optical cable—are based on sand. The digitization of information has had a huge impact on the capacity for transferring, storing, and processing information.
- It is virtual. The virtual organization is just one example of the transition from real to virtual work made possible by digitization and networking (Hagel and Singer, 1999). The growing role of virtual (i.e., electronic)

money, virtual transactions, virtual communities, virtual vacations, and virtual sex are dissolving the boundaries between the real and imaginary worlds to the point where futurist Watts Wacker (Wacker, Taylor, and Means, 2000) claims that we are entering an age where anything we can dream we can do.

- It is fast moving. The new economy is subject to rapid change. Partly because of the rapid pace of innovation and partly because of the efficiency of communication that results in speedy diffusion, the pace of technological change has accelerated sharply. Evidence of this is produced by the compression of product life cycles. The automobile and the safety razor required more than a decade to transition from their "introduction stage" into their "growth stage," and even for the microcomputer the lag between introduction and rapid market penetration was about six years. By contrast, during the past decade and a half, CD-ROMs, personal digital organizers, digital PCs, telecommunications, and satellite TVs entered their growth phases almost immediately after their introduction. The combination of speed, intangibility, and connectivity has created what Stan Davis and Chris Meyer (1998) call the "blur" aspect of the modern economy. The high-velocity business environment calls for a rethinking of firms' strategies (Brown and Eisenhart, 1998).
- It is better performing. Although Japan and much of Western Europe are too affected by sluggish overall demand to appreciate the benefits of the "new economy," the U.S. "Goldilocks" economy reveals with remarkable clarity the capacity of the knowledge-based economy to reconcile high growth and high employment with price stability.

These various trends have combined to produce a number of structural changes within the business sector. These include the dissolving boundaries between firms and markets and the growing role of collaborative organizational forms that are neither firms nor market transactions. Also prominent has been *disintermediation*—the tendency for firms to transact directly with final customers without the need for distributors, wholesalers, and agents to act as intermediaries. A further implication has been globalization. Once seen as a result of trade liberalization and the activities of multinational corporations, globalization is now knowledge driven. As Drucker remarked, "Knowledge knows no boundaries." The jungle tribes of Papua New Guinea and the bushmen of the Kalahari are almost as knowledgeable about Monica Lewinski, the death of Princess Diana, and the O.J. Simpson verdict as CNN watchers in North America and Europe. Global communication and information networks, the Internet in particular, have permitted the smallest enterprises to engage in international transactions. Finally, the distinction between producers and consumers is becoming less clear. Interactive media result in consumers being drawn into designing their own news bulletins, vacations, and automobiles in a process that Don Tapscott (1997) calls "prosumption."

Looking Beyond the Hype

The danger of this approach is that by lumping together all significant changes that have occurred in the modern economy and labeling them as features of the "knowledge economy," we will fail to analyze current trends. If we are to understand the contemporary business environment and plot its trajectory into the future, then it is essential that we look systematically at the drivers of change.

Many of the alleged characteristic features of the so-called "new knowledge economy" do not stand up to scrutiny. Take the much-discussed trend toward disintermediation. In the electronically interconnected age, firms do not need to distribute their wares through wholesalers and retail; they can sell direct to the consumer. Publishers can supply articles and complete newspapers and journals in directly downloadable form. House sellers do not need the services of realtors; they can locate buyers directly through the Internet. Yet, these examples represent, not so much disintermediation, as the displacement of one type of intermediately by another. The new intermediaries are Internet portals and ISPs such as AOL and Excite, telecom companies such as MCI-Worldcom that provide the communication infrastructure, Visa International that processes the transactions, and Federal Express that makes the physical delivery.

Similarly with the supposed convergence of industries. Are industries really converging, or is it simply that technology and deregulation are redrawing their boundaries? While communication and computing, commercial and investment banking, and TV and telephony converge, other industries fragment and diverge. For example, the once-monolithic computer industry has fragmented into industries supplying components, assembled computers, operating systems, applications software, and computer services. Similar observations could be made of the telecommunications industry.

The idea that we have moved from an economy based on land, labor, and capital to one based on knowledge is nonsense. All major human advances since the beginning of civilization have been based on knowledge. The building of Stonehenge and other megalithic monuments in Northern Europe at around 2,000 B.C. coincided with the economic growth arising from the knowledge revolution in the form of the introduction of agriculture. The agrarian and industrial revolutions of the eighteenth and early nineteenth centuries were also consequences of the development and diffusion of new knowledge. The econometric analysis of economic growth since the pioneering work of Kuznets (1966) and Denison (1968) has been consistent in identifying advances in knowledge as the primary driver of increasing real income per capita. Hence, apart from the simple fact that knowledge accumulated over time and its growth pattern may well be exponential, it is not apparent that knowledge plays a fundamentally different role in today's economy than it did a hundred or even a thousand years ago. The basic difference is that a greater stock of knowledge supports a far higher level of productivity.

Similar observations may be made about the so-called "knowledge worker." Such a concept relies on some restrictive assumptions about what constitutes knowledge. It is not obvious to me that a computer software engineer or a lawyer is any more a knowledge worker than a shepherd, a sculptor, or a Buddhist monk. The key point is that different workers use different types of knowledge, and it is difficult to compare the knowledge intensity of different occupations. Does a pharmacist use more knowledge than does a bus driver? Certainly the conventional distinction between working with one's hands or with one's brain is of little help. Is an office clerk more of a knowledge worker than a manual worker such as Antonio Stradavari or a brain surgeon? The most that can be said is that different types of knowledge are differentially distributed among individuals, that different types of knowledge take different lengths of time to acquire, and that without knowledge the human being is completely unproductive. The challenge, then, is not to talk vaguely about the knowledge-based economy and knowledge workers, but to explore in precise terms the features of knowledge and its use that are different today than in previous periods of time.

Productivity and Increasing Returns in the Software-Based Economy

The defining feature of today's knowledge-based economy is the digitization of information. Digital technologies embodied in semiconductors, computers, computer software, and communication systems have resulted in huge reductions in the costs of storing, processing, and transferring explicit knowledge. The "soft revolution" has two main elements. First, knowledge is no longer embodied exclusively in people and capital equipment; it is embodied in software. Software takes the form of recipes, computer programs, movies, management systems, and all other codified representations of information, science, and creative expression. Second, the economics of such software is fundamentally different from the economic principles associated with traditional factors of production. Traditional factors of production are associated with diminishing returns; explicit knowledge is subject to increasing returns. Explicit knowledge embodied in software is costly to create, but once created it can be reproduced and distributed at close to zero marginal cost. In contrast to the traditional sources of scale economies—the benefits from the specialization and division of labor in Adam Smith's pin factory—the extent of scale economies in the movies, recorded music, and computer software are huge. The exploitation of these increasing returns is the primary driver of globalization in today's economy.

Nor are these increasing returns associated with explicit, codified knowledge restricted to information technology and media industries. The value-

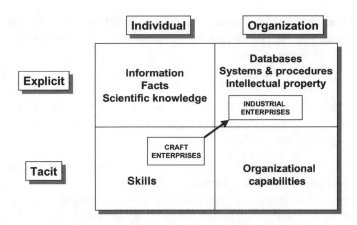

Figure 2.1 *The Systematization of Knowledge from Craft Enterprises to Industrial Enterprises*

creating potential associated with the low-cost replication of explicit knowledge offers huge incentives for systematizing existing knowledge, and then replicating it over and over again to exploit its value. The major impact of digital technologies is in facilitating the systematization of knowledge into codified form and in greatly lowering the costs of its replication. This process of systematizing tacit knowledge is represented in Figure 2.1.

If knowledge exists in two principal forms, explicit and tacit, and at two major levels, the individual and the firm, then there are major benefits to the firm in shifting its primary knowledge base from individually held tacit knowledge, to firm-held explicit knowledge. First, explicit knowledge offers greater potential for value creation because of its replicability potential. Second, the firm's potential for appropriating this value is greater if ownership lies with the firm rather than with the individual. The systematization of tacit, individually held knowledge into explicit, firm-held knowledge is the primary force behind the evolution of craft trades into industrialized trades. This process of industrializing craft businesses has been the basis of many of the most outstanding business successes of this century. For example:

- Henry Ford's mass production system for the manufacture of automobiles took the tacit knowledge of skilled craftsmen and embodied it into machine tools and an industrialized system that could be replicated throughout the world.
- Ray Kroc's genius was in recognizing the potential for converting the McDonald brothers' San Bernardino hamburger joint into a system that could be replicated many thousands of times over in a global chain of franchised hamburger restaurants.

- In a similar process, Starbucks took the traditional Seattle coffee house and reduced it to a set of formulae capable of precise replication throughout North America, and now the world.
- Andersen Consulting took the business of systems integration, one based on the experiential knowledge of IT professionals, and built a set of systems that allowed the creation of a worldwide business based on the systematic training of fresh, young graduates and equipping them with package solutions to IT management.

In the field of management consulting Hansen, Nohria, and Tierney (1999) have observed that a fundamental difference in firm strategies is between those that pursue a "codification strategy" based on a "people-to-documents" approach that permits extensive knowledge reuse, and a "personalization strategy" offering customized solutions based on the expertise of individual consultants and one-to-one consultant–client dialogue. Andersen Consulting and Ernst & Young have pursued codification strategies, and McKinsey and Bain epitomize the personalization approach. While Hansen et al. do not argue for the superiority of any one approach, our analysis suggests that, in principle, a codification strategy that exploits economies of reuse should offer greater potential for rent generation and appropriation.

The productivity gains associated with conversion of tacit into explicit knowledge and its subsequent replication on a global scale are fundamental to the rapid rates of economic growth experienced during the past few decades. Paul Romer has estimated that the growth in real output per hour of work achieved by the world's leading economy has accelerated over the past three centuries (see Table 2.1). As the new information technologies increase the speed and lower the cost at which new forms of software can be created, replicated, and diffused, it is likely that long-term rates of productivity growth will continue to accelerate. "New recipes," whether they be Starbucks systematized approach to producing cappuccinos or Wal-Mart's cross-docking system of receiving and shipping goods to and from warehouses, are permitting unparalleled productivity improvements in service activities. But, according to Romer (1999), the real gains are still to come; electronic commerce in particular offers the potential for massive efficiency gains in the distribution of goods and services—traditionally a low productivity sector.

Standards and Winner-Take-All Markets

Any markets subject to scale economies will tend toward high levels of concentration due to the cost advantages of large firms over small firms. The extent of the scale economies arising from the low cost of replicating information and other forms of explicit knowledge has been an important force driving rapidly increasing concentration across a range of once-fragmented industries ranging from management consulting to pizzerias. Although the primary sources of industrial concentration were economies in large-scale

Table 2.1
Growth in Real Output per Hour Worked by the World's
Leading Economy, 1700-1979

Period	Country	Annual Growth of Real Output per Hour (%)
1700–1785	Netherlands	0.1
1785–1820	U.K.	0.5
1820–1890	U.K.	1.4
1890–1979	U.S.A.	2.2

Source: Paul Romer, "The New Economy." Presentation to the Strategic Leadership Forum Annual Conference, Chicago, April 19, 1999.

manufacturing processes in sectors such as steel making, automobile manufacture, and petrochemicals, it is scale economies in information reuse that explain Microsoft's dominance in the market for microcomputer software and McDonalds's dominance in the world hamburger market.

However, the present trend toward "winner-take-all" markets is not solely a consequence of the economics of software replication—it is also a result of interconnectivity within the networked economy (Shapiro and Varian, 1999). In many industries, the extent of concentration goes well beyond the requirements for the minimum efficient scale of operation. The tendency in the markets for computer operating systems and video game players is for a single company to establish a position of near-unassailable market dominance. This phenomenon is associated with markets that combine low-cost replication with network externalities—the situation in which a consumer's utility from a product is dependent on the number of other users consuming that product. For such products this relationship was expressed more precisely by Robert Metcalfe, the founder of 3Com. Metcalfe's Law states that the utility of a network increases at the square of the number of members. While the "killer app" is no new phenomenon—the stirrup was a killer app of the eighth century—network externalities in the interconnected, digital economy have greatly increased the number of, and speed of dissemination of, such innovations (Downes and Mui, 1998).

Network externalities may arise from a number of factors. The most basic is direct linkages between consumers—as in the case of a telephone system—in which the usefulness of the product depends on direct linkages between users. It may also arise from user mobility in the face of significant training costs. Thus, the emergence of Microsoft PowerPoint as the dominant presentation software was encouraged by the ability of users to take their presentation skills to any organization without the need to learn a different software package. Network externalities may also arise from the availability of complementary products. The tendency for computer software, videotape formats, and computer game consoles to move toward a single market-dominating product or system arises primarily from the linkage between product leadership and the availability of applications software; the disadvantage with ownership of a minority standard, whether it is a Sony Betamax VCR or an Apple Macintosh microcomputer is that most producers of applications—whether movie studios or software developers—will be producing their products for the dominant standard.

The implications for competition are far-reaching. Because the winner takes all, the competition for market leadership is intense. The "battle of the browsers" competition between the two key players quickly resulted in both Netscape and Microsoft offering their products free. Similar trends are evident in other areas of Internet competition. By mid-1999, competition between Internet service providers in the UK had resulted in many leading players offering free service. The quest for standards-setting market leadership had also resulted in the tendency toward coalitions of players. The critical importance of winning standards battles often produced some strange bedfellows—arch rivals Kodak and Fuji collaborating in developing and marketing the Advanced Photo System for a new generation of films and cameras, and Microsoft collaborating with both Sun Microsystems and AOL-Netscape over technical issues.

Implications of the New Economy for Knowledge Management

My proposition, thus far, is that there is nothing fundamentally new about an economy based on knowledge. What distinguishes the present economy from a knowledge perspective is the sheer accumulation of knowledge by society, the rapid pace of innovation and, most important, the advent of digital technologies that have had far-reaching implications for the sources of value in the modern economy. These characteristics of the new economy have been important drivers behind the explosion of interest in knowledge management over the past six years. In particular, four key aspects of knowledge management stand out.

1. *Property rights in knowledge.* There is an increased recognition of knowledge as the most valuable and strategically important of resources used by firms together with the increased embodiment of knowledge within recipes, designs, computer software and other forms of software has resulted in increased attention to ownership. Looking back, the lack of interest in property rights by pioneers of research and innovation seems remarkable. For most of the post–Second World War period AT&T's Bell Labs simply gave away many of the foundations of the microelectronics revolution. Indeed, it was not until Texas Instruments revealed the huge revenue potential from patent licenses that most companies began to manage their patent portfolios as income-generating assets (Grindley and Teece, 1997). Recognition of the value of pro-

prietary knowledge has propelled the strengthening of intellectual property regimes by legislatures and judicial systems over the past two decades. Among both companies and their industry associations, the enforcement of intellectual property in the form of patents, copyrights, and trademarks has become a central asset-management activity and a key issue in international economic relations.

2. *Accelerating knowledge creation and application.* The increasing pace of technological change has placed substantial pressures on companies to increase the speed at which they develop and apply knowledge. This emphasis on speed is particularly evident in new product development in which, across a wide range of industries, companies have struggled to shorten their product development cycles. In automobiles, for example, U.S. and European manufacturers have fundamentally redesigned their approaches to new product development in an effort to cut the time from drawing board to market launch from five to three years (Clark and Fujimoto, 1991). According to Brown and Eisenhart (1998, pp. 163–168) the fundamental force behind Intel's sustained success is its "time pacing"—the time pacing of product development through continual minor innovation with periodic "mid-life kickers," together with a nine-month cycle of fab construction.

3. *Converting tacit into explicit knowledge.* If most knowledge is tacit and embodied within individual employees, its rent potential for the firm is limited by its high costs of replication and the inability of the firm to appropriate its value. As Kogut and Zander (1992, p. 390) acknowledge: "Unless able to train large numbers of individuals or to transform skills into organizing principles, the craft shop is forever simply a shop." However, what Kogut and Zander refer to as the "paradox of replication" is that the codification of knowledge required for internal replication may also facilitate imitation by other firms. The challenge is to build barriers to external replication through linking the firm's internal systems to knowledge that cannot be replicated by outsiders. Thus, all the major purveyors of systematized knowledge, whether McDonalds Restaurants or Andersen Consulting, invest heavily in brand building. The other is to reconvert codified knowledge into organizational routines that operate at the tacit level. Thus, the training undertaken by McDonalds at its Oak Brook, Illinois, Hamburger University or by Andersen Consulting at its Lake Charles, Illinois, training center emphasizes socialization and cultural integration conducive to the replication of organizational routines. Recognition that the value of the firm is generated by the low-cost replication of its systematized knowledge has encouraged a fundamental rethinking by many firms of their strategy and identity. In the same way that it is often remarked that Apple Computer's fundamental error was mistaken identity—it was a software company that thought it was a hardware company—so other firms are recognizing that their value lies not in their products but in their systems. Nike's success and value lies in its system for managing the design, supply chain, and marketing of lifestyle products to the

youth market. It has replicated this system worldwide and from athletic shoes to sports and casual clothing, into sports equipment and accessories. Wal-Mart's fundamental strength is its retail system that integrates point-of-sale technology and in-store management with its procurement and distribution system. This system has been replicated not only throughout the United States, but also increasingly to other countries, and from its Wal-Mart stores to Sam's Club warehouses, and now to acquired retail chains such as Asda in Britain.

4. *Competing for standards.* The past two decades have seen a remarkable development in the understanding of the role of standards in the economy and far greater sophistication in the strategies used by companies in standards battles. In retrospect, the errors made in earlier standards battles make the players seem naïve. In the battle of the personal computers, Apple's failure to license its operating system and IBM's failure to establish any proprietary interest in the PC standard seem to be remarkable misjudgments, as was Sony's failure to license its Betamax technology. Recent standards, whether for digital wireless telephony (GSM vs. TDMA vs. CDMA), recordable digital audio media, and Internet browsers, have all been characterized by a vastly greater insight into both the value of owning, or even influencing, standards and into the dynamics of standard setting. Thus, the recent standards battles have involved the willingness of the participants to forego current profits in order to invest in market leadership and the building of broad-based coalitions around particular standards. These coalitions have typically involved competitors as well as suppliers, customers and providers of complementary goods and services.

THE DISCOVERY OF KNOWLEDGE MANAGEMENT

Despite the increasing importance of knowledge within the economy and the far-reaching changes caused by the digital revolution, I am not convinced that the recent surge of interest in managing knowledge is primarily the result of external changes in the business environment. More important, in my opinion, has been the burst of intellectual activity that has accompanied the recognition of knowledge as a productive resource, the rediscovery of the discussion of knowledge by writers such as Hayek (1945), Polanyi (1962), Arrow (1962), and March and Simon (1958), and the wave of new thinking concerning the characteristics of knowledge and its role within the firm.

Thus, most of the developments in the concepts and techniques of knowledge management that appeared during the 1990s were not specific to the present digitally based, postindustrial economy. Indeed, some of the powerful tools of knowledge management that have recently emerged concern the development and application of tacit knowledge as opposed to the management of codified knowledge. Taken as a whole, the main contribution of knowledge management has been in shedding light on the fundamental issues of management that have long been central to strategy, organization, and human resource management. What knowledge management offers us is insight into aspects of management that we have failed to understand properly because of our failure to consider the nature and characteristics of knowledge.

Seeing Management Through the Knowledge Lens

Consider, for example, two of the most important developments in management thinking during the twentieth century: scientific management and total quality management. Although these two important and highly influential management paradigms are largely incompatible and to a great extent conflicting, we can reinterpret these approaches to management from a knowledge-based perspective. The result is not only insight into the implicit assumptions about knowledge in each, but also recognition that the differences between the two paradigms can be traced to these different assumptions.

Knowledge and Scientific Management

Fundamental to the emergence of the modern corporation has been the development of management as a specialized body of knowledge. The earliest manifestation of this, the "scientific management" movement at the turn of the century, was founded on the idea of a division of labor between workers and managers: workers do the work, while managers, as experts in management, specialize in decision making. However, as with all production tasks, specialization requires integration; the manager's knowledge of organization must be brought together with the workers' skills and their familiarity with workplace conditions. Because managers possess superior intelligence and specialized knowledge of the scientific principles of management, then managers must be given decision-making rights over workers. However, a critical assumption of the approach is that managers can access all the knowledge held by the workers. Thus, Fredrick Taylor's description of the application of scientific management to shoveling coal and iron ore at Bethlehem Steel is based on the assumption that the manager has full knowledge of the skills of shoveling and of the range of situations encountered by shovelers (Taylor, 1916).

This implicit assumption that managers can access the knowledge of their subordinates is a striking weakness, not just of scientific management but of hierarchical models of decision making more generally. In a hierarchy, decision making over routine matters is delegated downwards through rules and procedures. Decision rights over complex and strategic issues tend to be retained in the upper organizational levels. Yet, if these upper-level decision makers are unable to access the knowledge available at lower levels of the organization, then efficiency of decision making is constrained not only by "bounded rationality," but also by bounded access to relevant knowledge.

Knowledge and Total Quality Management (TQM)

It is interesting that TQM, like scientific management, is based on the application of the principles of the scientific method to decision making and the organization of work. TQM applies cause-and-effect decision trees to the diagnosis of problems and statistical analysis to the analysis of defects. Yet, despite these commonalties, TQM gives rise to quite different management methods and allocations of decision rights than those of scientific management.

The critical difference between scientific management and TQM lies in their assumptions about the distribution and characteristics of knowledge. While scientific management assumed that managers are capable of accessing all the knowledge possessed by workers, TQM recognizes that knowledge is not easily transferable. Given that good decisions require the application of the knowledge relevant to those decisions, TQM favors the transfer of decision making concerning each employee's production tasks to the employees who are undertaking the tasks. Hence, in addressing Taylor's "shoveling problem," TQM results in a fundamentally different allocation of decision than that recommended by Taylor. Although TQM focuses on quality as the primary performance variable, the same principles also can be applied to efficiency. If know-how about shoveling coal and iron ore accrues to those who undertake the work, and this know-how is not easily transferred to a manager or foreman, then it is the shovelers who are best able to improve productivity through improving job design and working techniques. The second assumption about knowledge implicit in TQM is that all human beings are intelligent and capable of learning. Hence, it is easier to instruct the worker in those "principles of management" necessary for the worker to make optimal decisions concerning his or her work than it is to transfer the worker's knowledge to a manager. Thus, a key feature of TQM is training workers in the statistical process control and "scientific" approaches to the analysis of problems.

Knowledge and the Structure of Decision Making

The examples concerning scientific management and TQM point to the fact that our assumptions about the distribution of general intelligence between individuals and the characteristics of knowledge have fundamental implications for the distribution of decision making within the firm. In order to generalize our discussion, let us consider the relationship between characteristics of different types of knowledge and the optimal distribution of decision making within an organization. We begin with the premise that the quality of a decision depends on the extent to which decision making is co-located with the knowledge required for informing that decision. Such co-location can be achieved in two ways: decision making can be devolved to where the knowledge resides, or this knowledge can be transferred to the seat of decision-making authority.

The critical issue here is the mobility of knowledge, which is a
its codifiablity. Where knowledge is fully codifiable (e.g., inform
ventories within the firm), not only can the knowledge be transfer
cost, it also can be aggregated within a single location. Given economies of
scale in decision making, it is desirable to decentralize such decisions. Hence,
in most companies, treasury functions, including cash management and foreign exchange hedging, are centralized in a single corporate treasury. Conversely, highly tacit knowledge is not capable of codification and is extremely
difficult to transfer and to aggregate. Hence, where the relevant knowledge is
tacit, then decision making power must be distributed to where the tacit
knowledge is located. Thus, the productivity of lathe operators and other ma-
chinists depends critically on their tacit skills; because their sensitivity to and
awareness of their machines cannot easily be codified, this implies that decision about maintenance and settings should be delegated to the operatives.

Recent trends toward "empowerment" have been justified primarily in
terms of motivation and philosophies of individualism and self-determin-
ation. Our knowledge-based approach provides a purely technical basis for
empowerment decisions; where knowledge is tacit or is not readily codifiable
for other reasons, then decision-making quality is enhanced where decision-
making authority is delegated to those with the relevant knowledge. At the
same time it points to situations in which decisions should be decentralized
and situations in which centralization is more efficient. Although the dominant trend of the 1990s was toward decentralization, developments in information technology and artificial intelligence promise to increase the potential
for knowledge to be codified. Such a development may encourage increased
centralization of decision making. Such centralization trends are apparent
within fast-food chains, where the information technology has encouraged a
shift of decision making over menus, pricing, and production scheduling
from individual restaurant managers and franchisees to the corporate and regional headquarters.

However, as Jensen points out, there exists a trade-off between the benefits of co-location of decision making and knowledge and the costs of agency.
As decision making is devolved to those with the know-how relevant to those
decisions, so the costs of agency arising from the inconsistent objectives of
different organizational members tend to increase. Hence, there is an optimal
degree of decentralization where, at the margin, the cost reductions from distributing decision rights to individual employees is equal to the rising agency
costs associated with moving decision rights further from the CEO's office.

The Emerging Knowledge Based View of the Firm

At the root of the intellectual contributions of knowledge management is a
theory of the firm that establishes the existence and the role of firms on different premises from those on which both the microeconomic and sociologi-

cal approaches have been based. The work of Demsetz (1988), Kogut and Zander (1992 and 1996), Connor and Prahalad (1996), and Grant (1996), among others, point toward a theory of the existence and the nature of firms that is somewhat different from the transaction-cost based approach of the new institutional economics.

Appreciating the characteristics of knowledge and the organizational challenge of integrating the knowledge assets of multiple individuals can provide considerable insight into the organizing role of firms. Although transaction cost economics (TCE) can demonstrate the sources of market failure in knowledge transactions, simply showing the inefficiencies of market contracts in synchronizing team-based production does not provide us with much insight into the design of an administrative system capable of maximizing team performance.

Kogut and Zander present the firm not so much as an institution that economizes on the transaction costs of markets, but rather as a social institution capable of coordinating human behavior in ways that are impossible for pure market contracts. They argue that "organizations are social communities in which individual and social expertise is transferred into economically-useful products and services by the application of a set of higher-order organizing principles. Firms exist because they provide a social community of voluntaristic action structured by organizing principles that are not reducible to individuals" (Kogut and Zander 1992, p. 384). The precise nature of these social communities, the social expertise that they possess, and the organizing principles under which they operate are not made entirely clear. Grant (1996) discusses some of the mechanisms through which firms (and other organizations) achieve the integration of individuals' knowledge into the production of goods and services. The key to efficiency in knowledge integration is to create mechanisms that avoid the costs of learning: If each individual has to learn what every other individual knows, then the benefits of specialization are lost. The analysis of coordination was pioneered by James Thompson (1968), who classified the types of interdependency between individuals and units. Thompson viewed the modes of interdependence between individuals as exogenously determined by the technology of production and its component processes. Using a knowledge-based perspective, we may view coordination mechanisms as choices made by the firm as to how it achieves the integration of the specialist knowledge of multiple individuals. The most important of these mechanisms are rules and directives and organizational routines.

The case for the existence of the firm as a unit of economic organization rests on the superiority of the firm over markets in supporting these knowledge integration mechanisms. To achieve coordination through these different mechanisms of integration requires authority (to permit direction), centralized decision making, co-location, and common knowledge (to permit communication). All these connotations are provided more readily within the firm than in any other type of organization.

KNOWLEDGE MANAGEMENT'S CONTRIBUTION TO MANAGEMENT PRACTICE

Thus far, I have discussed knowledge management and the emerging knowledge-based view of the firm primarily from a theoretical viewpoint. However, the surge of activity among corporations and consulting firms during the past six years has been driven less by the contribution of the knowledge-based thinking to advances in the theory of the firm than it has been driven by the potential for the techniques of knowledge management to directly impact company performance. The range of knowledge management tools and techniques has been broad. For years firms have been involved in actively managing particular types of knowledge and particular knowledge processes. For example, information systems, financial reporting and control systems, strategic management processes, and research and development are all management systems involving knowledge creation, knowledge transfer, and information management. The primary contribution of the recent knowledge management movement has been to look broadly at the entirety of knowledge and knowledge processes within firms in order to extend the scope of knowledge management activities to types of knowledge and knowledge activities that have been under-managed by firms, and also to achieve increasing integration across different knowledge management activities.

The Pioneers of Knowledge Management

Pioneering developments in knowledge management have occurred in a diversity of organizations. Most prominent have been the management consulting firms. Their leading role in knowledge management has been the result of two factors. The first factor has been the internal challenges they have faced in managing their own development and deployment of knowledge. These have focused on the need to ensure that the learning gained from individual consulting projects is retained and transferred within the firm. The second factor is the recognition that knowledge management provides attractive opportunities for revenue growth for the firms. The consulting firms were among the first organizations to create internal systems for knowledge management and, in many cases, followed this by creating knowledge management practices. These include:

- Andersen Consulting's Knowledge Xchange, which is at the heart of its dynamic matrix structure that links employees, clients, knowledge databases, reporting systems, and consulting tools.
- Arthur Andersen's Knowledge Enterprises.

- Ernst & Young's Center for Business Knowledge in Cleveland, which links a technological IT infrastructure with consultant interest groups and affinity groups.
- KPMG's KWEB knowledge management infrastructure and "Cyber Park Avenue."
- McKinsey & Company's "practice development" process, which seeks to codify consultants' learning from client engagements and research projects. In addition, McKinsey is a leader in the development and exploitation of social networks that provide informal knowledge exchange mechanisms. These networks extend to McKinsey former consultants ("alumni") who are encouraged to keep in contact with the firm.
- Bain & Company's "Experience Knowledge Base," which documents and distributes consultant learning from client engagements.

Firms that have emerged as leaders in particular areas of knowledge management include:

- IBM's contributions to knowledge management are many, including one of the first attempts to provide a company-wide knowledge architecture for mapping the vast amount and range of information within the company. IBM's Guide to Market Information was a "catalog of catalogs" in integrating the information available within IBM and linking each information area to a contact person (Davenport, 1997, pp. 164–167).
- Bechtel's Global Knowledge Network, overseen by Bechtel's Web Advisory Board, is a company-wide initiative that aims to disperse mission-critical knowledge across Bechtel's 20,000 employees throughout the world. It includes the BecWeb intranet that provides standardized formats for storing and distributing documents, engineering designs, standards, and client information.
- Dow Chemical has pioneered the systematic management of knowledge through its Intellectual Asset Management Model, the core of which is Dow's portfolio of over 30,000 patents, which it values and links with the strategies of Dow's individual businesses. Intellectual asset management is supported by 75 multifunctional teams, each aligned with a business, and each responsible for the development and exploitation of a segment of Dow's intellectual capital (Petrash, 1996).
- Skandia, the Swedish insurance company, has been a world leader in intellectual capital accounting: identifying, valuing, and measuring the performance of intellectual capital. Under the leadership of Skandia AFS's director of intellectual capital, Leif Edvinsson, Skandia has published since 1992 an intellectual capital supplement to its annual report and in 1993 launched its "Business Navigator," an integrated system for linking intellectual capital management with strategy and performance measurement (Marchand and Roos, 1996).

- Texas Instruments turned to knowledge management after an extensive program of cost reduction and business process reengineering. The knowledge management program was launched in 1994. Cindy Johnson, director of Collaboration and Knowledge Sharing noted: "We felt we needed to find a new paradigm for reaching the next level of improvement. We had to find ways to become more agile and learn faster so that we can innovate faster than our competitors. This is not about cutting people or bringing in new machines. It is about facilitating the flow of ideas, practices and knowledge" (O'Dell and Jackson, 1998, pp. 152–153). The emphasis was on sharing best practices. Chairman Jerry Junkins observed: "We had pockets of mediocrity right next door to world-class performance simply because one operation did not know what was happening at the other operation." The TI Business Excellent Strategy (known as I-BEST) provided a common methodology and common language for defining excellence, assessing progress, identifying opportunities for improvement, and establishing and deploying action. The first major initiative was transferring best practices around TI's 134 fabrication plants. In 1994 TI created an Office of Best Practices to facilitate best practice identification and transfer. At the heart of the system was a Best Practices Knowledge Base based on Lotus Notes.
- Hewlett Packard's position as one of the oldest and most adaptable of the leading companies in California's Silicon Valley owes much to the company's ability to acquire, reconfigure, and redeploy knowledge—even though these processes were established in HP well before the term "knowledge management" had achieved common currency. Like most companies, many of HP's knowledge management activities have focused on the management of explicit knowledge and have been heavily IT based. In addition, HP has been especially concerned with the management of tacit knowledge. As chairman and CEO Lew Platt observes: "Successful companies of the companies of the 21st century will be those who do the best jobs of capturing, storing, and leveraging what their employees know." HP's "Knowledge Links" system shares knowledge about product generation and at HP Consulting, knowledge sharing has extended beyond GroupWare and knowledge mapping to include informal groupings with common interests called "learning communities" and "project snapshots" that collect and lessons from project teams (Martiny, 1998).
- Looking further beyond the use of IT to store and transfer explicit knowledge to the more complex challenges of developing and deploying tacit knowledge, 3M has done more than any other company to create organizational systems that promote the transfer of tacit knowledge and its integration into new products. 3M aims to create "an atmosphere of generosity, freedom, and safety in which innovation can flourish" (Brand, 1998). Lifetime employment and internal mobility develop communication and knowledge sharing. Tolerance for mistakes is central to creativ-

ity: 3M began with a mistake (the acquisition of a worthless mine) and has continued to develop success out of failure (Post-it Notes used a new adhesive that did not stick; the ceramics business was also founded on a series of mistakes). Central to 3M's knowledge management is the combination of "knowledge by design" (defining customer needs that could use 3M technology) with "knowledge by emergence" (the informal process through which all employees are permitted to devote 15 percent of their time to developing new ideas).

Not-for-profit organizations have also been among the leading innovators in the development of knowledge management concepts and techniques. In particular, the U.S. Army has enhanced experiential learning through a systematized approach to identifying the lessons learned from both actual experience and experiments, then feeding back these lessons into procedures and policies. The Center for Army Lessons Learned at Fort Leavenworth, Kansas, collects the lessons learned from a wide variety of activities, codifies them, and distributes them. "The analysts quickly learned that the more hectic the operation, the more important is an organized system of collecting lessons learned. . . . The remaining challenge is to ensure that lessons are applied. . . . After the 1994 invasion of Haiti, CALL had experts interview soldiers about incidents with mobs and confrontations with local authorities, observe after-action reviews, read intelligence reports, and compile lessons. They developed 26 training scenarios for use by replacement units. In the next six months, these units actually encountered 23 of these scenarios" (*Wall Street Journal*, 1997b).[2] The 1995 Bosnian operation involved even more intensive efforts to distill experience gained and disseminate it quickly— every 72 hours a list of new lessons was distributed.

Key Areas of Knowledge Management

A fundamental distinction in knowledge management is between those activities that involve the application of existing knowledge and those that generate knowledge that is new to the organization. Most management principles deal with the organization of existing knowledge. According to Spender (1992), the two types of activity are distinguished by the fact that knowledge application is formalized, while knowledge generation is institutionalized: its structure is not dependent on the knowledge necessary for the task at hand— that knowledge has to be generated—but on some other social patterning such as professional affiliation or membership in a creative team. If knowledge-generating activities are to be successful in resolving uncertainty, then some form of alternative non-knowledge-based structure is essential. An implication, therefore, is that knowledge application and knowledge generating activities need to be organized differently within the firm. For example, in 3M there is a formal structure for managing 3M's existing businesses with their more than 30,000 separate products. At the same time there is a parallel, informal structure whereby the members of the formal structure engage in product development activities through an institutionalized system of "bootlegging" through which they appropriate time, materials, and technical support. Starting from the distinctions between knowledge generation and knowledge application activities, Figure 2.2 offers a classification of different knowledge management activities.

To date (Summer 1999), most organizations' knowledge management efforts have remained at a fairly basic level. The primary area of activity has been in the capture, storage, and transfer of knowledge. At the most basic level, organizations have attempted to identify the knowledge that resides within them in order to make it accessible by others in the organization. An interesting feature of management is that, despite recognition of knowledge as firms' most productive asset, formal systems of asset management have focused on the tangible assets identified and valued within firms' financial accounting systems. Until recently, very few organizations had any formal system for establishing an inventory of knowledge. Knowledge identification and transfer occurred informally—"If you want to know about warehousing bought-in widgets, speak to Joe. He worked for Widgets International before he came here." IBM's Guide to Market Information provides a mapping of information resources only. More ambitious is Teltech's "KnowledgeScope" system, which combines a thesaurus of technical terms with biographies of employee expertise, thus allowing both customers and employees to identify expertise relevant to their queries (Davenport, 1997, pp. 172–173). At Hughes Communications, Adrian Ward developed a "Knowledge Highway" using organizational ethnography and archaeology to discover and document the company's tacit and explicit knowledge, competencies, and communities and relationships (Ward, 1999).

Continuing with the contrast between the management of knowledge assets and the management of tangible assets, a feature of accounting systems for tangible assets is an overriding concern with valuation. By contrast, progress in measuring, let alone valuing, knowledge assets has been limited. The principles for valuing assets are well known: if there is an external market for the asset, use the market price (based on comparables where necessary); if there is not an external market, then estimate the net present value of the future returns to the asset. In the case of knowledge, neither approach is typically viable: market failure in knowledge transactions is widespread, the returns to knowledge are not readily identifiable, and most knowledge is embodied within people, systems, or products. Although progress has been made in the valuation of many intangible assets—brands in particular—the valuation of knowledge assets remains elusive. The approach adopted by Skandia and several other companies has been to value knowledge as the residual of the stock market valuation of a firm over and above the book value

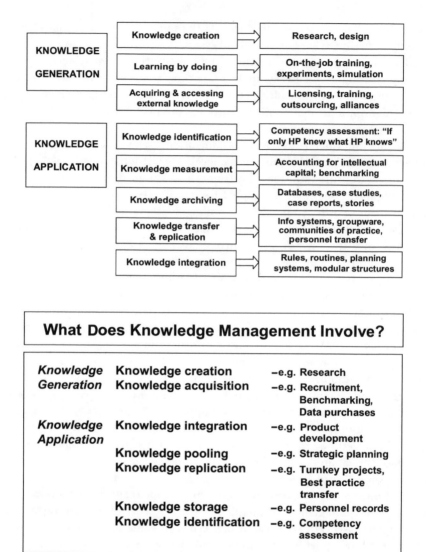

Figure 2.2 *The Dimensions of Knowledge Management*

of tangible assets. Although such an approach can indicate the magnitude of intangible asset valuation, it does not permit the valuation of individual knowledge assets and is distorted by all the errors involved in the variations of tangible assets. The difficulties in applying the common measuring rod of monetary valuation to knowledge assets has resulted in the use of a variety of indicators of knowledge stocks and investments in knowledge. Thus,

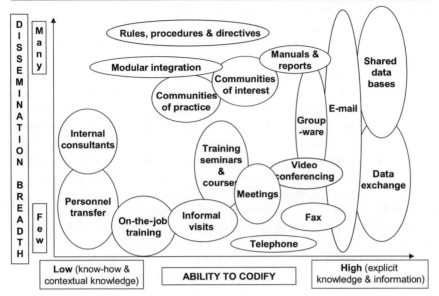

Conclusion: Designing a Knowledge Management System

- What are the knowledge processes that are critical to creating value and competitive advantage? (E.g., for Dow it is creating and exploiting patents; in semiconductors it is designing Ics with increased functionality and accelerating process innovation)

- What are the characteristics of the relevant knowledge?

- What mechanisms are needed for the generation and application of the relevant knowledge?

- What organizational conditions need to be in place in order for the knowledge management mechanisms to work?
    - Organizational structures
    - Incentives to contributors and users
    - Behavioral norms and values

Figure 2.2   *The Dimensions of Knowledge Management (continued)*

Skandia uses a variety of metrics for monitoring the development and utilization of its intellectual capital, ranging from days of training per employee per year to introductions of new products.

Looking beyond the mapping and measurement of existing knowledge is the capture and storage of new knowledge. The challenge is to build systems that collect the learning arising from projects and ongoing activities, to systematize and archive that knowledge, and then to distribute it to those members of the organization likely to benefit from it. The management consulting companies have been leaders in this area, and virtually all of them have created systems through which the learning from individual client assignments is standardized and stored within a central repository. The knowledge bases are typically accessed by consultants through intranets with specially designed search tools. March and Garvin (1997) describe the knowledge management databases constructed by Arthur Andersen and Ernst and Young.

Within the industrial and service sector more broadly, the major emphasis of knowledge management has been knowledge transfer and replication within corporations, particularly "best practice transfer." If learning and innovation are continuous processes that occur in all parts of a company, and if similar activities are being conducted in different locations within the company, then value can be created through the rapid internal diffusion of such knowledge. Among multinational enterprises in particular, it is increasingly recognized that one of the greatest benefits of multinationality is distributed learning. However, the major source of value creation from such learning occurs from the rapid replication of superior practices, products, and processes. Unilever's head of marketing has noted that across the thousands of products that Unilever markets in hundreds of countries, many similar problems and opportunities are encountered. The potential for transferring the knowledge gained in tackling these issues is huge. The intense interest in best practices transfer arises not simply because of the importance of such transfers in terms of performance enhancement, but also because of the difficulty of such transfers. These difficulties arise, first, from the nature of the knowledge— best practices often involve organizational routines that are dependent on the tacit knowledge of team members and complex patterns of interpersonal interaction—and second, from the impediments of organizational structures, systems, and behaviors. Gabriel Szulanski's (1996) analysis of "stickiness" in the transfer of best practices looks beyond the inherent complexity of the knowledge being transferred to explore the organizational conditions that hamper knowledge transfer, including the relationship between the parties to the knowledge exchange and the motivation of each party.

Although information and communication technology from e-mail to groupware, the Internet, and intranets have made huge strides in classifying, storing, and transferring explicit knowledge, it is in the management of tacit knowledge that the major challenges remain. It is widely believed that for the great majority of companies know-how rather than know-what is the more important productive resource and the primary basis for competitive advantage. But if knowledge cannot be codified, how can it be managed? Three considerations appear to be important in designing approaches to managing tacit knowledge.

1. *What is the degree of tacitness of different types of knowledge?* Some knowledge is so deeply embedded that it is completely nontransferable. Consider the skills of a fragrance expert. The ability to recognize and diagnose minute differences in fragrance requires olfactory skills that may well be genetically based. It is useless to train fragrance experts unless they have particular aptitudes to begin with. Effective management of fragrance analysis knowledge requires the intense use of the company's few experts, requiring their mobility around the company to wherever their skills are needed. Where skills are transferable, then training processes and communication mechanisms need to be designed to match the characteristics of the know-how being transferred. If knowledge acquisitions require learning by doing, then training seminars and courses are likely to be of limited value.

2. *What social context is conducive to the tacit knowledge transfer?* Brown and Duguid (1991) point to the roles of narration, collaboration, and social construction in learning, knowledge transfer, and the interpretation of experience. These occur within informal social groups they call "communities of practice." The importance of these observations is the recognition that experiential, uncodifiable knowledge can be transferred, integrated, and enriched within the appropriate social context. With narratives as the principal medium of communication, tacit knowledge is transferable where there exists a common language, common interests, and a common knowledge basis. The implication of this work has been intense interest in the existence of such communities of practice within organizations and efforts at managing and creating such groups as instruments of knowledge management.

3. *Even if tacit knowledge cannot be readily transferred, can it be integrated?* The key challenge of the enterprise is in achieving coordination between multiple specialists such that their different knowledge bases can be integrated to produce goods and services. Such integration does not necessarily require knowledge transfer. Knowledge transfer is critical for the purposes of replication, but for the purposes of production the key is to efficiently integrate different specialist knowledge. A critical issue in the design of processes is to integrate the specialist knowledge of different individuals without the costs of their having to learn from each other. The trend toward modularity in product design is one approach to efficient knowledge integration (Sanchez and Mahoney, 1996; Bayliss and Clark, 1997). Thus, the key to Microsoft's success in designing huge software programs such as Windows NT, Internet Explorer, and Microsoft Office that require the coordinated efforts of close to 500 software developers is to modularize these programs using its "synch and stabilize" system (Cusumano, 1997).

CONCLUSIONS

Three main conclusions arise from this chapter. First, the current surge of interest in knowledge management is not, primarily, a product of some "knowledge revolution." Although there are features of knowledge usage that are different today as compared with 30 years ago, digitization in particular, the scope of knowledge management is much broader. The importance of the current enthusiasm for knowledge management is that (a) it directs attention toward the most important and productive of the resources deployed by companies, and one that is the most inefficiently utilized, (b) by explicitly considering the role of knowledge within the enterprise, we are being forced to reconsider the most fundamental principles of management.

Second, in any fashion trend that is as pervasive and encompassing as knowledge management, there are likely to be elements that are worthwhile and enduring and others that will prove to be blind alleys. Which aspects of knowledge management are likely to offer the greatest potential for insight and value generation? An interesting feature of management activities in the corporate sector has been its emphasis on fundamental, even simplistic aspects of knowledge management. Can we identify and draw up an inventory of the knowledge within the organization? How can we distill and archive the new knowledge that is being generated within a company? How can knowledge be transferred from one part of an organization to another? Although these are basic issues of knowledge management, their solutions are not necessarily easy. The remarkable fact is that only recently have most companies addressed these issues on a systematic basis. Looking ahead, firms will need to look at the more complex aspects of knowledge management, especially with regard to the transfer and utilization of tacit knowledge and the redesign of organizational structures and processes in order to facilitate knowledge generation and utilization.

Which aspects of knowledge management are likely to prove of limited potential? The enthusiasm for knowledge accounting—the valuation of intellectual capital for example—seems to offer a low ratio of output to input. Given close to 3,000 years of philosophical debate as to what knowledge is, the ability to value what we do not yet understand seems unlikely. Ambiguity over the ownership of knowledge further compounds the problem of valuation. With the exceptions of knowledge forms for which property rights have been legislated—patents, copyrights, and trade secrets—ownership both of explicit and tacit knowledge is ill defined. A second area of dubious activity relates to organizational learning. Clearly, the ability to acquire knowledge from experience is critical to building a knowledge base. However, interest in organizational learning has tended to the obsessive in some quarters. The critical questions are what to learn and by whom? Learning is an investment, it is costly, and these costs need to be justified by potential further returns. Much learning may offer little return, or even negative returns. Consider the enthusiasm for cross-functional learning. Clearly, the ability to integrate the knowledge of different functional experts is critical to successful new product development. But the key to such knowledge integration is to retain the benefits of specialization in knowledge integration. If engineers, financial analysts, and marketing experts spend their time learning one another's specialties, the danger is that they will become mediocre engineers, financiers, and marketers.

Finally, how are managers to steer their way through the plethora of concepts, tools, and techniques of knowledge management to ensure that they select wisely without being overwhelmed by the onslaught of new practices and terminology? Two considerations are paramount. First, what are the characteristics of the knowledge being managed? The distinction between tacit and explicit knowledge is fundamental to virtually every aspect of knowledge management. If knowledge is explicit, its identification, storage, and transfer involve few problems—these can all be handled by the organization's information systems. The issues surrounding the management of tacit knowledge are entirely different, and the creation of value from such knowledge may require fundamentally new approaches to organizational structures and management systems. Knowledge also differs according to its importance. Which types of knowledge are critical to a firm's performance and competitive advantage? Despite the widespread interest in organizational capabilities and competency modeling, most firms have a poor understanding of which types of knowledge are critical to their future success. Second, what are the purposes and characteristics of the knowledge management processes? There has been a profusion of glib talk about the need to learn, to transfer knowledge, to absorb knowledge from competitors and partners, and the like. The danger is that we use knowledge management processes that are not suited to the task at hand. Consider the example of managing relationships with strategic alliance partners. The type of knowledge management that is appropriate depends on the knowledge goals of the alliance. Is it a "learning alliance" in which the firm is attempting to acquire the partner's knowledge? Or is it a "knowledge accessing alliance" in which the goal is to access the partner's knowledge base to maintain one's focus on core competencies? As with the internal transfer of knowledge, is the goal to replicate in another location the knowledge that is in one location, or is it simply to gain wider utilization of the knowledge that exists within a single location?

NOTES

1. *Wall Street Journal*, 1997a, "Saatchi's manager of knowledge keeps track of what's trendy," February 28, p. B16.
2. *Wall Street Journal*, 1997b, "Army devises system to decide what does and does not work," May 23, pp. A1, A10.

CHAPTER 3

A Thematic Analysis of the Thinking in Knowledge Management

Charles Despres and Daniele Chauvel

INTRODUCTION   The idea has certainly come of age: coura-
geous are those who would argue with the
idea that knowledge management (KM) is
one of the most ramified topics in the busi-
ness lexicon. Much of this amplitude can be attributed to the number of fields
that lay claim to the idea, or some part of it, including computer and information science, business strategy, macroeconomics, and interpersonal
dynamics to mention only a few. KM's proponents generally claim that this
symphony of schemes is appropriate given the important, transversal, and
imminently practicable nature of knowledge management. Its critics, on the
other hand, are hearing either a remix of older refrains, schizoid melodies, or
an outright cacophony.

All parties agree that we are nonetheless witnessing an explosion of interest in the term "knowledge management" and all that it may or may not imply. As an indicator of this we have reported elsewhere (Despres and Chauvel,
1999) that the number of new knowledge management articles registered in
the ABI/INFORM database has more than doubled each year over the past decade[1] (Figure 3.1).

Some consider this body of literature to be the latest hype in the progression from MBO to OD to TQM to BPR. Others view it as the harbinger of a
new age in management and economics. Whichever side of this divide the
reader prefers, we find that knowledge management is on the slippery slope

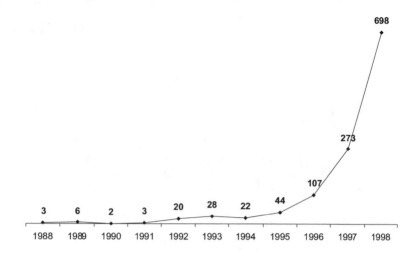

Figure 3.1 *Keyword "Knowledge Management" in the ABI/INFORM Database, 1988–1998*

of becoming intuitively important but intellectually elusive. Important because, "With rare exceptions, the productivity of a modern corporation or nation lies more in its intellectual and systems capabilities than in its hard assets. . ." (Quinn, Anderson, and Finkelstein, 1996). Elusive because, "To define knowledge in a non-abstract and non-sweeping way seems to be very difficult. Knowledge easily becomes everything and nothing" (Alvesson, 1993).

Knowledge management is clearly rife with this *everything and nothing* dilemma. It is variously at the center of global economic transformation (Bell, 1973; 1978), organizational success (De Gues, 1988), new forms of work (Blackler, Reed, and Whitaker, 1993), the forthcoming paradigm shift from infowar to knowledge warfare (KWarfare) (Baumard, 1996), and the eventual demise of private enterprise capitalism (Heilbruner, 1976). Competitive advantage is located in *learning organizations* (Mayo and Lank, 1994), *brain-based organizations* (Harari, 1994), *intellectual capital* (Stewart, 1994), and the *economics of ideas* (Wiig, 1997). Knowledge has achieved this centrality in conjunction with sweeping changes in organizational forms[2] and the dawning of the postindustrial and information revolutions (Postman, 1993).

Our general conclusion is that proponents and critics alike find it difficult to weave these trajectories into some coherent whole. Lacking, we believe, are the organizing themes that lay the sense-making ground, which permit other fields of endeavor to function with relative cohesion. In this chapter we will attempt the following:

1. Fix the current state of diversity in knowledge management as a normal development in the sociology of a body of knowledge

2. Outline the current dimensions of thought around which the field appears to be organizing itself
3. Extract the major thematic elements

AMBIGUITY

Emerging phenomena are fuzzy phenomena, and particularly so when their importance is fundamental, or evokes something fundamental. This is the case with knowledge management; despite its intuitive importance there is neither agreement nor clarity on what, exactly, constitutes the concerted effort to capture, organize, share, transform and reinvent the knowledge that is considered important to a corporation. The literature is similarly unclear on the socioeconomic drivers involved, the historical antecedents and—especially—the future implications. Instead, there exists a patchwork of subdomains in and around knowledge management that deal with one set of issues while ignoring others.

One basic part of the problem stems from the definition of knowledge itself. But more telling is that rather than offering a stable set of principles and models to anchor thinking in this domain, knowledge management provides a substantial variety. The resulting fluster is remarkably similar to organizational culture's struggle with conceptual clarity during the 1980s—which has been likened to the allegory involving an elephant and the truth-seeking blind. It is possible to take a meta-analytic view, however, in order to discern the themes underlying the variety of principles and models. That is the purpose of this chapter, and the first step is to approach matters with the sociology of knowledge.

COMMUNITY

Sociologists are familiar with confusions of this type and in particular, those who have concerned themselves with the sociology of knowledge. A frequently cited figure in this regard is Thomas Kuhn, who argued that scientific knowledge is ". . . intrinsically the common property of a group or else nothing at all" (Kuhn, 1970, p. 201). Rorty (1979) and others have expanded this thesis to assert that all knowledge, not just scientific knowledge, is founded in the thinking that circulates in a community. The sociologists of science claim that in any discipline, what we normally call reality, knowledge, thought, facts, and so on are constructs generated by a community of like-minded peers. These constructs become, in turn, symbolic devices that define or constitute the communities that generate them. The validity of what we know is community bound; the community is, in fact, its only source. As Barabas writes, ". . . there is no universal foundation for knowledge, only the agreement and consensus of the community" (1990, p. 61).

If one accepts this premise, the excited confusion that forms the hallmark of knowledge management is an expected outcome. The functional task becomes clear as well: the community must consciously crystallize the main elements of its discourse and assemble around an agreed set.

Defining the Community

It is from this base and for these reasons that we attempted to identify the main thematic elements in contemporary knowledge management discourse. The choice of literature in this type of work is critical and given the difficulties previously outlined, we constrained the field, which, obviously, is an exercise that defines the community. The literature domains, which we investigated for this review, include the emerging field of knowledge management itself, business management and strategy, information systems, managerial and organizational cognition, organization studies, economics, and library science. From this set we privileged works that addressed managerial, strategic, or organizational concerns and left aside those that focused on more technological issues.

A search of this literature was conducted within the ABI/INFORM database to locate models or classification schemes that have achieved a level of acceptance in the field. We utilized the descriptors and classification codes of ABI/INFORM and searched for the terms *knowledge management* or *intellectual capital* with *model*, or *taxonomy*, or *classification*, or *typology*. There were 1,179 articles that appeared with the keywords *knowledge management* or *intellectual capital* as of October 1999. These were crossed with *model*, or *taxonomy*, or *classification*, or *typology* to yield 74 titles of interest. A first review triage of these texts discarded those deemed irrelevant to our purposes, and the remainder were added to titles we had previously gathered in the Theseus *KMC²* database to form the bank of 72 books and articles that appear in Appendix 1. These 72 titles, spanning the period 1978 to 1999, were reviewed by both authors, and a subset was informally selected for discussion later in this chapter. The assumption is that this bank of 72 titles either substantially represents views in the community, or informs the thinking of members, or both.

We approached the second methodological step in a general rather than an exacting way. Thematic analysis is a rigorous ethnographic methodology that typically involves a painstaking examination of the words and meanings in a text (such as a transcript) and, less commonly, of action or objects observed in some social or organizational setting. Given the scope of the literature involved and the constraints of time, we opted to examine prevailing constructs rather than texts as they are represented by models and classification schemes of knowledge management. Our assumptions are as follows:

1. Thought and discourse are guided by the conceptual models that achieve acceptance in a community.

2. Conceptual models reported in different parts of the knowledge management community represent some part of the thinking in play.
3. A thematic analysis of these conceptual models will provide a good indication of the dimensions on which the knowledge management discourse is operating.

Models and Classification Systems

Given that science has become the portal of truth for the Occidental mind, it is perhaps appropriate that we fix the place of models and classification systems in the overall scheme of scientific inquiry. We begin with the truism that science aims at not only describing regularities in what we observe (empirical phenomena) but also at explaining those observations (prediction, control). The scientific mind assembles these phenomena to create concepts and constructs that fix their place in a larger scheme. Although concepts are the building blocks of science, they are also human creations that attempt to define and communicate the essence of perceptions and phenomena that are, a priori, undefined and nameless. Constructs complicate the matter by assembling sets of concepts at higher levels of abstraction in service of some theoretical purpose. We will refrain from entering into postmodern discussions of the wicked problems that beset such attempts at definition and order, and note only that they are weighty indeed.

Classification systems or taxonomies are networks of description that assemble concepts or constructs in some orderly way, with the intent of establishing relations among the phenomena of interest. Classification systems have definitional effect insofar as they establish meaning between the phenomena being classified. Models are more highly formalized representations of phenomena and their interactions and, in most cases, are established in order to predict or control the phenomena in question.

Models in the Community

The following is a selection of models and classification systems that appeared in the literatures defined in the preceding paragraphs. These are, in our opinion, representative but certainly not an exhaustive collection of such devices in what may be termed the domain of knowledge management. The following sections present a brief description of each model or classification system and constrain the discussion to its dimensional structure.

SECI (Nonaka)

Ikujurio Nonaka, a professor at the Japan Advanced Institute of Science and Technology and the University of California at Berkeley, articulated a model of "knowledge creation" in a series of articles and books dating from the early 1990s. The SECI (Socialization, Externalization, Combination, Internalization) model first appeared in 1991 and attained recognition as a useful and rigorous approach to describing the ways knowledge is generated, transferred and re-created in organizations. In brief, the model incorporates the following:

1. Two forms of knowledge (tacit and explicit)
2. An interaction dynamic (transfer)
3. Three levels of social aggregation (individual, group, context)
4. Four "knowledge-creating" processes (socialization, externalization, combination, and internalization).

The model proposes that a "knowledge-creating company" consciously facilitates the interplay of tacit and explicit forms of knowledge. This is accomplished through systems and structures, and a corporate culture that facilitate the interaction of four knowledge-creating processes, per the following:

- *Socialization*: the sharing of tacit knowledge between individuals through joint activities, physical proximity
- *Externalization*: the expression of tacit knowledge in publicly comprehensible forms
- *Combination*: the conversion of explicit knowledge into more complex sets of explicit knowledge: communication, dissemination, systematization of explicit knowledge
- *Internalization*: the conversion of externalized knowledge into tacit knowledge on an individual or organizational scale; the embodiment of explicit knowledge into actions, practices, processes, and strategic initiatives

Critical for Nonaka is the interaction dynamic between forms of knowledge and levels of organization. He proposes that the spiral resulting from the exchange of tacit and explicit knowledge across different organizational levels is the key to knowledge creation and re-creation. The prescription is that companies should recognize the importance of this interaction dynamic and imbed the mechanisms that make it possible. Schematically, the model appears in Figure 3.2.

In 1998 Nonaka & Konno introduced the concept of *Ba*, which relates to the English concept of place. A *Ba* in knowledge management is a space for dynamic knowledge conversion and emerging relationships. Four *Bas* are defined by Nonaka (Figure 3.3):

- *Originating Ba*: a space where individuals share feelings, emotions, experiences, and mental models.
- *Interacting Ba*: a space where tacit knowledge is made explicit. Two key factors are dialogue and metaphors.

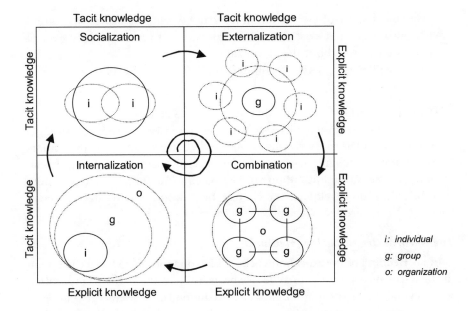

Figure 3.2 *The SECI Model (Adapted from Nonaka, 1998, pp. 40–54)*

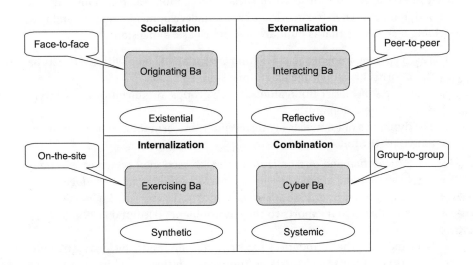

Figure 3.3 *Ba and the SECI Model (Adapted from Nonaka, 1998, pp. 40–54)*

- *Cyber Ba*: a space of interaction in a virtual world. Implicates the combination of new and existing explicit knowledge to generate new explicit knowledge throughout the organization.
- *Exercising Ba*: a space that facilitates the conversion of explicit knowledge into tacit knowledge.

Ba calls attention to the fact that knowledge is context dependent; it cannot be separated from its "place" in any meaningful way. Each knowledge-creating process therefore requires a *Ba*, a phenomenal space whose importance should be recognized by the organization. The organization, in fact, should focus significant attention on the development of its *Bas* because more is to be gained by developing the environment around knowledge processes than by efforts directed at the processes themselves.

The N-Form Organization (Hedlund)

Gunnar Hedlund of the Stockholm School of Economics introduced the notion of the N-Form corporation in 1994. He proposed that the N-Form corporation goes beyond the M-Form in that it better accommodates the emerging imperatives of knowledge-based organizational design, drawing its synthetic wisdom from the ". . . gray zone between economics, organization theory and strategic management" (Hedlund, 1994, p. 74). Hedlund suggests that a principal attribute of the model is its conjoint analysis of two sets of concepts: tacit/explicit knowledge, and four levels of social aggregation. He injects into these a set of dynamics related to knowledge creation, development, transfer, and use, yielding a structure that is built around three basic dimensions:

1. Two types of knowledge (tacit and articulated), and within each type three forms of knowledge (cognitive, skill, embodied)
2. Four levels of carrier (individuals, small groups, organizations, the inter-organizational domain)
3. The dynamics of knowledge transfer and transformation, which are articulated by the following processes:
   - *Articulation* and *internalization*, the interaction of which is *reflection*
   - *Extension* and *appropriation*, the interaction of which is *dialogue*
   - *Assimilation* and *dissemination*, which refer to ". . . knowledge imports from and exports to the environment" (Hedlund, 1994, p. 76)

Hedlund lays the foundation for his dynamic model by distinguishing between types, forms, and levels of knowledge. In brief, he juxtaposes tacit and articulated knowledge (attending closely to definitional issues) with different levels of social aggregation. This results in a classification scheme that assumes cognitive, skill-based, and embodied forms of knowledge exist in both tacit and articulated forms across the range of organizational levels (Figure 3.4).

	Individual	Group	Organization	Interorganizational Domain
Articulated Knowledge / Information Cognitive Skills Embodied	Knowing calculus	Quality circle's documented analysis of its performance	Organization chart	Suppliers' patents and documented practices
Tacit Knowledge / Information Cognitive Skills Embodied	Cross-cultural negotiations skills	Team coordination in complex work	Corporate culture	Customers' attitudes to products and expectations

Figure 3.4   *Types, Forms, and Levels of Knowledge (Adapted from Hedlund, 1994, pp. 73–90)*

On this foundation Hedlund then situates the dynamics of knowledge transfer and transformation. He writes that most existing works speak, ". . . primarily in terms of storage of information, and only secondarily about its transfer, whereas its transformation is left outside most analyses" (Hedlund, 1994, p. 76). Knowledge transfer, storage, and transformation are presented as a set of processes whose interactions, across the different types and levels of knowledge, privilege knowledge creation and, in turn, argue for the N-Form organizational design. The articulation of tacit knowledge, and the internalization of articulated knowledge, may occur at any level of carrier and the interaction, termed reflection, is held to be a primary source of knowledge creation (Figure 3.5).

The acquisition of tacit or articulated knowledge by lower agency levels, termed appropriation, and the dissemination of tacit or articulated knowledge to higher agency levels, termed extension, signal the movement of knowledge through different levels of carrier. Their interaction is termed dialogue, whose ". . . quantity and quality are hypothesized to be important determinants of the type and effectiveness of knowledge management in an organization" (Hedlund, 1994, p. 77).

These and related concepts are developed both theoretically and concretely, discussed in the context of Western and Japanese management systems, and then operationalized in the idea of an N-Form corporation, the outlines of which are summarized in six main themes as displayed in Table 3.1.

Knowing and Knowledge (Earl)

Michael Earl of the London Business School is known for the work he has conducted on the information systems function in organizations, the role of the CIO, and more recently, the role of the CKO. His more recent works pro-

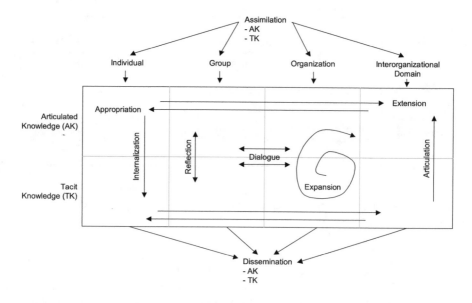

Figure 3.5   *Knowledge Types and Transformation Processes (Adapted from Hedlund, 1994, pp. 73–90)*

Table 3.1
Basic Characteristics of the N-form and M-form Corporations

	N-form	*M-form*
Technological interdependence	Combination	Division
People interdependence	Temporary constellations, given pool of people	Permanent structures, changing pool of people
Critical organizational level	Middle	Top
Communication network	Lateral	Vertical
Top management role	Catalyst, architect, protector	Monitor, allocator
Competitive scope	Focus, economics of depth, combinable parts	Diversification, economics of scale and scope, semi-independent parts
Basic organizational form	Heterarchy	Hierarchy

Reproduced from Hedlund, 1994, p. 83.

Table 3.2
A Classification of Data, Information, and Knowledge

	Data	*Information*	*Knowledge*
Content	Events	Trends	Expertise
Form	Transactions	Patterns	Learnings
Information task	Representation	Manipulation	Codification
Human element	Observation	Judgment	Experience
Organizational intent	Automation	Decision making	Action
Value test	Building block	Uncertainty reduction	New understanding

pose a set of heuristics that situate the CKO knowledge function within organizations and prescribe its activities.

One distinction he makes, often discussed by others, is that between data, information, and knowledge. Earl proposes the classification in Table 3.2 and writes, "Trite and imperfect as this classification is, it suggests that knowledge comprises expertise, experience, know-how, skills and competence. . . ." (Earl, 1998, p. 7).

Going further, he recognizes two organizational states that are relevant to knowledge management: knowledge and knowing. If these constructs are set at right angles, four states arise as displayed in Figure 3.6.

Earl proposes that an organization may usefully concern itself with the creation, protection, and leveraging of its knowledge assets by attending to four functions:

1. *Inventorising*: mapping individual and organizational knowledge
2. *Auditing*: assessing the nature and extent of planned ignorance and then developing knowledge through learning activities
3. *Socializing*: creating events that enable people to share tacit knowledge
4. *Experiencing*: addressing the problem of unknown ignorance by learning from experience and action, and by handling unusual situations

The OK Net and the OCS (Carayannis)

Elias Carayannis (George Washington University) has recently proposed a ". . . synergistic symbiosis between information technology and managerial and organizational cognition" (Carayannis, 1999, p. 219) the conjunction of which is knowledge management. IT is approached as a value-adding technological infrastructure, managerial/organizational cognition as the ". . . capability for individual and collective reasoning, learning, emoting and envisioning," and knowledge management as ". . . a sociotechnical system of tacit and

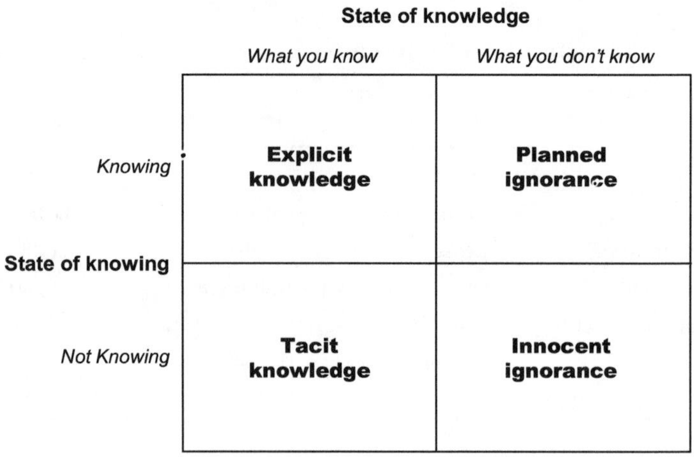

State of knowledge
What you know
What you don't know
Knowing
Explicit knowledge
Planned ignorance
State of knowing
Not Knowing
Tacit knowledge
Innocent ignorance

Figure 3.6 *Knowledge and Knowing (Adapted from Earl, 1998, p. 8)*

State of knowledge
What you know
What you don't know
Knowing
Explicit knowledge
Inventorizing
Planned ignorance
Auditing
State of knowing
Not Knowing
Tacit knowledge
Socializing
Innocent ignorance
Experiencing

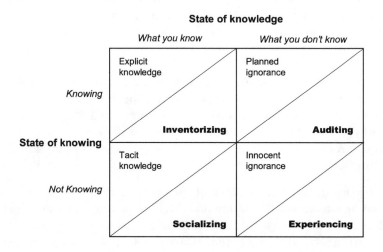

Figure 3.7 *Prescriptions for States of Knowledge and Knowing (Adapted from Earl, 1998, p. 9)*

explicit business policies and practices" (Carayannis, 1999, p. 219). In general terms, Carayannis attempts to define the systems and structures, both real and virtual, that would allow an organization to maximize the efficiency and effectiveness of its cognitive processes.

The crystallized form of this effort is termed the *Organizational Knowledge Network* or OK Net. Carayannis specifies a number of concepts to lay its foundation, including the key elements of metacognition, metalearning, and metaknowledge. A familiar theme in the organizational learning community, Carayannis states that the relationship between knowledge (K) and metaknowledge (MK) is critical in knowledge management. He defines a 2 × 2 matrix that ". . . consists of successive knowledge cycles where an individual or an organization can transition or traverse 4 stages of awareness and ignorance" (Carayannis, 1999, p. 224). Four possible states of organizational knowledge management obtain (Figure 3.8):

- Ignorance of ignorance (K̲, M̲K̲)
- Ignorance of awareness (K, M̲K̲)
- Awareness of ignorance (K̲, MK)
- Awareness of awareness (K, MK)

Organizations may thereby plot their situation(s) in one of these cells and a development effort is aimed at managing the transitions from one state to another. The ideal is awareness—of knowledge, of ignorance—and the willingness to move from the latter to the former. Transitions may be accomplished via two paths: connectivity or interactivity. Connectivity is enabled by information technology and held to be the efficiency-driven path. Interactivity denotes sociotechnical phenomena and emphasizes the tacit/explicit interplay in human interaction. Managed correctly, the movements from Cell I to Cell IV engender not only a spiral of increasing wisdom (metaknowledge), but also learning how to learn.

The organizational design implications resulting from this are outlined in the Organizational Knowledge Network: ". . . an organizational knowledge management network for the support, monitoring, capturing, measurement, and enrichment of organizational cognition in an eight-stage process" (Carayannis, 1999, p. 223). The OK Net begins with an assessment of the firm's in-

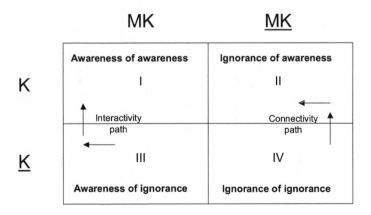

Figure 3.8 *Knowledge and Metaknowledge (Adapted from Carayannis, 1999, pp. 219–231)*

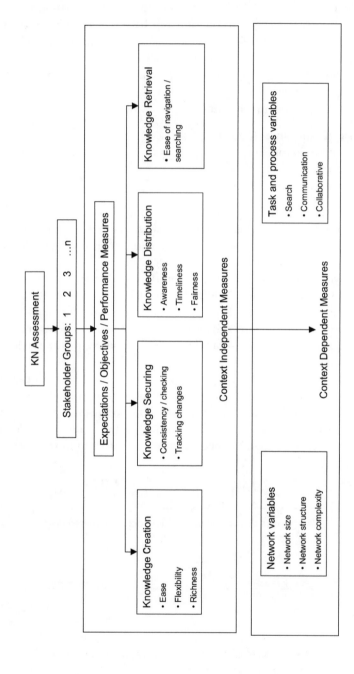

Figure 3.9 *The OK Net (Adapted from Carayannis, 1999, pp. 219–231)*

tellectual capital, accounts for the interests of key stakeholders, and then unfolds a rational system that details the creation, securing, distribution, and retrieval of knowledge together with relevant measures and technological prescriptions (Figure 3.9).

By "stakeholders" Carayannis implicates all the actors that typically participate in a firm's affairs including employees, teams, customers, suppliers, and complementary (but nonbranded) organizations. For each, the idea is to identify and capture knowledge that is deemed relevant, store it in various knowledge repositories and schemata, apply sociotechnical and IT methods to maximize its availability and use, and promote the development of meta-knowledge and learning.

Three Pillars of Knowledge Management (Wiig)

Karl Wiig is one of the pioneers in the field of knowledge management and was among the first to publish a series of texts that assembled management-relevant concepts focusing squarely on the topic. His overarching framework is based on three pillars and a foundation (Figure 3.10).

Wiig proposes that the foundation of knowledge management is comprised of the way knowledge is created, used in problem solving and decision

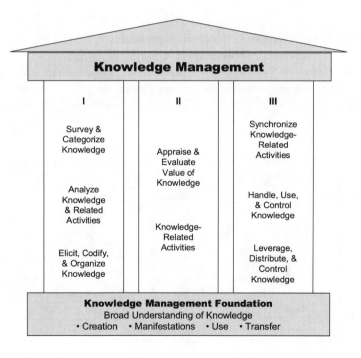

Figure 3.10   *Pillars and Functions of Knowledge Management (Adapted from Wiig, 1993, p. 20)*

making, and manifested cognitively as well as in culture, technology, and procedures. On this foundation he situates three pillars, which categorize the exploration of knowledge, its value assessment, and its active management. This framework summarizes the main areas on which a KM initiative should focus.

A Model of Intellectual Capital (Edvinsson)

Leif Edvinsson of Skandia achieved notoriety in the field of knowledge management after being named the first CKO in 1991. He publicized his work within Skandia and later developed his thinking in a series of publications. The focus of Edvinsson's interest is intellectual capital management and the valuation of knowledge assets. His core model is a scheme for organizing a firm's assets, which defines four major components of intellectual capital and their interactions for value creation (Figure 3.11):

1. *Human capital* relates to a firm's human resources, including the knowledge and know-how that can be converted to value. This is said to reside in people, organizational routines, and procedures. Intellectual assets include codified, tangible, or physical descriptions of specific knowledge to which the company can assert ownership rights and readily trade in disembodied form.
2. *Structural capital* relates to the firm's supporting infrastructure. This is defined as both physical infrastructure (building, computers, etc.) and intangible infrastructure (history, culture, management).
3. *Business assets* are defined as the structural capital a firm uses to create value in its commercialization process (processing facilities, distribution networks).

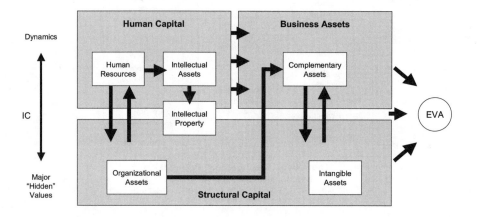

Figure 3.11 *A Model for Intellectual Capital Management (Adapted from Edvinsson, 1996, pp. 356–364)*

4. *Intellectual property* relates to the intellectual assets of the firm for which legal protection has been obtained.

The dynamic aspect of this model relates to the creation of value, for which Edvinsson proposes there are two fundamental sources. The first are those innovations that are generated by the firm's human resources into legally protected intellectual assets, and the second are the products and services that result from the commercialization of innovations.

The Ecology of Knowledge Management (Snowden)

David Snowden, who directs IBM's Institute for Knowledge Management, EMEA, has developed an approach to implementing knowledge management programs in a series of articles that rest, in general terms, on a foundation of cognitive science, semiotics, and epistemological pragmatics. In these works, Snowden elaborates an action-oriented knowledge system that embraces four major elements:

1. Explicit/tacit knowledge
2. Knowledge assets
3. Trust
4. The certainty/uncertainty of decisions relative to (a) objectives and (b) causal relations

These are developed, together with their interactions, in a system of thought that is focused on action: the value of knowledge, he writes, ". . . comes from its exercise, not from its existence per se" (Snowden, 1999, p. 4). This is woven together into a fabric that recognizes trust as a fundamental arbiter of knowledge dynamics, humans as the vessels of tacit knowledge, and external systems and structures as the holders of explicated knowledge. The approach to knowledge in organizational contexts is from a decision-making perspective, particularly with regard to the level of certainty pertaining to means, ends, and causal relations. From this and other elements the model in Figure 3.12 is developed.

Snowden argues that the first step is to map the stock of tacit and explicit knowledge in an organizational unit. Explicit knowledge thus identified and considered valuable is channeled into artifact-creating systems and structures (e.g., a knowledge base). Tacit knowledge assets pose the conundrum of being more valuable but also more problematic, leading to the explication of tacit assets that can be readily articulated, and the creation of competence management systems for those that cannot.

A decision matrix provides a starting point for the judgment as to whether tacit knowledge assets should be explicated. This contrasts the ". . . uncertainty of objective . . . with uncertainty of cause and effect. It provides four environments, each of which requires a different balance of tacit and explicit knowledge" (Snowden, 1999, p. 4).

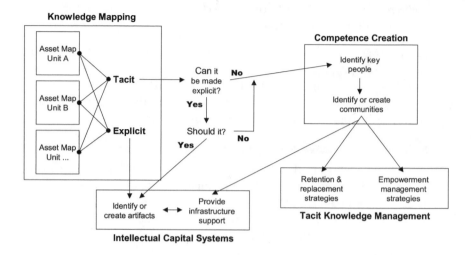

Figure 3.12 *A Decision-Making Approach to Managing Knowledge (Adapted from Snowden, 1998, pp. 1–9)*

This decision matrix and the model described in Figure 3.13 suggest that organizations will manage four types of transitional activities:

1. Sharing explicit knowledge through systems and structures
2. Sharing tacit knowledge through psychosocial mechanisms
3. Transforming tacit to explicit knowledge through BPR, documentation and related
4. Releasing tacit knowledge through trust and its dynamics

The balanced and adapted management of explicit and tacit knowledge is said to lead to knowledge management ecology within a firm.

Knowledge Management Processes (Inkpen and Dinur)

Andrew Inkpen and Adva Dinur, of Thunderbird and Temple University respectively, introduced an empirical model of knowledge management designed to explicate learning and knowledge transfer between partners in strategic alliances. They begin with the idea that ". . . the firm is a dynamic system of processes involving different types of knowledge" (Inkpen and Dinur, 1998, p. 454) and go on to explore how firms acquire and manage new knowledge, particularly with respect to alliance arrangements.

The model they propose distinguishes between tacit and explicit knowledge and holds that a key challenge is the conversion of tacit individual knowledge to explicit organizational competence. They state that, ". . . organizational knowledge creation should be viewed as a process whereby the

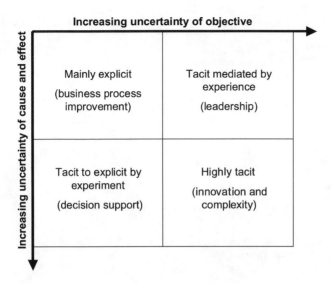

Figure 3.13 *Managing Tacit Knowledge Assets (Adapted from Snowden, 1998, pp. 1–9)*

knowledge held by individuals is amplified and internalized as part of an organization's knowledge base" (Inkpen and Dinur, 1998, p. 456). Knowledge conversion, creation, and learning occur in a multilevel context that invokes different processes depending on the level in play. At the individual level, interpretation and sense making are key; at the group level, integration; and at the organizational level, integration and institutionalization.

Organizations therefore have "a range of types of knowledge and carriers of knowledge" (Inkpen and Dinur, 1998, p. 457) and the issue becomes understanding the importance of different types of knowledge specific to an organizational situation, and how organizations transform and manage this knowledge. They propose Figure 3.14 as a basic representation. The vertical dimension of this model—tacitness—is a continuum that carries the assumption that the more tacit the knowledge, the more difficult it is to codify and transfer. The horizontal dimension straightforwardly distinguishes the different organizational levels at which knowledge may reside.

This base model is joined by the notion of mechanisms and processes, either formal or informal, which are invoked to encourage or accomplish knowledge transfer. Forty-two partner joint ventures in the automotive industry formed the empirical context in which Inkpen and Dinur applied this model to investigate knowledge creation and transfer. Their results, which are significantly abridged for present purposes, outline the various ways in which different types of knowledge may be transferred and integrated across the organizational levels of a partner participating in an alliance (Figure 3.15).

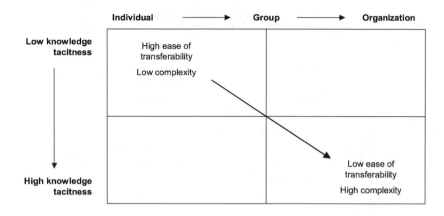

Figure 3.14 *Type and Transferability of Knowledge (Adapted from Inkpen and Dinur, 1998, pp. 454–468)*

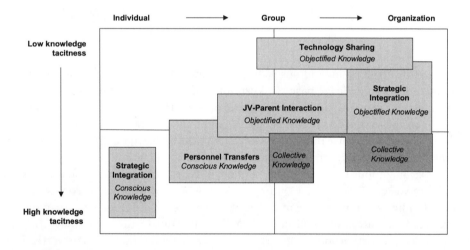

Figure 3.15 *Methods for Transferring Knowledge (Adapted from Inkpen and Dinur, 1998, pp. 454–468)*

Intellectual Capital Management (Van Buren)

Van Buren, a senior associate with the Research & Enterprise Solutions unit of the American Society for Training and Development (ASTD), has reported a model developed by the ASTD Effective Knowledge Management Working Group, a virtual organization composed of knowledge management practitioners in various industries. This group has created an intellectual capital management model, the goal of which—much akin to a benchmarking exercise—is a standard set of measures that can be used to assess knowledge man-

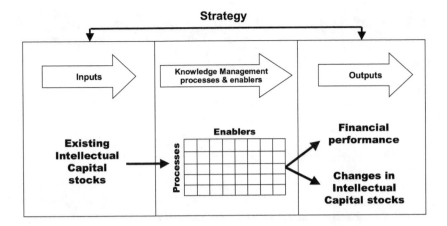

Figure 3.16 *A Model of Intellectual Capital Management (Adapted from Van Buren, 1999, pp. 71–78)*

agement activities across different companies. The model includes two sets of measures:

1. Those pertaining to intellectual capital stocks, including (a) human capital, (b) innovation capital, (c) process capital, and (d) customer capital
2. Those pertaining to financial performance and business effectiveness

The starting point resides in the firm's stock of intellectual capital, the identification of which serves as input for knowledge management processes and enablers (Figure 3.16). Despite their lack of visibility, these are held to constitute "the critical leverage points for enhancing the firm's knowledge management capability" (Van Buren, 1999, p. 76). The critical knowledge management processes, which are imbedded in the firm's activities and initiatives, are held to be the (a) definition, (b) creation, (c) capture, (d) sharing, and (e) use of knowledge. The enablers are, in brief, those corporate functions/systems/structures that define, leverage, and structure the firm's activity: leadership, corporate culture, communication, technology processes, human resources policy, and so on. These two dimensions are plotted in a matrix, which allows a firm to chart specific knowledge management activities (Figure 3.17). This therefore highlights the interaction of processes and enablers, all of which is placed in the context of a firm's business strategy: knowledge management efforts should be driven by strategic intent rather than the reverse.

Outputs are made as concrete as possible through measures associated with financial performance and changes in the stock of intellectual capital. Van Buren suggests a range of financial performance measures including market-to-book value, return on equity, revenue per employee, and value added per employee. He suggests a total of 50 intellectual capital measures

	Leadership	Structure	Culture	IT	Rewards	Measurement	Skills / Abilities	Management
Define								
Create								
Capture								
Share								
Use								

Figure 3.17   *Functions and Activities for Managing Knowledge (Adapted from Van Buren, 1999, pp. 71–78)*

distributed across four categories—human capital, innovation capital, process capital, and customer capital—and including such items as educational levels, time in training, the number of copyrights and trademarks, average age of patents, IT accesses per employee, and annual sales per customer.

A Taxonomy of Knowledge Management (Despres and Chauvel)

The authors of this chapter launched its precursor as a research program that aimed to systematically review the various literatures associated with applied knowledge management and construct from these a classification that accounted for activities in the field. This review led us to conclude that the field is dominated by "islands of discourse" that are in various states of agreement. Based on this, we suggested that four dimensions cut across many of the discussions:

1. *Time*: referring to a linear and simplified representation of cognitive processes, including the (a) mapping, (b) acquisition, (c) codification, (d) storage, (e) application, and (f) transformation of knowledge or its elements
2. *Type*: referring to tacit and explicit knowledge
3. *Level*: referring to different levels of social aggregation
4. *Context*: referring to sense making, in that no knowledge element has any meaning outside of a given context

We assembled these in a classification system that purports to situate actions in the field. In structural form it appears in Figure 3.18. This device allows one to situate both the knowledge management practices commonly employed by companies, and the products and services offered by vendors. After reviewing anecdotal and case evidence from this ensemble, we concluded that seven major clusters of activity are currently active in knowledge management (Figure 3.19).

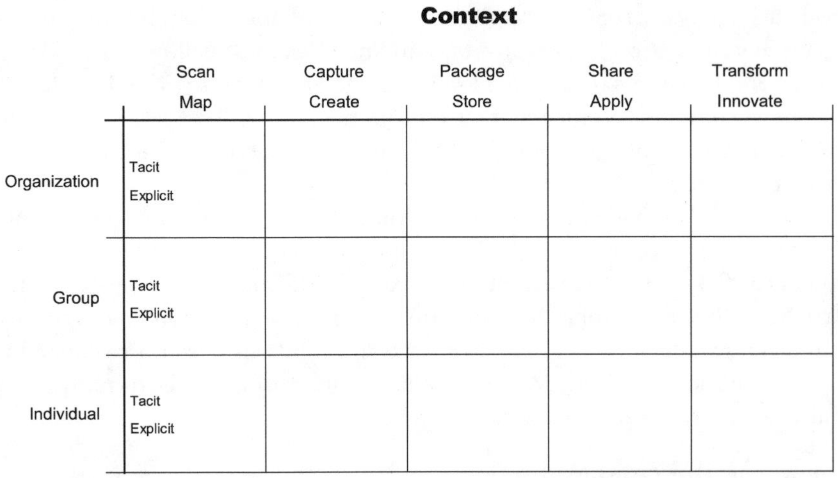

Context
Scan
Map
Capture
Create
Package
Store
Share
Apply
Transform
Innovate
Organization
Tacit
Explicit
Group
Tacit
Explicit
Individual
Tacit
Explicit

Figure 3.18 *Taxonomy of Applied Knowledge Management (Adapted from Despres and Chauvel)*

Context
Scan
Map
Capture
Create
Package
Store
Share
Apply
Transform
Innovate
Organization
Tacit
Explicit
Business
Intelligence
DataWarehousing
Innovation
Communities
of Practice
Benchmarking
Groupware
Virtual teaming
Synergies
Group
Tacit
Explicit
Creativity
Individual
Tacit
Explicit
Learning, Competencies,
Employee Development

Figure 3.19 *Regions of Practice in Knowledge Management (Adapted from Despres and Chauvel)*

Our claim is that the majority of behaviors and practices associated with knowledge management can be located in this classification, which we liken to a map that permits the plotting and tracking of KM initiatives. We draw the practical implication that managers working in the field should realize that knowledge management is more than groupware or an intranet (Group

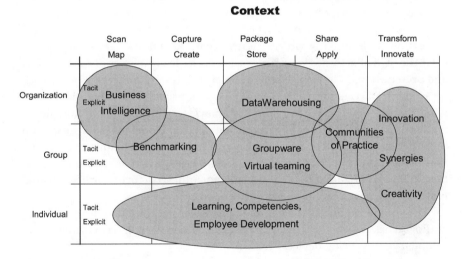

level Package-Store & Share-Apply in the *KM Map*), more than business intelligence (Organization level Scan-Map) and more than a "yellow pages" database of employee CVs (Individual level Package-Store). This research indicates that most companies implement such projects on a small, experimental scale and then expand into other areas of the "map," which is itself a chart of the feasible options.

We have also made the point that although knowledge management has always been rooted in the individual and his or her behavior, the formalization of the field has shifted attention upwards in the map toward systems and structures that encourage the generation, transfer, application, and reinvention of knowledge in a company. Much of this shift has been occasioned by the information technologies that facilitate one-to-one, one-to-many, and many-to-many communication.

Themes in the Community

Assuming that the models and classification schemes in this review are a representative set, an analysis should reveal the major streams of thought in knowledge management. What, then, do they reveal?

The first finding is perhaps obvious: each of these devices is marked by two fundamental aspects, one structural and the other prescriptive. Each author structures thought with a set of concepts that constrains and directs the perception and thinking process with regard to knowledge management. Once the field of action is structured, each device leads to a set of explanations and prescriptions. The first aspect is structural, the second prescriptive. Earl, for example, directs one to see that people and organizations may not know what they do not know. The aspects of *knowledge* and *knowing* in knowledge management are his primary structuring devices. Nonaka's basic model, on the other hand, directs one to see other realities and in particular, the interaction of tacit and explicit knowledge. *Socialization, externalization, combination,* and *internalization* become the fundamental structuring devices around which Nonaka weaves the rest of his thinking.

The second finding is the commonality of basic concepts with which the authors work. We divide these into two sets, which we will term primary and secondary structuring devices (Table 3.3).

Primary structuring devices are held in common across all the models and classification systems reviewed for this chapter. They relate to fundamental issues and enjoy a high degree of commonality—frequent use and relatively stable definitional agreement. Secondary devices are those that authors employ frequently but dissimilarly. There is less definitional clarity in the way these devices are used, although the concepts being communicated are similar. Taken together, these seven devices appear to synthesize the thinking in the field of knowledge management. Only one author, Hedlund, includes all in his work while others focus on some subset. We discuss the varieties of meaning associated with each device in the following sections.

Table 3.3
Themes in the Community

Primary structuring devices	Time	
	Types, Forms, Embodiments	
	Social Space	
Secondary structuring devices	Context	
	Transformations and Dynamics	
	Carriers and Media	
	Knowledge Culture	

Greater commonality ↑

Time

An epistemological fundamental in Western science, it comes as no surprise that all of the authors in our review explicitly or implicitly employ time in some part of their work. It is explicitly present in Despres and Chauvel, Nonaka, Carayannis, and Van Buren, for example, where a longitudinal view of the cognitive process is used to organize matters. It is less explicitly cited in Hedlund, Snowden, and Inkpen and Dinur but still clearly implicated. Given that it is difficult to conceive of the thinking process in a frozen, static state, it appears that the implication of time in knowledge management is a primary requirement. This argues against conceptions of knowledge as a store in organizations and instead points to the importance of knowledge processes.

Types, Forms, Embodiments

All of the authors in our review make reference to a classification of knowledge of some sort. The tacit/explicit distinction popularized by Polanyi (1966) is so often employed it may achieve the status of a banality in the near future. Other typologies of knowledge include the metaknowledge (knowledge of knowledge, awareness, consciousness) found in Earl and Carayannis, the different embodiments of knowledge (products, routines, processes) found in Hedlund and Snowden, and the more commercial approach of intellectual capital which views knowledge as stocks and assets (Van Buren, Edvinsson). Like the factor of time, the attempt to type knowledge is no stranger to epistemological musings. Frank Blackler, for example, has outlined five different types: embrained (conceptual skills abilities), embodied (acquired by doing), encultured (acquired through socialization), embedded (organizational routines), and encoded knowledge (signs and symbols). And even cursory research in the history of science will reveal that the discussion goes far beyond: there is, in fact, little agreement on a universal classification of the types of knowledge but wide consensus that they are multiple and consequential.

Social Space

Once classified and fixed in time, all of the authors locate knowledge phenomena somewhere in social space, albeit with different levels of specificity. The most common approach is that involving the levels of social aggregation usually employed in organization studies: individuals, groups, and organizations. Carayannis and Hedlund go a step beyond to explicitly include the stakeholders outside a company's boundaries (industry and interorganizational context), the importance of which has clearly been demonstrated by institutional theory and others. In the discussions that ensue most authors also recognize that the cornerstone of knowledge management is the individual, and that organization-level knowledge is a fiction. But having given individuals their due, most also recognize that knowledge is an inherently social construct, for how could anyone recognize a phenomenon inaccessibly locked in the confines of some brain as knowledge? This branches to a larger discussion on knowledge as action (activity theory), which we will leave aside to make the simpler observation that all authors define some unit of social space.

Context

Context is another fundamental if one accepts the proposition that nothing has any meaning outside of a context. As a way of introducing a broader view of the idea, we cite Pierre Teilhard de Chardin who, at the beginning of this century, conceptualized a web of determinate human knowledge he termed the *nöosphere* and announced that it enveloped human consciousness on Earth. He believed this knowledge web gave substance to physical and social phenomena and that without it, we were senseless as to the phenomena of gravity, rainfall, or the displacements of matter that constitute architecture. Business is to knowledge management as the *nöosphere* was to de Chadrin's concept of life on this planet. All authors recognize that a business context anchors their knowledge management devices, but they do so differently, varying from the firm's strategy, to human interaction, group dynamics, and technological infrastructure. While some clearly set the boundaries of a context (Edvinsson's approach to the rents generated by thinking and knowledge in a firm) others are more elusive (Despres and Chauvel's use of values, culture, systems, and structures). That said, all make reference to the context of knowledge management in some way, but because of the lack of definitional agreement, we view this as a secondary structuring device.

Transformations and Dynamics

This is a normative and prescriptive device in that it carries the caveat that unless knowledge is transformed or dynamized in some way, it is essentially useless. The root idea is that knowledge becomes useful only when it goes into the forge of social interaction. Examples of transformations and dynamics include Nonaka's *socialization – externalization – combination – internalization*, Earl's *inventorising – auditing – experiencing – socializing*, Hedlund's *internalization – articulation – reflection – dialogue – expansion*, Carayannis' *interactivity* and *connectivity* paths, and aspects of Van Buren's *enablers*. This is also consistent with authors like Edvinsson who work on the transfer of human capability and knowledge to organizational structures, and those like Hedlund who specifically target organizational routines.

Carriers and Media

Perhaps a subset of the preceding theme, we nonetheless distinguish *carriers and media* because of their presence in the literature. With this theme we mean to bring into evidence the systems and structures that specifically aim to facilitate the transfer and transformation of knowledge in an enterprise. While the theme *transformations and dynamics* points squarely at knowledge processes, *carriers and media* are concerned with technologies of all kinds, both human and machine. They are, in a sense, the infrastructure of trans-formative/dynamic processes. Examples of this device include Nonaka's emphasis on physical proximity and interpersonal interaction for knowledge externalization; the participation, in-company training, and cross-function-alism encouraged by Hedlund; Snowden's emphasis on storytelling as a core knowledge mechanism; the *auditing* and *socializing* advised by Earl; the ensemble of Van Buren's *enablers*. Obviously included are the machine tech-nologies familiar to anyone working in the field, including data warehouses, document management systems, groupware, Web-based communication, and so on. To the extent that transformations and dynamics are objectives in a knowledge management effort, carriers and media are the methods; the for-mer are the "what" and the latter, the "how."

Knowledge Culture

Finally, a set of authors in our review make it clear that managing knowledge involves far more than the structures and systems that shuffle ideas back and forth. More important than knowledge itself, they say, is the context or ecol-ogy in which knowledge phenomena are nestled. This clearly branches to the organizational learning notion of double-loop learning where rather than a given learning, "learning how to learn" becomes the critical competence. Having learned is one thing but understanding the elements and dynamics of the learning process itself is quite something else. This is analogous to what we have termed knowledge culture. Authors such as Hedlund and Nonaka clearly emphasize the importance of knowledge management processes, which encourage awareness and knowledge creation over systems and struc-tures that manage existing stores of knowledge. A knowledge culture re-quires such foundations but goes beyond. In the end, this device argues for reconceptualizing the firm as, for example, an N-Form Corporation or a knowledge creating company.

CONCLUSIONS

We begin the conclusion with a caveat: this review has dealt with structural models and classification systems and, thereby, ignored more literary treatments that propose text-embedded devices that are also designed to influence thinking. This is a limitation. The review is also limited to published practitioner/academic material and ignores devices that are certainly in wide circulation within the consulting community.

That said, it seems that knowledge cultures bring us full circle in a way. The models and classification systems reviewed in this chapter are, in part or in whole, aiming at a broader concept of organizing and the modern firm. They do so from different orientations and objectives, even while authors build their arguments on some or all of the seven devices outlined previously. Knowledge management becomes complex once the surface is scratched, providing opportunities to address the multifarious complexity that every company is. The 72 works cited in Appendix 1 are all trying to concretize an abstraction, but the majority, in our opinion, succeed in completing only a piece of the emerging, multidimensional mosaic.

All the works in this review wrestle with a certain antagonism in the term "knowledge management." They negotiate with different degrees of success the conflicted idea that knowledge can be managed the way one manages a distribution system, or inventory, or a production process, or a treasury. Here we find two basic distinctions. One is drawn by fundamental assumptions concerning the era in which we live: "industrial age" thinking applied to knowledge management does not yield the same design, nor the same vision, as that which informs the "information age." The second, and related, distinction pertains to one's conception of knowledge itself: is it a variable or a root metaphor? The industrial age counted its assets and converted them into variables that furnished great stochastic systems, but attempts to do likewise with knowledge appear, to us, seriously misinformed.

Finally, knowledge management writ large would seem to have ambitions that go beyond the management of knowledge, over to the unending potential that arises from the random association of certain humanistic fundamentals: individuals, knowledge, creativity, community, contribution, and certainly others. Try this, for example: (a) individual contributions to creative knowledge communities; (b) communities that contribute through creative individual knowledge; (c) creative communities from the contributions of knowledgeable individuals. This jeu could go on but the point would remain the same: the terms are reflexive and mutually reinforcing. Individuals, the fundamental reality of knowledge and organization, are "senseless" outside a community which itself is a void absent the individuals; knowledge has no meaning without its induction into a social context, hence a contribution of some kind. Taken at this level, the field of knowledge management holds itself out to be our latest, best hope for fundamentally reshaping the organizations, which we enact and then live in. Hopefully, we will not let this opportunity slip by.

NOTES

1. The ABI/INFORM database contains 800 journals of popular and academic merit in fields related to business. This search recorded the number of new articles that included the keywords "knowledge management" each year between 1988 (three articles) and 1999 (320 articles). Over the ten-year period, this represents an average increase of over 100 percent per year.
2. The move has been from rational (engineered, segmented, bureaucratic) to natural (organic, psychosocial, humanistic) to open and multiply connected organizational forms (Perrow, 1973; Scott, 1987; Nohria and Eccles, 1992; Despres, 1996).

APPENDIX 1

Albino, V., A. Garavelli, Claudio, and G. Schiuma, 1999, Knowledge Transfer and Inter-Firm Relationships in Industrial Districts: The Role of the Leader Firm. *Technovation*, 19(1): 53–63.

Allerton, Haidee, 1998, News You Can Use. *Training & Development Journal*, 52(2): 9–10.

Anderson, Neil. 1998, The People Make the Paradigm. *Journal of Organizational Behavior*, 19(4): 323–328.

Belasco, James, 1993, The New Organization. *Executive Excellence*, 10(4): 15–16.

Bienayme, Alain, 1988, Technology and the Nature of the Firm. *International Journal of Technology Management*, 3(5): 563–578.

Blanning, Robert, 1984, Expert Systems for Management: Research and Applications. *Journal of Information Science Principles & Practice*, 9(4): 153–162.

Buell, Hal, and Amy Zuckerman, 1999, Information, Please. *Journal for Quality & Participation*, 22(3): 52–55.

Bukowitz, Wendi, and Gordon Petrash, 1997, Visualizing, Measuring and Managing Knowledge. *Research-Technology Management*, 40(4): 24–31.

Carayannis, Elias, 1999, Fostering Synergies Between Information Technology and Managerial and Organizational Cognition: The Role of Knowledge Management. *Technovation*, 19(4): 219–231.

Carayannis, Elias, 1999, Knowledge Transfer Technological Hyperlearning in Five Industries. *Technovation*, 19(3): 141–161.

Chang, Ai-Mei, Clyde Holsapple, and Andres Whinston, 1993, Model Management Issues and Directions. *Decision Support Systems*, 9(1): 19–37.

Cisco, Susan, and Karen Strong, 1999, The Value Added Information Chain. *Information Management Journal*, 33(1): 4–15.

Cohen, Laurie, Joanne Duberley, and John McAuley, 1999, The Purpose and Process of Science: Contrasting Understandings in UK Research Establishments. *R & D Management*, 29(3): 233–245.

Cohen, Stephen, Nena K. Backer, 1999, Making and Mining Intellectual Capital: Method or Madness? *Training & Development Journal*, 53(9): 46–50.

Davenport, Thomas, David De Long, and Michael Beers, 1998, Successful Knowledge Management Projects. *Sloan Management Review*, 39(2): 43–57.

Davies, Jan, and Alan Waddington, 1999, The Management and Measurement of Intellectual Capital. *Management Accounting-London*, 77(8): 34.

Demarest, Marc, 1997, Understanding Knowledge Management. *Long Range Planning*, 30(3): 374–384.

Dolk, Daniel, and Benn Konsynski, 1984, Knowledge Representation for Model Management Systems. *IEEE Transactions on Software Engineering*, SE-10(6): 619–628.

Dove, Rick, 1998, A Knowledge Management Framework. *Automotive Manufacturing & Production*, 110(1): 18–20.

Dove, Rick, 1999, Managing The Knowledge Portfolio. *Automotive Manufacturing & Production*, 111(4): 16–17.

Dove, Rick, 1999, The Avoidance of Real Knowledge Management. *Automotive Manufacturing & Production*, 111(5): 16–17.

Doz, Yves, and C.K. Prahalad, 1987, A Process Model of Strategic Redirection in Large Complex Firms: The Case of Multinational Corporations. In A. Pettigrew (Ed.), *The Management of Strategic Change*, Basic Blackwell Ltd, Oxford, pp. 63–83.

Earl, Michael, 1997, Knowledge as Strategy: Reflections on Skandia International and Shorko Films. In Larry Prusak (Ed.), *Knowledge in Organizations*, Butterworth–Heinemann, pp. 1–17.

Earl, Michael, 1998, What on earth is a CKO? M. Earl & Ian Scott, Survey IBM. London Business School.

Edvinsson, Leif, and Paul Sullivan, 1996, Developing a Model for Managing Intellectual Capital. *European Management Journal*, 14(4): 356–364.

Edvinsson, Leif, 1997, Developing Intellectual Capital at Skandia. *Long Range Planning*, 30(3): 366–373.

Ford, Nigel, 1989, From Information to Knowledge Management: The Role of Rule Induction and Neural Net Machine Learning Techniques in Knowledge Generation. *Journal of Information Science Principles & Practice*, 15(4,5): 299–304.

Frappaolo, Carl, 1998, Defining Knowledge Management: Four Basic Functions. *Computerworld*, 32(8): 80.

Grantham, Charles, Larry Nichols, and Marilyn Schonberner, 1997, A Framework for the Management of Intellectual Capital in the Health Care Industry. *Journal of Health Care Finance*, 23(30): 1–19.

Guenette, David, 1997, Enterprising Information. *EMedia Professional*, 10(11): 38–50.

Harvey, Michael, and Robert Lusch, 1999, Balancing the Intellectual Capital Books: Intangible Liabilities. *European Management Journal*, 17(1): 85–92.

Hedlund, Gunnar, 1986, The Hypermodern—a Heterarchy? *Human Resource Management*, 25(1): 9–35.

Hedlund, Gunnar, 1994, A Model of Knowledge Management and the N-Form Corporation. *Strategic Management Journal*, 15(Special Issue): 73–90.

Hedlund, Gunnar, and Nonaka Ikjurio, 1993, Models of Knowledge Management in the West and Japan. In P. Lorange et al. (Eds), *Implementing Strategic Process, Change, Learning and Cooperation*. Basil Blackwell, London, pp. 117–144.

Hildebrand, Carol, 1994, The Greater Good. *CIO*, 8(4): 32–40.

Inkpen, Andrew, and Adva Dinur, 1998, Knowledge Management Processes and International Joint Ventures. *Organization Science*, 9(4): 454–468, July–Aug.

Johnson, William, 1999, An Integrative Taxonomy of Intellectual Capital: Measuring the Stock and Flow of Intellectual Capital Components in the Firm. *International Journal of Technology Management*, 18(5,6,7,8): 562–575.

Joyce, Teresa, and Bonnie Stivers, 1999, Knowledge and Innovation Focus: A Classification of US and Canadian Firms. *International Journal of Technology Management*, 18(5,6,7,8): 500–509.

Kerssens-Van Drongelen, Inge, Petra de Weerd-Nederhof, and Olaf Fisscher, 1996, Describing the Issues of Knowledge Management in R&D: Towards a Communication and Analysis Tool. *R & D Management*, 26(3): 213–230.

Lee, Thomas, Steven Maurer, 1997, The Retention of Knowledge Workers with the Unfolding Model of Voluntary Turnover. *Human Resource Management Review*, 7(3): 247–275.

LeRoy, Stephen, 1989, Efficient Capital Markets and Martingales. *Journal of Economic Literature*, December, 27(4): 1583–1621.

Liyanage, Shantha, Paul Greenfield, and Robert Don, 1999, Towards a Fourth Generation R&D Management Model—Research Networks in Knowledge Management. *International Journal of Technology Management*, 18(3,4): 372–393.

Lynn, Bernadette, 1998, Performance Evaluation in the New Economy: Bringing the Measurement and Evaluation of Intellectual Capital Into the Management Planning and Control System. *International Journal of Technology Management*, 16(1–3): 162–176.

Malone, Michael, 1997, New Metrics for a New Age. *Forbes ASAP Supplement*, April 7: 40–41.

Mascitelli, Ronald, 1999, A Framework for Sustainable Advantage in Global High-Tech Markets. *International Journal of Technology Management*, 17(3): 240–258.

Maurer, Hermann, 1998, Modern WISs. *Communications of the ACM*, 41(7): 114–115.

Mirchandani, Dinesh, and Pakath Ramakrishnan, 1999, Four Models for a Decision Support System. *Information & Management*, 35(1): 31–42.

Nahapiet, Janine, and Sumantra Ghoshal, 1998, Social Capital, Intellectual Capital, and the Organizational Advantage. *Academy of Management Review*, 23(2): 242–266.

Nightingale, Paul, 1998, A Cognitive Model of Innovation. *Research Policy*, 27: 689–709.

Nonaka, Ikjurio, 1989, Organising Innovation as a Knowledge Creation Process: A Suggestive Paradigm. Working Paper N OBIR-41, University of California at Berkeley, CA.

Nonaka, Ikjurio, 1990, Redundant, Overlapping Organizations: A Japanese Approach to Managing the Innovation Process. *California Management Review*, 32(3): 27–38.

Nonaka, Ikjurio, 1991, The Knowledge Creating Company. *Harvard Business Review*, November–December, 96–104.

Nonaka, Ikjurio, 1998, The Concept of "Ba": Building a Foundation for Knowledge Creation, *California Management Review*, 40(3): 40–54.

Nonaka, Ikjurio, 1994, Dynamic Theory of Organizational Knowledge Creation, *Organization Science*, 5(1): 14–36.

Odem, Peggy, and Carla O'Dell, 1998, Invented Here: How Sequent Computer Publishes Knowledge. *Journal of Business Strategy*, 19(1): 25–28.

O'Hara, Margaret, Richard Watson, and Bruce Kavan, 1999, Managing the Three Levels of Change. *Information Systems Management*, 16(3): 63–70.

Oliver, Amalya, and Julia Liebeskind, 1997/1998, Three Levels of Networking for Sourcing Intellectual Capital in Biotechnology: Implications for Studying Interorganizational Networks. *International Studies of Management & Organization*, 27(4): 76–103.

Peters, Tom, 1996, Know Thy Service. *Forbes ASAP Supplement*, October 7: 144.

Ram, Sudha, Stephen Hayne, and David Carlson, 1992, Integrating Information Systems Technologies to Support Consultation in an Information Center. *Information & Management*, 23(6): 331–343.

Silverman, B.G., 1985, Toward an Integrated Cognitive Model of the Inventor/Engineer. *R & D Management*, 15(2): 151–158.

Simatupang, Togar, and Angus White, 1998, A Policy Resolution Model for Knowledge Acquisition in Quality Management. *Total Quality Management*, 9(8): 767–779.

Snowden, David, 1998, The Ecology of a Sustainable Knowledge Programme. *Knowledge Management*, 1(6): 1, 13–14

Snowden, David, 1998, Thresholds of Acceptable Uncertainty. *Knowledge Management*, 1(5): 1–9.

Snowden, David, 1999, Creating a Sustainable Knowledge Programme. Proceedings from Optimizing Knowledge Management conference, IIR Ltd, London, September 9–10, 1999.

Stauffer, David, 1999, Why People Hoard Knowledge. *Across the Board*, 36(8): 16–21.

Swanson, Richard, and Elwood Holton, 1998, Developing and Maintaining Core Expertise in the Midst of Change. *National Productivity Review*, 17(2): 29–38.

Templeton, Gary, and Charles Snyder, 1999, A Model of Organizational Learning Based on Control. *International Journal of Technology Management*, 18(5,6,7,8): 705–719.

Van Buren, Mark, 1998, Virtual Coffee Klatch, *Technical Training,* 9(5): 42–46.

Van Buren, Mark, 1999, A Yardstick for Knowledge Management. *Training & Development Journal*, 53(5): 71–78.

Ward, Arian, and Victor Leo, 1996, Lessons Learned on the Knowledge Highways and Byways. *Strategy & Leadership*, 24(2): 16–20.

Wiig, Karl, 1993, *Knowledge Management Foundations*, Vol 1. Schema Press, Texas.

Younger, Jon, and Kurt Sandholtz, 1997, Helping R&D Professionals Build Successful Careers. *Research-Technology Management,* 40(6): 23–28.

PART II

Knowledge-Intensive Management

CHAPTER 4

Dynamic Business Systems for Knowledge Creation and Utilization

Ikujiro Nonaka and Patrick Reinmoeller

A knowledge management system is simply an information processing system if it is defined by closed circuits and routines for sharing knowledge. Such systems neglect contextual knowledge. Organizations must develop a dynamic business system to create and utilize knowledge effectively and efficiently. Dynamic systems integrate structural and procedural components and are open to continuously changing contexts. Business systems aim at stabilizing sporadic organizational processes in order to develop efficient routines, but dynamic business systems develop creative routines to generate and utilize knowledge. Creative routines for dealing with knowledge and using contexts in motion emerge from the juxtaposition of hard and soft technologies, synchronic and diachronic processes.

Creation and utilization processes in knowledge creation theory are briefly introduced in the first section of this chapter. This section presents hard and soft components and structural and procedural perspectives of dynamic systems, creative routines, and hard and soft components of dynamic systems for knowledge creation and utilization. Three levels of knowledge creation and utilization are identified and the context-dependency of knowledge in improvising is analyzed in depth. Two case studies of Seven-Eleven Japan and Toyota Motor Corporation illustrate how dynamic systems and creative routines are applied in section two. The conclusion presents implications for developing creative routines supported by dynamic systems of contexts in motion.

THE SECI MODEL: KNOWLEDGE CREATION AND UTILIZATION

Knowledge management systems currently emphasize the capturing and sharing of existing knowledge. The set of standardized tools or best practices in such systems is not enough to innovate and sustain competitive advantage, however; organizations must build business systems that create and utilize knowledge efficiently and effectively to succeed. Knowledge management currently recommends partial and static information processing systems for the routine utilization of knowledge. Instead, dynamic systems are needed (Amabile and Conti, 1999) that support knowledge creation and utilization through established structures and processes. The media and key constituents of such dynamic systems are routines for innovation. Routines preserve and refine organizational structures (Nelson and Winter, 1982), but they can also be impediments for innovation and change. Therefore, creative routines and human intervention in contexts are necessary as media and modules of Dynamic Systems for Knowledge Creation and Utilization (DKCU).

Organizations create and utilize knowledge through the interaction between explicit and tacit knowledge, the processes of knowledge conversion. There are four modes of knowledge conversion: socialization, externalization, combination, and internalization (SECI) (Nonaka, 1990; Nonaka and Takeuchi, 1995). Through these conversion processes, tacit and explicit knowledge expands in terms of quality and quantity.

Socialization and externalization are processes that emphasize the creation of knowledge. Socialization (from tacit knowledge to tacit knowledge) is a process of converging new tacit knowledge through shared experiences. Sharing the same experience through joint activities such as being together, spending time together, or living in the same environment is a key for this conversion. Walking around inside and outside of an organization provides experiential access to tacit knowledge. Externalization (from tacit knowledge to explicit knowledge) is a process of articulating tacit knowledge into explicit knowledge. By making tacit knowledge explicit, it can be shared by others and become the basis of new knowledge. Tacit knowledge is often articulated through metaphors, analogies, diagrams, or prototypes.

Combination and internalization focus on utilization of knowledge. Combination (from explicit knowledge to explicit knowledge) is a process of converging explicit knowledge into more complex and systematic sets of explicit knowledge. Knowledge is exchanged and reconfigured through documents, meetings, or communication networks. Data mining in large-scale databases is an example of this process. Internalization (from explicit knowledge to tacit knowledge) is a process of embodying explicit knowledge into tacit knowledge. It is closely related to learning by doing. Through internalization, knowledge is shared throughout an organization; it broadens and changes

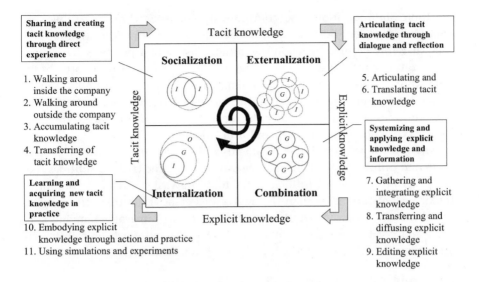

Figure 4.1 *The SECI Model of Knowledge Creation and Utilization (Sources: Nonaka and Takeuchi, 1995; Nonaka and Konno, 1999)*

organizational members' mental models. When knowledge is internalized into mental models or technical know-how, it becomes a valuable asset.

The tacit knowledge of an individual is then again shared through socialization within the group; the new knowledge created in the group expands outwards to the organization and its interorganizational networks. Creation and utilization processes continuously unfold side by side (synchronic) and in sequence over time (diachronic); they are not limited to one organizational level.

Current knowledge management emphasizes static information technology systems such as databases or enterprise systems. Few organizations emphasize the creation of knowledge, but many focus on utilization of knowledge through information technology. Both approaches tend to become static, infused in either an existing or an automated order.

Dynamic systems promote knowledge creation and utilization processes; they establish a dynamic balance on the fine line between exploration and exploitation (March, 1996) and develop creative routines to promote the spiral of the SECI process.

Knowledge is commonly utilized in everyday business routines. Routines are fundamental to sustainable social life and organizational processes (Giddens, 1993; Nelson and Winter, 1982). They emphasize repetitive action, replication, and standardization; they thus become barriers to the exploration and creation of new knowledge. Changing the static routines that influence the way people work is difficult; it is even more difficult to encourage innovation, improvisation, and continuously challenge the ways things are done. Standardized and static routines are visible and can be quickly imitated; they therefore become items on the laundry list of best practices. Therefore, organizations need to develop creative routines, that is, action patterns for innovation. Creative routines are dynamic action patterns promoting innovation by creating and utilizing authentic knowledge on a daily basis. Creative routines are simultaneously the media and the constituents of dynamic systems for knowledge creation and utilization.

Organizations must build reliable dynamic systems for knowledge creation and utilization (DKCU) that generate and use the creative routines that are generally embedded in tacit individual knowledge. Dynamic organizational systems are more than the aggregated creative routines of organizational members (Clippinger, 1999). DKCU systems integrate changing contexts and creative routines. They synchronically and diachronically create and utilize knowledge in everyday organizational practice.

Hard and Soft Components for DKCU Systems

DKCU systems integrate shared contexts in motion (Japanese *Ba*) (Nonaka, Toyama, and Konno, 2000). Creative routines are embedded in such contexts. Artifacts (e.g., telephones, office environments, computer interfaces), people (e.g., colleagues, competitors, personal networks), and contextual knowledge (information and shared experiences, ideas, ideals), or any combination of these can elicit creative routines. Frequent face-to-face contact or virtual meetings on the Internet, as well as informal dialogues over lunch, at the copier, or in front of the water cooler, are creative routines that are embedded in integrated hard and soft systems.

The literal meaning of context (Latin *contexere*) is "putting together, to interweave." Contexts generate relationships or meanings. Consequently, knowledge is information in contexts. Contexts encompass the resources provided by continuously changing conditions and circumstances of the before and after (diachronic context) and the now (synchronic context). Actions and knowledge processes are juxtaposed in contexts (Granovetter, 1985; Suchmann, 1987; Nonaka and Konno, 1998; Ueno, 1999). Different contexts define actions and knowledge, the same way that the contextual interdependence of acoustics and visuals influence human perception of ensembles.

The Japanese art of Kabuki juxtaposes different resources including music and sound, rhythm, costume, movement, dance, text, and the spatial arrangement of stages during each performance. These resources are equally important components of the context, and as the performance proceeds they create a dynamic and meaningful context (Eisenstein, 1953; Ueno, 1999).

The ways actions and knowledge shape contexts are influenced by the use of time. Management practice and theory emphasizes the importance of time to increase cost-efficiency (Stalk and Hout, 1990; Northey and Southway,

1993; Fine, 1998). Only recently is the potential in a variety of time concepts being discovered. The relevant time concepts include synchronicity (Jaworski, 1996), strategy under the condition of complexity (Brown and Eisenhardt, 1998), and the multiplicity of time as an enabling context for all knowledge processes (Reinmoeller, 1999a; Reinmoeller, 1999b).

DKCU systems juxtapose structural (hard) and process (soft) components to create contexts in motion (*Ba*). Such contexts are transient, unstable phenomena in time. They emerge and develop, thus they need to be seized at the right moment. DKCU systems promote such contexts on a constant basis and develop creative routines to seize the moments. To do so effectively and efficiently, human intervention in automated processes is necessary.

The Structural Perspective: IT and Organizational Systems

The structural perspective includes information technology and organizational systems. These systems are important in developing creative routines for knowledge utilization in everyday business. IT systems promote routines for systemizing and disseminating knowledge; organizational structure promotes routines for exercising and practicing new knowledge.

Information technology provides the structure in which explicit knowledge is created and exploited. IT in knowledge management has three major advantages: efficiency, effectiveness, and velocity (Ciborra, 1993; Earl, 1996; Churchill and Snowdon, 1998; Choo, 1998; Cohen, 1998; Davenport and Pearlson, 1998; Davenport and Prusak, 1998; Ruggles, 1998; Kelly and Allison, 1999).

First, tools to appropriate information include software agents, browsers, search engines, and indices. Voice-mail systems, for instance, force customers to respond to questions structured like a decision tree, and help organizations to appropriate information about customers.

Second, databases, hyperlinks, or software discern relationships between documents from different sources and automatically connect dispersed information. Software programs automatically connect information on individuals, and build extensive user profiles and databases by interacting with people (Shout, 1999; Turban, McLean, and Wetherbe, 1999).

Third, tools such as e-mail, intranets, or programs to customize information to be sent to individuals increase efficient sharing and dissemination. Software can help write logical documents and groupware for collaborative prototyping allows numerous members to interact through computer networks.

Fourth, tools supporting better utilization of information and knowledge include workflow management software to support decision-making processes in product development projects and concurrent engineering. Visualization through HTML-based browsers, graphical user interfaces (GUI), agents, or navigators support easy and fast access to databases and help to utilize information (McKenna, 1997; Nonaka, Reinmoeller, and Toyama, 2000).

Fifth, increasing possibilities of free access requires protection of proprietary information and knowledge. Tools such as firewalls around intranets or encryption technology for interactive exchange, net-based communication, or e-commerce are needed to protect knowledge and information from unauthorized access.

The American retailer Wal-Mart and Amazon.com, the online bookstore, are two companies that illustrate how IT tools are used for appropriating, connecting, disseminating, utilizing, and protecting information. Wal-Mart is a leader in the use of information technology. The goal of automatic data accumulation and extraction of knowledge is pursued with high investments in centralized information systems (Nonaka, Reinmoeller, and Toyama, 2000). Further, Wal-Mart deals with its vendors through the Internet to maximize interaction efficiency. Amazon.com, the rapidly diversifying American online bookstore, has patented technology that illustrates the use of hard systems in the context of the Internet. Repeat viewers who return to Amazon's Web site after an online purchase are offered a "one-click-shopping" service. During their first purchase the technical data of the customer's PC, and personal data such as address, phone numbers, and the credit card number, are captured. When the customer returns to the Web site from the same PC, Amazon welcomes them and offers a customized list of books and other goods. Because these data are already available, the customer can shop by clicking the desired merchandise.

But there are problems with the current focus on IT tools in knowledge management. Efficient IT is fast becoming standard practice (Schank, 1997; Davenport, De Long, and Beers, 1998; Ishida, 1998) and therefore less helpful for attaining competitive advantage. Further, the contexts of knowledge and the embeddedness in social relationships escape such tools (Granovetter, 1985; Clancey, 1997; Dyer and Singh, 1998). Recently, however, the increasing reach and richness of communication media and tools for visual real-time communication is addressing these problems.

The structural perspective includes organizational systems. Knowledge is embedded in the context of organizational systems and it is necessary to employ them to effectively enhance learning and application. Human resource and career development programs are examples of systems promoting internalization of explicit knowledge.

Corporate universities are metaphors for technology-enhanced learning environments within companies. The corporate university at Daimler-Chrysler combines the technological infrastructure of global computer networks and social architecture, including communities of practice for new learning programs that include real-time online teaching, learning, and teamwork worldwide.

Creative routines for internalization rely on the learning disciplines of individuals or teams; team members can belong to different organizations

(Nonaka and Konno, 1998) or be part of network relationships in regions (Nonaka and Reinmoeller, 1998). On-the-job training is a well-known way to structure learning processes. Sharing time and space on the site is necessary for learning and refinement of new skills. Continuous self-improvement through learning in apprenticeship models or communities of practice and mentorship is important.

Communities of practice (Senge, 1990; Lave and Wenger, 1991; Brown and Duguid, 1991; Wenger and Snyder, 2000) are used for sharing skills and learning. Professional communities of engineers in functionally structured organizations are an example for such communities. The apprenticeship and Kaizen models of incremental perfection are particularly diffused in manufacturing. Quality circles are applications of communities of practice.

Mentorship systems focus on learning by doing under the guidance of a senior mentor. Such systems are important to convey practices to pupils. The continued focus on exercising specific practices helps to refine routines. Internal consulting departments often apply systems similar to mentorship.

The focus on internalized routines reflects the closed nature of communities of practice and mentorship models. Such closure emphasizes the execution of existing routines and protection of traditions rather than improvisation with creative routines.

The Procedural Perspective: Sharing and Improvising

The procedural perspective represents the soft and transient side of DKCU systems, focusing on shared disciplines to capture new meanings in changing contexts. DKCU systems have to develop creative routines that promote inter-

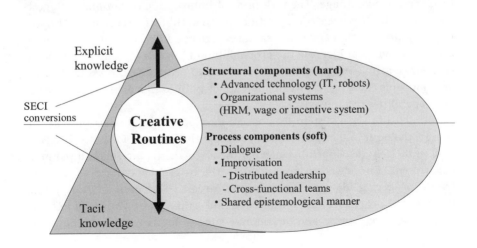

Figure 4.2   *Creative Routines in Dynamic Business Systems*

nalization and externalization in everyday business. Hard systems can trigger and support dialogue and improvisation, but they fail to take account of contexts. The capabilities, commitment, and discipline of people are required to utilize tacit knowledge and contexts in motion. Soft systems integrate such contexts in motion, discovering meanings through creative routines, including dialogue, improvisation, and shared epistemological manner.

Systems for dialogue are needed to promote externalization. DKCU systems support the development of routines for sharing and articulating of tacit knowledge. Occasional contact with members of other departments, customers, or clients is not enough to share tacit knowledge. Systems for dialogue create physical, face-to-face interactions as effective ways to capture the full range of physical senses and psycho-emotional reactions (e.g., joy, ease, or discomfort) and to transfer tacit knowledge and generate emotional knowledge assets.

The Japanese retail chain Mujirushi has several systems for sharing the tacit knowledge of customers. Each shop floor is an important place for face-to-face interaction between customers and employees. A Mujirushi summer camp offers a holiday experience in a Mujirushi environment. Here customers use new and old Mujirushi products that include food, toiletries, apparel, and so on. Employees who are committed to engaging in dialogue with customers can spend time camping with them to elicit tacit knowledge. During the camp, employees absorb tacit knowledge by experiencing the customer's life with Mujirushi products.

Systems for improvising integrate individuals' mental models and skills through a dynamic process of co-creation. Individuals share mental models with others in intensive dialogue, that is, joint acting and reflection, and by using creative language. The metaphor of improvising or jamming suggests the best of both worlds. Competition and playfulness, structure and openness, beginner's mind and professional experience, introspection and simultaneous extraversion increase the probabilities of serendipity and spontaneous emergence of meaning. DKCU systems need to promote contexts that juxtapose multiple resources allowing individuals with complementary knowledge and capabilities to improvise.

Mujirushi uses a system for concept development and selection with the roles of dialogue and improvisation prominently featured. Ideas are discussed and tentatively developed by internal members of the buying and planning department. The ideas are presented to the external members of a design team, triggering dialogue and improvisation. The design team judges whether the proposals match the vision and strategies of Mujirushi in terms of quality, image, price, and fit and may suggest improvement or oppose the development.

Shared epistemological manner is a set of creative routines based on the use of contexts in motion, the SECI spiral, and knowledge assets (Nonaka and Toyama, 1999). Leaders integrate these elements of knowledge creation to establish a company's "shared epistemological manner" so that effective and efficient knowledge creation becomes second nature in the organization.

The epistemological manner shared by organizational members at Honda, for instance, is characterized by self-reflection (Who am I? Why do I want to do this?) and the pursuit of knowledge as the goal. The intrinsic motivation to serve customers and create unique products is based on the assumption that humans want to explore, know, and create. The results of knowledge creation are justified according to authentic criteria, including aesthetics. Such epistemological manner is different from extrinsically motivated exploitation of knowledge. Knowledge sharing with best practices at GE, for instance, is justified by success over the competition and not by the knowledge created.

Three Levels of Knowledge Conversion

For developing creative routines and DKCU systems, three different levels of knowledge conversion processes need to be analyzed. The parties involved can belong to internal departments or outside organizations; they can be individuals, groups, and organizations. DKCU systems have to prepare and energize the creative routines of conversions between these parties.

There are three different levels of knowledge interactions between two parties (Figure 4.3). Knowledge conversions can involve (1) only explicit knowledge, (2) only tacit knowledge, and (3) tacit and explicit knowledge. The three levels differ according to their time requirements; the first level of conversion requires only instants while the second and third need longer periods of time. Furthermore, the third level requires synchronic interaction.

DKCU systems support these three levels in different ways. Each level comes with specific contexts and needs creative routines to maintain a dynamic balance between structural (hard) and procedural (soft) components. At level 1, explicit knowledge is gathered, combined, and utilized through communication media. The time required to transmit explicit knowledge with IT is reduced to real-time, that is, a point in time. On this level two problems have to be solved. The first is a problem of technology. The transfer of explicit knowledge requires hard systems to make efficient exchange possible. Information technology and organizational systems solve this problem most effectively. Systems that automatically provide access or disseminate data are used in data mining or intranets inside organizations. The second problem is that of incentives. Within companies, the transfer of explicit knowledge needs to be systematically linked to compensation systems. Organizational members will be inclined to share explicit knowledge when the incentive system and markets for knowledge provide compensation (Davenport and Prusak, 1998).

At level 2, the different parties help each other to articulate tacit knowledge. The second level of conversion from tacit to explicit knowledge requires intensive dialogue in shared contexts in motion (*Ba*). The time that is required for such dialogue is a period of synchronic interaction. During this period of

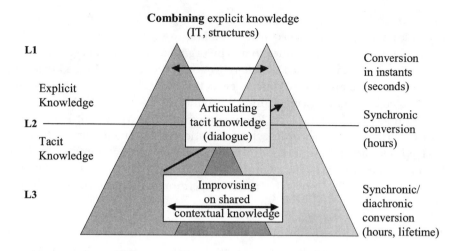

Figure 4.3   *Three Levels of Creating and Utilizing Knowledge*

synchronic experience, the participants develop shared tacit knowledge and begin to understand each other's mental models. If this time is spent together without sharing the same context, for example through chat on the Internet, mutual understanding can lack depth.

Two problems need to be solved on this second level. First, face-to-face interaction is important for dialogue. Information technology is not yet able to fully substitute for face-to-face interaction because it omits context. Second, dialogue needs creative routines to elicit the conversion of tacit into explicit knowledge. IT can provide triggers to meet face to face or opportunities to discover causal relations. However, people have to seize opportunities; people's skills determine the value of IT systems for DKCU. Organizational systems such as human resource management, incentive systems, meeting schedules, operating procedures, patterns for problem solving, and dialogues are effective means for developing creative routines.

At level 3, both parties share their tacit knowledge and externalize it to promote innovation. The third level of conversion requires longer periods of time spent together. The time required for improvising includes longer synchronic and diachronic experience for the sharing of rich tacit and contextual knowledge. Mutual understanding of deep tacit knowledge is based on shared experiences of multiple and long periods of time (diachronic). On the third level, knowledge is not articulated and the creation and utilization of knowledge remains tacit. Here knowledge is created and utilized by improvising and bricolage (Mirvis, 1998), serendipity, crafting strategy, creative sparks, or jamming (Mintzberg, 1988; Quinn, 1988; Kao, 1996; Crossan et al., 1996; Crossan, 1998; Leonard and Swap, 1999). In this sense, if mutual understanding and trust has developed, knowledge is created at the spur of the moment when conceptual insight and practice are merged in action.

Level 1 is the domain of current knowledge management. Digital technology links explicit knowledge in real-time and provides instant access to large databases. Some information technology, such as groupware, has become widely used on level 2. However, the dynamics of synchronous dialogue and improvisation in shared contexts (*Ba*) have not been emulated by digital technology. Level 3 of knowledge creation and utilization is most difficult but also most important. This level provides sustainable competitive advantage because tacit knowledge and processes are authentic, hidden in contexts, distributed, and therefore difficult to imitate.

DKCU Systems for Improvising

Creative routines for improvisation include the use of symbolic language, systematically distributed knowledge, leadership, cross-boundary teams, and epistemological manner.

Symbolic language, including metaphors, analogy, and narratives, is based on common tacit knowledge. Symbols and images convey insights and are intuitively understood. Narratives such as "war stories" of experiences at the "frontline" are important (Shaw, Brown, and Bromiley, 1998). 3M and Xerox have systemized creative routines for storytelling. At Xerox Parc, analogue storytelling is the basis for Eureka, a digital system that accumulates the personal success stories of copier repairmen. Eureka offers a rich source of local and sticky knowledge via computer networks to support problem solving globally. DKCU systems interweave symbolic language, distributed knowledge, and cross-boundary teams in everyday work.

Distributed leadership is necessary for the co-creation of prototypes in a group. Using experts with different complementary knowledge is important to broaden the scope of improvisation. DKCU systems integrate the different perspectives of people who share a common goal.

Leadership is distributed simultaneously over place, time, and knowledge (expertise). People who promote knowledge creation and utilization by volunteering tacit knowledge become temporary leaders. Systems for distributed leadership allow flexible integration of individual knowledge. Leaders emerge from peers by creating and utilizing knowledge in new ways. Systems foster the emergence of volunteers by facilitating improvisation in shared space and time.

Honda achieved several breakthroughs during the development of the humanoid robot (Tagami, 1998). Furthermore, Honda recruited mostly external people with the knowledge needed to develop the robot at Honda R&D laboratories. The shared dream of a friendly robot was an important criterion for the selection of people. Leadership within the team changed according to the knowledge required within the project (expertise) and individual energy.

Cross-functional teams link members with different expertise to support improvisation. A common base of tacit knowledge and a diversity of perspectives are important. Knowledge maps, knowledge yellow pages, or the design of offices with self-assigned seats facilitate the formation of cross-functional teams (Nonaka and Reinmoeller, 1999). DKCU systems also provide cues that energize and sustain the dynamic balance between creation and utilization by milestones or deadlines. Cross-functional teams rely on a common perspective, specialized knowledge, and they improvise to realize the vision.

Using such teams has become a routine at Sharp for fast development of new products. Sharp's strategically important products are developed by Urgent Project Teams with members from different departments and professions. The project leader in charge selects the team members. The team leader is generally a senior manager with extended personal networks and knowledge about employees and their capabilities. The team enjoys full support of the organization because it creates and utilizes knowledge of strategic value for Sharp.

Nonaka and Toyama (1999) propose the concept of shared epistemological manner as routines of knowledge creation and utilization. Such manners also promote improvisation. They increase the common base of contextual knowledge through shared vision and methods to pursue a common purpose. Shared epistemological manners provide creative routines, including the use of metaphors and analogies or patterns of dialogue.

Integrating DKCU Systems in Business Practice

The general model of DKCU systems is summarized in Figure 4.4. The horizontal axis shows the value chain and related organizational activities covered by headquarters. The vertical axis shows the three DKCU levels. Level 1 is fundamental to DKCU systems and mainly built with tangible resources, information technology, and organizational systems. Headquarters maintains this level and provides opportunities for the real-time combination of knowledge.

On level 2, creative routines promote externalization and visualization. Creative routines are situated in *Ba*. Juxtaposed soft and hard systems support visualization, dialogue, and improvisation to articulate new ideas. Knowledge processes on level 3, including the internalization of skills and socialization with suppliers, colleagues, and customers in everyday business processes, take more time. Diachronic accumulation and continuous interaction are the keys to anticipating and detecting fluctuation. Fluctuations can occur, for instance, on the assembly line or shop floor.

DKCU systems visualize or articulate these fluctuations and trigger the creative routines of dialogue and improvisation to create new hypotheses about possible solutions. Means for visualization include images, metaphors, or stories. Creative routines concentrate the distributed knowledge in the organization (people, perspectives) and energize processes of iterative testing

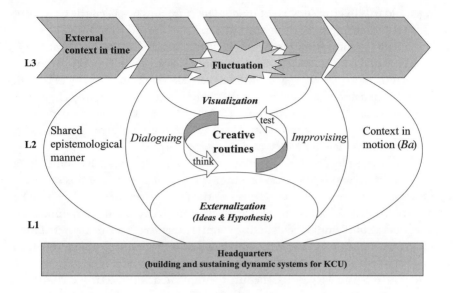

Figure 4.4 *DKCU Systems of Creative Routines*

and thinking (compassion, momentum) about new solutions to avoid fluctuations and improve business processes. Creative routines juxtapose testing and thinking, synchronic creation of new ideas, and diachronic utilization of expertise in *Ba*. The routines of generating the dynamic ensemble of diachronic and synchronic patterns, in both soft and hard systems, are creative routines. Symbolic language, distributed knowledge, leadership, and cross-functional teams prepare contexts in motion in which creative routines can take place.

CASE STUDIES

The following cases, Seven-Eleven Japan and Toyota Motor Corporation, show how DKCU systems and creative routines are used to create and utilize knowledge in retail and manufacturing business. Both companies have built authentic DKCU systems in which human interventions provide important contextual knowledge and new ideas.

Seven-Eleven Japan

In 1973 Ito-Yokado, a Japanese supermarket chain, and Southland Corporation, the operator and franchiser of Seven-Eleven convenience stores in the United States, reached a licensing agreement. Ito-Yokado established Seven-Eleven Japan and opened the first Seven-Eleven stores in 1978. In 1991 it acquired the Southland Corporation. Seven-Eleven Japan is considered to be setting standards in efficiency worldwide. The company has been the most profitable retailer in Japan both in absolute and sales–profit ratio terms.

Critical to understanding Seven-Eleven's success is the fact that it is a franchiser and does not sell goods (although it runs several stores for experiments) (Okamoto, 1998; Usui, 1998). Seven-Eleven provides services to franchisees by creating and utilizing market knowledge. The company charges its franchisees for the continued flow of new products, the services it provides them, royalties for trademarks, and leasing fees for equipment such as information systems, display racks, and refrigerated cases.

Each Seven-Eleven store of about 100 square meters sells some 2,800 items, of which about 70 percent change every year. To sustain this stream of innovations and provide new services to the franchisees, Seven-Eleven makes extensive use of quintessentially explicit knowledge such as manuals for store operation, employee training, and franchisee recruitment/training. This heavy reliance on explicit knowledge differentiates Seven-Eleven from most Japanese companies rather dramatically.

Recently Seven-Eleven has begun to implement an electronic commerce strategy that attempts to leverage the large retail network of 8,000 stores as a platform for cash and carry services of merchandise sold online. These new services are expected to increase profitability because the strengths of Seven-Eleven's DKCU systems can be exploited for an expanding range of products.

Dynamic Systems at Seven-Eleven

Seven-Eleven's outstanding success is largely based on new knowledge. A DKCU system strikes the balance between hard and soft systems, juxtaposing analog and digital, synchronic and diachronic processes in multiple creative routines.

Structural Systems   Digital technology is an important part of Seven-Eleven's dynamic system (Mitsugi, Takimoto, and Yamazaki, 1998); it is used to eliminate mediocre products and to support innovation. The POS system (point of sale system) offers real-time access to explicit knowledge from headquarters and instant access. It is used as the key tool for generating profitability listings. Such explicit knowledge is used to identify and replace products that perform below expectations. Bad performance quickly triggers replacement with new products and the development of a hypothesis about causal relations.

Constructing and verifying hypotheses is the key to Seven-Eleven's ability to innovate quickly. The POS system triggers building and testing of hypotheses. The POS system is partly automated; it induces reflection upon simultaneous display of important data, visuals, and contextual information such as weather conditions. The system offers options on how to analyze, understand, and test the present situation to make the generation of hypotheses as easy as possible. On this level 1 of DKCU, the speed of combination and access to databases is important; Seven-Eleven analyzes new data on a daily basis and provides access in real-time. The new fifth-generation POS system includes satellite transmission from headquarters, data mining, and free access and queries from all stores.

Seven-Eleven has designed its systems to build creative routines for knowledge conversions. Soft and hard systems are linked so that the data and intuition of employees trigger synchronic building and diachronic testing of hypotheses. Creative routines take place on the shop floor (micro) and in headquarters (macro). When placing orders, people on the shop floor hypothesize what items would sell well, how many, and how to sell them. Each hypothesis is tested by actual orders and actual sales are again confirmed by POS data. At headquarters, the sales data of all stores are analyzed on a daily basis. The POS system visualizes fluctuations and elicits new ideas from people at headquarters. These ideas are used for 80 new or improved products per week and in the training programs. Afterwards, successful hypotheses are collected and disseminated throughout the company. Seven-Eleven has designed the hard system for the best use of the ingenuity of all employees within the company and all partners in the network.

Organizational Systems　　Seven-Eleven utilizes an ordering-replenishing system and emphasizes automated processes with human intervention (Suzuki, 1998; Kunitomo, 1998, p. 243). To develop creative routines, Seven-Eleven uses the POS data and organizational systems such as systematic training of store owners and human resource development for employees. The training of store owners includes intensive periods of preparation and simulations for running a Seven-Eleven store. Store situations allow new owners to internalize the explicit knowledge of the franchise system by engaging both body and mind. Such training builds routines to create and utilize knowledge more efficiently.

Human resource management at Seven-Eleven emphasizes OJT (on-the-job training) throughout the career path at Seven-Eleven. New employees start on the shop floor with their first learning experience, which is followed by assignments as store manager in one of the few directly managed stores, and later as field counselor. This variety of experiences is important for young entrants to internalize distributed knowledge in different contexts and to become familiar with different perspectives within the company. Managers who experience the different positions are multiskilled; they have internalized creative routines in different contexts. They are prepared to address fluctuations by providing tacit knowledge including perspectives, compassion, and momentum.

Procedural Systems　　Seven-Eleven's vision and guiding principles are continuously disseminated throughout the company to reinforce the consistency of Seven-Eleven's corporate culture. Seven-Eleven's vision, "adapt to changes and pursue fundamentals," is linked to four principles: freshness of goods; the best assortment of goods; cleanliness of stores, goods, and employee uniforms; and friendliness to customers. The vision provides criteria for all operational procedures and guidelines for store owners, part-timers, and employees who are responsible for the customer interface.

Mr. Suzuki, president of Seven-Eleven, has a key role in communicating the company culture. He took over management from the founding generations and developed a management system that integrates structural and process systems. Each week he interacts with several hundred field counselors directly and improvises on the company vision. His leadership imposes a system on employees that uses contexts in motion (*Ba*) to visualize and trigger creative routines in dialogue, improvisation, distributed leadership, and cross-functional teams.

Dialogue and Improvisation

Seven-Eleven has several systems for sharing the tacit knowledge of customers. Each shop floor is a place for face-to-face interaction with customers and employees. The shop owners, employees, field counselors, and walking-around employees are absorbing tacit knowledge by circulating inside and outside the company. On this third level of DKCU, employees and owners at the frontline continuously experience changes in customer mood and learn how to adapt to them. The changes in customer behavior are first spotted as fluctuations on the shop floor (micro). Face-to-face interaction is important to improvise on these fluctuations.

A system of meetings generates synchronicity and creative routines. For example, knowledge of changes in customer needs is captured in the 8,000 stores of Seven-Eleven through short dialogues with customers (synchronic) and repetition of interaction over time (diachronic). Local employees share their knowledge with other employees and in meetings with operation field counselors (OFC). On level 2 of DKCU, creative routines of dialogue and improvisation are used to share and externalize images of experiences.

The OFC visit stores frequently to consult the store owners and engage in dialogue with customers and employees. The problems detected are augmented by knowledge of the OFC (diachronic) and shared through OFC groupware and face-to-face dialogue (synchronic) at meetings in Tokyo.

The day before the field counselors meet in Tokyo, all managers (macro) get together every Monday for the weekly face-to-face meeting (synchronic). President Suzuki expects the managers who are facing problems to leave the meeting to solve their problems immediately (improvising) and to return to the gathering and report on the strategies implemented, actions taken, and show early results. Thus, President Suzuki triggers immediate action by synchronic face-to-face communication.

On the following day (Tuesday) all field counselors meet in Tokyo to attend a meeting; this synchronizes Seven-Eleven's market knowledge. During the meeting all field counselors listen to a speech by the energetic leader, Suzuki, who improvises on the company vision and current issues, including those discussed at the manager meeting. President Suzuki synchronizes Seven-Eleven's distributed expertise and prepares the integration of soft and hard technologies. He has generated creative routines to regularly create occasions for dialogue and improvisation.

Distributed Leadership

Seven-Eleven utilizes the distributed knowledge (expertise in local needs) of all employees and customers to improvise. Customer behavior and comments are observed and captured by employees on all hierarchical levels. Distributed ordering, for instance, means that ordering responsibilities for product categories are assigned to individual employees and jobbers who then develop specific knowledge for hypothesis building. The success of hypotheses and orders can be checked against the sales data of all stores. The OFC collect problems and new ideas through dialogue with employees and observation. They concentrate distributed knowledge for the meetings in Tokyo (level 2).

Similarly, leadership is distributed over knowledge, time, and place. The testing of ideas through actual orders is done where new ideas are conceived. Thus, employees in each store are empowered to lead Seven-Eleven and introduce new ideas. Furthermore, employees are responsible for sales floor and service, store managers for the economic success of stores, OFC for regional performance, and people in headquarters for overall success; each addresses fluctuations at different levels of complexity. The career path for top managers at Seven-Eleven requires years of experience in different positions including those of sales floor employee, shop manager, and field counselor. Through this system managers learn to manage and improvise on all three levels of DKCU.

Cross-Boundary Teams at Seven-Eleven Japan

The strength of Seven-Eleven lies in the leading role of its development teams that span the boundaries of organizations. Seven-Eleven systematically develops new products through strategic alliances with manufacturers that own complementary knowledge. This idea of an improvisational way of creating and utilizing knowledge among (potentially competing) organizations has been applied thus far to more loosely coupled teams of makers, trading firms, and Seven-Eleven.

The Seven-Eleven headquarters initiates the creative routine of team merchandising and forms a development team, together with experts from the manufacturers (supplier network). Briefly, the five-step process is as follows.

1. The new product development committee conceptualizes the topic and assigns appropriate members to the team.
2. Manufacturers' tacit knowledge materializes in trial products.

3. Some of the trial products are selected as prototypes. Ideas on how to improve them are generated by the team.
4. New prototypes are made based on these ideas.
5. These new prototypes are evaluated at the officers' meeting at Seven-Eleven. If the approval of Seven-Eleven is gained, full support in terms of know-how and data is given to finalize the prototype and start production.

Thus, the merchandising process at Seven-Eleven integrates soft and hard systems to enable improvising in alliances.

Team merchandising dynamically integrates the tacit knowledge of manufacturers with POS data and Seven-Eleven's DKCU system. However, the fast cycle of data analysis and replacement of poorly performing products creates continuously new products, but does not favor breakthrough innovations (Ogawa, 2000).

Epistemological Manner

Seven-Eleven has developed distinctive epistemological manners. The observation of customers and reflection on their behavior are engrained in everyday practice. Observation and reflection help to generate hypotheses on new ways to sell more. The testing of such hypotheses is key to knowledge creation and utilization. Several times each day, orders of merchandise are placed; they test whether hypotheses are good or bad predictors of future developments.

Toyota Motor Corporation

Toyota Motor Corporation, established in 1937, is the largest car manufacturer in Japan. Toyota is known for its efficient manufacturing system and is an industry leader worldwide in product development lead-time and efficiency of resource utilization. The evolving Toyota Production System, the prototype of "lean production," relationships with suppliers, and the design and development system have been critical for its success (Fujimoto, 1999; Sobek, Ward, and Liker, 1999; Besser, 1996; Cusumano, 1985). During the postbubble crisis, Toyota emerged as one of the strongest independent Japanese carmakers and has been expanding its global reach by opening more factories abroad.

In January 1992 Shoichiro Toyoda announced the new Toyota vision to all organizational members. He proclaimed that Toyota aspires "towards harmony with people, society and environment. . ." and asked each organizational member to help construct a new Toyota of the twenty-first century. One of the principles presented was that Toyota is to build a new company culture that elicits individual and team creativity. Open buyer-supplier systems for mutually stimulating research and innovation were mentioned by

Toyoda. The new vision articulates Toyota's environmental responsibility and the need to emphasize creating and utilizing knowledge.

During the late 1990s, Toyota's corporate renewal resulted in targeting younger segments. Besides several innovative marketing initiatives, Toyota has been able to introduce advanced environmentally friendly technology to the markets. Particularly noted in this regard was the sales start of Prius in 1997, the first hybrid car worldwide (Itazaki, 1999; Iemura, 1999).

Dynamic Systems at Toyota

The following presents the way Toyota integrates hard and soft systems to develop creative routines for knowledge creation and utilization. First we analyze the assembly line as part of the DKCU system (level 3). Then we consider Toyota's new approach to new product development with cross-boundary teams (level 2).

Toyota Production Systems   Just-in-time, automation, total quality control and continuous improvement (Kaizen), and other subsystems are described at length in the literature (Fujimoto, 1999; Spear and Bowen 1999). These subsystems at level 1 of DKCU systems are based on three fundamental principles: reducing non-value-adding activities, reducing irregular pace of production, and reducing workload.

Structural Systems   Structural systems, including advanced technology, for example robots and automated systems, are used on level 1 of Toyota's system. Toyota uses automation technology cost consciously, that is, automation equipment is bought with just enough functions and high reliability. Automated processes are used for cost reasons. However, Toyota has recently favored semi-automated systems over ones that are fully automated. Semi-automated equipment requires the intervention of skilled workers in automated processes.

Besides advanced technology and automated systems, Toyota utilizes simple and effective methods and manual work. One example for such methods is the Kanban system that reduces inventory by triggering production and parts delivery in response to consumption. The use of cardboard and simple routines regulates the flow of information and parts.

Organizational systems are very important for levels 1 and 2 of Toyota's DKCU system. This is illustrated in the following paragraphs by standard operating procedures, quality systems including quality circles, work teams or maintenance rules, and examples from human resource management and internal consulting.

Standard operating procedures for repetitive tasks explain specifics to the workers with visuals that are easy to understand. Such procedures are frequently revised to include successfully tested ideas that improve the overall result of the team, group, or assembly process. The visuals help all workers to quickly absorb the improvements made.

The system of quality circles is part of the organizational structure and culture. Standardized methods to increase the effectiveness of quality circles include the QC story (a standard sequence of analysis) and QC tools, a collection of visual material, all of which support workers in incremental innovation.

Toyota's culture is based on teams that share the view of partaking in a community of fate (Besser, 1996). Toyota's small work units consist of four to five peers. Enjoying working well, benefiting from incentive systems such as Kaizen awards, and avoiding a bad reputation all motivate team members and leaders to volunteer their energy and compassion. Clusters of such teams form groups that are considered teams. The company team consists of the locally employed who work cooperatively for the same goal. The corporate team encompasses Toyota and its networks. The nested structure creates shared context for locally developing creative routines.

Another system promoting creative routines is called Total Productive Maintenance (TPM), which, together with detailed 5 S rules (regarding cleanliness, order, and discipline), is disseminated throughout the organization. All workers, maintenance specialists, and engineers engage in preventive maintenance of the production equipment. Workers learn about the equipment they use by cleaning and checking the machines, occasionally performing minor repairs and tool changes. The statistical analysis of the machine's processes helps to develop deeper understanding of the equipment and its purpose in use. Such exercising and internalizing of knowledge about the equipment enables workers to develop creative routines in quickly assessing problems and finding solutions.

Skill accumulation is an important factor in Toyota's wage system. Toyota's human resource management promotes the multiskilled worker. Workers are paid by their ability to solve a variety of problems by creating and using knowledge. Leaders of small work teams, for instance, earn 5 percent more than team members because they have greater responsibility, coordination, and motivation tasks. This wage system is linked to job rotation and assignment of multiple tasks. Experience in different workplaces increases worker's knowledge and provides a wider set of creative routines.

The careers of shop floor supervisors are based on diachronic accumulation of knowledge during 10 to 15 years of experience at the assembly line (level 3). Shop floor supervisors are Toyota veterans with multiple experiences on different jobs. The experiences of supervisors are used to share and use creative routines in educational training or through troubleshooting at the production line.

Further, internal consulting groups are a part of the DKCU system that crosses the boundaries of Toyota's organization. They also support suppliers in mastering the Toyota Production System. Recently, Toyota has begun to consult clients outside of the group on the Toyota Production System.

Procedural Systems

Low-cost automation and the organizational systems mentioned previously are insufficient to continuously create and utilize knowledge. They are partial by design and require human intervention. Toyota's dynamic systems create contexts for creative routines. Visualization, distributed knowledge, leadership and cross-boundary teams trigger dialogue and improvising at the actual spot.

Visualization   Toyota uses visualization to sustain improvisation. The automatic detection of defects visualizes fluctuations by stopping the production line (and/on system) and is a strong signal of crisis. This is communicated visually together with detailed information to synchronize the worker's awareness of fluctuations and to elicit a fast solution. Hypotheses are generated (externalization) and tested on the spot to overcome the fluctuations.

The standard operating procedures visualize actions that have proven to be superior in the past (diachronic). Displays, tables, and other visual cues communicate tasks, problems, and performance levels along the assembly line. Several systems such as the Kanban system, vehicle specification sheets on each body, colored lines separating sections on the floor, and different colors to classify boxes make fluctuations visible and create a shared knowledge base for all workers. The visual cues trigger actions such as ordering parts in the Kanban system. The 5 S rules for cleanliness, order, and discipline create a homogeneous background of normality. This state of normality helps to detect fluctuations visually because they are immediately visible as disorder.

Other visual cues are used to discourage and avoid action. The foolproof prevention of problems (poka-yoke) blocks the view on equipment parts that could cause false operation. Such fool-proofing focuses the context on important actions.

Distributed Knowledge and Leadership   Toyota's automatic detection of defects and shut-down of machines uses distributed knowledge in a systematic way (and/on systems). This and/on system interrupts the flow of production if it detects a defect and creates a crisis for all workers on the line. This crisis calls experienced workers for help to use contextual knowledge for solving problems on the spot. This system integrates the contextual knowledge distributed along the assembly line with the tacit knowledge of workers to improve overall performance.

Furthermore, workers can manually stop the assembly line when they detect a problem by pulling a stop cord at several locations along the assembly line. The and/on signboard displays what kind of problem occurred and where (Fujimoto, 1999). This concentrates attention on the actual spot and calls workers with relevant knowledge to join in improvising new solutions. Thus the and/on system visualizes fluctuations and triggers creative routines.

The team structure of working at Toyota creates contexts where individuals share goals, cooperative workstyles, close relationships, and mutual understanding of each member's role. The local contexts in motion concentrate different perspectives, distributed expertise, and resources at the spot when and where fluctuations occur. Team members engage in dialogue with open feedback and aim to create solutions.

Similarly, fluctuations can trigger improvisation in the supplier or sales network. In the supplier network, "face-to-face" competition (Ito, 1989) puts pressure on suppliers to cooperate and innovate. The sales network of Toyota's dealers provides a continuous flow of distributed customer knowledge that influences new product development.

Distributed leadership at Toyota can be illustrated through the quality circles or the and/on system previously noted. Any worker at the assembly line who detects a problem and triggers Kaizen processes, or who takes responsibility, can assume leadership. In the case of Kaizen activities in quality circles, such leadership may receive a small recognition. Taking responsibility at the assembly line can prepare one for leadership of teams or groups.

Toyota emphasizes multiple skills and trains workers so that they have a variety of experiences and understand different perspectives. Shop floor supervisors are multiskilled veterans. Some of them are work team leaders and others are group leaders responsible for several teams. Finding new solutions when fluctuations occur requires a broad range of experience. This puts multiskilled workers in charge of the improvisation process.

Cross-Functional Teams   The Prius hybrid car project goes back to different projects linked to the new corporate vision of environmental responsibility. The development project of the Prius began in January 1996. It represents Toyota's new effort to build cross-functional teams and to use distributed expertise (Nonaka and Toyama, 1999). Each product development phases required knowledge different in scope and depth, and leaders changed accordingly. For the first time, Toyota installed a "team room" for the members of the cross-functional project team (level 2), and used extensive computer networks to link team members, thereby facilitating communication and providing access to databases (level 1).

Further, different design departments in locations such as California, Europe, and Tokyo were involved in the design process. They participated in the internal, international competition that organically linked the distributed knowledge of different communities of practice.

An important breakthrough was achieved by combining different areas of expertise. Vice president Wada had interrupted the development process and forced the team members to abandon old mental models. He created a crisis and urgent need to improvise. Uchiyamada, the chief engineer and project team leader, managed to integrate the necessary technical and design knowledge inside and outside of the company boundaries. Different groups within Toyota such as the R&D group developing the hybrid system, and the Electric Vehicle group, were developing in parallel without knowing of each other's intentions and mutual relevance (diachronic). The time pressure synchronized the battery and the Prius development group, and revealed complementary knowledge assets that they then integrated. Further, the external expertise at Panasonic provided critical knowledge to develop the battery for Prius.

The Prius project was an important experience for Toyota. First, improvising with internally and externally distributed knowledge was never before accomplished to this extent. Second, synchronizing different diachronic histories of professionals in cross-functional teams was very effective. Third, the project has generated new creative routines. Since the project concluded, cross-boundary dialogue and improvisation has been used companywide.

Toyota continuously evolves its production system with emphasis on utilization of knowledge at the assembly line. Recently, it has created a new department promoting new ventures. Here the creation and utilization of innovative concepts is required. In addition, Toyota has begun to cooperate in alliances with other companies to combine existing technologies and capabilities. Alliances with Sony or Kao, a Japanese detergent maker, offer access to advanced marketing knowledge. Forging of such alliances across company boundaries illustrates new creative routines and the transformation of Toyota's system.

Epistemological Manner

Knowledge is defined as justified true belief. Toyota engages in fundamental inquiry to justify true beliefs every day. Shared epistemological manners help organizational members to rigorously question their own hypotheses. To find true cause-effect relationships, Toyota's organizational members ask five times "why." Such patterns make hidden relationships visible and justify hypotheses on a daily basis.

CONCLUSION AND IMPLICATIONS

Shared contexts in motion (*Ba*) are the platforms for knowledge creation and utilization. Such contexts are opportunities in time and space that need to be seized. To provide and to seize such opportunities, organizations have to develop DKCU systems. DKCU systems are open and they continuously prepare *Ba* by juxtaposing soft and hard systems, structural and procedural, internal and external, diachronic and synchronic perspectives.

The creation and utilization of knowledge needs human intervention whenever contextual knowledge in *Ba* is important, which is always the case in innovation. The procedural perspective in DKCU systems allows creating contexts in motion and tapping such contextual knowledge.

To use contextual knowledge and to seize opportunities, static routines are ineffective. Organizations need creative routines to visualize fluctuations and create, test, and develop new ideas. The individual cases of companies have shown creative routines in *Ba* of the assembly line and on the sales floor. Companies that develop dynamic systems for creative routines continuously create and exploit Schumpeter's gales of creative destruction (Schumpeter, 1942, 1962).

CHAPTER 5

Tools for Knowledge Management

Anthony K.P. Wensley
and Alison Verwijk-O'Sullivan

INTRODUCTION

W e have deliberately drawn a wide net in the following discussion of tools for knowledge management. The first part of the chapter could have been restricted to information technology (IT) tools, but although these are becoming increasingly important to knowledge management, they are by no means the only tools available. We feel that it is important to investigate many of the issues surrounding the use of tools in knowledge management using a more general view of the matter. This affords an opportunity to investigate the nature of knowledge management tools in general before focusing on some of the IT tools that are now available in an ever-increasing supply.

The following chapter is divided into two sections. In the first we discuss knowledge management and the nature of the tools that we may have at our disposal to manage knowledge. The second section presents an annotated list of some of the Web-based (IT) tools that are available, and is presented in Appendix 1. This list is necessarily incomplete but we hope that it will give the reader some grasp of the range of tools available. We would also encourage the reader to undertake a voyage through the many Web sites that are referenced. There is really nothing to replace first-hand experience. In the opinion of many, the Web will, in coming years, present us with a rich set of new tools for managing knowledge. This will primarily arise from two of its characteristics: First, it provides an extremely rich common language for representing knowledge—we have only just begun to explore the true nature of this richness. Second, it is an intensely interactive medium allowing for the sharing and cooperative development of knowledge. But more of these issues later.

It is interesting to note that much of the work in Web-based knowledge management tools derives considerable strength from what have been fairly mainstream research and applications in artificial intelligence. This relationship is likely to broaden and deepen in future years, as we will indicate in more detail in the rest of the chapter.

KNOWLEDGE MANAGEMENT

Many researchers in the field of knowledge management seem to think that the field sprang into existence de novo a few years ago. This is demonstrated by a delightful attribution of the definition of knowledge as "justified true belief" to Nonaka when, in fact, such a definition, though not in precisely the same words, was provided by Plato in the Socratic dialogues! Hubris of this order may be attributed to a number of factors. In the first place, knowledge management as a concept seems to have taken flight from the ashes of business process reengineering and a variety of other ideas first promulgated by management consulting firms. Newness and originality are often ascribed to old concepts on the belief that one can charge higher fees as a result! Second, information technology has given us data management, information management, and now, logically, knowledge management. Information technology, from this perspective, created the opportunity for "really" managing knowledge by using information technology.

Having unfairly set up two straw men, let me set them aflame in good pagan fashion. Is knowledge management a new phenomenon? No. Although we certainly see ways in which knowledge management can be seen to have been born of such movements as business process management, customer orientation and the like knowledge in business is certainly not a new phenomenon. Further, with respect to the part that information technology has to play, its existence is neither a necessary nor a sufficient condition for knowledge to be managed. As we hope will be indicated in this chapter, information technology and the tools it provides can certainly support some aspects of knowledge management, but knowledge management does not begin and end with information technology. We concede that data management probably does begin and end with information technology. In many ways information technology created the notion of data today; it allowed for the reduction of information into data and thus it would seem relatively uncontentious to argue that data management is only really possible with information technology. However, we certainly do not believe that this is true for information, let alone knowledge.

Knowledge management has to do with the management of all stages in the generation, codification, refinement, and transmission of knowledge. To the extent that we have any unique perspective in this area, it is as a researcher who has been intimately involved in creating and codifying knowledge in specialist domains for at least a decade and a half. Although we are no longer directly involved in such creation and codification, our research is now directed to many of the issues that arose during this period of prior research.

We have stated that the stages of knowledge management are generation, codification, refinement, and transmission. What is involved in each of these stages? Ruggles (1997, p. 1) elaborates on the stage of knowledge generation as follows: "Knowledge generation includes all activities which bring to light knowledge which is 'new,' whether to the individual, to the group, or to the world. It includes activities such as creation, acquisition, synthesis, fusion, and adaptation." Similarly, he expands on the concept of knowledge codification as follows (1997, p. 2): "Knowledge codification is the capture and representation of knowledge so that it can be re-used either by an individual or by an organization." Finally, he defines knowledge transfer (1997, p. 2) as follows: "Knowledge transfer involves the movement of knowledge from one location to another and its subsequent absorption."

He further notes (1997, p. 2) that: "Generation, codification, and transfer all occur constantly, so management itself does not create these actions. The power of knowledge *management* is in allowing organizations to explicitly enable and enhance the productivity of these activities and to leverage their value for the group as well as for the individual." With respect to a definition of knowledge management tools (1997, p. 3), he states: "Knowledge management tools are technologies, broadly defined, which enhance and enable knowledge generation, codification, and transfer."

Having created a very large canvas, we will now proceed to examine a small portion of it. We will investigate how technology can be used to facilitate each stage of knowledge management. But first, we would like to talk a little about technologies and tools.

A distinction is often made between technologies and methodologies. We shall consider here that a *technology* is some human construct or artifact that potentially can enhance and enable human activities. Typically the way in which a technology is used is directed by some *methodology*—a set of ways of interacting with the technology. A *tool* is one aspect of a technology that is typically used to achieve some specific purpose or related set of purposes.

METHODS, TOOLS, AND CONTEXTS

We think that it is appropriate to observe that mankind has, over the millennia, developed many different approaches to knowledge and knowledge management that have informed both methodologies and technologies. These approaches are typically embedded in what Wittgenstein referred to as "forms of life." As Collins notes (1997, p. 148): "If, so much knowledge rests upon agreements within forms of life, what is happening when knowledge is transferred via bits of paper or floppy disks? We know that much less is transferred this way than we once believed, but something is being encapsulated in symbols or we would not use them. How can it be that artifacts that do not share our forms of life can 'have knowledge' and how can we share it?"

Clearly, one of the reasons that tools can support knowledge management is that they are embedded in particular ways of acting and value systems. Consider, for a moment, the Delphic Oracle. One could say that some of the tools for managing knowledge in this case were the women who made the oracular responses to questions. The women functioned as providers of knowledge partly through the implementation of a methodology concerning the interpretation of the oracular responses by the priests. Thus the tools gain their ability to be part of a knowledge management process through the use of methodologies that lead to the embedding of the tools in a particular "form of life."

When we make the popular distinction between tacit and explicit knowledge, it is easy to forget that even explicit knowledge is only explicit because of a deep and richly understood context that allows us to interpret so-called explicit knowledge. This shared context is such a natural part of our existence that it is easy to ignore its existence until we discover/explore its richness to find that there can be alternative interpretations of what constitutes knowledge and understanding.

Our central point here is that no knowledge management tool stands alone. It can only be understood in the context in which it is used and the methodologies that are associated with it. If we focus too much on the tools of knowledge management we may blind ourselves to this richness. So-called knowledge management tools can potentially be used to manage superstition and falsehood when used in inappropriate contexts.

It is also worth remembering that much esoteric knowledge is difficult to understand and requires expert interpreters. To some extent, though, this very esotericism can be created deliberately. Knowledge confers power and power is often gained and jealously guarded in this manner. Any admission of the pedestrian nature of a particular type of knowledge would make it available to everyone! We still see many of the vestiges of this "form of life" in organizations the world over. Esoteric knowledge is often considered to be dangerous, particularly in the hands of the uninitiated. Secret societies are established with rites of initiation, stages of progress, and secret documents to protect the knowledge and retain its power. In these contexts, knowledge management tools may either be resisted or given token acceptance. Some aspects of organizational knowledge may be represented using the tools but much may be deliberately left out.

Of course, one of the most well-developed sets of tools and methodologies are those of the scientific method. Over many centuries this approach has been enhanced and refined. Technologies have been applied and tools developed to "create" knowledge along with methods. In addition, there is a well-developed social context for the assessment and refinement of scientific knowledge. Scientific knowledge has to be accepted by the scientific community before it becomes scientific knowledge.

The relevance of coming to understand something about what we might call scientific knowledge management is that it can direct our attention to potential gaps in our understanding of knowledge management in organizational contexts. Organizations have evolved into many interrelated "forms of life." The creation of functional disciplines has resulted in there being many different types of knowledge residing in organizations. Some of this knowledge certainly has the status of scientific knowledge—research and development departments often have strong scientific cultures. They have many of the tools that are typically used by the scientific community. On the other hand, much of the marketing department's understanding of consumer behavior may be grounded in scientific disciplines but may also be just as much hunch and intuition as science.

The recognition that there are many different types of knowledge within an organization is the source of much of the richness of organizations. It is often the source of their complexity, the course of their flexible responses to the external environment, the source of competencies that are very difficult for their competition to copy. The fundamental issue at stake, however, is that we ignore such richness at our peril. If we place too much emphasis on one particular type of knowledge or knowledge culture, we are likely to "hollow out" the knowledge of the organization and leave it competitively vulnerable. Knowledge management tools must be used to explore this richness rather than be used to slavishly enforce one particular type of knowledge or knowledge culture.

There are some more general lessons that we can learn from the previous points with respect to knowledge management tools.

- Many tools may have very different functions, depending on the context within which they are used. For example e-mail may provide the basis for sufficiently rich communication between individuals within the scientific community. It may be a tool that facilitates the creation, refinement, and transfer of knowledge in this context. In contrast, when members of the general public share e-mail it may only be the source of rumor and innuendo.
- A particular tool may enforce a particularly restricted approach on the user. This is unlikely to be because there is some inherent inflexibility in the tool itself. It is likely to be the case that in many contexts the tool is perceived in a particular way. A parallel of this problem is the basis of the sociotechnical systems approach. There are many different social contexts into which a particular technology may "fit." The different contexts may have very different values, behaviors, and indeed, knowledge.

One other word of caution with respect to knowledge cultures. It is important to recognize their richness within an organization. It is also important to recognize instances of the inappropriate identification of a particular knowledge culture. When investigating the knowledge cultures within the organization we must compare their knowledge practices with their understanding of these knowledge practices. Some groups may feel that their knowledge is essentially scientific knowledge. On closer inspection we may find that the knowledge is not open to verification, that it comes from unsubstantiated sources, and so on.

Before moving to consider some of the Web-based knowledge management tools that are now available to knowledge management practitioners we would like to review, in a little more detail, the various stages of knowledge management, starting with knowledge generation.

Knowledge Generation

As noted previously, Ruggles (1997, p. 2) states that knowledge generation includes the activities of knowledge creation, knowledge acquisition, knowledge synthesis, knowledge fusion, and knowledge adaptation. One of the most interesting features of most of these activities is the need for intensive communication, and a culture that is accepting of new ideas and is prepared to support exploration. In addition, interestingly enough, there is a need to provide barriers. New knowledge will not be created if there are not barriers to rail against. There needs to be some structure, some established knowledge that catalyzes the process.

What are the tools that aid knowledge generation? Perhaps the most obvious are those that allow for the sharing of knowledge in the first place. It is only through the sharing of knowledge that we become aware of the gaps in our knowledge. In the case of many businesses and organizations it is critically necessary to be able to surface current knowledge and assumptions. It is particularly important to surface fundamental assumptions (the tacit context within which the business operates), the unwritten rules of the organization. In many organizations there have been examples of traditional "knowledge" that has been handed down from one generation to the next. Sometimes this knowledge has been explicitly handed down in company manuals or in training sessions. More often than not, however, it has been embedded in company processes—hidden from view but very much there. Knowledge management tools can be used to surface this knowledge and make it available for critical scrutiny. As we will see in the next section, the artificial intelligence community has built a variety of tools over the years that allow us to represent knowledge, tools that will become central to some aspects of knowledge management over the coming decades.

Knowledge Codification and Refinement

Traditionally, we have codified knowledge in a variety of ways. Artificial intelligence research has provided us with a much clearer understanding of both the strengths and limitations of the approaches we have adopted. One popular approach is to codify our knowledge in terms of rules. This was first exemplified by Aristotle with his syllogism—the rules of correct argumentation, rules that would guarantee that if we started with true propositions we would end up with true deductions. Over the 1980s and 1990s, vast numbers of researchers made use of a variety of tools to encode these rules and investigate their behavior. Tools, such as those based on the programming language Prolog, provided a unique opportunity to investigate the interaction of rules and the range of deductions that could be made from them. In some cases this led to the refinement of the knowledge in question. In other cases it led to the recognition that the knowledge being investigated could be only partially represented in the form or rules or not represented at all. An interesting example of this arose in the law. On the surface, the law would appear to be rule based and it is reasonably so in some areas. However, in many areas of the law a very significant amount of knowledge is needed to interpret the rules and it does not appear that this knowledge can be embedded in the rules themselves.

Unfortunately, we do not have time or space to investigate all the tools that are available for codifying and refining knowledge. Readers who want to explore this area are best advised to seek out the artificial intelligence literature. However, along the lines of our previous discussion, a severe caution is in order about tools that can be used to codify knowledge. These tools typically provide for one way of representing knowledge (though some are somewhat more flexible). The knowledge that you wish to represent may not be representable in this way, or may be only partially representable—as in the case of the law and a rule-based approach. Further, it may take considerable skill and knowledge to be able to interpret the knowledge and represent it using a particular representation. Many of us in the expert systems field spent many years learning how to represent specific knowledge in relatively "simple" rules. Finally, you should always be concerned that knowledge has been lost through the use of too restrictive an approach to representing that knowledge.

Knowledge Transmission

As we have noted previously, the Web provides for the transfer of very rich information in a timely and machine-independent way. Thus, many of the tools that are used for knowledge codification and refinement can be made directly available to anyone who has access to the Web. This potentially allows for the transmission of many different varieties of knowledge.

However, to assume that the Web can "deliver" knowledge is as naïve a belief as the idea that knowledge can be "extracted" from individual experts and embedded in computer programs. The contextual importance of knowledge cannot be overstressed. Interestingly enough, the intensively communicative nature of the Web and the Internet may allow for the building and extension of context in ways that were formerly only possible in face-to-face communities. However, we suspect that there are many other aspects of social context that can be established only through traditional social processes such as assimilation. Having put some boundaries on the potential capabilities of Web-based (enabled) knowledge management tools we will now proceed to investigate some of the major types.

WEB-BASED (-ENABLED) INFORMATION TECHNOLOGY TOOLS FOR KNOWLEDGE MANAGEMENT

There are a number of reasons for focusing on Web-based (or -enabled tools). The most important is that the Web offers a very powerful platform for tools supporting all stages of knowledge management. The Web is an intensively interactive medium providing for rich communication between any user regardless of his or her location or equipment. The Web allows for an unprecedented degree of integration of different representational and communicational media. This allows us to make the most of existing tools while developing a variety of new tools—thus our reference in the following section to some pre-Web tools as well as some unique Web tools.

Traditional Database Tools

More and more sophisticated database modeling tools have been developed over the years. These tools attempt to allow users to create general data properties implicitly within a database. For example, they allow for the creation of objects that have certain properties, can communicate with other objects, and so on. Though the creation of databases we have encapsulated much knowledge from many domains. Some of the clearest examples of knowledge creation arise from the analysis of large amounts of data in databases. Giving structure to data is one of the key stages to statistical analysis. It is no surprise that at the core of the statistical analysis package SAS is a powerful relational database.

Many will argue that, by themselves, these tools do not constitute knowledge management tools. They are data management tools and only become even information management tools through extensive interaction with users. As we have indicated previously, however, it is our belief that all knowledge management tools require extensive interaction with their users.

Process Modeling and Management Tools

In recent years more and more attention has been focused on organizational processes. In the past, the major focus of process knowledge was related to manufacturing processes. Processes that involved the transformation of physical material have been the focal metaphor. Tools that have been built to support these processes may encode considerable knowledge of the process. For example, knowledge relating to the order in which particular activities may be carried out is implicitly present in a particular implementation of the process model. However, it is worth noting that the reasons why particular precedence relations exist may not be encoded in the process management implementation. This can cause problems when the transformation technologies change. In these cases we expect the production engineers to be able to appreciate opportunities for reengineering the process.

Workflow Management Tools

These tools have grown out of traditional flowcharting tools. In a sense they are the process management tools for information-intensive organizations. Workflow tools allow for the specification of the movement of documents in information processes. Interestingly enough, many organizations learn about their information processes through modeling them using workflow management tools. Workflow tools can also be used to implement and manage processes.

As these tools have evolved, they have begun to have capabilities for representing both the knowledge of the workflow process and the knowledge that is processed using the workflow process. However, there is clearly much more work to be done in this area.

Enterprise Resource Management Tools

There is little doubt that Enterprise Resource Planning and Enterprise Resource Management (ERP/ERM) applications embed significant knowledge about the organization and, increasingly, suppliers and customers. At the center of SAP systems are a variety of models of the organization's processes, organizational structure, strategic plans, and so on. There are two key issues here. First, to what extent is this knowledge available explicitly for enquiry, modification, and refinement? Generally speaking, it is not possible to formulate enquiries about the nature of the processes, organizational structure, and so on. The second issue relates to the ability of the various packages to deliver knowledge to the appropriate activities.

Enterprise modeling tools are being developed that provide all the modeling capabilities of ERP/ERM systems along with the explicit representation of organizational and environmental knowledge. Most of these tools are still in the research phase of their development. One system that has been implemented on a variety of test sites was developed by Mark Fox and his coresearchers at the University of Toronto (www.eil.utoronto.ca).

One of the key challenges of ERP packages is to be able to integrate the many different types of knowledge that they represent and present it to many different types of users in a meaningful way.

Agent Tools

These tools rely on *agents*, relatively autonomous programs that can perform a variety of tasks. One example of the use of agents is with respect to finding information. Agents may be provided with the specifications of the information that the user is interested in and they will then search the Web and specified other databases to find the information. Early versions of information-seeking agents did little more than the existing first-generation search engines. New versions of information-seeking agents are more "intelligent" and better able to identify relevant information—they are more aware of the context of queries for information and make use of this knowledge in constructing queries for databases and in selecting information from the Web.

Information agents may facilitate initial activity by the user—as the user attempts to "pull" information by posing particular questions. On the other hand, agents may track the behavior of users and try to anticipate the user's needs for information. These types of tool make use of a "push" strategy.

An interesting development in this area of "push" tools is the Active Collaborative Filtering (ACF) tools. These tools, widely used by such companies as amazon.com, Musicboulevard.com and many other consumer-oriented e-commerce companies, attempt to predict user interests based on the interests of users with similar profiles. This becomes an increasingly powerful technology as the number of users increases and it can also be used to develop profiles of knowledge communities. An interesting, if somewhat breathless, discussion of the potential of ACF can be found at www.lucifer.com/~sasha/articles/ACF.html.

At another level, information-seeking agents can act in a consultative fashion with users. In this mode they are somewhat like human librarians; when the user poses a question the librarian asks further questions of the user in order to refine the question. The refinement function is based on the librarian's knowledge of the structure and content of the databases that are likely to be searched, metaknowledge, and also some knowledge of the domains of knowledge that are liable to be of interest to the user.

Search Engines, Navigation Tools, and Portals

Among the most significant applications for the Web were search engines such as Yahoo, Excite, AltaVista, and the like. There are now many thousands of search engines—some of them essentially generic while others address narrow niches. The first generation of these search engines varied in the quality of information they returned to the user. Some of the search engines performed automatic text-only searches while others relied on human "interpreters" who would access Web pages and then analyze and classify them. The second generation of search engines developed somewhat more sophistication in looking both for specific terms and also related terms, attempting in this way to identify more accurately what the questioner was looking for. In addition, these second-generation search engines used a variety of methods to weed out uninformative hits.

The development of these search engines continues as they begin to become, in part, knowledge navigators. This is hardly a new phenomenon and again draws on earlier work in computer science and, in particular, artificial intelligence. Users are provided with support as they navigate themselves through a knowledge domain in order to locate the knowledge that they are seeking. As these navigation aids become more sophisticated they are having to take account of the user's initial knowledge of the domain and, in some cases, providing instruction as the search proceeds such that the user provides answers that guide subsequent navigation.

In the listing in Appendix 1 we have not provided details of these tools but we do hope to provide a detailed discussion of developments in this area in the coming year. Should the reader be interested in this area please feel free to e-mail Anthony Wensley at wensley@home.com.

Visualizing Tools

The increasing power of computers and the development of high-resolution monitors has given us access to a variety of very powerful visualization tools. Some of these tools have been used for data visualization in areas from financial markets to molecular biology. Other tools have been developed to investigate the structure of knowledge domains and knowledge within domains. We have not provided a detailed listing of these tools since they are only just becoming Web enabled. We do expect that these tools will become increasingly powerful and popular over the next decade.

Collaborative Tools

As indicated previously, one of the key aspects of knowledge and knowledge management is that most stages are to some extent or other collaborative. Over the years, a wide variety of collaborative tools have been developed and many of them are now available through the Web. In Appendix 1 we have provided some examples of collaborative tools but there remain, of course, many tools that are not referenced. Some tools provide for setting up bulletin boards and others provide for real-time videoconferencing, whiteboards, and chat rooms. The potential for the development of new collaborative tools is vast.

Virtual Reality

In addition to collaborative tools that provide support for direct communication, others provide environments for collaboration through interactive model building and analysis. We have only just begun to tap some of the power of virtual realities in this area. Virtual realities provide an active laboratory for investigating, representing, and refining knowledge. These realities can also be excellent tools for sharing knowledge.

APPENDIX 1

The following survey of Web-based and Web-enabled software tools for knowledge management was compiled by Alison Verwijk-O'Sullivan. It is presented in alphabetical order and refers to a wide range of Web or Web-enabled tools. Some of these tools are basic e-mail or e-mail filtering tools, some are tools for document management, and others are sophisticated tools for building Intranets and analyzing their structure and performance.

The descriptions of the products provided in the listings are those supplied by the firms themselves. The assessments of the products do not necessarily represent the assessments of the authors, nor should they be taken as any expressed or implied endorsement of the products by the authors.

In the following listing we have used the Ernst and Young categories of the activities involved in knowledge management to give an initial "cut" at the capabilities of each of the tools. As a further refinement, the following categories have been identified:

- Acquire
- Store
- Deploy
- Add value

We plan to make a more refined version of this catalog available on the Web. If you are interested in this project please send an e-mail to wensley@ home.com so that we can update you on the progress of the project.

Table 5.1

Web–Based and Web–Enabled Software Tools for Knowledge Management

E&Y Category	Company Name	Product Name	www Address	Notes/Description
Acquire	Eloquent Software	Eloquent Presenter!, Presenter! Server Consulting	www.eloquent.com	Eloquent is a complete turnkey solution. The Eloquent Presenter! Software lets users navigate easily to information they need through a powerful multimedia player from a CD-ROM or the Presenter! Server that efficiently delivers Eloquent content over both corporate intranets and the Internet. The Eloquent Services group leverages this power to deliver complete multimedia applications in a fraction of the time required by traditional multimedia tools.
Acquire	Infoseek	Ultraseek Server	www.infoseek.com/products/ultraseek	Harness the power of Infoseek's award-winning search and spidering technology for your own Web. Whether it's a single public system, a huge corporate intranet, or anything in between, our hands-off approach to administration will get you up and running immediately. From the user's perspective, natural language queries that yield the most relevant results and an index that is always complete and up-to-date make Ultraseek a real favorite.
Acquire Add value Deploy	WebCrossing	WebCrossing	www.lundeen.com	WebCrossing® is the world's leading discussion and chat software, the most commonly used discussion and chat software, the top choice online among high-profile sites, is the most scalable, reliable discussion software, is the most flexible and customizable solution, offers the greatest functionality and capability. Dialogue—distance learning, online collaboration software.
Acquire Add value Deploy	Semio Corp.	SemioMap 2.1— SemioMap Server, SemioMap Client	www.semio.com	SemioMap® is text-mining software that provides the ability to discover and leverage new value in the glut of textual information on corporate intranets. Semio is a pioneer of text-mining software that enables medium-to-large-sized organizations to increase the value of undiscovered knowledge buried within large volumes of unstructured, text-based data. Supports document formats in text, HTML, PDF. Knowledge management.

Table 5.1
(continued)

E&Y Category	Company Name	Product Name	www Address	Notes/Description
Acquire Deploy	Seeker Software	The Seeker Workplace™	www.infoxpress.com/ acc/ knowledgemanagement/	Seeker Software™ is the leading provider of employee and managerial self-service intranet Web applications for the enterprise. The Seeker Workplace™ is a suite of HR and financial applications that even un-trained users can access via standard Web browsers to automate everyday workplace transactions, previously paper-based. These applications deliver immediate bottom-line benefits through improved productivity, employee service, and satisfaction.
Acquire Deploy	Well Engaged	Well Engaged Discussions Server 3.0	www.wellengaged.com	Well Engaged provides the total solution for creating thriving online collaboration and online communities by creating an interaction between people and content with the leading discussion board software; Chat software; Extensive consulting services. Dialogue distance learning, online collaboration software.
Acquire Store	Cogito Inc.	None yet. . . consulting	www.cogito-software. com	This year, Cogito will move its focus more fully toward Internet-based solutions, building interactive Web sites for its clients and developing real-time intranet-based document imaging and management systems. Internet-centered development (interactivity through Perl, Java, etc.), forms, automated responses, etc., online databases, searchable resources, live computational activity sites.
Acquire Store	FileNet Corporation	Panagon Family including "Panagon Web Publisher"; Watermark	www.filenet.com	Filenet offers a modular suite of off-the-shelf products that are highly scalable, tightly integrated, and yet flexible enough to configure to a client's specific requirements. For transaction-intensive environments and other applications that can benefit from structured organization, workflow processing and retrieval of scanned records, Filenet integrates and supports industry leading document imaging, workflow, and Computer Output to Laser Disk (COLD) software. Document management. NOT WEB ENABLED

	Company	Products	URL	Description
Acquire Store Add value (indexing) Deploy	MicroSearch Corp.	re:Search, CDSearch, Online re:Search, PDL, EmailBox	www.microsearch.net	Internet and CD-ROM Quick Access Solutions—electronic publishing solutions to help organizations meet their research information access and distribution goals. (1) Easy-to-use, customizable Quick Access interface. (2) Index of every word and number in the library. (3) Quick Access to valuable information and images. (4) e-Commerce enabled for Internet, CD-ROM sales.
Acquire Store Add value Deploy	DataBeam	neT.120 Conference Server, DataBeam Learning Server, DataBeam MeetingTools, FarSite	www.databeam.com	A leader in the market for multimedia communications technology, DataBeam's products range from application software to servers to developers' toolkits for the Internet and dial-up networks. (1) neT.120 Conference Server—our award-winning software for real-time collaboration and conferencing over the Internet. (2) DataBeam Learning Server—a software-only server for live web-based training and distance learning. Now a part of the Lotus LearningSpace Family! (3) DataBeam MeetingTools—advanced presentation and whiteboarding software for Microsoft's popular NetMeeting. (4) FarSite—our award-winning client software for application sharing and whiteboarding—the perfect compliment to neT.120.
Acquire Store Deploy	Arbortext	Epic, Adept Series of Web page development tools, Consulting	www.arbortext.com	Web publishing and document management. ArborText develops and supports software that makes the process of capturing and delivering knowledge more effective. Global 5,000 organizations use the company's products to author, catalog, and reuse information stored in document databases. "Epic is open, scalable software that streamlines the product information flow."
Acquire Store Deploy	askSam Systems	askSam 3.0/ Professional	www.asksam.com	askSam 3.0/Professional—The fast, flexible way to organize your information. **Web Publisher—The easy way to put full-text searchable databases on the Net. **Electronic Publisher—Distribute information on disk or CD-ROM. **Resume Tracking System—Track and organize resumes with askSam. **SurfSaver—The Searchable Filing Cabinet for Web Page.

Table 5.1
(continued)

E&Y Category	Company Name	Product Name	www Address	Notes/Description
Add value	InterNetivity Inc.	dbProbe 2.0	www.InterNetivity.com	dbProbe 2.0 is a Java-based decision support tool that offers access to, and analysis of, multidimensional data over the Web. The dbProbe client sets the standard in Web-based user interfaces, providing solid desktop integration, connectivity to OLE DB for OLAP compliant servers and more. Its architecture also makes dbProbe the ideal complement for other applications, such as e-commerce, ERP, and others. Leading tool for Web-based OLAP and reporting.
Add value Deploy	Time Vision	OrgPublisher for Intranets	www.infoxpress.com/ acc/ knowledgemanagement/	OrgPublisher for intranets generates organization charts for intranet distribution. Editions are available for creating organization charts automatically from employee data or manually. Employees can view, search, and print published charts using their Web browsers. You can publish charts with hotspots. Download a free 30-day trial from www.timevision.com.
Deploy	Ardent Software	RedBack	www.vmark.com	RedBack—A comprehensive, database-independent solution for building and delivering scalable, transactional applications for the Internet and corporate intranets. RedBack lowers Web technology barriers and makes it easier to integrate Web-based systems with existing data and applications.
Deploy	Diffusion Inc.	Diffusion	www.diffusion.com	The Diffusion System is designed for fast-paced information transactions. Distribute information from any source file in each individual's preferred communication channel. The Diffusion customer relationship management (CRM) solution, a leader in the category, provides full-service customer relationships by leveraging your existing IT and Web infrastructure investments. Diverse touch points automatically work together to enable higher levels of individualized service without increasing your costs—a deadly combination that your competitors can't match.

Category	Company	Product	URL	Description
Store	Chrystal Software	Astoria 2.0	www.chrystal.com	Astoria is a high-performance document component management system. Xerox New Enterprises launched Chrystal Software as an independent company. Chrystal Software's Astoria was originally developed and marketed by Xsoft. Document management.
Store	Hyperwave	Hyperwave Information Server 4.0	www.hyperwave.de/hw-man/wavemaster	Info publishing server solutions. Hyperwave offers solutions and services enabling organizations to turn information into knowledge. Web site in German.
Store Add value	Dvorak Internet Development, Inc.	WebSprite™	www.WebSprite.com	WebSprite™ is a "Web scrubber" that specializes in gathering specific data automatically from the Web. By allowing a wide variety of support links, WebSprite™ ensures that the user is provided links back to sites and specific pages that enhance the headline, and make Web usage a targeted and highly effective experience.
Store Add value Deploy	Action Technologies	ActionWorks™ Metro	www.actiontech.com	ActionWorks™ Metro, the market-leading Web-based workflow software suite, is designed to rapidly deliver collaborative and administrative business applications across intranets and extranets. Metro enables professionals, managers, and executives to work together on high-impact business interactions that speed customer acquisition, product development, and service delivery. Metro manages 100% of work, including not only structured business processes, but also the collaborative projects and ad hoc tasks that account for a majority of knowledge work. Intranet management, document management.
Store Deploy	Aviator Software	Aviator R2.1 (coming soon)	www.aviatorsoftware.com	Aviator is the easiest, most cost-effective document management system for your Lotus Notes users. Aviator is fully integrated with Lotus Notes and can be deployed within minutes on any Lotus Notes platform and the Internet.
Store Deploy	Baker, Thomsen Associates	Benefit Internet Communicator	www.infoxpress.com/acc/knowledgemanagement/	Benefit Internet Communications allows employees to access information regarding group benefit plans. Saves costs, minimizes report preparation and staff time. Increases employee satisfaction—takes advantage of FAQs available on carrier sites, links employees to provider directories. Electronic Safeharbor for DOL, SPD, and SMM reporting, saves time, lets the Internet answer questions.

CHAPTER 6

Managing Knowledge Assets in Diverse Industrial Contexts

David J. Teece

INTRODUCTION There is increasing recognition that the competitive advantage of firms depends on their ability to build, utilize, and protect difficult to imitate knowledge assets. The shift to knowledge assets as the basis of competitive advantage is rather ubiquitous as the liberalization and expansion of markets domestically and internationally enables components/inputs to be available to all firms everywhere at similar prices. Even if components don't trade freely, firms can frequently locate where they can access low-cost components. Fueled by free-market philosophy and assisted by new information technology, these developments are having a leveling effect with respect to competitive advantage. The trend is well established, and unlikely to be reversed.

In this chapter, certain general implications are distilled. Managerial challenges that flow from the centrality of knowledge and intellectual property are rather different from those from a bygone era in which physical assets were key. Furthermore, there are also major differences in knowledge management requirements from situation to situation according to the underlying cost and demand logic at work, the appropriability regimes in which the firm operates, the importance of compatibility standards, the nature of innovation at issue, and the richness of the technological opportunity facing the firm. This chapter analyzes knowledge management requirements in these different contexts. But first, some background.

CREATING VALUE WITH KNOWLEDGE ASSETS

The nature of knowledge assets is such that they cannot be readily bought and sold. Because they frequently cannot be bought, they must be built in-house by firms, and they frequently must also be exploited internally in order for full value to be realized by the owner. This observation flows from the fact that the market for know-how is far from complete, and where it exists it is far from "efficient." This condition derives from the absence of commodity-like markets for knowledge assets, caused in part by the nature of knowledge itself and in particular, the difficult to articulate and codify "tacit dimension." These transactional difficulties are mainly associated with organizational knowledge. Personal knowledge can, of course, be more readily bought and sold. Transactions in personal knowledge occur every day, when particular (individual) talent is hired and fired. Organizational knowledge or organizational competence is a different matter, being embedded as it is in organizational processes, procedures, routines, and structures. Such knowledge cannot be moved into an organization without the transfer of clusters of individuals with established patterns of working together. This is most frequently accomplished through mergers and acquisitions of business units, if not entire enterprises.

In short, the absence of a well-developed market for knowledge renders it imperative that firms innovate internally. Put differently, innovation cannot be outsourced in its entirety, even though internal efforts can be successfully augmented through external acquisition activities (Chesbrough and Teece, 1996). Specification of the internal environment and processes adapted to support rapid innovation is, of course, a topic on which much has been written and a good deal is understood. Accordingly, this topic will not detain us further in this chapter, despite its great importance. Rather, attention is given to several related aspects of knowledge management: extracting value through (1) disembodied transfer inside the firm (internal technology transfer and utilization), (2) disembodied external transfer, and (3) bundled sale of technology (embodied in an item or device).

But first, a basic observation. Much knowledge is of limited commercial value unless bundled in some way. A line of software code is of little utility until it is combined with other pieces of software to constitute a program. (For example, units of software smaller than "applets" cannot typically be bought and sold.) The absence of markets (due possibly to high transaction cost) is the reason that this is so. More frequently, know-how does not command external value until it is embedded in products. Only then can it be an item of sale.[1]

There are exceptions. Even when they are not an item of sale, knowledge assets relating to production processes can generate great value inside the firm. The internal technology transfer and use of process know-how is less compromised by the absence of a market for know-how. Indeed, the very essence of a large, integrated firm can be traced in large part to its capacity to facilitate (internal) exchange and transfer of knowledge assets and services, assisted and protected by administrative processes (Teece, 1980; 1982). We examine each mode of extracting value from knowledge, as each raises distinctive knowledge management issues.

TRANSFERRING KNOWLEDGE ASSETS

Given that technology transfer inside the firm is not significantly impeded by proprietary concerns, one would think that technology transfer and use inside the firm would be straightforward. However, this is definitely not the case. As Lew Platt, CEO of HP once put it: "If only HP knew what HP knows, we would be three times more productive!" The large size of many enterprises, their global reach, the importance of knowledge to competitiveness, and the availability of tools to assist knowledge transfer has sharpened the competitive importance of accomplishing knowledge transfer inside the firm.

In the 1960s and 1970s, knowledge transfer inside the firm was viewed as being mainly one way: out from research and development to the divisions, and out from the United States to the rest of the world. Now, if not then, the flow is in all directions. Research and development is no longer as centralized organizationally as it used to be. Moreover, the sources of knowledge are diffused geographically, requiring flows from the periphery to the center, and from one node on the periphery to another. Casually formed networks no longer suffice to diffuse best practice and new knowledge more generally. As Larry Prusak asks, if the coffeepot was a font of useful knowledge in the traditional firm, what constitutes a virtual one? How do we manage face time in a firm of tens of thousands? The requirement is to use (information) technology creatively.

We know very little about how to transfer technology inside the firm. Economists and other social scientists frequently have a poor grasp of this topic and are often content to assume that the transfer is costless, when clearly it is not (Teece, 1976). Managers are not much better informed, although top management in many companies (e.g., British Petroleum, Hewlett Packard) has flagged the importance of knowledge transfer issues. Moreover, the knowledge that needs to be transferred is not simply technological. Knowledge about competitors, customers, and suppliers is also a part of the mix, as is managerial experience. Such knowledge is often embedded in operating rules and practices; in customer, supplier, and competitor data banks; and in the company's own history. As mentioned earlier, there is also an important tacit dimension that is difficult to transfer, absent the transfer of people.

In the information age, there is both the need and the opportunity to match information and knowledge needs with availability in ways that have hitherto been impossible. Knowledge that is trapped inside the minds of key employees, in file drawers, and databases is of little value if not supplied to the right people at the right time. Information "float"—the time lapse between knowledge discovery/creation and transfer/use—is extremely costly, at least in opportunity cost terms. Corporate intranets and the Internet itself can help facilitate the flow of such information. However, information itself rarely constitutes knowledge, so IT tools are never the entire solution. Moreover, knowledge and competence are often widely diffused in an organization. Some may lie in research and development laboratories, some on the factory floor, and some in the executive suite. Often what is critical is the capacity to weave it all together. Although universities can frequently avoid the imperative of cross-disciplinary activities, firms cannot eschew the need for cross-functional and geographical integration without paying a heavy penalty in the marketplace.

Although proprietary barriers to internal knowledge transfer are typically absent, within the firm transfer is not friction free and costless, as noted previously. Merely finding the person or group with the knowledge one needs is often quite difficult. In addition, issues such as absorptive capacity (Teece 1976) rooted in education and experiences, social, professional, and hierarchical contexts also appear to be important (Seely Brown and Duguid, 1998, p. 102). "Gatekeepers," "translators," and "internal knowledge brokers" are often needed to effectuate transfer (ibid, p. 103).

External transfer, from one organization to another, occurs either as a consequence of deliberate transfer (under learning and know-how agreements), of inadvertent transfer (e.g., spillovers in the context of alliances), or through the imitative activities of competitors. Clearly, the external flow of that knowledge protected by intellectual property rights (e.g., trade secrets) is impeded (to the extent that intellectual property law is effective or deemed to be so), as compared to flows inside the firm. However, much knowledge is not protected by intellectual property law. Indeed, Seely Brown and Duguid claim that "knowledge often travels more easily between organizations than it does within them" (1998, p. 102). Their claim appears to derive from the observation that "knowledge moves differently within communities than it does between them. Within communities, knowledge is continuously embedded in practice and thus, circulates easily" (p. 100). This is undoubtedly true, but as a general matter, internal transfer is easier.

Firms often enter into licensing and technology transfer arrangements. This can dramatically accelerate the transfer of technology because it not only removes intellectual property barriers, but also is frequently accompanied by technology transfer agreements that provide technology transfer assistance. The challenges associated with such external transfers are significantly softened (as compared to the internal challenge) by the frequent absence of a requirement for the subsequent transfer of updates and improvements. It is substantially easier to transfer a known technology for which there is operating and transfer experience than it is to constantly and continuously transfer state of the art.

Perhaps the most frequent way that knowledge assets are transferred is by bundling know-how (because consumers aren't interested in know-how per se, but the utility/functionality it provides to goods and services) with the services of complementary assets, and producing an item for sale, which is then shipped to the customer. Indeed, this is the familiar way that knowledge assets come to yield value to the enterprise (Teece, 1986).

INFORMATION MANAGEMENT AND KNOWLEDGE MANAGEMENT

Much of the excitement around knowledge management has been propelled by advances in information technology. However, information transfer is not knowledge transfer, and information management is not knowledge management, although the former can certainly assist the latter. Indeed, the very success of information technology in making information accessible at low cost highlights the difference between information and knowledge. Individuals and organizations now frequently suffer from information overload. Just as the winner of a national quiz show may never go on to do anything beyond the mediocre, so might a corporation with excellent IT systems have trouble competing. Knowledge is not primarily about facts and what we refer to as content. Rather, it is more about context. Knowing how to select, interpret, and integrate information into a usable body of knowledge is a far more valuable individual and organizational skill then simply being able to know the answer to a discrete question or a series of questions. Accordingly, data warehousing and date mining exercises are useless, absent other knowledge and other sense-making statistical and organizational processes.[2] This is not surprising, given the tacit nature of much organizational knowledge. Information technology assists in the storage, retrieval, and transfer of codified knowledge; but unassisted by other organizational processes, the productivity benefit from information technology is generally quite limited.

However, the combination of information technology and co-aligned organizational processes can significantly enhance learning and competitive advantage. In addition, the conversion of tacit to codified or explicit knowledge can make the firm more innovative and more productive (Nonaka and Takeuchi, 1995). Once knowledge is made explicit, it is easier to store, reference, transfer, and hence redeploy. Cutting the other way is the fact that once it is codified, it is sometimes harder to protect. Once data is held electronically, it can be sent almost anywhere in the world in seconds. In the wrong hands, it can "leak out" comprehensively and quickly. However, the absence of strong intellectual property protection is usually not sufficient to warrant managerial strategies in favor of suppressing the conversion of tacit knowledge to explicit knowledge, as such suppression harms the owner's ability to use, reuse, and combine such knowledge. Moreover, in most jurisdictions, there is some form of trade secret protection, thereby providing a medium of protection against the misappropriation of explicit knowledge.

KNOWLEDGE MANAGEMENT AND THE DESIGN OF FIRMS

Structural Issues

The migration of competitive advantage away from tangible assets to intangible helps highlight some fundamental aspects of the business firm. Firms are sometimes portrayed as organizations designed to protect specific physical, locational, and human capital assets (Williamson, 1985). The protection of asset values from recontracting hazards will be an ending feature of the business enterprise. In the global economy we now confront, it is intangible capital that is preeminent; but in addition to protecting such capital against recontracting hazards, one must also focus on generating, acquiring, transferring, and combining such assets to meet customer needs.

In order to be successful in these activities, firms and their management must be entrepreneurial. They must exhibit capabilities that I have labeled elsewhere as dynamic. To be entrepreneurial, firms must be organized to be highly flexible and responsive (Teece, 1996). That in turn requires a set of attributes that include:

1. *Flexible boundaries*: a presumption in favor of outsourcing and alliances[3]
2. *High-powered incentives*: to encourage aggressive response to competitive developments
3. *Nonbureaucratic decision making*: decentralized, or possibly autocratic; self-managed to the extent possible
4. *Shallow hierarchies*: both to facilitate quick decision making, and rapid information flow from the market to decision makers
5. *An innovative and entrepreneurial culture*, which favors rapid response and the nurturing of specialized knowledge

As Charles Leadbeater[4] points out, orthodoxy both from the left and the right does not always find the new emphasis on entrepreneurship agreeable. The left has demonized entrepreneurs as profit-hungry exploiters of the weak and the poor. Meanwhile, many orthodox economists on the right have no place for the entrepreneur in their intellectual frameworks. In the perfectly competitive world of equilibrium economics, the entrepreneur is superfluous. It is mainly in the Austrian school that one finds a ready acceptance for the critical role of the entrepreneur in economic development. More recently, the role of entrepreneurship in management is beginning to be recognized (Teece, 1998).

The modern corporation, as it accepts the challenges of the new knowledge economy, will need to evolve into a knowledge generating, knowledge integrating, and knowledge protecting organization. Although many companies have performed these functions with proficiency for decades, if not centuries, the global transformations taking place are quite radical in their implications for management of many old-line enterprises, requiring and enabling an entirely new level of proficiency in knowledge management. In the new economy, significant premiums are being placed on the entrepreneurial capacities of management, and on the capacities firms develop for building, protecting, transferring and integrating knowledge—both productive knowledge and customer knowledge. The ability of an organization to exhibit dynamic capabilities is critical to success. Absent the organizational capacity to make sense of the evolving reality, the corporation will fall upon hard times. Entrepreneurial leaders must be able to make good decisions based on limited information. They must understand the evolving needs of customers in market contexts that are changing at high speed.

Compensation and Employment Issues

If hierarchy is antithetical to performance of knowledge based firms, how can one gain confidence that members of the organization are working for the organization and not against it? The answer lies, in part, with performance pay and equity based compensation systems. Providing clear performance based metrics facilitates high autonomy; if well designed it also facilitates goal congruence. Equity provides a sense of membership and belonging.

The use of equity pay is still largely a U.S. phenomenon, and significant reliance on it tends to be mainly confined to high-growth Silicon Valley–type companies. It has worked very well in a variety of diverse contexts. For the individual, it can provide spectacular returns if the company does well; for the company, it can facilitate a strong sense of "belonging" when there may not be much else. It can also save on cash compensation, which may well be advantageous when cash is tight or earnings are marginal relative to market expectations.

The use of equity based compensation works better when there is good liquidity (a publicly traded security complemented by a publicly traded option; or at least a prospect of each). Indeed, in the United States, the possibility of receiving stock in an entity is frequently a spur toward uncommon efforts and uncommon sacrifices, to the benefit of the enterprise and its members.

In a high-flex organization, such equity compensation ought not be limited to those traditionally thought of as "insiders" or "employees." Independent contractors and suppliers can, and should, be linked in where possible. Even customers can be included if the customer is accepting uncommon purchaser risk, as when a customer helps with early product adoption and testing, or when a customer places a large up-front order to help legitimize the company and its products.

Highly flexible Silicon Valley–type firms, where there is a presumption in favor of outsourcing, but where critical knowledge assets are built and protected internally, are likely to be a favorite organizational form in some sectors of the new knowledge economy (Teece, 1996). The corollary is that the employment relationship will continue to evolve, with distinctions between "inside" the firm and "outside" the firm becoming increasingly blurred.

Successful companies will always have those with whom they collaborate, be they other firms (located upstream, downstream, and laterally), individuals, or universities. When the sources of knowledge are widely dispersed, such collaboration is likely to be extensive. Networks are thus frequently critical to the knowledge based firm. But even though networks have been of growing importance for at least a couple of decades, one should not presume that this means that the integrated corporation is doomed. It is here to stay. As explained elsewhere (e.g., Chesbrough and Teece, 1996), the corporation cannot outsource its key systems integration capability where specialized knowledge assets are required for competitive advantage; these should be developed and practiced internally. But it can outsource functions not critical to the firm's core activities. Indeed, it will frequently find providers who specialize in such "routine" support functions. Such firms can provide a level of service that the firm might not be able to provide for itself, possibly because of scale, or possibly simply because the supplier has developed other relevant knowledge. Clearly, one is unlikely to be able to beat one's competitors with respect to a function if one sources that function externally; but if one is behind, one can certainly catch up through outsourcing.

INDUSTRIAL CONTEXT

In this chapter, and in a series of articles over the past decade, I have advanced the proposition that competitive advantage (superior profitability) at the enterprise level depends on the creation and exploitation of difficult to replicate nontradable assets, of which knowledge assets are the most important. Although this proposition is advanced as having general applicability, its strength is likely to vary according to industrial context. Putting to one side sectors of the economy shielded from competition by government regulation (where political access and regulatory influence are key drivers of firm performance), it would appear that other aspects of the environment also impact the strength of the proposition and affect appropriate managerial responses. In this section, we explore how the underlying cost and demand dynamics and other factors affect knowledge management, and strategic management more generally.

There is even greater variability in competitive dynamics as one looks across activities in the economy that use different knowledge assets, or possibly no proprietary knowledge assets. That is not to suggest that the knowledge economy is or will be confined to just a few activities or industries. All industries open to competition will be affected. But the underlying cost/success drivers are different in different contexts. Understanding the relative role of knowledge assets and dynamic capabilities is obviously of some importance. Perhaps we can begin by looking at extremes. Where is the new logic of organization likely to have its greatest impact? Where is it likely to have the least impact?

Identifying environments where there is already, or will soon be, a significant premium associated with the ownership and orchestration of knowledge assets is not difficult. Multimedia, Web services, electronic banking, and brokerage are just a few obvious examples. Less obvious, but equally important, is agriculture. Technology has always been critical to agricultural productivity, but new information technology coupled with satellite surveillance and active futures market participation is enabling more astute decision making with respect to crop selection and harvesting. Biotechnology is meanwhile creating a more visible revolution with respect to plant and animal selection and growth. Ironically, education is one of the least impacted sectors, in part because of its public ownership and the limited competition that exists in many locales. Traditionally low-tech activities like retailing are meanwhile undergoing a revolution, enabled by information technology, and confronted by the Internet as an alternative and competitive distribution channel.

Physical assets will, however, remain important in many industries. We will still need steel mills and petroleum refineries, though they will be run in quite different ways. Take the oil business, for example. Once the current wave of consolidation has leveled gross capacity utilization differentials, firms will be able to compete either through new technology (better and cheaper ways of finding, transporting, refining, or distributing oil), or through political influence (being better at winning in the political allocation of rights to explore for, produce, and transport oil). The physical assets will not, however, provide a source of significant differentiation. Indeed, global competition and the expansion of intermediate product markets (including futures markets) means that one can compete downstream as a "virtual" refiner, outsourcing supply while protecting oneself in financial markets from the risk thereby involved. Accordingly, there is no easy metric for carving out sectors of the economy that might be insulated to some degree from the fundamental dynamics described earlier. One cannot do it based on R&D sales, because so much R&D is "outsourced" in one way or another, and because R&D in one industry impacts the competitive dynamics of another, as when biotech research impacts agriculture.[5] Nor can one do it solely on the basis of the underlying cost dynamics that characterize the industry.

There is a need to identify factors that make knowledge management salient. Figure 6.1 is an attempt to identify several factors. Each factor that helps define relevant dimensions of industrial context is briefly described in the following paragraphs.

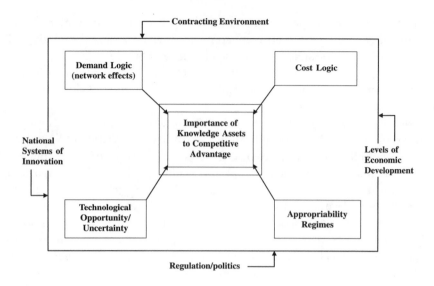

Figure 6.1   *Factors Impacting Knowledge Management*

Increasing Returns

In many industries today, and in particular in the information industries themselves, increasing returns are the norm. This is not just a matter of increasing returns to scale, as the phenomenon flows from both demand- and supply-side considerations. The effect is that whoever gains advantage, ceteris paribus, gains further advantage. Whoever loses advantage will tend to lose further advantage (e.g., Apple Computer in the early 1990s). Momentum lost is difficult, though not impossible, to regain, as Apple Computer is demonstrating.

There are at least three reasons for this phenomenon. The first is cost. High-tech products involve large development costs—perhaps more than $250 million for the first disk of Microsoft Windows 95. The second disk could be created for almost nothing, and if distributed over the Internet could be distributed for next to nothing. Although there are up-front fixed costs in many of the older industries (e.g., steel and autos), scale economies would tend to become exhausted before industry demand was substantially satisfied. The second reason is because of demand-side factors. The bigger a network gets, the more utility is associated with being on that network. This is because the product might well become a standard, actual or de facto. The third reason is the development of user knowledge, familiarity, and skills with the product. One might become familiar with WordPerfect, or Microsoft Word, and so if upgrades are available, the user will go with the product that builds on the user's skills.

These demand- and supply-side factors work together to produce increasing returns. They also tend to make markets unstable in that there is an absence of smooth substitution possibilities among products or platforms. The market may tip one way, and then possibly another. There is a tendency for the market to "lock in" once one firm's product gets ahead, whether due to superior acumen, small chance events, clever strategizing, government regulation, or judicial blundering; but one should not think that whoever gets started first will necessarily win. Moreover, lock-ins may be quite weak and easily surmountable because switching costs are low. Like the presidential primaries, there is much that can happen between New Hampshire and California, although it typically doesn't hurt to win in New Hampshire. But even if one loses there, one can catch up through the use of complementary assets (e.g., advertising programs) and clever strategy, good luck, and hard work. In product markets, one needs to focus on trying to get bandwagons going. Having a good product that is attractively priced helps immensely in increasing returns contexts.

Industry position may well become established for a while, but certainly not forever. Lotus 1-2-3 dominated spreadsheets for a while, Digital dominated minicomputers for a decade, and Microsoft may have DOS/Windows as the standard for the PC OS for a few more years; but all eventually get overturned.[6] It is not that competition stops once dominance[7] is achieved. It simply takes on a new form. Once a standard is anointed by the market, competitors push for a new standard and may have to develop a radical new technology to make it happen. Monopoly power, if attained, is transient, not permanent. Competition in the market gets displaced by competition for the market.

When competition is of this kind, competitive strategies must adjust. The payoff to market insight—figuring out where the market is heading and investing heavily to get there first—is high. The strategic challenge is therefore in part cognitive. However, even if an organization is good at figuring out the future, to succeed one must be good at responding quickly. Directed strategies, quickly and comprehensively implemented, are what is required: witness Bill Gates's response at Microsoft in 1995 once he figured out the significance of the Internet. The ability to sense and then seize such opportunities is in part an organizational capability. In Section II and elsewhere, it has been referred to as dynamic capability (Teece, 1998; Teece, Pisano, and Shuen, 1997; Teece and Pisano, 1994).

In increasing returns environments, the challenge is to engineer products and services that can potentially become industry standards. Superior technology clearly matters, but it will not succeed alone. Not only does one need complementary assets, one also needs the capacity to build a bandwagon effect, suggesting the importance of disseminating information about marketplace successes, the willingness to price low to build an installed base, and strong dynamic capabilities to sense and then seize opportunities. Virtual structures may well be ideal early on, when the payoff to flexibility is high.

Once anointed as the flag bearer, firms must keep innovating as staying ahead is by no means inevitable. Failure to engineer the next generation of products satisfactorily could well unseat the incumbent. The incumbent is also confronted by competition for the market. The stakes escalate as the market grows. The main reason for technology transfer is not to keep the product on the frontier of technology—although that matters—but to maintain the standard by licensing others (complementors) to keep supporting and developing the established standard.

Constant Returns

Large sectors of the economy are still characterized by constant returns to scale. Getting ahead is desirable, but it need not confer much advantage to profit margins, even though total profits may expand. Professional services (e.g., accounting, consulting, law) may well fall into this category, together with scalable industries like food processing, book publishing, copiers, printers, paints, pharmaceuticals, adhesives, and shoes. In these industries, the outcome of competitive battles depends on cost, quality, and product and process innovation.

Knowledge management is important. The ability of firms to create new products that meet customers' needs requires a constant tuning of product offerings. Market share is gained in little bites, and dominance, if attained, is not protected through "lock-in" effects or switching costs. Competitive advantage is built the old fashioned way, by keeping customers happy. Because competition is within the market, rather than for the market, the threat from inside the industry is relatively more important than the threat from the outside. Learning is key to staying competitive, and licensing is critical to keeping technologies and products refreshed.

Because technical expertise is of great importance in firms that compete in these contexts, the management of knowledge assets is critically important. The entrepreneurial factor is less significant because innovation can be more "routinized." The techniques and tools of knowledge management must find their full expression here, if competitive advantage is to be built and maintained. Constant returns environments also offer opportunities for the global expansion of the business. There are no diseconomies associated with expansion.

Constant returns industries may vary in their research and development intensity. Some, like drugs, specialty chemicals, and robotics are highly research/knowledge intensive; others, like tobacco, consulting, and petroleum refining, are less so. Needless to say, knowledge management is especially critical in the research and development intensive industries, but is not unimportant in the others. Indeed, in the less research and development intensive industries, effective knowledge management can lead to differentiation that wasn't hitherto possible, allowing better customer information and knowledge to be parlayed into superior service. Management consulting is a case in point. Consultants learn a great deal from client engagements. In many cases, there are significant portions of this learning that are not proprietary to the client. The ability of a consulting firm to learn from its projects, store useful insight and analysis, and redeploy this in other engagements can assist firms in winning new business. Few large firms do this well. Honing and supporting this capability can clearly be a source of competitive advantage.

Diminishing Returns

Diminishing returns implies that the enterprise confronts rising costs as it endeavors to expand. This is because of some fixed "factor of production," which limits profitable growth. The Napa Valley vineyard, the local, sole proprietor construction contractor, and the small-town real estate management firm are cases in point. Although superior knowledge management can push back the effects of the fixed factor, they are unlikely to overcome it, though opportunities do exist.

In such circumstances, knowledge management can be an important component of competitive strategy, as it will assist the firm in pushing the limits of its business model. Indeed, it could become the very foundation of its competitive success, as it may enable customer capital (e.g., customer databases) to be leveraged more effectively. In general, however, knowledge management is unlikely to enable the firm to completely unshackle itself from the disabilities of diminishing returns. Mauna Loa of Hawaii may be able to improve its performance, but if land suitable for macadamia nut production is limited, superior knowledge management is unlikely to completely remove those shackles.

Appropriability Regimes

In a world of strong appropriability (i.e., where patents or trade secrets and copyrights are an effective isolating mechanism), innovators can keep imitators and followers at bay, at least for a while. This gives the innovator the ability to line up complements and seek strategic partners; and do so from a position of relative bargaining strength. Lead time in the market is more confidentially assured, and the chances of competitive success are higher if the firm astutely uses the intellectual property protection that it has. Dynamic capabilities are therefore less critical to success because of the protection already available through intellectual property. The converse is also true. Dynamic capabilities will become more critical as the advantage from intellectual property weakens.

The advantage from intellectual property weakens if several firms have strong intellectual property rights in the same competitive space. Competitive advantage will then be eroded, although not destroyed. Cross-licensing among the owners of complementary intellectual property will lead to at least the partial dissipation of rents, but firms that have not contributed to the technology in any way will have to pay a competitive license fee. Competitive advantage might thus be somewhat preserved inasmuch as the free riders will be excluded.

Intellectual property protection is also likely to be jurisdiction specific. The level of protection available in the United States is generally higher than that available in Italy, Brazil, Turkey, Japan, or China. Still, an advantage in a key market like the United States can sometimes enable the innovator to build sufficient scale and complementary assets to compete effectively where there is less intellectual property protection—and possibly also in the period after the patent expires.

Compatibility Standards

This is related to the section on increasing returns, inasmuch as one of the reasons for increasing returns to scale, at least on the demand side, is the existence of compatibility standards. When such standards exist, some degree of customer "lock ins" may exist, possibly resulting in significant switching costs for the consumer if the innovator is offering an incompatible standard.

If standards issues are not permanent, then battles over standards will not be a major strategic factor. The ability of the firm to compete by simply being better at the basics—including, of course, innovation—is likely. However, when incompatible standards are being advanced by significant contenders for a major market, the entrepreneurial and strategic capabilities of top management and their ability to marshal the requisite resources will become paramount.

In particular, the capabilities of the firm to sense and possibly shape the likely course of advancement will be of particular importance. In such circumstances, there is high risk and the rules of the game are by no means transparent. With such high uncertainty, failure is likely to be frequent. Still, superior sensing and celebrating of the opportunities (and hence superior decision making) will be of great importance.

Technological Opportunity

Knowledge assets and dynamic capabilities command a higher premium when there is rapid growth. Some environments are likely to support much greater demand growth than others. Judging from the valuation of Internet IPOs, businesses that support or use the Internet are widely regarded, at least by investors, as providing significant opportunity. 3D graphics accelerator chips are likewise experiencing rapid growth as performance is provided at lower prices. Demand for caskets, on the other hand, its not predicted to grow very much, because the death rate appears quite stable in advanced countries and there is little scope for selling more than one casket for each deceased person. Accordingly, the mortuary business is likely to be significantly more stable, and growth less robust, than Web services, or multimedia, or 3D graphics computers. Although there are frequently surprises with respect to traditional businesses, and an environment that has low opportunity in one epoch may have high opportunity in a subsequent epoch, there nevertheless are businesses where the payoff to astute knowledge management is higher than others.

Role of Political Influence

Government regulation has proven time and time again to stand in the way of innovation.[8] Not only does it tend to limit market competition, it also diverts managerial effort away from competing on the merits and in favor of competing by using the regulator and the regulatory process to limit the competitive activities of one's rivals.

Accordingly, when environments are characterized by circumstances in which market forces are muted by regulation, the payoff to good management (be it of knowledge assets or any other assets) is likely to be significantly compromised. However, if an environment is transitioning toward competition and away from regulation, then developing dynamic capabilities is likely to be both especially difficult and especially valuable. It will be especially difficult because the basic instincts and routines of a regulated enterprise are not going to be oriented toward embracing competition. It will be especially valuable because deregulation will occasion rapid change and the opening up of commercial opportunities that have been suppressed by regulation or government control.

The Nature of Innovation

Distinctions can be made between autonomous and systemic innovation, the latter requiring much greater integration of both tacit and codified knowledge (Teece, 1997). Although the management of innovation is always a significant challenge, the nature of the managerial challenge is much greater with systemic innovation. Almost by definition, one cannot look to the market to effectuate the requisite coordination when innovation embraces multiple systems and subsystems. The firm's ability to develop and use high-performance organizational and managerial processes to achieve this integration will be a significant performance differentiator.

CHALLENGES TO ORTHODOXY

The imperatives of the knowledge economy require new paradigms for management and a revised understanding of the role of markets and firms. In this section, we briefly summarize some of the key contentions developed in this chapter.

1. Development, ownership, protection, and astute development of knowledge assets, not physical assets, provide the underpinnings for competitive advantage in the new economy.
2. Because property rights have fuzzy boundaries, and because knowledge is not resident in some hypothetical book of blueprints inside the firm, figuring out how to protect and retain knowledge inside the firm is a key challenge for management. It is not just an intellectual property issue that belongs with the law department.
3. The new environment favors organizations (firms) designed to protect knowledge assets from recontracting; but it also favors firms that can build, buy, combine, recombine, deploy, and redeploy knowledge assets according to changing customer needs and the changing competitive circumstances. Successful firms in the future will be high flex and knowledge based.
4. It makes little sense to talk about labor markets in isolation from the market for know-how. Much that is interesting about the former emerges from the study and understanding of the latter.
5. The entrepreneurial function of firms in the new economy is more critical than the administrative ones. Administrative functions can frequently be outsourced without loss of competition advantage.
6. The globalization of financial markets and the narrowing of information asymmetries between borrowers and lenders are eroding access to capital as a major determinant of competitive advantage.
7. Compensation structures need to be more equity based. Rewards need to be geared toward individual and team outputs, not inputs.
8. Virtual structures are frequently virtuous; the presumption should be to outsource all except the development and combination of knowledge assets and knowledge routines.
9. Managing knowledge is not the same thing as human resource management. Besides human resource management, knowledge management involves managing intellectual property; that is, managing the development, transfer, and development of industrial and organizational know-how. It is far more multifaceted than simply managing people.

The boundaries of the firm can no longer be defined with reference to equity stakes. Networks that do not involve equity are likely to be an integral part of the firm as a functioning entity.

CONCLUSION

The thesis advanced in this chapter is that competitive advantage flows from the creation, ownership, protection, and use of difficult to imitate knowledge assets. That being so, superior performance depends on the ability of firms to be good at innovation, protecting (intangible) knowledge assets, and using knowledge assets. Using knowledge assets obviously conceals complex processes surrounding (1) the integration of intangibles with other intangibles, and with tangible assets, (2) the transfer of intangibles inside the firm, and (3) the astute external licensing of technology where appropriate. This set of activities requires management to refocus priorities, to build organizations that are "high flex" to accommodate such activity, and to display an uncommon level of entrepreneurial drive.

These challenges obviously will not simultaneously confront all firms at the same time in the same manner. Context is important. But the new norms required for success are already evident in many of the high-tech industries in the United States, Europe, and Japan. Those enterprises that are slow to recognize the paradigm shift, and respond appropriately, can expect to experience performance declines. Many of the new start-up firms being born in Silicon Valley and elsewhere understand the logic articulated here. Many incumbents are beginning to recognize the new logic, but have as yet failed to effectuate transformation. Clearly, such firms are at risk.

NOTES

1. Process Technology is the exception as it can yield value by lowering costs and/or improving quality inside the firm.
2. For examples of knowledge management projects, see Davenport and Delong (1998).
3. The only situation in which this presumption ought to be overturned is innovation itself, as discussed previously.
4. *Living on Thin Air: The New Economy*, draft (January 1998).
5. Another good example is data services and telecommunications. Few service providers engage in R&D. Most of the technological innovation is driven by equipment companies like Cisco and Lucent.
6. Unless government intervention moves in to freeze the status quo.
7. I am using the term "dominance" loosely. I do not mean to imply dominance in any legal sense.
8. That is not to say that government R&D spending (e.g., the NIH) doesn't sometimes provide a great assist.

CHAPTER 7

Managing Knowledge Systems

J.-C. Spender

INTRODUCTION	This chapter focuses on the ways a knowledge based analysis might advance our thinking about organizations and their management. There is already a considerable volume of knowledge management literature. It would not be too uncharitable to point out that the bulk deals with the old topics of designing and managing organizations in essentially old ways, albeit with a gloss of new terminology. But the important thing about the knowledge based approach to the firm is that it does, in fact, make it possible to address entirely new problems and old problems in new ways.

One way to illustrate this is to categorize the current literature and ask (a) what is new, and (b) what is not covered. At the end of this process we shall conclude that a knowledge based approach opens up new topics and methods only to the extent that we understand the difference between an organization's knowledge assets and those that are of more conventional types.

Much of the conceptual difficulty in approaching the new topics arises because knowledge is such a slippery and difficult to define term. Knowledge has features that are familiar, but it also has features that do not fit into traditional economic or organizational analyses. Knowledge, we discover, has characteristics of extensibility and contextuality, which render it a public good as well as a private good. By *public good* we mean valuable simply because it is available to all. But it is also difficult to analyze because, unlike normal (private) goods which are created and consumed, public goods often grow in extent and value simply because they are being used. It is these additional features that make a knowledge based approach exciting, able to lead us to new topics, both theoretical and empirical, and so to new challenges and solutions for practicing managers. In particular, I argue for a concept of knowledge systems, highlighting the dialectic between the public goods that give organizations their sense of identity and place in the world, and the private goods that are their more evident interacting components.

WHAT DO MANAGERS WANT FROM KNOWLEDGE MANAGEMENT?

Today's managers are hyper-conscious of the new dynamics and constraints of their relationships with customers, suppliers, and competitors. When they speak of moving into the Information Age, or the age of "knowledge work," they are telling us that their strategic possibilities and constraints are no longer based on limited capital, demand, production capability, or access to foreign markets. Today's business constraints derive most of all from the shortage of the people available to drive the business forward into the global economy. By "people," of course, they do not mean unskilled labor. They mean the human agents who can bring a variety of intangible resources together with the resources that can be managed conventionally and focus the result on increasing customer value.

But these notions are neither easily understood nor implemented. What managers want from consultants, academics, and the other commentators and pundits on knowledge management is help that enables them to bring human capital to the center of their analysis. By *human capital* we mean knowledge and skills, as well as the self-reflexive ability to identify and find sources for the knowledge and skills they do not possess—what managers sometimes call initiative, or creativity, or an entrepreneurial capability.

Many managers presume, quite correctly, that their information technology investments leverage the skills of all of those people working in the company, as well as those "outside" working with the company. Thus ERP (enterprise resource planning), improving information flow within the organization, is complemented by EDI (electronic data interchange) with customers and suppliers. These managers look for guidance about how to make more effective use of their IT investments, how to get better value from what are rapidly becoming the largest and most perplexing elements of their capital spending programs. If they get these investments right, they considerably improve the levels of corporate integration and responsiveness. If they get them wrong they find themselves accused of not considering their users or customers, and of threatening their firm's entire process. Managers believe that their ability to maximize customer value depends on the effectiveness with which information technology is used to leverage, integrate, and deliver their employees' knowledge and skills. They are looking for ways of analyzing these questions so that they can improve their chances of success.

Today's managers are aware that the extent, depth, and scope of the firm's knowledge and skills increasingly drive its competitive chances. There is awareness that there is little difference, from the managers' point of view, between the human capital that "goes home in the evening" and that which becomes available through strategic alliances. Dealing with the uncertainties presented by knowledge based competition requires firms to develop (a) a keen sense of themselves, their strengths and their weaknesses, and (b) the ability to embrace and manage the risks of increasing their dependence on others.

In the following sections we address these challenges by making some general comments about the knowledge management literature, and summarizing some of its more useful aspects. We are left with deep questions about data and meaning. Not much of the knowledge management literature tells us how the data that individuals generate and exchange, by speaking or through electronic systems, gains its meaning. The problem of meaning is the analytic wedge that allows us to separate the more problematic aspects of knowledge assets from those that can be dealt with in a conventional analysis.

Meaning, we shall argue, arises from the organizational context, the ways it operates and embeds its activity in the world. We shall also understand that activities, and their associated tools and data, are not embedded in the world on their own. They are individual elements of complex activity systems. It is these knowledge and activity systems—or *actant systems*—that are the source of the meanings that the people who work within them use to understand, reason about, and direct their activities. Our primary objective in this chapter is to draw attention to managers' need to comprehend how the identifiable and discrete elements of organizational knowledge are embedded in the organization's knowledge system.

KNOWLEDGE AS OBJECT VERSUS KNOWLEDGE AS PROCESS

As we look at the knowledge management literature we should be struck by the fact that much of it treats knowledge as an object to be created, bought, possessed, or sold, just as one might treat a piece of production equipment, a piece of real estate, or any other organizational asset. This literature lets us focus on the difficulties of identifying and storing a firm's knowledge assets. There is real value in this literature and the managerial advice it generates. Most organizations have extensive but fragmented knowledge bases. Not all of their data is stored in paper or electronic form. Some of it may be stored in objects, such as failed as well as successful products. Some of it may be stored in the rules created for dealing with particular situations. Some of it may be stored in unexpressed or informal practices, the things that people have to learn about when they join new firms or departments. Much of this kind of knowledge may be useful at other locations, or under circumstances not yet considered. It is fragmented not only because it is not coherent, fitting within a single integrated set of organizational objectives and ideas, but also because it is not always available to people at the right time. There is obvious value in inventorying this knowledge and using the power of modern technology to make it readily available to whoever needs it.

This agenda actually goes back to the work of Frederick Taylor and his scientific management colleagues at the beginning of the twentieth century. Like many in the Victorian era, they were concerned with minimizing waste and thereby maximizing efficiency. Most managers are anxious to prevent their organizations from "reinventing wheels," and the idea of centralized and carefully managed inventories of organizational knowledge seems an obvious and powerful use of information technology resources. Indeed, scientific management was largely popular among managers because it was a way they could finally achieve complete control over and optimize the organization's knowledge and activities.

The literature that treats knowledge as an object is complemented by another literature that focuses on the process of knowledge creation. This is also a key element of scientific management that we can see as the precursor of our interest in knowledge management. Taylor and his colleagues saw that the structure of the organization and its patterns of authority would have a significant impact on the incentive to create and share knowledge. Much organization research since that time sought to differentiate authoritarian and democratic management styles in terms of their impact on employees' motivation and creativity. This debate continues. *Learning organizations* may be a new term, but it is an old concept that refers to a group that is structured or motivated to respond intelligently to market changes and competitive challenges. Scientific management paid great attention to organizational structure. Its techniques, and those that have emerged from a century of criticism, can now be complemented by modern information technologies.

Although these two literatures overlap (knowledge as object and knowledge as process), they carry different messages for managers trying to understand what knowledge management means for them. The first literature pays little attention to people, individually or collectively, unless the knowledge asset being considered cannot be separated from them. This is why so much of the knowledge management literature attempts to deal with *tacit knowledge*, a complex term used to identify knowledge that cannot be stored in an inanimate form, and so be transported or traded.

This leads to a concept of knowledge management as the activity of surfacing and making explicit the knowledge that is embedded in the organization's individual or collective practices. This agenda, of course, is precisely that of scientific management. Many current techniques such as expert systems, data warehousing, and business process reengineering reflect this agenda. While the first literature seeks to abstract knowledge from the people who create and implement it, the second literature, focused on knowledge as process, embraces the individual and social processes of creativity, innovation, motivation, and communication. In this sense it is both a more complex and a more conventional sociological and psychological literature.

At this stage we can see the first literature as inherently modernist, looking to machines, computers, and quasi-scientific measurement systems to objectify human knowledge and, through careful choice and design, to achieve greater control human activity. Managers are being advised to bring knowledge assets into the same accounting, administrative, and trading frameworks that they use to make decisions about the organization's tangible assets. The second literature, while recognizing that knowledge is a fundamental fuel for organizational growth and development, conceptualizes it more broadly as a facet of the organizational processes, which are directed and energized by executive insight and leadership. This view, we might argue, derives directly from the work of Chester Barnard, whose model of the firm comprised interacting systems or "economies."

CONTEMPORARY KNOWLEDGE MANAGEMENT PRACTICE

At this stage we see that managers can get some good advice from those writing and talking about knowledge management. First, knowledge is an important corporate asset that needs managing. Although this may well be more important in the Information Age of knowledge intensive firms (KIFs) and knowledge work, it clearly has always been true. Knowledge cannot be managed unless it is identified. Knowledge assets also present special management problems when knowledge needs to be transported, transferred, traded, or stored. As von Hippel (1994) and others have shown, knowledge can seem both sticky and leaky. Sometimes it seems perishable, at other times it seems to grow.

The problems of managing knowledge assets require managers to pay special attention to the institutional and legal arrangements that enable organizational knowledge to be pinned down and objectified. Much of the empirical literature deals with patents, the principal example of knowledge that has been so objectified, or turned into a tradable object. Some have criticized this work, pointing to considerable divergence between those industries, such as pharmaceuticals, in which patenting has considerable strategic importance and others, such as software, in which patenting plays a far smaller or even negligible role. Perhaps these writers could have done more to indicate what other arrangements managers have at their disposal to capture knowledge as private property. The medieval guilds, for instance, were set up, in part, to protect the value of specialized knowledge. Nowadays, contemporary industrial societies offer a far richer set of legal and institutional arrangements, such as union membership, government testing laboratories, or regulated professional qualification.

Once identified and objectified, whether in terms of institutional and legal arrangements such as a patent or a license to practice, knowledge assets can be valued. With this comes the idea of accounting for the costs of generating and sustaining knowledge assets. The best-known examples of "knowledge accounting" are those of the Buckman and Skandia corporations. Clearly there is little merit in considering knowledge as a corporate asset unless the costs of its creation or acquisition, maintenance, storage, transfer, and application can be integrated into the practices that managers already use to deal with the organization's tangible assets.

Business process reengineering and expert system analysis help the organization make its embedded and tacit knowledge explicit. For many writers, such as Nonaka and Takeuchi (1994), this is the core of knowledge management. Once knowledge is identified, valued, and costed, managers begin to get a real handle on the organization as a bundle of knowledge assets. They can begin to focus on the structural issues of making sure that the right knowledge is in the right place at the right time, and on the ongoing productivity issues of optimizing the communication and knowledge transfer processes.

Finally, considering the organization as a system of knowledge generating, communicating, and applying activities helps managers to think through the ways of maximizing its responsiveness to changing market conditions, and competitive ability to think "out-of-the-box." Creativity, both individual and collective, is becoming increasingly important as the pace and unpredictability of markets increases.

AN EXAMPLE OF KNOWLEDGE MANAGEMENT FROM THE FIRST UNION BANK (U.S.)

Retail banking is one of the many industries being transformed by modern information technology and the efficiencies it creates. It is easy to overlook the way consumers' expectations are rising, along with their incomes, and so driving change from outside the financial services industry. Management's challenge is to think beyond how modern technology can reduce the cost of providing an unchanged service, toward considering the new products and new business models the new technologies can facilitate. Although this is generally true, it is especially true of those industries whose principal service component is knowledge, such as knowledge about the money in one's account, the value of one's portfolio, whether bills have been paid, or payments received, and so on.

Modern technology enables retail banking to deal with a large variety of customers whose circumstances differ. Banks understand that if they are able to integrate everything that they know about the customer and his or her circumstances into every interaction, they can create a tight bond of customer loyalty, which has enormous commercial value. The U.S. auto industry estimates the net present value of a "customer-for-life" to be in excess of $600,000. That is worthwhile taking seriously as a business investment objective. For the First Union Bank, it has become a slogan that the value of the organization is based not on its products, services, branches, or technology, but on its ability to understand its customers and to react quickly, to gain, keep, and grow long-term customer relationships. They have understood that modern technology enables them to adopt a customer relationship marketing (CRM) model that is both new to retail banking and puts considerable pressure on competing banks.

To implement this strategy they pulled all the legacy data together into a relational database system that they call the "customer data mart." This was technologically challenging, expensive, and time consuming. Once achieved, the data mart became the foundation of their new business model. They were able to develop new executive information systems and business analysis tools in which it was possible to both categorize different lines of business and different types of customers, and their corresponding costs and profit potentials. It was also possible to drill down to particular customers and transactions. Most important, it provided a data platform for forecasting business trends and simulating the impact of new financial products. Likewise, the customer data mart enabled management to offer a sales and service activity uniquely customized to every customer. Now, every interaction between the bank and the customer could reflect everything that the bank knew about the customer. This facilitated add-on sales for good customers and a focused method of dealing with bad customers. Such a customer-by-customer approach, sometimes called one-on-one marketing, is the essence of the CRM model that First Union Bank implemented by taking a knowledge management approach to their business.

As an investment project, First Union likes to report that their data warehouse contains information on 16 million customers, stores several years of transaction data, pulled together 24 legacy systems, and is likely to produce a net return of $100 million a year.

This kind of knowledge management is serious stuff, whatever academics might think about the purity of the theories behind it. It is true that little of what First Union Bank has done requires us to consider the special nature of knowledge or the special managerial difficulties that might be posed by knowledge assets. But at the same time, it may be that the bank's down-to-earth, practical conception of the customer relationship marketing model misses some of the managerial challenges to making it work, as well as some of its potential benefits and limits.

In the next section we consider whether knowledge management offers more than an important new design rubric for implementing modern information technology.

KEY TOPICS IN A KNOWLEDGE BASED APPROACH TO ORGANIZATIONAL MANAGEMENT

In the previous sections we have focused on how to help managers come to terms with the rising knowledge intensity of today's economy, and with the increasing capacity of information systems to support organizations and open up the prospect of new business models. In the following sections we explore how a focus on knowledge can open up a new universe of ideas about how organizations operate and how they might be managed. The path to this new universe lies in appreciating the fundamental differences between knowledge and the corporation's other assets.

It is easy to use the term *knowledge* and assume that it is going to clarify what managers do. Yet we should bear in mind that knowledge is one of the most perplexing notions in our vocabulary. The problems of understanding what knowledge is, how it is to be justified or warranted, and its extent and permanence have been the subject of vigorous philosophical debate for many thousands of years. Much is understood, but much is also still under debate.

The promise of a knowledge based approach grows out of regarding knowledge not merely as an asset, or a facet of the organization's process, but as something deeply problematic. The knowledge management literature should begin, not end, with the notion that knowledge is not simply data. We argued previously that scientific management can be seen as the precursor for much of today's knowledge management discussion, but scientific management had an excessively naïve view of what knowledge was, of how it might be abstracted from the organization's processes, and of how it might be optimized. The challenge of a knowledge based approach is that it invites us to go beyond such naïve views and penetrate the subtleties of the way human and organizational knowledge is produced, and of the way it shapes individual and collective activity.

To deal intelligently with knowledge we must confront the paradox that statements about knowledge are themselves only another form of knowledge. We must not ignore the inherent circularity of definitions or statements about knowledge. As a result, it is not clear that there exists any form of metaknowledge, or higher level of knowledge, that gives us a special handle on the applied knowledge possessed or used by an organization's managers or employees. To put this another way, it is not clear that the knowledge that academics create and exchange is in any way fundamentally different from the knowledge applied in an organization. There is no reason to think of theories as fundamentally different from other types of knowledge. Much of the debate in the philosophy of science is about whether there are distinctively different levels or types of knowledge—whether, for instance, scientific laws are different from observation reports. Little of this prolonged epistemological debate is reflected in the knowledge management literature. Nonetheless, there are profound epistemological choices to be made about how to address organizational knowledge questions.

The most fundamental choice is one's position on the possibility of truly objective knowledge. The debates about positivism, relativism, and postmodernism turn on this assumption. Only if one assumes that objective knowledge is available can one seriously attempt to demonstrate how objective knowledge might be distinguished from the other forms of knowledge of which humans are clearly capable. In what follows we shall take a somewhat contrary position. We shall attempt to avoid the incipient anarchy of relativism, arguing that while no knowledge can be truly objective in the sense used by many philosophers of science—that it reveals the nature of the physical universe—it can be objective in that it is embedded in the parallel reality of our social processes. It is in this sense that a knowledge based approach can help managers embrace not only the challenge of managing tangible assets and competition in the physical universe of properties and objects, but also the challenge of managing processes and activities in the social and cognitive universes of behaviors and perceptions. To recall a point from the writings of John Seely Brown and Paul Duguid (1998), two of the more thoughtful researchers in our field, there is a crucial difference between knowledge (an object) and knowing (a consideration of the consequences of knowledge on the social process).

In the interests of a managerial approach, and rather than an excessively philosophical approach to these matters, we shall consider three aspects of how knowledge may be understood to be present in and influence social processes at the level of the firm. We shall consider (1) embeddedness, (2) boundedness, and (3) the public goods nature of knowledge. We shall try to illustrate these ideas with some practical examples.

We begin this, of course, by adopting a broad set of assumptions about organizational knowledge. Rather than lay these out and examine them in philosophical terms, we can quickly restate our position in the language familiar to those who read the knowledge management literature. First, the term *knowledge* must extend beyond patents or the knowledge embodied in human artifacts, to embrace the knowing revealed in the problem-solving and productive practices of individuals and groups within the organization. Whether it is economically or theoretically feasible to make such knowledge explicit is beside the point. It makes no sense to restrict the term knowledge to that which can be scientifically validated. Socioeconomic behavior is as often shaped by fad, fashion, misinformation, and emotion as it is by fact. It follows that a knowledge based approach to management must go beyond what can be captured in terms of empirically measured and scientifically justified theories.

Second, the fundamental weakness of both forms of literature considered previously, whether we treat knowledge as an object, or focus on the processes of knowledge production and application, is that the analyses fail to consider the problem of meaning. Where does the meaning of data come from? The positivist assumption that knowledge reveals the nature of reality trivializes the question of meaning. In ordinary business discourse we would not normally consider it necessary to explain how to attach meaning to terms such as *customer*, *employee*, or *profit*. At best, these are subordinated as problems of measurement. In practice, it is not obvious what the terms used by the First Union Bank actually mean. We simply assume they are meaningful, and that they can be readily integrated into the bank's practices.

Third, it is necessary to make some assumptions about the knowledge possessed by individuals and by collectives. Are they the same types of knowledge, or different, or related at all? For academics these questions raise ancient unease about whether there are knowing entities other than individuals. Many authors try to avoid the question by asserting that collective knowledge, such as might be exhibited by what a group of people reveal in their collective behavior, is nothing more than an individual's knowledge shared, and that only individuals can know. In modern sociology the debate goes back to Durkheim and Halbwachs (1974). The position that we shall adopt is eclectic. Individuals clearly differ in what they know. But groups that have become socialized know things that often go beyond what any individual can identify and are able to sustain this knowledge even though their individual members change.

The implication is that knowledge management goes beyond the scientific management tradition of identifying knowledge and communicating it to individuals who then implement it. We believe knowledge management takes us into the realm of corporate culture, reputation, value systems, and those other evidences of the social nature of man. We shall argue that the meaning of all individual knowledge is actually grounded in collective practice. This is no more than an alternative expression of institutional theory, the assumption that a society's or an organization's behavior can be best understood in terms of the institutional structures that shape its choices and so constrain its actions.

From the foregoing assumptions we can see several aspects of the model being put forward. Most obvious is that individual knowledge is located within a system of knowledge, while that system is bounded as a coherent set of social practices. This suggests a dialectical interplay between individuals and the context in which they are collectively embedded. Giddens's (1984) work on structuration theory is especially relevant here. We can also see that managers need to be concerned with both levels of the dialectic, both with the knowledge and practices at the individual level, and with the knowledge and practices at the collective or systemic level. In what follows we try to flesh out some immediate consequences of our assumptions.

THE PROPER OBJECTIVE OF A KNOWLEDGE BASED APPROACH

There is no point to a knowledge focused approach if it only captures the same phenomena and produces the same advice as a conventional positivist decision-making approach. If we can extend organizational analysis and management theory beyond the phenomena that can be captured and dealt with in a rational scientific framework, then we have the promise of helping managers deal with the many matters of judgment, value conflict, image management, and emotion that confront them in the workplace and the market.

We can say that the proper objective of a knowledge-system approach is to develop a conceptual framework in which managers can identify (1) new organizational and business models, (2) the managerial problems peculiar to knowledge and its differences from the organization's other assets, and (3) new heuristics or forms of advice that extend their understanding, options, and means of influence.

EMBEDDEDNESS

Much of the knowledge management literature notes the difference between data and information. Authors typically make some assumptions that are, of course, fundamentally causal to everything they say afterwards. We shall do the same. Data is a signal or a sign without meaning. Information is a signal whose meaning can be sought in a system, whether that be an information system or a coherent system of practice. Information is, by definition, embedded in a host system and can take no other form other than that permitted by the system. Here we adopt a typical Wittgensteinian view.

Information cannot be abstracted from the system that gives it meaning without its losing that meaning; the information would become a document written in a dead language. Similarly, information inevitably carries with it implications of action, preference, value, and moral burden which can only be perceived and understood by reference to the host system and its implicit moral and cultural commitments. A knowledge system is a type of system in which knowledge is integrated and embedded at many different levels. A functioning computer system has its designers' and implementers' knowledge embedded within it, as does any human artifact. But it is a dead system. It is not capable of generating new knowledge or responding under conditions of uncertainty.

The real complexity of thinking about organizations as knowledge systems is that we must presume them to be capable of generating knowledge. This is a corollary of presuming them to be knowing entities, unlike a computer system or a mechanical system such as a machine tool, which cannot adapt or change the boundaries of its operating envelope.

The importance of paying attention to tacit knowledge is that much of the meaning embedded within the host system cannot be revealed in the languages available. Polanyi's allusion to people knowing more than they can say is actually double-edged. On the one hand, people know much that they cannot verbalize for lack of insight and verbal skills, but on the other hand, they know much that can never be verbalized because it goes beyond the possibilities of language. Pierce (1963) founded pragmatism with the argument that the meaning of an idea could be determined best by its practical consequences. But he also noted the "indexicality" of language, the impossibility of separating meaning from the context of an idea's practical consequences. He argued that terms like "here" and "now" would have no meaning for a listener without that additional unspoken information. Thus statements about the world can never be complete, speakers must always presume that the listener has available some unexpressed and probably unexpressable underpinning or background information.

The argument is that managers recognize the importance of managing both information and meaning, and in a knowledge system such as an organization, both are embedded in the individual and the social practices of that system. The relationships between information, meaning, and practices are dialectic. Neither has logical, temporal, or epistemological priority. We can contrast this with the conventional bureaucratic model of management that presumes that all organizational action follows from managerial decisions—that is, the choice of organizational objective and means of its implementation has logical priority—and that all such decisions can be made or explained using a rational theoretical framework deriving from that objective. Even the most extreme theorist knows this is false. Many contemporary theorists remain undecided as to whether it might be possible, through continued research, to improve the rational approach to the point where it captures many of the phenomena that now seem irrational or a-rational, or whether an entirely new class of thinking is called for.

Giddens's structuration theory is an attempt to create a new kind of framework. In terms of a theory of knowledge management, we can see that managerial decision often leads to activity, but as that activity becomes integrated into the social system it precipitates changes, which sometimes call for further decisions. The managers' influence over the pattern of activities is indirect, mediated by the cognizing system's own knowledge and sense of self. In the same way as we might argue that politics is the art of the possible, so managers need a keen sense of the options implicit in the current pattern of activities. This brings us to the well-known distinction between incremental and architectural change in the system, between that which the system already "knows" and can exhibit without changing its knowledge base, and those changes that are beyond its current knowledge. Likewise the host knowledge system has its own cognizing capabilities which become manifest not only in the new meanings that become attached to existing language, but also in the evolutionary tendencies that become evident in new practices. These reshape the decision space for managers.

We shall illustrate these rather dense ruminations later in the chapter. The main point is that knowledge gains its meaning from being embedded in a system of practice. Jean Lave and Etienne Wenger's work (1991) on "communities of practice" can be seen as a direct attempt to analyze and deal with these patterns of activity and the way they comprise the source of the organization's meaning and evolution.

BOUNDEDNESS

We can explore the boundedness of one of these knowledge systems much as an anthropologist or ethnologist would, by determining the boundary around the social group, which used a particular language, or social institution, or cultural artifact. There is value in taking the same approach to organizations. The substantial amount of research into organizational culture and the problems of culture clash when organizations interact, merge, or attempt to come into strategic alliance, indicates that culture, and much of organizational practice, is sharply bounded and tied up with the historical evolution of the organization. The psychological tendencies and value systems of past CEOs are also likely to be embedded in the firm. This is especially true for the firm's founders.

But it would be a mistake to think that culture is an adequately powerful metaphor to capture all that we mean by the collective and bounded context. Toennies (1971) made a classic distinction between purely social practice, which cannot usefully be described as purposive, and organizational practice, which is purposive by definition. From a knowledge management theory point of view we can say that much of the organization's knowledge context is like a culture, without purpose, even though we must recognize that the functional nature of that culture is under constant review by its members. Although the organizational knowledge system has cognizing properties, managers are continuously attempting to harness these to the organization's objectives. This is the other side of the dialectic. The managers' creativity is continuously challenged by the evolutionary tendencies of the background knowledge system in which they are embedded.

It may be useful to track one way in which the dialectic develops between (a) the individuals who comprise the knowledge system and (b) the background in which they are embedded. Imagine a basketball team. When they first meet, the players are simply individuals with their own knowledge of their own capabilities. Under a good coach, as they begin to play together, particularly against other teams, they begin to form collective knowledge, what Fayol called "esprit de corps." On a basketball court this is evident in the ease with which players anticipate each other's moves and so accelerate the pace of the game, giving them a profound advantage over teams that still depend on overt signaling to underpin their collaboration. The coach knows success not only in whether the team wins, but also in the degree to which the players surprise themselves with what they can do individually and collectively. In this case the boundaries around the knowledge system are somewhat subtle. Every team has more players and maybe more coaches than are evident in any particular game. The boundary around the knowledge system, or community of practice, can be defined in terms of those changes to the line-up that are productive and increase the team's capability, and those that do not.

Other kinds of team work, especially that involving scientific knowledge, requires different kinds of communication, often more verbalization and a deep understanding of the limitations and structures underpinning the knowledge. Kidder's analysis in *The Soul of a New Machine* (1982) shows the importance of developing new language when new ideas and new practices are required. Such language is often called *jargon* and is typically incomprehensible to those who are not participants in the knowledge system. In this case the boundaries around the knowledge system are relatively easy to identify. Both examples indicate the importance to managers of effective boundary management. Managers need a keen sense of how to manage the boundaries around the knowledge system on which they are focusing and for which they are responsible.

Both of the previous examples focus on people, on moving them in and out of the knowledge system. Real management is more complex than a sports or research team. Although management is about getting things done through people, it is also about providing these people with the tools, equipment, and knowledge to do specific jobs. Much of this equipment, especially when it comes to information and technology intensive work, is also systemic in nature. By this we mean that any specific job requires a complex of other apparatus, capabilities, and activities to be in place other than that being used by the particular individual. There are discrete boundaries around such equipment systems.

In the operations of modern retailing organizations such as the Gap or Home Depot, we can see the complexity of the interplay between the rational decision making about the financial, merchandising, and information systems, and the emergent, dynamic, and evolutionary properties of the social system which uses these tangible assets.

The auto industry always exhibits extremes of managers' challenges and skills. Although modern production line work might look comprehensible to those who have seen Chaplin's film *Modern Times*, they would likely miss the background systems on which it actually depends. From the customer's ability to order a vehicle to be built precisely to her or his specification, to the plant's inventory systems' automatic ability to call up additional just-in-time parts from a supplier through EDI, the real production system extends vastly beyond the individual workers on the visible line. In particular, modern central computer–controlled auto-assembly equipment is capable of detecting "out-of-tolerance" conditions and sending automatic corrections to the upstream stations, thus diminishing or even removing the possibility of human error on the line. It is this kind of enhanced integration of non-animate systemic features with the widely understood sociotechnical issues that makes understanding the background so important for contemporary managers.

PUBLIC GOOD ASPECTS

The theory of the firm we are sketching here is a two-level system of knowledge. At the individual level there are both people and resources such as information, real estate, and equipment. By people, of course, we mean individuals with the knowledge and skills necessary to engage in the system of activity, which results in progress toward the organization's objectives. The more constraining and specific the systemic aspects of the equipment and information they use, the more specific and narrow these skills, and the more important their training processes.

If we think of the ability to work with corporate jargon as a key resource for the individuals engaged in a responsive and effective organization, we confront the public goods aspect of language. Public goods have a complex nature that we are familiar with in practice but have some difficulty analyzing, in spite of Samuelson's work (1995).

A key characteristic of a public good is that it is shared by a community in ways that make it difficult to price. Yet it is still valuable to a community because it facilitates its processes. One of the economist's favorite examples is the lighthouse, which guides ships away from hazards and toward their destinations. It would seem impossible to price this service in a way that truly reflects its value. A tonnage-based tax would fail to reflect the value of the cargo carried, or the passengers carried, or the variable hazards presented by the weather. Another example might be a bridge across a river. When the bridge is built it facilitates economic growth. Although traffic across the bridge can be charged a toll, thus making the bridge a private good providing a priced service, it may make better sense to the community to let traffic cross the bridge for nothing. The social benefits (economic spillovers) from the resulting activity may be greater.

A key feature of public goods, illustrated by both these examples, is their extensibility—they can serve an entire community without being consumed. As Arrow noted (1974), knowledge is the preeminent public good. One person can give another information without the giver's stock of information being diminished. Language is similarly a public good. Far from being consumed by use, language exhibits *network externalities*—that is, its value increases the more it is used. Economists often illustrate the concept of network externalities with the telephone, the usefulness and value of which increases as more people are connected.

The point here is not to produce a thorough understanding of public goods, but merely to draw attention to the fact that the background of practice and meaning in which the organization's individuals are embedded is largely made up of public goods that are specific to that system. The boundaries around a knowledge system are often marked by the systems of contributions to and the protection and use of the system's public goods or systemic features.

A community of practice is more than a collection of knowledge-sharing individuals and their interactions. For these individuals and activities are also embedded in a sharply bounded universe of meaning that enables them to collaborate under conditions of uncertainty. Under conditions of certainty, such as are presumed in most organizational theorizing, the rules and processes of collaboration can be designed ahead of their use. Under conditions of uncertainty, the ability of the organization to hold together and respond to the unanticipated lies at some other level. Weick (1993) has commented on the "glue" that makes mindful collaborative activity possible. Here we are arguing that this glue is actually behavioral evidence of the presence of public goods shared across the knowledge system being analyzed.

It might seem more straightforward to call these resources the institutional structures of the organization. But this would imply, in the spirit of Toennies, that they are purely emergent, that they are not at all dependent on management's decisions. The whole point of adopting this two-level dialectical model is to argue that managers can and must influence the creation, acquisition, application, and husbandry of resources at both levels, albeit indirectly. Samuelson's treatment of public goods accepts that they have to be managed into existence and are costly. Likewise Hardin's famous paper on the "tragedy of the commons" (1968) reminds us that the capacity of real public goods is always limited and that they can be destroyed by overuse. We can see how that would apply to both the lighthouse and the bridge.

Now we can begin to come back from the realm of philosophy and close the loop with the first sections of this chapter. One of the most important public goods in the contemporary organization is its information system. The First Union Bank example illustrates the additional value available once all the information systems are coordinated into a single customer data mart. At the same time, we can sense the difficulty of framing the creation of public goods within a conventional capital project analysis. Indeed, one of the most perplexing aspects of modern organizations is determining the return on their information technology investments. Because they establish patterns of meaning against which organizational activities can be measured, the organization's accounting and budgeting systems also have many public goods aspects about them. Again, it would be difficult to determine the rate of return on an accounting system. If asked, many managers think about the public goods that they need to put in place for their organizations in terms of a "cost of doing business," that is, of taking part in the competitive economic situation.

By defining a knowledge system as one that has cognizing and knowledge-creating abilities, we propose a system with the resources at both levels of the dialectic. First, at the level of individual system components, individual people, and the interactions between them; and second, at the level of the collective meanings and practices. The system exhibits a dynamism and indeterminacy quite different from that associated with the static bureaucratic mechanical model that underpins conventional organization theory. In the theory proposed here, managers are repositioned as components of these organizational knowledge systems so that they have limited influence over both levels. They are no longer in a position to design and control the system, as they are positioned by traditional organization theory. On the contrary, the knowledge system is quasi-autonomous, partly self-organizing, partly constrained to an evolutionary trajectory.

SOME MANAGERIAL HEURISTICS

As we suggested previously, the real purpose of a knowledge based approach to organizations is to reach for a new model or theory of the firm. Its value is dependent on the ability to reach beyond conventional analysis to capture and analyze new phenomena. Ultimately, as Pierce (1963) might have suggested, its value lies in its ability to give managers greater insight into and influence over the systems of activities and community of practice that we call organizations and for which they are paid to act responsibly.

First, a knowledge based theory relocates managers relative to the rest of the organization. Instead of being either the organization's designers or mere cogs in its rational problem-solving mechanism, managers are more like gardeners shaping the knowledge system's natural growth processes. The classic notions of bureaucratic direction are replaced by the subtler notions of executive leadership explored by Barnard (1938).

Second, a knowledge based theory redirects managers' attention. In conventional organization theory managers are designing, resourcing, and controlling the organization, as crisply captured by the POSDCORB (Planning, Organizing, Staffing, Directing, Coordinating, Reporting, Budgeting) acronym. In the model we sketched here, managers are certainly resourcing the organization, but at two levels: the system's components and the system's public goods. They are certainly designing, but in the knowledge that the outcome is mediated by the inherent vitality of the knowledge system for which they are responsible. Much of the organization emerges from the interactions between the components that managers make available. We are reminded of the classic distinction between the formal and informal organizations.

Third, the managers' means of influence is as much to do with boundary management as it is to do with resourcing. Economists often argue that a system's behavior is determined by the activities at its margins. Correspondingly, it is possible to define having a business strategy as knowing when to say "no" to an offer. In practice, a business's strategy is often implemented merely by selecting a specific set of product-market interactions. This is simply expressing the concept of boundary management in different terms.

Fourth, managers are challenged to create and shape the public goods that provide meaning for those active within the system. The examples we have noted would be extremely difficult to administer using conventional accounting principles. Yet we believe most good managers develop an intuitive sense of the public goods they need to put in place if the organization is to be healthy and display the vitality and responsiveness necessary to survive under the uncertain circumstances they typically experience in their markets.

Fifth, economic thinking about public and private goods tends to treat them as totally different things. In practice, within a bounded system, there is likely to be some privatization of its public goods, as well as much making of private goods available to a wider public. It is clearly possible to transform one into the other. Some of the knowledge management literature is about distributing knowledge that was previously held within a small part of the organization. The two-level models we are proposing imply that this may not always be wise. For example, as Adam Smith noted, a division of labor is crucial to organizational efficiency. Although it is useful for marketing people to have some familiarity with the problems of production, it makes no sense to have everyone in the organization operating with the same knowledge. It is quite different if we have every employee embedded in a communication system that gives him or her individualized access to the sum total of the organization's knowledge. We can presume that employees will access only the knowledge that is relevant to their own activity.

Sixth, the notion of a boundary around the knowledge system or community of practice that provides the actors' source of meaning, shares something important with Penrose's (1959) theory of the growth of the firm. She noted that the value of assets brought into the firm would be transformed by its managers' knowledge—or ignorance. In this sense we can say that the true parents of a modern dynamic knowledge system theory of the firm are on the one hand scientific management, and on the other Penrose's dynamic and quasi-autonomous model of the firm.

At various points in this chapter we have tried to illustrate some of the more complex notions with examples from the world of business. The more complex notions are (1) embeddedness, (2) boundedness, and (3) the public goods nature of the second level of knowledge. Thinking about the First Union Bank again, we can see that the contents of the data warehouse gather meaning only in the very specific context of the bank's practices. How its customers are categorized, and how the system of categorization is related to the bank's action alternatives is not drawn out in their explanation of how the system was built. Yet these are the system's crucial operational consequences. These relationships may seem so obvious that they are scarcely worth noting. Yet another bank would almost certainly establish a different set of relationships. Both would explain that these are the ways "things are done around here." The point, of course, is that these relationships are aspects of the background level of the firm's knowledge system—like its culture.

SOME CONCLUSIONS

In this chapter we first considered knowledge as an asset that can be privatized and objectified as, for instance, in a patent. We recognized that much knowledge management is about identifying and subsequently protecting and exploiting such knowledge. Another branch of the literature is about managing the processes of invention and innovation. A third branch deals with managing information systems. All three branches tend to overlook questions of how knowledge or data gets its meaning for those within and working with the organization.

We argued that meaning is inevitably grounded in the systems of practice that make up the organization and its relationships with others. We suggested a dialectical relationship between the elements of the organizational knowledge system and the systems of meaning in which they are embedded.

Most important is that our model repositions managers. They are no longer the designers and controllers implied in classical organization theory. They become participants in a social process that is beyond their immediate control. But they have several ways of influencing the organization. At one level they can change the inventory of resources and shape the interactions between them. But at another level they can influence the emergent processes that yield the system's public goods. They do this by managing the boundary around the organizational practices, and by influencing the transformation of private goods into public goods and vice versa.

But the model proposed here calls attention to the absence of a really applicable theory of managerial power and influence, in the same way that Penrose's theory calls attention to the absence of a real theory about what managers do for their firms. A more sophisticated knowledge based theory of the firm might advance our thinking simply because it implies that managers both have skills that go beyond rational decision making, and have duties and responsibilities that include shaping the public goods and cultural and moral contents of the workplace.

PART III

Knowledge-Intensive Organizations

CHAPTER 8

Designing for Business Benefits from Knowledge Management

Peter Murray

INTRODUCTION: DESIGN AIMS

All business managers want results. This desire applies just as much to the practice of knowledge management (KM) as it does to any other proposition that claims to aid better business performance. Just what kind of results a business might expect from KM and how to go about demonstrably getting them is a reasonable demand for a business manager to make before committing resources to a KM program.

This chapter develops a program of action for organizations that are seriously considering KM or that have perhaps abandoned earlier attempts. It draws on a survey of 260 European businesses conducted by the Information Systems Research Centre at the Cranfield School of Management. This survey, backed up by a number of interviews, was designed to uncover what businesses are thinking, planning, and doing about KM. Although the survey data have been published elsewhere ("The Cranfield and Information Strategy Knowledge Survey—Europe's State of the Art in KM"), this chapter focuses on the key issues that need to be addressed in practical terms if an organization wishes to attempt KM, as revealed by the experience and learning of the companies participating in the survey. It examines the perceived need for KM, its nature, how success can be ascertained, and what barriers there are to effective KM, and suggests some practical ways of implementing a KM program. The scope is deliberately constrained to KM in business organizations—which is still a large domain. Other writers and researchers have attempted a wide historical approach embracing anything from ancient Greek philosophy to timetables, but we found that, in businesses, successful investment in KM was always linked to some business purpose or desired result. This framing provided by a business aim helped enormously in understanding KM initiatives and developing strategies for KM because it answers the basic question, "Why do KM?" A model is proffered that locates knowledge and knowledge management in a results–oriented framework (the DIKAR model).

THE CONCEPT OF KM IN COMPETITIVE MARKETS

It is now regarded as axiomatic, especially in the United States, that the knowledge a business has is one of its most precious assets. Arguments eloquently expressed elsewhere assert that a company's knowledge may be the one thing that allows it to be competitive because all other resources are to a large extent reproducible.

It follows that the management of such a resource is important. Furthermore, the changing nature of the marketplace has put even greater emphasis on knowing how to operate competitively. Being competitive in marketplaces that are increasingly globalized, liberalized, and deregulated means that companies have to be innovative (a knowledge activity itself), and also know in some depth what competitors are doing or are likely to do. As more and more products and services become commoditized, the added value required of an organization that wishes to be a chosen supplier becomes more one of know-how about customers' needs and preferences rather than straightforward product excellence.

Knowledge of what specific resources exist in a business is essential for the management of its operation. Here the term *resources* covers not just money, equipment, plant, and people, but also structures, responsibilities, processes, and roles with their attendant skills. Ensuring that there is an appropriate supply of these resources is a business competence, as is their exploitation. In a highly competitive environment, a further knowledge characteristic is required. This is the knowledge of how to integrate any or all the resources at a business's disposal in such a way that it will distinguish itself from the competition. A capability will thus be created that potential customers will deem unique or preferable. KM as a management practice is aimed at exploitation of both levels of knowledge—at the specialist levels and at the competitive integrative capability level. It seeks through appropriately developed methods, and usually with the aid of certain information technologies, to deliver to senior managers the ability to collect, create, store, disseminate, and exploit a company's knowledge to some business benefit.

An example will illustrate the features of the resource-based approach to knowledge in organizations and the role knowledge plays. Consider a team of managers and specialists meeting and working together to formulate a bid for a major piece of international business. The bid is a complex one involving not just product specialists and deal-makers but also expertise in contractual law, tax, exporting, global supply chains, complex sourcing, costing, and finance. Furthermore, the bidding activity will not be the straightforward sequential application of one expertise after another, but is more likely to be the iterative exploitation of the expertises because a change in one expert's input could have consequences elsewhere. In a gathering of such experts each will bring his or her functional competence to bear on the bid-making activity set. However, to make a successful bid will require more than the sum of the parts; what is needed is the managerial know-how necessary to integrate these into a successful bid process. To develop such a capability will mean winning business— without it the organization is likely to respond to potential new business with a flurry of activity rather than a coherent business process.

The knowledge of each expert can in a sense be thought of as a knowledge "package," some of it even codifiable. The knowledge of acting together to create a capability will be much more diffuse and will reside within the bid team and will be much harder to document, let alone codify. However, the outcomes of the team's activities will be documentable, and these can form the basis of learning—more on this later. How to manage specialized "packaged knowledge" and how to integrate it with and manage "diffuse knowledge" such as exists in teams is one of the key goals of KM.

THE DIKAR MODEL: KM FOR RESULTS

A model that helps locate packaged knowledge and diffuse knowledge within a business-related framework is the DIKAR model (Data, Information, Knowledge, Actions, Results). This model has proved useful in understanding and framing KM issues. Represented in simple diagrammatic terms it has the form shown in Figure 8.1. The conventional way of interpreting and using the model is to view it from left to right, that is, to start with Data and progress through a series of "enriching" stages to worthwhile business Results. The labeled stages should not take attention away from the linkage lines. These links represent how the organization achieves the enriching steps between stages and include procedures, systems, processes, organizational structures, administration, skills, and so on. They will vary even between very similar organizations because of history, culture, various constraints, and most important, management's worldview on how business is done. Within any company the set of linkages between any two stage boxes will also differ; basically, the further to the left (the Data end) the more we can expect to see defined procedures and the extensive application of technology, while to the right (the Results end), what occurs will depend much more on people—as individuals, as groups, and as directed by management.

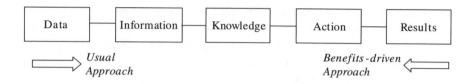

Figure 8.1 *DIKAR Model*

Using the DIKAR model in left-to-right mode is very useful in understanding (in a knowledge and information sense) how business is actually done. For an organization's core processes, senior managers should have a firm and detailed grasp on how DIKAR applies to those processes—that is, it implicates their business model. The application of experience, knowledge, technology, or sometimes flair to the linkages can, over time, improve the overall core process in a targeted incremental fashion.

However, when the organization steps outside its day-to-day processes and instead sets itself new goals or new results targets, the left-to-right use of the model cannot explain how to achieve them. Examples of this would be how to launch a new competitive offensive, how to break into a new market, how to innovate or indeed to effect any radical change. The data/information/knowledge/action chain does not exist. The DIKAR model can still be helpful by reversing the usage to right-to-left. In its RAKID direction it poses a set of questions: Given a desired results set, what actions are needed to achieve them? Given a set of actions, what do we need to know to perform the actions? What information and data constructs are required in order to be in a sufficiently knowledgeable state? These questions are all knowledge questions located within a results-driven framework.

The linkages in the RAKID mode of the model are essentially integrative—given an endpoint, what resources do we have to bring together to get there and how do we bring them together? The necessary resources will consist not just of the obvious such as money, manpower, equipment, and skills, but are likely to include processes, structures, roles, and knowledge. It is perhaps the knowledge of how to integrate such a range of resources in a new way to achieve new results that is the most potent form of KM. Traditionally, businesses focus more management attention on physical things and resources that can be measured, which means the "softer" resources such as process, roles, and knowledge never enter ROI evaluations. But in a competitive environment these are perhaps the most valuable because they are less reproducible as well as being the vehicles for innovative approaches to new demands. The effects of globalization, liberalization, and deregulation on markets has been to generally make those markets harder to survive and prosper in—there are potentially more competitors and more substitutions competing for customers' interests. The appropriate response to this is unlikely to be to "turn up the wick" on traditional resources and their deployment. Instead, companies have to find ways of demonstrating new capabilities that distinguish them in the marketplace from existing or potential competitors. These capabilities will arise only if management is competent in integrating all of the resources (as defined previously) in new value-adding ways.

The role of KM in this "new results" scenario is to marshal knowledge and experience—not just of all the necessary specialisms but also the ability to integrate them into a new capability that the market will place value on. For example, the resources required to make a bid for a major piece of business in a new market may involve expertise such as commercial, legal, tax, technical, regulatory, and production. Winning the bid also requires knowledge of how to deploy those expert resources in a way that the competition fails to do and that the customer finds attractive. In practice, bids such as that just described are treated as one-offs, as a task outside the expert's "proper" job, and the experience accumulated in winning or losing the bid is not retained as corporate learning. The wheel is therefore reinvented many times and no one is apparently alarmed by this. Losing a bid tends to be put down to more straightforward causes such as price, lead-time, or how the value proposition was put, rather than examining how the organization went about creating the value proposition.

Thus we need to contemplate at least two kinds of knowledge in a business-oriented KM program: basic information-type knowledge with its associated "standard expertise" (such as tax law) and also, when in a competitive situation, integrative knowledge which is needed to bring together the resources in the organization into a capability that distinguishes the business in the marketplace.

THE LOCATION OF KNOWLEDGE AND THE ISSUES FOR A KNOWLEDGE MANAGER

Referring to the DIKAR diagram, a knowledge manager, located in the center, can view knowledge and its management issues from two perspectives: downstream toward the Data end and upstream toward the Results end.

Starting from the knowledge box in the DIKAR model and looking toward data and information, the knowledge manager has a certain set of issues to contend with which are different from the upstream view. An example would be if a worker at a research establishment has knowledge about XYZ that the knowledge manager's company could benefit from in its own R&D program or market planning. This could be laboratory or survey work or something similar. Such knowledge in this circumstance can be thought of as a body of information, formally written down and capable of being readily digested into the interested company's systems. The issues of KM here are identifying the knowledge and its location, validating it and verifying its value, obtaining it in a useful form at a reasonable cost, determining where it is most useful in the business and making it available there in an appropriate form, using suitable technology, and finally ensuring that the knowledge is used beneficially.

Looking upstream, the knowledge manager is now operating with a set of issues around the kind of knowledge that determines actions, and actions that need certain knowledge—the domain of know-how. This kind of knowledge is more diffuse and invariably resides in peoples' heads. An example could be a business that wants to move into a new overseas market—they will need somebody who knows how to quickly set up supply chains into that market, knows the business scene there, the relevant legal and tax factors, the culture, and so on. This is primarily experiential knowledge, although some of it can be made explicit to a degree (e.g., tax laws). Someone who knows the working relationship between businesses and a country's civil servants has knowledge that is hard to code. The knowledge manager has to operate in a much more personal domain—the motivation to share hard-won knowledge of the experiential kind is not usually high, the individual is "giving away" his or her value and may be very reluctant to lose a position of influence and respect by making it available to everyone.

There is nevertheless a strong desire, almost a belief, that as the information software and systems get "more intelligence" this know-how can be captured (e.g., expert systems) and suppliers of "knowledge systems" are keen to press the point. The assumptions may be too simplistic. Although at one level it is clear that rules that have evolved over time can be encoded, some behaviors owe more to chaotic factors than to logical left-brain activity. Many times in the interviews managers referred to the organic nature of knowledge, and how "mind-maps" are more appropriate than information architecture diagrams.

A more complex variation on know-how is the team. Here knowledge is distributed among a group of people. Furthermore, the team itself can create knowledge by its activities. Teams also represent an effective way of generating learning, of marshalling knowledge and disseminating it. Here the knowledge manager has to contend with facilitation of team activities, providing frameworks for more formal knowledge handling, and ensuring its recording so that learning can occur. Typically, companies interviewed saw the gradual buildup of knowledge repositories, which, if carefully constructed and subsequently used intelligently, can ramp up learning curves and remove duplication and re-invention. The three stances on KM revealed in the preceding paragraphs are summarized in Table 8.1.

Table 8.1
Three Approaches to Knowledge Management

	Knowledge as Body of Information	*Knowledge as Know-How: The Individual*	*Knowledge as Know-How: The Team*
Nature of Knowledge	• Explicit • Codifiable • IS can play a part	• Tacit • Personal	• Tacit • Fluid • Dependent on team dynamics
KM Issues	• Finding it • Validation • Value assessment • Obtaining at reasonable cost • Integration with own system • Making available to the right population in the right form • Sensible use of technology • Ensuring subsequent beneficial use	• Establishing suitable processes for extraction • Tight ownership • Reluctance to impart • Motivation and reward • Experiential so hard to encode • Trust • Finding suitable way of passing on learning • Limited role for technology	• Formal management of essentially free-form activity • Establishing suitable frameworks and processes • Members' own perception of their role • Mutual trust—need 100% buy-in • Formal learning mechanisms • Dissemination • Creating and using knowledge repositories • Technology has a background role
Common KM Issues	• Knowledge about knowledge: knowing it exists and where: its context and hence its importance • Ownership and buy-in to KM processes • Updating and reuse of knowledge • Demonstrating causal link between KM activity and business benefit		

Notwithstanding the factors posed by the location of knowledge as just indicated, there still remains the issue of how an organization approaches the topic of knowledge overall. Approaches do differ and the various perspectives currently being adopted are discussed in the next section.

EIGHT ORGANIZATIONAL PERSPECTIVES ON THE MANAGEMENT OF KNOWLEDGE

The survey work referred to earlier revealed a range of approaches currently being used in the field of KM. They fall into eight clusters.

Intellectual Capital

This approach, developed and made well known by Skandia, seeks to recognize and where possible codify the valuable knowledge an organization has, then apply the principles of asset management to the identified knowledge assets. This includes putting a book value on the asset. This is less difficult when the knowledge is codified, and more difficult when it still resides in peoples' heads, so the terms "human capital" and "structural capital" have been coined to distinguish the provenance of the knowledge asset. Additionally, under this approach KM will invoke programs designed to move knowledge out of people's heads and usefully disseminate it to selected parts of the business, that is, to change human capital into structural capital. In the DIKAR model this is a left-to-right approach and seeks to enrich the Knowledge component such that a wider range of actions can be contemplated or taken. The quality of the actions and the certainty of their outcome are potentially improved.

Knowledge as an Individual Skill

This approach recognizes that sufficient numbers of knowledge-competent personnel are always needed to achieve appropriate actions or results and thus seeks to improve the stock of such people. Management development programs and career planning processes, for example, are consciously including knowledge-acquisition elements. The knowledge sought is experiential knowledge, such as how to do business in the Indian subcontinent. Out of necessity, R&D managers have known and practiced this competency approach for a long time, but the formal recognition by other branches of management for developing such competencies has been late in coming.

Philosophical

This approach is a high-level attempt to "think out of the box" by posing deep knowledge questions about the knowledge pool in the organization. As such it can only be part of a solution viz the initial review but, if successful, will no doubt create a valuable framework of understanding that will inform later initiatives. An example might be to ask questions concerning competitiveness, which is not always evaluated in formal ways. Thus, "What do we know that we know about competitors?" is seeking to establish some certainty that the management team all agree what they do know concerning the competition. Not infrequently there is disagreement or surprise in getting answers to that question, but at the end there is more understanding of the team's collective awareness on competition and how the knowledge is distributed and might be shared. For those who can hang on to the probing nature of this line of questioning it can be extended: "What do we know that we don't know about the competition?" aims at uncovering known pools of ignorance about competitors; for example, we know that we are unaware of their R&D pipeline, we are ignorant of their expansion plans in several of our key overseas markets, and so on.

There is also a strong belief among senior management, confirmed in the survey, that useful knowledge often already exists in the organization but no one is sure where it is. This is an example of "What do we not know that we know?"

Technological

In the DIKAR model this is a strongly left-to-right-driven approach. It enshrines a belief that knowledge is completely codifiable—if not now, then at some time—and that technology can manage it by looking after its capture, storage, dissemination, deployment, and growth. To a limited extent this is true, but so far most companies installing intranets (the most popular of knowledge technologies) have been unable to demonstrate people working in any new ways as a result of being "knowledge-enabled," let alone demonstrate those new ways of working resulting in any business benefit. Most claims for benefit turn out to be low-level task improvements—things are a little easier, a little quicker, and a little less costly to do. Often the biggest benefit claimed is the lower cost of IT, which is not knowledge related.

Interviews indicated strongly that technology should never be the first step because KM is above all a people and process issue, with technology as an enabler. This has received further confirmation from ongoing research into getting benefits from intranets.

Teams as Knowledge Agents

Several companies, especially those operating internationally, are investing in constructing virtual organizations. These are primarily designed to overcome the barriers of geography and functional organization without resorting to creating new organizational structures. They appear to serve businesses best when the concurrent application of several expertises is required, such as the large complex bid described previously. From time to time something approaching a team or even a virtual department is created to tackle a complex task or set of tasks, where the necessary expertise and know-how is spread around the organization. The management issues in these arrangements are centered on ownership, roles, process, knowledge sharing, and trust. The use of technology is a secondary consideration until the people and process factors are in a manageable state. Companies in which this virtual organization approach is being developed seriously also take steps to insert formal learning loops into the processes, thereby amassing a knowledge repository of how to do business in this way.

The support technologies are frequently a combination of intranets, e-mail, document management, and workflow plus specialized applications attuned to the task set (e.g., planning packages) assembled in a proactive mode of operating. This mode is needed because first, the team members' prime jobs lie elsewhere and the distributed nature of the team means that members are not usually confronted with the immediacy of contact with other team members, unlike in their day-to-day work environment, so it is easier for tasks to languish. Second and more important, the technology provides some momentum for the virtual team to function, if properly implemented. If, for instance, a team member receives a key document—for example, the legal member gets some new regulatory information—then when putting the document into the registry he or she will be asked to add expert comments. Furthermore she or he will also be asked to rate the importance of the document. Depending on its rating, e-mails will automatically be dispatched to other team members. This also overcomes the problem of the passive nature of intranets: how does anyone know if there is something important on the Web without time-consuming frequent accessing?

Strategic

This approach takes two forms. The first is a fundamental reappraisal of the business in knowledge terms, and in some ways is linked to the intellectual capital approach except that the latter will not challenge existing organizational forms and structures whereas the more strategic approach could redefine them in more appropriate forms that, by design, utilize and exploit internal knowledge rather than just perform stewardship on it.

The other form of the strategic approach is the formal take-up of knowledge management concepts into the strategic management processes. This is a key consideration for businesses that rely on innovation in order to survive and prosper. Strategies are always assumed to be the province of the most senior executives, but in an innovation-based organization the executives would recognize the value of innovation although they themselves do not provide it. The innovation providers probably reside some levels below the senior executives and are remote from the strategy creation process. Under these circumstances, how can a strategy that must rely on innovation make meaningful contact with the innovators? It is to this problem that considerations of knowledge management might be applied. Thus a KM-based strategy would contain and foster knowledge frameworks to encourage and sustain innovation.

Process

This also takes two forms. The first form involves making knowledge management itself into an available business process. This takes the form of KM expertise available to managers who are, for example, attempting analysis or improvement programs. A documented and supported process is on offer to be used in the initiative.

The second variation is to examine business activities and processes to determine whether application of KM techniques and approaches will leverage business benefit. This approach, invariably in combination with other approaches mentioned previously, appears to have yielded the most business benefits so far. The reason is almost certainly that by focusing on a current business issue a concentrated approach can ensue, in contrast with the opposite wherein enormous amounts of so-called "knowledge" are collected in the hope that someone with a technology aid (e.g., data mining) will spot something beneficial to the business. The latter exists but usually it is pattern seeking in highly structured data sets (e.g., insurance companies finding correlations among their policy data, their claims data, and their customer data sets allowing them to spot high and low risk clients).

This approach also seems to be accompanied by a degree of transformation of activities into processes. Not infrequently there are "assemblages" of activities such as the large bid described earlier, or account management for instance, which are important to the business. Such assemblages do not generate revenue directly, but if performed well do yield inputs into the revenue-generating processes. Because in some senses they are adjacent to the main processes they receive less attention from senior managers, and they are largely people-only activities that are difficult to measure—two other characteristics that appear coincident with lack of senior management interest. As such there is informality, lower ownership, and lower focus than on the core processes in the business, which probably have representation at board level. The people-centered nature suggests KM might be of assistance and where this does yield benefits it almost always results in the activity set being remodeled into a knowledge-centric process. Thus ownership, workflow, knowledge sharing, learning, and focus on benefits become much clearer. Also reinvention, length of learning curves, and the confusion of roles can drop significantly because of the formal knowledge sharing and the useful discipline that such a process enforces.

Combinations

Most organizations pursue some combination of the seven approaches already discussed, usually containing elements of technology, process, and intellectual capital approaches.

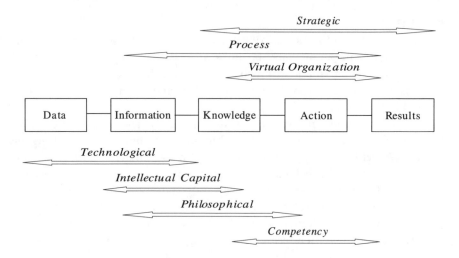

Figure 8.2   *Approaches for the DIKAR Model*

Mapping the Approaches onto the DIKAR Model

In order to assess the perspectives separately and collectively, use is once more made of the DIKAR model. It enables comparisons of foci and scope and as will be seen indicates the merits of a combination approach.

The strategic approach spans most of the Knowledge stage (perhaps excluding only very detailed knowledge) through to Results and possibly beyond because even desired results have to be determined within a wider framework of corporate objectives and drivers.

The process approach does not attempt to embrace all results but has the virtue mentioned previously of focusing on a particular set. It extends back into the Information stage, picking up specific requirements in the Action and Knowledge stages, and importantly, in the linkages as well.

The teams-as-knowledge-agents approach (virtual organization) concentrates on removing the barriers to synergy among Knowledge that is residing within distributed expertise, and the Action programs needed for particular results.

Currently, the technological approach extends from Data through Information and just into the lower reaches of Knowledge, where it mainly acts as a channel or conductor for knowledge sharing.

The intellectual capital approach sets itself the goal of identification, codification, and stewardship of knowledge and as such iterates usefully between the Information and Knowledge stages.

The philosophical approach attempts first, deeper understanding then radical reframing of the Action and Knowledge stages and their connections, and second, new directions for the information sets required to perform in the newer way of working.

The competency approach aims to tackle the central people issues in the Action stage with reference to the (longer term) results needed and the fundamental experiential knowledge that has to be acquired and exploited.

None of the approaches spans all elements of the model or even all the aspects of the stages—which emphasizes the value of the combination approach as the most likely route to business benefit.

It is worth emphasizing the key role that linkages play in the model: all the approaches span at least one or two stages and thus embody, at a minimum, one set of linkages. Any practical approach needs to embrace both a right-to-left approach (Definitional) and a left-to-right (Delivering) approach.

HOW ORGANIZATIONS ARE PROGRESSING IN KNOWLEDGE MANAGEMENT

Based on the survey and subsequent work, the following observations are offered on the current sate of progress of organizations that are investing in KM programs.

Stage of Evolution of KM

It is still relatively early to judge the merits of KM programs. Most CKOs or their equivalents have been in posts only a short while—6 to 24 months, which is not long given some of the transformational goals being attempted through KM. They appear to have spent their early months wrestling with definitions, concepts, and levels of understanding in their business about what KM might be for their organization, and are now in the throes of marketing to management colleagues what KM might do for them. Further support for this observation comes from an analysis of the findings by industry sector, which show some differences but not many. Likewise, between large and small companies the differences are of degree rather than large gaps, which indicate that some businesses are further down the track than others. In two years' time, the effect of specific market changes should show that some industries have tuned KM activity directly to the needs of their markets, thereby producing distinct differences according to the nature of business.

The real test will be the demonstrable delivery of business benefit from KM with a clear causal chain showing that KM delivered a business capability leading to real benefits. This was emphasized in the survey returns, which showed that 93 percent of the respondents agreed or strongly agreed that KM is an issue of "applying knowledge to some benefit."

Evidence exists that companies have instituted enabling changes and activities, which are prerequisites to achieving knowledge-leveraged benefits, but few businesses have gotten as far as actually delivering the benefits in a consistent way. Apart from the time taken to put the appropriate mechanisms in place and overcoming various barriers, the significant benefits from KM are not short term. R&D, for instance, was voted the number one function for useful KM and the overall reason for doing KM—competitive advantage—is not the kind of benefit that materializes overnight, no matter where it originates.

It is likely that KM advantages and benefits will emerge relatively slowly. Claims for faster achievements are often relabeled cost-cutting exercises elevated by the use of the latest KM buzzword. This is the usual trap for any new approach and usually hastens its demise. The activities of knowledge managers will be crucial if the early work is not to subside into an over-hyped under-delivering fad.

The Cost of KM

KM is expensive to do and also—if a business is in highly competitive markets—expensive not to do. Referencing the DIKAR model, companies that have disparate infrastructure platforms have not invested in data management; and those whose executives have never seriously debated the role of information in their business activities are unlikely to make headway in KM before those issues are sorted. There are basic issues of codification of knowledge (most companies report this takes far longer than they first hoped), education, and sometimes changing an organization to value knowledge sharing. All these take time, money, and senior management attention.

There is a significant management cost because KM is not a low-level technique. On the contrary, where it works it is very much a collective managerial activity. To promote such a paradigm requires the appointment of knowledge managers who command respect and have resources at their disposal. The cost of achieving the right level of buy-in is time and quality management effort. Also, any form of collectivism usually constitutes a behavior change if not a value-set change. This means that KM must have leadership. Knowledge sharing must be demonstrated and rewarded by senior managers, otherwise organizational fiefdoms will prevail. Depending on how territorial a business is and its developmental stage in the KM process, the aggregation of these costs may seem an excessively high price but there appears to be no shortcut. Conversely, global companies that perceive their marketplace to be highly competitive believe that it is expensive not to do KM.

THE NATURE OF KM AND ITS IMPLICATIONS

Knowledge management is more organic in its nature and execution than is information management. This is because knowledge resides primarily within people or groups of people; thus, it has complexities not found in defined procedural activities. Knowledge sharing often has aspects of trust and politics associated with it and needs its own managerial approach to be developed. Attempts to bypass organizational politics (e.g., functional barriers) with technology are to be resisted if conflicts or apathy further down the line are to be avoided.

The personal and organic nature of knowledge has to be managed head-on. Where communities of practice have been constructed, managers reported that they only succeeded when buy-in and contribution was 100 percent; anything less led to degradation because people felt others were not matching their effort and the desire to withdraw prevailed. As mentioned earlier, leadership appears to be key in achieving a truly open knowledge environment.

THE ROLE OF TECHNOLOGY

Technology is needed but it should never be the first step. KM is primarily a people and process issue. Once these have been sorted out, then the created processes are very amenable to being supported and enhanced by the use of IS/IT. This is certainly the case in global companies where geographical barriers to knowledge movement and sharing are large. The degree to which information technology can directly contribute to business activity attenuates according to a left-to-right progression across the DIKAR model. The nature of the IS/IT contribution alters around the Knowledge point in the model. To the left, IS/IT can actually work directly on data/information and even create inputs, but in significant knowledge exchange this is not currently the case.

As indicated earlier, knowledge sharing is complex, personal, and organic. The most effective modality is face-to-face conversation in which more happens than the mere exchange of words. This can be hugely uneconomic and impractical, however, and especially so for international companies. The role of IS/IT alters to being that of a communication channel or conduit, and its success lies in how well it can emulate the richness of the conversation channel. Desktop videoconferencing currently comes closest to being such a channel. This is not the mere provision of a facial image on a PC screen—it operates according to indigenous rules and is backed up by high-bandwidth infrastructure carrying shared access to data, images, video clips, searchable documents, and so on. BP Exploration has invested heavily and successfully in this technology and claims significant cost savings in new drillings through shared learning curves around the globe.

Other technologies that are making a contribution "on the right of DIKAR" are interactive intranets and the combination of document management and workflow management. The latter is especially true in situations in which large complex multipart documents such as contracts or regulatory submissions require concurrent attention from several experts who may be in different countries.

KM HAS TO BE MANAGED

There seems little return in just collecting knowledge, making it accessible, and then waiting for some evolutionary process to emerge that turns the business into something better purely through the increased presence of increased knowledge. Management must intervene to leverage the benefits, and the appointments of CKOs so far reflect this—nearly all are appointed by a CEO, and virtually all those interviewed who are making progress had a wide business background, commanded some respect in their organization (and outside of it), and exhibited drive and the will to change things.

IMPACT OF KM

Certain features are present where KM seems to be producing the greatest business benefits. First, a process-oriented view has been taken and the places where knowledge is key to a process or activity have been identified and worked on. Mapping rather than modeling seems more successful due to the organic nature of knowledge. Knowledge has a shared attribute with money in that it seems of value only when it is moved and used. Acquisition and dissemination are only the beginning of a "knowledge trading market," which is where the value adding occurs.

The survey and interviews show that the areas in which active knowledge management is producing business benefit are usually not the core business processes. KM at the main business process levels has always been a reality. This is not surprising since a manufacturing manager would, of necessity, have to be knowledgeable about the processes central to and supportive of manufacturing itself. Thus the gains for KM at the core process levels are likely to be small. If an organization were truly unknowledgeable about its core business processes, it would not stay in business very long. Fourteen percent of respondents in the survey, when asked to identify the responsibility for KM replied, "It is everyone's job," which implicates the process level and was confirmed in interviews.

WHERE KM IS DELIVERING BUSINESS BENEFIT: FEEDER PROCESSES

Although core processes can and do benefit from knowledge, the survey revealed other processes that gain significant benefit from active KM. These non-core processes can be thought of as "feeders" to the main business processes. An analogy is the relationship between a river and its tributaries: as long as the tributaries supply fresh oxygenated water the river can continue to function as a transport system and an ecosystem.

An example of such a feeder activity is winning large international supply chain contracts. Constructing a bid for such business requires the marshalling of many types of expertise, usually in compressed timescales. One company interviewed had decided to increase their rate of winning such business. They assembled the key experts into a knowledge group whose aim was to effectively create a "large bid" process. Initially this was a meeting of the relevant men and women who really knew the practicalities of international logistics but focused on how to rapidly construct competitive and profitable bids. When the process emerged with some clarity, they then created support for it with appropriate technology to minimize the need for face-to-face work and to make it a more efficient and easier process.

The characteristics of knowledge feeder processes are as follows:

- In contrast to core business processes, feeder processes do not usually generate income but rather create inputs to the main processes—often significant inputs.
- Feeder processes involve the concurrent application of a wide range of knowledge and expertise—usually in a compressed timescale.
- The interaction of expertise can be complicated—even language may be an issue, such as between a biotechnologist and a lawyer, each using a specialist vocabulary.
- They are knowledge-intensive—particularly when involving experiential knowledge.
- They work best when operated as a team or community activity.
- Documents and workflow are important. "Documents" in this sense are not just pieces of paper; rather they are significant items such as contracts, key technical papers, and expert reviews. Such documents are subject, particularly in global companies, to review by many experts. Who has commented, who has seen those comments, and what has occurred as a result can be critical at certain stages. Version management can become a key issue because if several people around the world are contributing, it is clearly vital that they all work on the same version, hence the need for workflow management.
- Typically, feeder processes may have not been viewed by the organization as processes at all in the past but rather as sets of activities that the relevant people "just get on and do."
- Because of the many functions involved, ownership is not as clear as it is for the main processes.
- There is a high degree of interaction with the outside world and the interaction is usually iterative.
- Unlike the main process, there is a "one-off" aspect to the feeder process. The latter can inhibit learning, especially learning from failure. If a large, complex bid fails, it takes real effort to extract learning about the bid process—especially if another bid prospect is ready and waiting. But in a true knowledge process learning is critical and the process should have this designed into it.

THE KNOWLEDGE MANAGEMENT BARRIERS THAT EXIST IN ORGANIZATIONS

There are structural, cultural and managerial barriers to KM as well as the usual issues of the time and money required to mount such initiatives. Paraphrasing the outcomes of the survey's interviews, it can be said that both the path and the barrier to successful KM lie in an organization's people. They have the potential to deliver or frustrate KM plans and programs. The root of this lies in the fact that knowledge sharing is not natural—there is a reluctance to divulge years of hard-won experience, especially if the divulgence is also associated with possible redundancy. Furthermore, experienced business-winners, such as senior consultants in a consultancy or senior partners in a law firm, may acknowledge the value of sharing their know-how with less experienced staff but typically will still rate one hour of fee earning well above one hour of knowledge sharing. Changing that outlook as a hearts-and-minds issue rather than a training issue.

In such circumstances value has to be demonstrably placed on knowledge sharing and corporate knowledge creation and stewardship. In most companies this will mean leadership by example from the top. Reward structures need to be visibly in place. These need not necessarily be financial rewards—formal peer recognition is often a high motivator for experts. Organizations also require formal learning loops and best practice sharing mechanisms to maximize the exploitation of their people's knowledge.

Sitting over all of this is the need to have some declared overview or policy on what KM is for the business and how it is linked into business drivers and plans. In several businesses KM still sits outside mainstream management activity. As such it will struggle to deliver any demonstrable tangible benefits. Mere assertions, however strongly delivered, that knowledge is a vital asset and needs to be handled as such have little chance of inducing the necessary changes for knowledge-leveraged benefits to appear.

Analysis of the Knowledge Barriers

At the top of the list of concerns is corporate culture. Turning a "We don't do it like that," attitude into "Who knows how to do it better?" demands a sea change in working practices and relationships. The survey reveals that European management identified knowledge barriers ranging from learning-averse individuals, to the whole framework of the business. Respondents were asked to identify the main obstacles they face in regard to knowledge management. People and cultural issues dominated as both the necessary means, but also the key inhibitor to sharing and exploiting knowledge. Forty percent didn't rate their company at all as a "learning organization." The set of obstacles cited can be tabulated as in Table 8.2.

People either don't want to change, or can't be changed quickly. Working styles are often ingrained into organizations and in many cases the produc-

Table 8.2
Knowledge Barriers

People	Management	Structure	Knowledge
• Inertia to change	• The fear of giving up power	• Inflexible company structures	• Extracting knowledge
• Too busy—no time to learn	• The difficulties of passing on power	• Fragmented organizations	• Categorizing knowledge
• No discipline to act	• Challenging traditional company style	• Functional silos	• Rewarding knowledge
• Motivation		• Failure to invest in past systems	• Understanding knowledge management
• Constant staff turnover	• Imposed constraints		• Sharing between key knowledge groups
• Transferring knowledge to new people	• Lack of understanding about formal approaches		• Making knowledge widely available
• Teaching older employees new ideas			

tion and sharing of knowledge—as opposed to a more tangible product—is still regarded as distracting or even career threatening in many physical and manufacturing industries. The task is not helped in many organizations by the nature of their own internal structures—often inflexible, fragmented, and separated into functional silos. It would appear that there are still serious issues to face in sharing that knowledge between key groups, and making some of it widely available inside and perhaps outside the company among partners, suppliers, or even customers.

THE WAY FORWARD FOR KM-ORIENTED ORGANIZATIONS

This section proffers organizations a framework for treating knowledge and its management as a business competence and also develops a management checklist designed to promote the achievement of business benefits from KM.

KM as a Business Competence

The first organizations that will benefit from managing their knowledge better will be those that have a balanced framework in which to locate the KM activity and an appropriate set of organizational competencies to direct and deploy knowledge. Such a framework is suggested in Figure 8.3. Its components are supply of knowledge, exploitation of knowledge, a knowledge strategy, and the three links between each. The existence or absence of any of

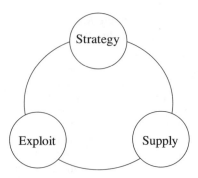

Figure 8.3 *The Knowledge Competency Model*

these six will determine how knowledge competent a business is and where it should direct its KM efforts.

Supply of Knowledge

An organization needs to be competent in the supply of knowledge. Assertions are made that increasing the amount and flow of available knowledge in an organization through, for example, an intranet will have a cultural effect, moving the organization from a "push" style of communication to a "pull" style. Often all this amounts to is the provision of a large amount of information and people who are left to make the best of it. There is also a tendency in organizations that see KM as a supply-side issue to then identify all KM problems as the fault of the knowledge manager or the IS function.

Exploitation of Knowledge

A knowledge business needs to be ever more competent in its exploitation of knowledge. If being competitive is the key driver—as indicated in the survey—then knowledge needs to be exploited for increased customer intimacy, product/service leadership, and improved operational excellence.

Strategy for Knowledge

Supply and exploitation need direction; the business must have a strategy to guide KM. This can take the form of a business strategy that clearly locates knowledge activities in its schema and where it sees KM leveraging the achievement of the strategy. Alternatively, it may develop specific knowledge strategies to address certain drivers, as in innovation-based companies that might have specific knowledge strategies for their R&D processes.

The other three competencies required are those that successfully link strategy, supply, and exploitation. Each linkage works in both directions.

Strategy-Supply

If there is little or no strategic direction, the knowledge supply activity runs the risk of collecting and disseminating increasing quantities of nonuseful or irrelevant knowledge and not supplying the value-adding knowledge. In the other direction, awareness of what knowledge is available, or could be made available, can influence strategic thinking.

Supply-Exploitation

Too much exploitation is driven by what the technology pushes forward. This competency is essentially getting the "what" properly in front of the "how" and driving the supply side from the demand side—insisting that all knowledge activities are keyed to specific business benefits. In the reverse direction, a competency of identifying opportunities arising in the supply side and taking them forward for exploitation also needs to be developed.

Strategy-Exploitation

This link tends to be the weakest of all the competencies. Without it, business plans are not going to be supported by targeted exploitation of knowledge, and conversely effort in exploitation will find its way into areas outside the business strategy.

A PRACTICAL PROGRAM FOR KM THAT WILL DELIVER BUSINESS BENEFITS

Tying Down the Concept of KM: The First Responsibility of Senior Management

As long as the concept of KM remains vague or ambiguous in an organization, then progress will be minimal or unnoticeable and success criteria will be misunderstood and even challenged. The key, as in many management domains, is focus. The first focus point is to enunciate what the company is looking for from its KM program—in business terms. The survey respondents overwhelmingly opted (from a list of eleven contenders) for competitiveness followed by profitability.

The second focus point is to be clear about how knowledge is going to leverage the advantage (e.g., competitor intelligence, innovation). Companies are often very vague about what they *need* from KM, but still seek "the answer," usually one involving a technology such as an intranet. Nearly all business-related knowledge needs are driven primarily by the market, and those needs will always change over time and in different circumstances. The market always needs watching and knowledge must be accumulated on its behavior and trends. Hence KM is an eternal and enduring discipline for all managers. It is not external to top team activity; it is core, and there will never be an "answer" that lasts for very long, only various tools and approaches that assist the management process. In a sense, the greater the constraint an organization puts on the meaning of "knowledge management," the more likely it is to see some improvements

Be Sure of a Likely Return on Investment

Do not spread KM everywhere—it will not turn up benefits in all or even most of a business's activities. Many activities are not amenable to KM-leveraged improvements. Pick only those business activities that are likely to have a significant chance of being affected by having their knowledge components overhauled.

Applying that stricture to competitiveness, for example, suggests the following: being competitive in marketplaces that are increasingly globalized, liberalized, and deregulated means that an organization has to be innovative (a knowledge activity itself) and also know in some depth what its competitors are doing (sometimes just knowing who they are). As more and more products and services become commoditized, so the added value that an organization has to have to be a chosen supplier becomes more a one of know-how about customers' needs, preferences, and so on rather than straightforward product excellence. This is where KM is likely to give maximum returns.

Retain a Focus on Useful Outcome and Measure It

Nearly all business activities can at some level be described in terms of the simple model in Figure 8.4. KM can be applied to any or all of the three elements of this model: input, activities, or output. Wherever it is applied the goal should always be the same: improvement in the output. Many KM initiatives attempt only to leverage the input side, and their chosen metrics (if they exist) tend to reflect that. For instance, many companies are content to provide an intranet as a way of knowledge-leveraging benefits. This is an input-only initiative and most companies in that group are content to measure success as the number of hits a Web page has had.

KM is most likely to lead to improvements when applied to the activity set itself in such a way that those performing the activities work in an improved fashion (i.e., they work in a new way, a better way, or can eliminate some as-

Figure 8.4   *Retain a Focus on Useful Outcome and Measure It*

pect of the activity set). Furthermore, the improvements must lead to ways of working that yield business benefits. It is insufficient, for example, just to save time unless that time saved is put to good use.

The simple activity model also suggests ways of measuring control of, and success for, KM actions. For instance, suppose a business has a set of activities that is performed throughout a number of sites. Sharing best practice could well be a KM-applied way of improving overall performance. The key metric is the desired improvement across the sites (i.e., lowest overheads, fastest stock turnaround, highest productivity). Everyone should be very clear on such goals and that they will be measured. Additionally, and in support of achieving the goal, it might be advisable to measure the rate of take-up and implementation of the agreed best practices as means of monitoring and controlling the progress of the initiative (measurement of the change in the activity set). If the changes are large and will take time, then it might also be worth measuring some of the inputs (e.g., revision of standards manuals, training of personnel, implementation of supporting IT, etc.).

Stakeholder Analysis

Analyze the various stakeholders' roles and commitments and develop action plans to influence and inculcate the new knowledge based approach. Some companies have induced the need for knowledge management by getting rid of what they had through delayering and downsizing. Usually it is middle-aged middle managers who go in these exercises, and they are the ones who know in depth how key parts of an organization actually work, particularly during the difficult times. Companies then find they have only one "knowledge hero" left and KM is a way of extracting that person's knowledge for dissemination. The learning here is by "auditing" the knowledge assets in the organization to identify key people who are repositories of the valuable knowledge that keeps a business going in its marketplace. All subsequent KM initiatives should take account of these key personnel and their stance and attitude.

Encourage Formal Capture of Learning

Whether it is sophisticated technology or simply very good paper records, the learning in making the changes should enter some corporate repository and be available for others. Thus, in the best practice example in the previous section, the first site to move in instituting shared practice should let its lessons in making the changes be shared with others, and so on. Learning will occur at two levels: first, accumulated learning within the initiative (the last site to adopt the practices should travel fastest and most economically by benefiting from the earlier adopters' experiences) and second, at a higher level the business will have data on how to introduce improvements in a multisite situation.

Publish Plans, Achievements, and Learning

KM activities benefit from sensible broadcasting. Arguably, because knowledge sharing is a central plank in KM, the approach should walk its own talk. More constructively, recognition (especially among peers) of the use of knowledge is a reward in itself to experts and an encouragement to more knowledge sharing. In that light, metrics should be chosen carefully and imaginatively to reflect both the value sets of key knowledge workers and genuine business benefit achievement.

CHAPTER 9

What Do We Know About CKOs?

Michael J. Earl and Ian A. Scott

I n 1997, we set out to study a newly emerging role with a pretentious title—the chief knowledge officer or CKO—and published the results in the form of both a report (Earl and Scott, 1998) and a journal article (Earl and Scott, 1999). Our purpose was twofold:

1. To understand the role and to see how it related, if at all, to the role of chief information officer, or CIO, which one of us had also studied (Earl and Vivian, 1993; Earl and Feeny, 1994; Earl and Vivian, 1999).
2. To provide a lens on the evolving practice of knowledge management.

Since that study, we have continued to monitor the experiences of CKOs and this chapter provides an opportunity to update our 1998 result, albeit with rather more anecdotal evidence. We draw five conclusions *pro tem*.

First, more CKOs are being appointed, particularly as a second wave of knowledge management enthusiasm takes hold in corporations. Second, some CKOs are falling by the wayside, either because of an inimical organizational context or because they do not fit our model of the ideal CKO. Third, it is difficult to see how knowledge management programs can be initiated and propelled without someone fulfilling the CKO role, even if they don't have the title. Fourth, it may be best to think of the CKO as a change agent, but one who is full-time. Finally, this is unlikely to be a long-term position.

THE CKO LANDSCAPE

CKOs have been in existence for about five years at most, although some pioneers may have been doing something similar in earlier years with different titles. Some directors of intellectual capital, organizational learning, and kindred folk may therefore feel they were early CKOs. When we started our 1997 study we had to work hard to find an acceptable sample size. We eventually settled for 20, reckoning that there were no more than 25 CKOs in existence worldwide! Our definition of a CKO was a senior executive leading a knowledge management initiative who had "knowledge" in his or her title. Even though we asked those CKOs we identified to refer us to other CKOs, we eventually had to "advertise" for CKOs on the World Wide Web. Our sample of 20 comprised 14 from North America and 6 from Europe.

On our definition, we estimate that there may now be 50 CKOs in the world and we have formed a CKO Network.[1] Our members look to this network to help them understand their role rather than to understand knowledge management. In other words, and unsurprisingly, if you are in a new role where there are no historical role models, you want to augment your personal action learning with that of others.

THE 1997 STUDY

We studied our 20 CKOs in three steps. First, we conducted face-to-face semi-structured interviews, which lasted from two to three hours. Then we administered a personality test using a well-known psychometric instrument. Finally, we held workshops with the participants in London and New York to discuss and refine our findings.

We collected data on why CKOs were appointed and how, what they did, their perceived competencies and their career histories, their experiences to date, and their own reflections on their role. Rather than repeat the results here, we choose to highlight some of the descriptive data, generalizing to a degree, and to present our central model.

DISTINCTIVE PEOPLE

Mostly, our CKOs had been appointed by the CEO and reported to the CEO. Their position was not on the organization chart and they did not expect the role to be permanent. The aim of the CKO was to initiate knowledge management and ensure that the philosophy and practice became embedded in the organization. So they were not establishing a function. Unlike CIOs, the CKOs did not have an operational set of activities to deliver; nor did they have obvious policy responsibilities such as technology and infrastructure planning that CIOs generally oversee.

In contrast, they had small staffs and small budgets, often working with "virtual teams" distributed around the organization or seconded to particular knowledge management projects. They spent time seeking out knowledge management champions who would pioneer ideas and sponsors who would fund and support these initiatives. However, they mostly realized that in time they might require more people and money as knowledge management initiatives prospered—and that they would require more time in the role of CKO to achieve substantial impact. Nevertheless, their goal was to work themselves out of a job and to have the line managers take over daily responsibility for knowledge management.

We described CKOs as "fun people having a fun time." They were typically bubbly and enthusiastic yet reflective and balanced. They were achievers and completers but willing to let others take the credit for any successes. They were broad-gauged and generally were catholic in their knowledge management orientations—as interested in explicit knowledge domains as in more tacit ones, ready to embrace technology or get involved in more organizational or behavioral endeavors. Indeed, they tended to be eclectic and pragmatic, backing any idea that made "knowledge sense" and ready to connect to other initiatives.

Forty percent of our CKOs were female. Most had a wide variety of experience not only in business, but also sometimes outside. But they also had several years' experience of working in their current organization and thus knew the culture while the key actors also knew them. The personality data indicated a degree of extroversion, an ability to be open to ideas and be flexible, ease of working with others, and a balanced attitude toward achieving results but not getting depressed by setbacks.

In their own eyes, they were fortunate to have been given the opportunity to be CKO; they mostly felt that their career experience had groomed them for the job and it was the best job they had had, working for a vision they really believed in.

THE MODEL CKO

Our interview data and the discussions in our two workshops led us to propose a model CKO (Figure 9.1). The CKO had to have two leadership qualities, being something of an entrepreneur and having the skills of a (strategy) consultant. All saw themselves as builders, starting a new activity, capability, or function, so the CKO must be a self-starter who is excited by business development and by growing something. The CKOs studied recognize the personal risks involved in taking on a newly created position, in particular one with a label that invites ridicule (although most valued having *knowledge* in their titles). However, all the CKOs studied seem stimulated by the risks. This spirit of newness, adventure, and risk taking invites the label of *entrepreneur*, and it is one with which the CKOs immediately identify.

A critical attribute of such entrepreneurship is being a strategist who can grapple with the implications of using knowledge management as a tool for corporate transformation. To a degree, the CKO is a visionary, able to see the big picture that the CEO has in mind, but also able to translate it into action, to think of new ways of doing things and yet focus on deliverable results. In

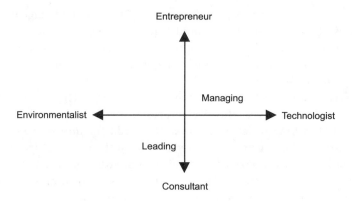

Figure 9.1   *The Model CIO*

short, the CKOs we have met are driven by building something and seeing it through. One CKO reflected that she "would hate to leave it undone." CKOs are thus entrepreneurs inside organizations.

However, vision and determination are not enough. The CKO is also a *consultant*. He or she has to bring in ideas and seed them, listen to other people's ideas and back them if they make sense and fit the knowledge vision. In other words, without ideas and projects, knowledge management is likely to be little more than rhetoric. So, as in classical management consulting, a valuable skill is matching new ideas with managers' own business needs and "buyer values."

Managing relationships is therefore an important capability. The CKO can operate only through influence, persuasion, and demonstration, and he or she must be willing to let others take center stage and receive the credit. One CKO described the role as "the most influencing job I've ever had." At the same time, it is important to be able to read the company's appetite for change and appreciate how to connect to, and work along with, other change initiatives. One CKO said she is "driven to make a difference to performance," but added that such goals are to no avail unless the CKO "understands the organization's business model and is clear on the kinds of knowledge that are relevant and will create value." This reflection reads like the key competence of a top strategy consultant.

On the managing axis, we proposed that CKOs ended up having to invite and manage two sorts of investments or interventions. Both involve design competencies; our CKOs stressed the verb "design" when they talked about what they actually do. First, they are technologists—to a degree. As a *technologist* the CKO has to understand which technologies can contribute to capturing, storing, exploring and, in particular, sharing knowledge. Several of these are emerging new technologies. Thus the CKO has to be sufficiently informed about technology to evaluate what works, to judge when to adopt a technology, to appreciate the opportunities enabled, and to assess any demanding implementation issues. On some occasions, the CKO is the sponsor of the IT project and nearly always has to work with the CIO or a senior IS executive. Thus the CKO needs the confidence to have credible discussions with technology partners. Among the CKOs we studied this was more likely to come from past involvement with IT projects than from formal IT training.

Such technology capability is not optional: the CKOs we studied recognize that they cannot operate in the organizational domain of knowledge management alone. Indeed, their first initiative is often based on IT, such as creating knowledge directories, developing knowledge sharing groupware, or building an intranet. As one recently appointed CKO reported, "we found we desperately needed an intranet to get people connected who did not know each other." And reengineering knowledge-intensive management and business processes, such as new product development or sales planning, often requires development of a knowledge sharing IT application, such as groupware to record experiences and ideas or a database to work from agreed or continuously updated know-how.

In contrast, the organizational domain and the management of much tacit knowledge require "softer" competencies. Here, the CKOs studied especially stress their design role, namely the creation of social environments that stimulate and facilitate both arranged and chance conversations or the development of events and processes that encourage more deliberate knowledge creation and exchange. The CKO is therefore also an *environmentalist*, which implies several things. It includes the design of space, such as designing office and relaxation areas or acquiring and furnishing retreats and learning centers. "I spend 90 percent of my time creating markets for conversations," reflected one CKO. It includes bringing together communities with common interests who rarely interact with each other. For example, all those in different functions who serve key customers or have information on them may be brought together or connected in order to exchange knowledge (especially experience and gossip).

Being an environmentalist also means radically redesigning performance measurement and executive appraisal systems to break down incentives centered on the individual, and instead to visibly encourage collective knowledge development and sharing, discourage people from avoiding risk, and encourage learning by experimentation. More basically, being an environmentalist means connecting to any management education and organizational development initiatives that increase the emphasis on, and enhance capacities for, knowledge creation. Examples include arranging experience-sharing events and experience-shaping projects and assignments for fast-track managers, and installing career development programs with broad and deep knowledge acquisition.

This model suggests that the CKO also has to be both broad and deep. Breadth applies to the need to acquire a range of competencies, probably through varied career experience. Depth refers to the need to acquire familiarity with, and respect in, the organization. We note that, in contrast, CIOs need to be stronger on technology but not so obviously environmentalists. And although being something of an entrepreneur helps, today CIOs inherit an established function with relatively clear responsibilities. Likewise, although having the attributes of a consultant could help, the CIO today is essentially a business executive running a critical function and becoming a fully fledged member of the executive team (Earl and Vivian, 1999). When we examine further what CKOs do, we see that they are mostly concerned with change and far less than CIOs with delivery.

WHAT CKOs DO

One year on from our study, we are beginning to see other patterns in what CKOs actually do. As first incumbents in the role, they have to create awareness of knowledge management, foster language and develop frameworks to help managers understand what it is, what is new and what can be done to sell the promise and to create support and demand for knowledge management initiatives. They are *evangelists* who have to help managers make sense of knowledge management. So they engage in propaganda by making presentations, issuing publications, arranging conferences, seminars, and so on. But they go only so far, sensing that simple models suffice and that actions speak louder than words.

So they also look out for projects. They sell ideas, they listen out for needs, and they latch on to existing initiatives where they feel that they can add on a knowledge perspective and raise the sights—whether it is a process reengineering project, a strategy exercise, an organizational development program, an information systems project, or whatever.

To do this effectively, they will be expected to bring concrete ideas of what is possible, so they have, and will need, a bag of *tools and solutions* to apply. They may not be the implementers of solutions, but they should know whom to bring in from inside or outside. They may well apply the analytical or conceptual tools to discover and prescribe the solution in conjunction with line management. Often they engage likely project champions to move an idea forward. They will also search out managers with quite individual needs to elicit how a knowledge management initiative could help their business unit or themselves. They may run workshops to discover knowledge management needs and opportunities.

When we reflect on these activities, it is clear to us that the model in Figure 9.1 tells us how to recognize in someone CKO potential to succeed in these endeavors, and it summarizes the competencies and experience required. The CKO has to be something of a consultant because there is no "to do" list; you

Figure 9.2   *The CKO as Change Agent*

have to analyze the organization and propose or discover ideas. The managing axis describes the two principal domains in which CKOs work, or the two sets of solutions available. Figure 9.1 is therefore a role description. A role specification is better provided by Figure 9.2, which summarizes the three sets of activities outlined in the previous three paragraphs.

If we stand back, we can see these three sets of activities—evangelizing on knowledge management, engaging supporters and doers, and applying tools and solutions—as typically those of the change agent role. In a most useful article, Markus and Benjamin (1996) analyze "change agentry" with respect to the world of information systems. They depict three models of the change agent role: the traditional IS (or systems analyst) model, the facilitator (or organizational development) model, and the advocate (or change leader) model. If we extrapolate from these three models, which they use to classify both direct and indirect work done on change agentry, we can see the typical change agent having to engage in the three activities in lower case in Figure 9.2, using Markus and Benjamin's terminology. We suggest preferred candidate descriptors for the CKO in upper case.

The real message of Figure 9.2 is that the CKO is a change agent. Whether CKOs prefer to be called *advocates* or *evangelists*, they are in the business of influencing minds and behaviors. They aim to get individuals and groups to accept and internalize the CKO's view that knowledge management matters and could yield a significant improvement to organizational performance and adaptation. They try to create an exciting vision of what could be possible, but they are flexible in spotting or connecting with different opportunities and ideas. So they freely embrace other initiatives or suggestions under the banner and program of knowledge management. And they are eclectic in choosing their form of propaganda—from language to framework to rhetoric to persistent persuasion.

As *facilitators*, they are more concerned with process consultancy than with advocacy. CKOs have to work with and through people and enlist sponsors, champions, and doers. Rather than be dogmatic about what knowledge management is, they prefer their partners or clients to invent, craft, and implement their own ideas. But they are skilled at shaping others' ideas and at knowing when to help. They are likely to be skilled at interventions, to be sensitive to group dynamics and individual characters, and to tolerate small steps as much as big moves. They prefer line managers to own projects and programs so that they both will make knowledge management happen and take the credit.

As *designers*, CKOs not only are technologists and environmentalists, but in particular they bring visions, ideas, and examples. They can analyze situations, ask good questions, and propose solutions, but they probably can't deliver the solutions. They know who can deliver and they may assist with implementation. Above all, they learn quickly about what is possible and what is not and about how to make knowledge management initiatives work. In this sense, they are like engineers.

The CKO is then perhaps the latest corporate change agent, following those who led Total Quality Management, Business Process Reengineering, and other similar initiatives. This is probably why our CKOs talked of seeing the job through but not of the CKO being a permanent position with an established function. In a nonpejorative sense, if the CKO is a change agent he or she will quite rightly be "here today and gone tomorrow." If people start to write about the "rise and fall of the CKO" this should not be a surprise—unless a particular CKO falls before the job is done, a weak trend we discern already.

THE FALLEN OR FALLING CKOs

We observe four categories of CKO demise. First, there is a change of CEO. The new CEO is typically appointed to remedy the situation left by the previous CEO. The departed CEO believed in knowledge management and appointed the CKO, therefore, the new CEO must abort knowledge management and fire the CKO. Such are the vicissitudes of corporate life!

Second, the CKO is asked to take on other—even more "urgent"—tasks as well. Three consequences may arise. First, the heat may go off knowledge management. Second, the organization can become confused about what the CKO is trying to do. Finally, the CKO may decide it is better to do something else.

Third, the CKO just gets frustrated with the rate of progress and concludes that it might be better to go back to a "real job." Typically, such CKOs have not really engaged the organization in knowledge management and have struggled to initiate anything worthwhile. They probably have shortcomings on our leadership axis of the model CKO. Put another way, they are not good change agents.

Finally, the organization—maybe the CEO or the executive team—declares victory in knowledge management. Something visible with real success has been achieved and it's time to move on to another venture. Mostly we think this is premature. The CKO thinks so, for there is more that can be done. And knowledge management is unlikely to be embedded in the organization after such a short time.

SO DO YOU NEED A CKO?

Most authorities will agree—as will many managers—that knowledge management is right for the time. The logic is compelling, either seeing knowledge as source of sustainable value creation or recognizing that we don't make the most of the knowledge we have—or indeed lose.

To do something about it involves change—a new IT system, a new office or spatial design, revised human resource policies, redesigned business and management processes, a cultural shift, and so on. Although in a fast-changing and uncertain world you can argue that everyone has to embrace and cope with change, as well as manage the routine and the present, changes on so many different fronts—and there is no single or universal prescription for knowledge management—are likely to need initiation, propulsion, and some coordination for learning. It seems most likely that without a senior executive, perhaps with a small team, to energize these activities, the goals of knowledge management will be more difficult to achieve.

In other words, a change agent helps. This is what a CKO does, and our 1998 model—entrepreneur, consultant, technologist, and environmentalist—informs on the attributes required. And the change agent description suggests that the CKO will not be a permanent position on organization charts, but could be a necessary one to get knowledge management moving.

NOTE

1. For more details contact the authors at London Business School.

CHAPTER 10

Communities of Practice: The Structure of Knowledge Stewarding

Etienne Wenger

Y ou are a claims processor working for a large insurance company. You are good at what you do, but although you know where your paycheck comes from, the corporation mainly remains an abstraction for you. The group you actually work for is a relatively small community of people who share your working conditions. It is with this group that you learn the intricacies of your job, explore the meaning of your work, construct an image of the company, and develop a sense of yourself as a worker.

You are an engineer working on two projects within your business unit. These are demanding projects and you give them your best. You respect your teammates and are accountable to your project managers. But when you face a problem that stretches your knowledge, you turn to people like Jake, Sylvia, and Robert. Even though they work on their own projects in other business units, they are your real colleagues. You all go back many years. They understand the issues you face and will explore new ideas with you. And even Julie, who now works for one of your suppliers, is only a phone call away. These are the people with whom you can discuss the latest developments in the field and troubleshoot each other's most difficult design challenges. If only you had more time for these kinds of interactions.

You are a CEO and, of course, you are responsible for the company as a whole. You take care of the "big picture." But you have to admit that for you, too, the company is mostly an abstraction: names, numbers, processes, strategies, markets, spreadsheets. Sure, you occasionally take tours of the facilities, but on a day-to-day basis, you live among your peers—your direct reports with whom you interact in running the company, some board members. And perhaps most important, you enjoy opportunities to meet other chief executives with whom you discuss a variety of issues when you play golf or when you attend the sessions of a business roundtable you belong to.

These people may or may not work together on a day-to-day basis, but they do value the learning that takes place when they spend time together. What they know may seem trivial or of great value, but their interactions with each other are crucial to their ability to do what they do. What these groups have in common is that engaging with each other around issues of common interest, sharing insights and information, helping each other, or discussing new ideas together are all part of belonging to the group.

Although we recognize knowledge as a key source of competitive advantage in business (and a key to the success of any kind of organization today, for that matter), we still have little understanding of how to create and leverage knowledge in practice. Traditional knowledge management approaches attempt to capture existing knowledge within formal systems, such as databases or Web sites. It may be good to capture information this way, but it is only half of the task, and I would argue, the second half. The first half is to foster the communities that can take responsibility for stewarding knowledge.

There are two problems with technology-based approaches. First, they can only capture the explicit aspects of knowledge. Some aspects of knowledge can usefully be described and codified, but a large part of what we know remains tacit. Second, technology-based approaches assume that knowledge exists in a social vacuum, that is, that it can be separated from the communities that own it. Many companies have ended up with large numbers of databases that nobody looks at. They have discovered that unless knowledge is owned by people to whom it matters, it will not be developed, used, and kept up to date optimally. Knowledge is not some substance that can be managed at a distance like an inventory. It is part of the shared practice of communities that need it, create it, use it, debate it, distribute it, adapt it, and transform it. These communities give it life. As the property of a community, knowledge is not static; it involves interactions, conversations, actions, and inventions.

What counts as scientific knowledge, for instance, is the prerogative of scientific communities, which interact to define what facts matter and what theories are valid. There may be disagreements; there may be mavericks. But it is still through a process of communal involvement—in spite of all the controversies—that a body of knowledge eventually emerges. And it is by participating in these communities—even when going against the mainstream—that members can claim to having produced scientific knowledge.

This process is not limited to scientific communities. We frequently say that people are an organization's most important resource. Yet we seldom understand this truism in terms of the communities through which individuals develop and share the capacity to create and use knowledge. Even when people work for large organizations, they develop knowledge through participation in more specific communities made up of people with whom they interact on a regular basis. These "communities of practice" are mostly informal and distinct from organizational units.

Under this view, "managing" knowledge is not primarily a technological challenge, but first and foremost one of community development. Focusing on knowledge and on communities cannot be separated. Systematically addressing the kind of dynamic "knowing" that makes a difference in practice requires the participation of people who are fully engaged in the process of creating, refining, communicating, and using knowledge. Knowledge has no value unless it is used, and the thrust to develop, organize, and communicate knowledge must come from those who will use it. What matters is not how much knowledge can be captured, but how documenting can support people's activities. Even though knowledge can to some extent be encoded in documents, knowing remains primarily a human act of meaning making. Communities of practice are the living repositories of their knowledge. Thus, they are a company's most versatile and dynamic knowledge resource and form the basis of an organization's ability to know and learn.

DEFINING COMMUNITIES OF PRACTICE

Communities of practice are nothing new. They have been around for a long, long time—as long as human beings have learned together. They were perhaps the first forms of knowledge organization, back when we lived in caves. In fact, the term *community of practice* was coined in the context of studies of traditional apprenticeship. Apprenticeship is often thought of as a relationship between a master and a student. Yet, we observed that learning took place mostly in interactions with journeymen and more advanced apprentices. Community of practice is the term we used to refer to this social structure, whose shared practice served as a living curriculum for the apprentice (Lave and Wenger, 1991). Once we had the concept, however, we started to see these communities in all kinds of other settings, where there was no official apprenticeship.

Communities of practice are everywhere. We all belong to a number of them—at work, at school, at home, in our hobbies. Some have a name, some don't. Some are recognized, some are largely invisible. We are core members of some and we belong to others more peripherally. You may be a member of a band, or you may just come to rehearsals to hang around with the group. And you may or may not be aware that the lunch group you belong to is one of your main sources of knowledge. You may lead a community of consultants who specialize in telecommunication strategies, or you may just stay in touch to keep informed about developments in the field. Or you may have recently joined a community and are still trying to find your place in it. Whatever form our participation takes, most of us are familiar with the experience of belonging to a community of practice.

A community of practice is different from a mere community of interest or a geographical community, neither of which implies a shared practice. A community of practice consists of three basic elements:

1. What it is about—the sense of *joint enterprise* that brings members together. Note that this joint enterprise reflects the members' own understanding of their situation. It is much more complex than a simple goal. For instance, a group of insurance claims processors I had the opportunity to work with not only learn to do what the company expects in terms of processing a certain number of claims per day, but also whatever it takes to create an acceptable atmosphere to work in. They hold each other accountable to the latter goal even more stringently than to the company's demand: it is OK to miss your daily quota, it happens to everyone at times, but it is not OK to make life miserable for your colleagues. A community's shared understanding of its enterprise allows members to decide what matters and what to hold each other accountable to. Whether the joint enterprise is to survive on the street for members of a gang, to invent a new style for artists in a café, or to understand how to upgrade city slums for development specialists at the World Bank, what characterizes a community of practice is shared identification fueled by a personal investment in a topic of interest.

2. How it functions as a community—the relationships of *mutual engagement* that bind members together into a social entity. Members learn with one another. They interact. They do things together. Having the same job or title, for instance, is not sufficient—even if it means a common passion for a topic. A community of practice is not an abstraction. You can all be CEOs and face the same kind of issues in your own companies, but unless you interact on a regular basis to develop your ability to do your job better, you will not form a community of practice. The degree to which any group is a community of practice depends on how they function together; it cannot be decided in the abstract. An ongoing history of mutual engagement is crucial because it creates a forum for building both the practice and the community. It is how learning takes place through joint activities, but also how relationships and trust are established, how the meanings of what members learn are negotiated, and how the joint enterprise is defined and redefined over time.

3. What capability its practice has produced—the *shared repertoire* of communal resources that members have developed over time through their mutual engagement. These communal resources include routines, lessons learned, sensibilities, artifacts, standards, tools, stories, vocabulary, styles, and so on. They range from very concrete objects, such as a tool or a document, to very

subtle displays of competence, such as an ability to interpret a slight change in the sound of a machine as indicating a specific problem. This repertoire embodies the community's accumulated knowledge. You can't be a real engineer unless you are familiar with the repertoire of your community: its language, its laws, its cases, its rules of thumb, its aesthetics. But this repertoire also embodies the community's potential for further learning; it provides the resources that members use to make sense of new situations and create new knowledge. Draw a quick circuit diagram using the right symbols, and you are ready to discuss a new idea with your engineering colleagues.

Members of a community of practice are informally bound by the value they find in learning together—from engaging in informal lunchtime discussions to helping each other solve difficult problems, from sharing new insights to dissecting the personality of a boss, from correcting a detail on a document to musing on the future of a profession, from broadcasting a tip on a Web site to establishing a standard or writing a complete manual. The value members find in their interactions is not merely instrumental. It also has to do with the personal satisfaction of knowing each other, of having colleagues who understand each other's perspective, and of belonging to an interesting group of people. Over time these interactions build up to a shared practice, which reflects the members' collective learning. They also build up to a community, which reflects the relationships and identities they have developed around that practice.

COMMUNITIES OF PRACTICE IN ORGANIZATIONS

I have insisted that communities of practice have been around since the beginning of history. Therefore, they are not a new kind of organizational unit or a new, passing business fad you can just wait out. Communities of practice exist in any organization whether or not the organization recognizes their value. They can be found:

- *Within businesses*: Communities of practice arise as people address recurring sets of problems together. So claims processors within an office form communities of practice to deal with the constant flow of information they need to process. By participating in such a communal memory, they can do the job without having to remember everything themselves. In a less visible way, nurses in a ward who meet for lunch and discuss patient cases do create learning value for each other and over time, a history of cases they all know about and can use to think about new problems together.
- *Across business units*: Important knowledge is often distributed in different business units. People who work in cross-functional teams often form communities of practice to keep in touch with their peers in various parts of the company and maintain their expertise. A large chemical company

may have safety managers in each business unit, who may gain from interacting regularly, solving problems together, and developing common guidelines, tools, standards, procedures, and documents. Again, they are a community of practice only to the extent that they interact, depend on each other for advice, learn together, and create a shared body of knowledge. When communities of practice cut across business units, they can develop strategic perspectives that transcend the fragmentation of product lines. For instance, a community of practice I knew once proposed a plan for equipment purchase that no one business unit could have come up with on its own.

- *Across institutional boundaries*: Because membership is based on participation rather than on official status, communities of practice are not bound by organizational affiliations; they can span institutional structures and hierarchies. In some cases, communities of practice become useful by crossing organizational boundaries. For instance, in fast-moving industries such as computer hard disks, engineers who work for suppliers and buyers may form a community of practice to keep up with constant technological changes, even though it is not part of their job description.

- *Across multiple organizations*: It is becoming more common for forums for shared learning to bring together people from different organizations, even direct competitors. In the oil industry, for instance, knowledge managers from various companies gather four times a year to exchange tips and discuss common issues even though they compete directly in the marketplace. Without revealing core company secrets, they find it more beneficial to share their knowledge and then benefit from their common pool of experience than to each hoard what they know.

Communities of practice have a variety of relations to the organizations in which they exist, ranging from completely unrecognized to largely institutionalized. Table 10.1 shows different degrees of institutional recognition.

The distinctions made in this table do not imply that some relationships are better or more advanced than others. Rather, these distinctions are useful because they draw attention to the different issues that can arise as the interactions change between a community of practice and the organization as a whole.

Looking at an organization through the lens of communities of practice emphasizes the learning that people have done together rather than, say, the unit they report to, the project they are working on, or the people they know. Communities of practice differ from other kinds of structures found in organizations in the way they are held together, exist over time, and define their boundaries.

- A community of practice is different from a *business or functional unit* in that it does not involve reporting relationships among members but is

Table 10.1
Relationships to Official Organization

Relationship	Definition	Typical Challenges
Unrecognized	Invisible to the organization and sometimes even to members themselves	Lack of reflexivity, awareness of value and of limitation
Bootlegged	Only visible informally to a circle of people in the know	Getting resources, having an impact, keeping hidden
Legitimized	Officially sanctioned as a valuable entity	Broader visibility, rapid growth, new demands and expectations
Supported	Provided with direct resources from the organization	Scrutiny, accountability for use of resources, effort, and time, short-term pressures
Institutionalized	Given an official status and function in the organization	Fixed definition, over-management, living beyond its usefulness

based on collegiality. Its purpose is to develop knowledge, not to allocate resources or manage people in order to deliver a product or service to the market. This does not mean that there are no differences in power among members of a community of practice. An expert will certainly have more power than a novice, but this power derives from the ability to contribute to the knowledge of the community, not from formal authority to control resources, give orders, or determine people's promotions.

- A community of practice is different from a *team* in that the shared learning and interest of its members are what keep it together. It is defined by knowledge rather than by task, and exists because participation has value to its members. It is held together by the passion of members for a topic and their identification with the enterprise of the community, not by commitment to a goal or a workplan. A community of practice does not appear the minute a project is started and does not disappear with the end of a task. It takes a while to come into being and may live long after a project is completed or an official team has disbanded. Its life cycle is determined by the value it provides to its members, not by an institutional schedule.
- A community of practice is different from a *network* in the sense that it is "about" something; it is not just a set of relationships. It has an identity as a community, and thus shapes the identities of its members. You can recognize members of a community of practice by the competence they display, not merely by the people they know or talk to. A community of

practice exists not just because there are individual relationships among its members, but because over time it produces a shared practice as members engage in a collective process of learning.

Communities of practice are not a separate kind of organizational unit, like a staff group, a corporate center of excellence, or an R&D department. People belong to communities of practice at the same time as they belong to other organizational structures. In their business units, they shape the organization and deliver products and services to their market. In their teams, they take care of projects and find solutions to problems. In their networks, they form relationships and spread information. And in their communities of practice, they develop the knowledge that lets them do these other tasks.

This *multimembership* is a very important principle. It is crucial to the creation of a learning process that connects the development of knowledge and the work of an organization. For instance, people work in teams for projects but belong to longer-lived communities of practice for developing their expertise. These "double-knit organizations," as Richard McDermott (1999) calls them, gain the flexibility of project teams while preserving the long-term orientation toward expertise typical of functional organizations.

Learning, of course, happens in teams as well, but to fully leverage this learning requires communities of practice. Project teams are temporary, so the learning they do is often lost. Functional teams are focused on their own task, so the learning that takes place in them often remains local. Communities of practice can serve as the organizational "home" for all this learning if the same people belong to both kinds of structures. As team members, they are accountable for performing tasks. When they face familiar problems they have opportunities to apply and refine their skills. When they face new problems they must invent new solutions. As community members, they are accountable to developing a practice. They bring their experience and receive help with their problems. They get a chance to discuss their new solutions, to share them with others, generalize or document them, and integrate them into the community's practice. Then they return to their projects equipped with expanded capabilities, which again face the test of application to real problems. And through this multimembership the learning cycle continues.

At DaimlerChrysler, engineering is organized around car-platform teams that develop a specific type of cars—large, small, minivans, and so on. The main affiliation of engineers is with their platform team so they can fully focus on working with other engineers to optimize the design of a model. But engineers have formed communities of practice across platforms to keep up with their specialty, coordinate standards, and share knowledge and lessons learned. Similarly, at the World Bank, development specialists work for projects around the world, but they belong to communities of practice in their areas of expertise—education, services to the urban poor, transportation.

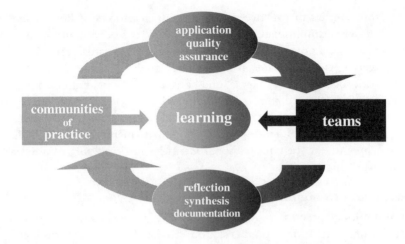

Figure 10.1 *The Learning Cycle (diagram developed in collaboration with Richard McDermott)*

THE VALUE OF COMMUNITIES OF PRACTICE

Communities of practice are important to the functioning of any organization, but they become crucial to those that recognize knowledge as a key asset. They fulfill a number of functions with respect to the creation, accumulation, and diffusion of knowledge in an organization.

Weaving the Organization Around Knowledge Needs

Communities of practice form around knowledge needs, not production requirements or formal units. In this sense, they represent a different cut through the organization. For instance, a community of practice that spreads throughout an organization is an ideal channel for moving information, such as best practices, tips, lessons learned, or feedback, across organizational boundaries. In other words, communities of practice fill the white spaces inherent in any organizational design by providing a context for the relevant exchange and local interpretation of information. They create the social fabric by which an organization can dynamically structure itself around knowledge needs.

Stewarding Specific Competencies

Communities of practice can sustain the capabilities necessary for an organization to achieve its goals. On the one hand, they can retain knowledge in "living" ways, unlike a database or a manual. Even when they routinize certain tasks and processes or document some practices, they can do so in a manner that responds to local circumstances and thus is useful to practitioners. Communities of practice preserve the tacit aspects of knowledge that formal systems cannot capture. For this reason, they are ideal for initiating newcomers into a practice. On the other hand, they can push knowledge forward, keeping the organization at the cutting edge. Members discuss novel ideas, work together on problems, and keep up with developments inside and outside a firm. When a community commits to being on the forefront of a field, members distribute responsibility for keeping up with or pushing new developments. This collaborative inquiry makes membership valuable, because people invest their professional identities in being part of a dynamic, forward-looking community.

Providing a Home for Identities

Communities of practice are not as temporary or local as teams, and unlike business units, they are organized around what matters to their members. Moving from one project to the next can be uprooting and being asked to focus on one task can feel limiting. Communities of practice can then provide people with a homebase that is tuned to their learning needs. They offer a stable form of membership that carries people from one task to the next while allowing them to find continuity in terms of professional trajectory and identity.

Developing an identity around learning is crucial because our identities help us sort out what to pay attention to and what to ignore, with whom to communicate, and what to aspire to. Issues of identity are central to participation in organizations. Consider the annual computer drop at a semiconductor company that designs both analog and digital circuits. The computer drop became a ritual by which the analog community asserted its identity. Once a year, their hero would climb the highest building on the company's campus and drop a computer, to the great satisfaction of his peers in the analog gang. The corporate world is full of these displays of identity, which manifest themselves in the jargon people use, the clothes they wear, and the remarks they make. If companies want to encourage people to learn, they must offer them forms of membership in communities that support and value their learning.

Communities of practice are ideal structures for the stewarding of knowledge. It is what they have been about for ages. What makes it possible is the combination of their three elements.

A *joint enterprise* around a topic creates a sense of accountability to a body of knowledge. You know what to put in the knowledge base and what questions to ask because you understand what your community cares about and where the leading edge of its knowledge lies. So you know the value of a lesson learned during a project or the importance of an idea that your team came up with. Participating in the process of sharing and developing knowledge is an integral part of your belonging. It both presupposes and asserts your membership. It presupposes your membership because you need to know what is relevant to communicate and how to present information in useful ways—an outsider would not appreciate why sharing this or that de- tail is important to the story. And it asserts your membership because it dem- onstrates to yourself and to others that you understand what matters to this community and that you are able to contribute something of value to its practice.

Mutual engagement allows for dynamic negotiation of both explicit and tacit aspects of knowledge. Knowledge comes alive in discussions and in joint problem solving. To the extent that members have built trust by interacting over time, they can ask probing questions without being overly afraid to ex- pose their ignorance. Knowing each other also makes it easier to call for help: you know who is likely to have an answer, you feel more confident that your call will be welcome, and if you are at the other end, you assume that the caller is competent enough not to waste your time. Belonging to an ongoing community can smooth the process of agreeing on standards and best prac- tices. As one engineer reported, you know that the issues can be revisited and that new issues will come up: You lose this one, you'll win another one.

Finally, a *shared repertoire* is a source of great efficiency in communication and joint problem solving. It implies a set of shared assumptions only few of which even need to be made explicit. When doctors talk about a patient, the specialized language and experience they share allow them very quickly to focus on the problem that matters by describing a few symptoms and sketch- ing a few hypotheses. Of course, this efficiency is also a source of boundary with outsiders and can make it difficult for doctors to communicate effec- tively with their patients. This is an issue communities have to deal with. Nevertheless, having a shared repertoire is a very useful resource.

Communities of practice can vary in the extent to which they explicitly undertake the stewarding of knowledge for themselves and for the organiza- tion. Some communities are content to exchange tips and lessons learned on an ad hoc basis. Some take responsibility for establishing and developing their practice and their community. Others even become strategic in their thinking, explicitly viewing the development of their practice as a strategic move on be- half of the organization. Finally, some communities undertake to transform the organization with the insights and new practices they have generated. These levels can be summarized as in Table 10.2.

Again, these levels do not represent a progression toward an ideal state. Each level has its value and is appropriate for some communities. But it is useful to see the range of what is possible and to be aware of the issues that communities face as they transition from one level to another.

Understanding the value of communities of practice as stewards of knowledge is not always easy because the effects of community activities on performance are often indirect.

- *Immediate value*: Belonging to a community of practice helps members do their job because they address problems that are close to their work, help

Table 10.2
Degrees of Stewardship

Degree of Stewardship	Definition	Typical Challenges
Sharing	Offering a social structure for the exchange of knowledge, tips, and lessons learned, and for help on problems	Haphazard knowledge development and lack of continuity
Proactive	Taking charge of developing a shared capability, establishing best practices, actively pursuing a learning agenda, and involving all the relevant participants	Finding the energy and time to take responsibility for knowledge
Strategic	Widely recognized and self-consciously central to the success of the organization and involved in strategic decisions	Short-term pressures, blindness of success, smugness, elitism, exclusion
Transformative	Capable of redefining its environment and the direction, structure, or culture of the organization	Relating to the rest of the organization, acceptance, managing boundaries

each other with issues they face, and coordinate their activities. By belonging to a community of practice, you don't need to know all there is to know in your domain.

- *Long-term value*: Communities of practice renew themselves and thus build capabilities that assure the long-term viability of their enterprise. They can benchmark their practice against world standards and join forces to make sure they stay at the leading edge.
- *Professional value*: Belonging to a world-class community of practice is an opportunity to develop professionally. In an era when companies can no longer promise lifetime employment, offering such development opportunities is a good way to recruit, develop, and retain talent.

From this perspective, an organization comprises a constellation of interconnected communities of practice, each dealing with specific aspects of the company's competencies—from the peculiarities of a long-standing client, to manufacturing safety, to esoteric technical inventions. Knowledge is created, shared, organized, revised, and passed on within and among these communities. This more or less recognized, more or less attended to fabric of communities and shared practices makes the work of the official organization effective and, indeed, possible.

It is important, however, not to romanticize these communities. Like any asset, they can be a liability. Their very success can be their undoing. Their passion for their enterprise can make them arrogant and exclusive. Their focus can become a blinder. Their engagement with each other can make them insular. And the communicative efficiency of their shared repertoire can prevent them from reconsidering their underlying assumptions. There is a paradox in the stewardship of knowledge by communities. Communities own their knowledge, and consequently no community can fully design the learning of another; but conversely no community can fully design its own learning because each community is hostage to its own locality. Communities of practice need interactions at their boundaries. It is therefore useful to consider communities not in isolation, but in the broader context of what I describe elsewhere as social learning systems, such as industries, regions, or alliances, that comprise multiple communities in interaction (Wenger, in press).

THE NATURE OF COMMUNITIES OF PRACTICE

Communities of practice can be a challenge to managers. Organizations will be able to leverage the full potential of communities of practice only if they understand the nature of these communities.

First, communities of practice move through various stages of development through their life cycle. They can look quite different at different stages. They engage in different activities. They have different kinds of interactions and relationships. They face different issues. They require different kinds of support and resources. Communities usually start as loose networks with latent needs and opportunities. As a consequence, you don't start a community of practice from scratch, but you build on the interests and relationships that already exist. Then the community starts to coalesce, sometimes very quickly, through a launch workshop for instance, sometimes more slowly as people discover the value of doing things together. As a community matures and grows, members take a more proactive responsibility for establishing a shared practice, a learning agenda, and a communal identity. Even when in full bloom, a community continues to evolve its practice and goes through cycles as new generations of members and leaders take over. Some communities last for centuries and some are short-lived, but all end up dispersing sooner or later as the need for their knowledge and the interest of members shift (see Figure 10.2).

These stages are merely typical. Different communities of practice go through them with different rhythms and intensity. Recognizing these various stages is useful for being able to foster communities: develop a sense of process, set realistic expectations, understand the issues a community faces, take productive action, and use evaluation criteria that are appropriate to a community's stage.

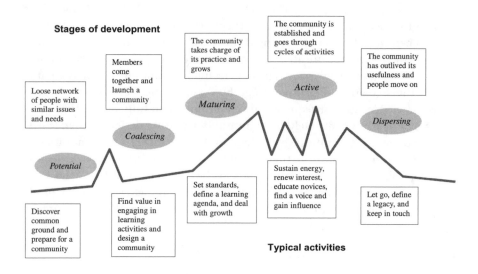

Figure 10.2 *Stages of Development*

Through all these stages, communities of practice involve multiple levels of participation. Because involvement can produce learning in multiple ways, the boundaries of a community of practice are more flexible than those of organizational units. Typical categories of membership and participation include:

- Core group—a small group of people whose passion and engagement energize the community
- Full membership—members who are recognized as practitioners and define the community (though they may not be of one mind as to what the community is about)
- Peripheral membership—people who belong to the community but with less engagement and authority, either because they are still newcomers or because they do not have as much personal commitment to the practice
- Transactional participation—outsiders who interact with the community occasionally to receive or provide a service without being members themselves
- Passive access—a wide range of people who have access to artifacts produced by the community, such as its publications, its Web site, or its tools

Levels of Participation

Different types of participants in a community of practice have different perspectives, needs, and ambitions. Note that people will move in and out of

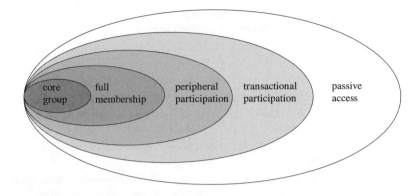

Figure 10.3 *Communities of Practice: Participation Levels*

these categories over the life of a community. Interactions and knowledge flows between these constituencies create many opportunities for learning. But there is a need for balance. On the one hand, peripheral members can be marginalized, but on the other, core members can be distracted and even overwhelmed by the demands of a wider periphery.

Not only do people participate with different levels of intensity, they also fulfill different roles. Communities of practice depend on internal leadership, but this leadership is diverse and distributed (Table 10.3). For instance, the role of community coordinator is often a key to the success of a community of practice in an organization, but this person is rarely a top expert. Recognized experts certainly need to be involved in some way in order to legitimize the community as a place for sharing and creating knowledge, but they may not do much of the work of maintaining the community. Rather than think in terms of leader and follower, it is more useful to think of roles in a community of practice in terms of an ecology of leadership. Internal leadership can take many forms.

These roles may be formal or informal. They may be concentrated in a small subgroup or more widely distributed. But in all cases, those who undertake them must have intrinsic legitimacy in the community. Indeed, whatever their relationship to an organization, communities of practice ultimately depend on internal initiative for their development. To be effective, therefore, managers and others must work with community leaders to develop communities of practice from the *inside* rather than merely attempt to design them or manipulate them from the *outside*.

Communities of practice develop around things that matter to members. Obviously, their understanding of what matters can change over time and the definition of a community's enterprise does evolve. Moreover, outside constraints or directives can influence this process, but even then, members de-

Table 10.3
Forms of Leadership

Type of Leadership	Definition	Typical Activities
Coordination	Keepers of the community	Organize events, talk to members, keep the pulse of the community
Networking	Keepers of relationships	Connect people, weave the community's social fabric
Facilitation	Keepers of conversations	Set agendas, watch over conversations, keep notes, provide pointers and summaries
Documentation	Keepers of the repository	Organize information in order to document practices, update and clean up the knowledge base
Expertise	Keepers of the heritage	Thought leaders and recognized experts uphold and dispense the accumulated wisdom of the community
Learning	Keepers of insights	Watch for nuggets, collect emerging pieces of knowledge, standards, and lessons learned
Inquiry	Keepers of questions	Notice emergent questions, keep them alive, outline a learning agenda, and shepherd "out-of-the-box" initiatives
Boundary	Keepers of connections	Connect the community to other communities or constituencies, act as brokers and translators
Institution	Keepers of organizational ties	Maintain links with other organizational constituencies, in particular the official hierarchy

velop practices that are their own response to these external influences. Even when a community's actions conform to an external mandate, it is the community—not the mandate—that produces the practice. In this sense, communities of practice are fundamentally self-organizing systems.

Organizations can't hope to start communities arbitrarily. A community requires identification with a topic that members care about and about which they can make a difference through their collective learning. If the domain of a community fails to arouse some passion, the community will flounder. Conversely, if the topic lacks strategic relevance to the organization, the community will be marginalized and have limited influence. The most successful communities of practice thrive at the intersection between the needs of an organization and the passion and interest of participants.

DEVELOPING AND NURTURING COMMUNITIES OF PRACTICE

You may well wonder whether anything can or should be done to develop communities of practice. Should they just be left alone? Can they be created, built, nurtured, or supported? Many communities of practice will exist whether or not the organization recognizes them. Some are best left alone and might actually wither under the institutional spotlight. But a good number will benefit from some attention, as long as this attention does not smother their self-organizing drive. Just because communities of practice arise naturally does not mean that organizations can't do anything to influence their development.

The best way I found to address this paradox is by analogy to gardening. Plants grow and they do their own growing. You cannot pull their leaves or petals to make them grow faster or taller. And yet there is a lot we have learned we can do to help plants grow: tilling the soil, making sure they have enough nutrients, supplying water; and securing the right amount of sun exposure. There are also a few things we know not to do, like pulling a plant out to check if it has roots. Whether you carefully planted the seed or whether the plant grew spontaneously, what you do to help it grow is not that different. Similarly, in organizations, some communities of practice grow spontaneously and some may require careful seeding, yet in both cases, a lot can be done to create a context in which they can prosper. Nurturing communities of practice in organizations requires attention to four areas.

Knowledge Strategy

Community development should be placed in the context of a broader knowledge strategy (Wenger, 1999). Organizations must develop a clear sense of how knowledge is linked to business strategies and use this understanding to help communities of practice articulate their strategic value. This involves a process of negotiation that goes both ways. It includes understanding what knowledge—and therefore what practices—a given strategy requires. Conversely, it also includes paying attention to what emergent communities of practice indicate with regard to potential strategic directions.

Organizational Orientation

The orientation of the organization toward the value of knowledge and learning is critical. Organizations can support communities of practice by legitimating participation and recognizing the work of sustaining them and by giving members the time to participate in activities. The attitude of management can make a big difference. Managers can show interest in what has been learned in a project as well as what has been achieved. To this end, it is important to have an institutional discourse that includes the value that communities bring. Merely introducing the term "communities of practice" into an organization's vocabulary can have a positive effect by giving people an opportunity to talk about how their participation in these groups contributes to the organization as a whole. Many organizations have created boards of senior management sponsors who constitute communities of practice initiatives. The mere existence of such a board sends the message that the organization values the work of communities of practice.

Organizational Systems

Though organizational systems are rarely the drivers of participation in communities of practice, they do matter because they reflect what is important to the organization. They may also inadvertently discourage participation. It is therefore important to tune these systems so they honor the work of community building and do not create unnecessary barriers. For example, issues of compensation and recognition often come up. Because communities of practice depend on passion and personal engagement with a topic, it is tricky to use incentives as a way to manipulate behavior or micro-manage the community. But recognition is important and many organizations have found it useful to include an explicit discussion of community activities and leadership in performance reviews. Managers also need to make sure that existing compensation systems do not inadvertently penalize the work involved in building communities. For instance, cutthroat competition among individuals and business units makes it more difficult for people to participate candidly in knowledge-sharing events and for managers to appreciate the time people spend on cross-unit communities of practice. Trade-offs between local and global contributions and between short-term and long-term goals usually require the breadth of purview and authority of senior managers and are another reason to establish a sponsoring board.

Organizational Resources

Communities of practice are mostly self-sufficient, but they do need some resources. There must be ways for communities of practice to gain access to such resources, for instance, time for community leaders, grants for learning projects, honoraria for outside experts, or travel budgets. It is usually good to have a company-wide support team that assists community leaders in their efforts. Such a team typically provides guidance and support when needed, helps connect community agendas to strategy, organizes resources, and coaches community leaders and managers. It also ensures compatibility of technology platforms across the organization as well as helps in designing specific applications, Web sites, and conversation spaces. Finally, it coordinates community development efforts and spreads success stories to create a momentum across the organization.

Communities of practice do not usually require heavy institutional infra-structures, but their members do need time and space to collaborate. They self-organize, but they flourish when their learning fits with their organizational environment. They do not require much traditional management, but they can use leadership and a voice in the organization. The art is to help such communities find resources and connections and to involve them in the running of the organization without overwhelming them with organizational meddling.

KNOWLEDGE STEWARDSHIP

Communities of practice are the Holy Grail of knowledge management, as it were. They are its future because they own their knowledge and thus are in the best position to manage it. Knowledge management so far has focused primarily on the structure of documentation of knowledge. It is time to turn our attention to the structure of stewardship of knowledge. Without such attention, our attempts at knowledge management will fail.

As the structures of knowledge stewardship, communities of practice are at the heart of organizing in the knowledge economy. They are the latest wave in our understanding of organizational structures. When we needed to organize large companies, we invented the functional organization. When we needed to focus on market segments and product lines, we created business units. When customer and technical demands required intensive project management, we organized around teams. And now that knowledge is the key concern, we need to understand communities of practice. We do not need to invent them; they have existed for as long as we have been around. But the new problem is how to fully leverage their value in the context of our organizations. Can we learn to design our organizations to be hospitable to these ideal, but nonconforming knowledge management structures? Can we master the art of balancing productivity and learning, strategy and passion, design and emergence?

A growing number of leading organizations are learning to do just that, including AMS, DaimlerChrysler, HP, IBM, Intel, Johnson and Johnson, Lucent Technologies, Shell Oil, the Veterans Administration, the World Bank, and many others. And each is taking a slightly different approach in line with its own culture and traditions. Some are a bit further along but all are really just beginning. They are each in their own way taking part in a large-scale experiment to devise the organizational forms of the knowledge economy. The real question for you now is not whether you need communities of practice. The question, rather, is whether you are ready to join this inquiry and truly learn how to lead a knowledge organization where communities of practice can thrive.

ACKNOWLEDGMENTS

This article reflects my discussions and work with many colleagues and clients, in particular Richard McDermott, George Por, and Bill Snyder. Thanks to all of them for their personal and intellectual companionship.

CHAPTER 11

Knowledge Transfer in Strategic Alliances

Nicolas Rolland and Daniele Chauvel

INTRODUCTION *K*nowledge *management* and *strategic alliances* are two complex concepts, voluminous in their literatures, that are of increasing interest for managers and academics. The business press regularly reports new bids, plans, projects, failures, and associated alliance activity. Since about 1990, knowledge management has shared the spotlight and, for some, become synonymous with a promising movement toward the further reaches of twenty-first-century management. Interestingly, as evidenced by several authors in this volume (e.g., Hedberg, Spender), the two concepts appear to increasingly occupy a felicitous cognitive space in business reality because to manage in today's economy, one must increasingly dissolve the integrated corporation and think in terms of the networks and knowledge among partners.

Previous chapters have adequately sketched the panorama of knowledge management (KM) and we will not repeat the wisdom already proffered. We point out only that the shift in economic thought that recognizes knowledge as a primary factor of production, source of wealth, and competitive advantage is significant and, in our opinion, durable. Firms are thus faced with the imperative of dealing intelligently with knowledge: their knowledge, their employees' knowledge, others' knowledge, others' employees' knowledge, public versus proprietary knowledge, and so on. Without privileging any given approach, we generally view KM as a mindset that necessarily permeates a firm in order to enhance the purposeful creation, use, and application of knowledge appropriate to its corporate context and strategic goals. The evidence suggests that this often requires a significant shift in corporate culture and managerial assumptions which, philosophers inform, is coincident with the passing of one age (Fordist, modernist, industrial) and the dawning of another (virtual, postmodern, informational).

Insofar as alliances are concerned, the evidence is that they are increasingly developed in core businesses and less for peripheral activities (Doz and Hamel, 1998), and are designed to achieve competitive advantage by gaining new markets, realizing scale economies, reducing time to new market niches, and acquiring or developing new competencies. Alliance structures have the practical benefit of protecting the identity of partners, concretizing a joint project, and prescribing rights and obligations. They may occur between competitors or noncompetitors, and different forms are feasible depending on strategic goals and structural implications.

Thus, the issues are numerous. We have therefore restricted our work to an intersection between knowledge and alliance where the keywords are *knowledge transfer* because, in a knowledge economy, for firms that must adapt to fast-changing environments, this ability is a source of competitive advantage. In the following chapters we investigate alliances in which the main motivation is the acquisition of new competencies, hence organizational learning broadly defined, and we will attempt to outline how the knowledge transfer operates in such a context. We first discuss theoretical approaches to "learning-based alliances" and then explore strategic and organizational characteristics that have been shown to favor efficient learning. We then embed this in a dynamic view of alliances to examine how specific conditions facilitate learning and can become drivers in the development of learning-based alliances.

THEORETICAL FUNDAMENTALS

Given the increase in alliance activity over the last two decades, theorists have tried to understand the phenomenon and the plausible explanations are multiple, if not numerous. Two major streams of thought on the matter devolve from industrial economics and transaction cost theory. In general, industrial economists view strategic alliances as an answer to environmental change and a practical way to achieve strategic advantage vis-à-vis competitors (Harrigan, 1986, 1988). The transaction cost perspective sees alliances as intermediate hybrid forms between the market and the hierarchy that can lead to "transaction cost minimization" (Williamson, 1985; 1991). These approaches, which are perhaps efficient in relatively stable environments, are proving less than satisfactory for firms in a "knowledge economy" in which innovation and the ability to respond to fast-changing environments is critical (Ciborra, 1991). But a third approach, composed of competence and knowledge, appears to be promising.

The classic approach to strategic analysis was developed in the 1960s and defines strategy as a confrontation between the strengths and weaknesses of a firm vis-à-vis the opportunities and threats in its environment. Initially, the idea of strategic choice augured for environmental and internal analyses but until the end of the 1980s, Porter's approach to industry analysis seemed the default mindset. With the economic shifts of the 1990s, more attention was paid to the resources available to a firm and how these could be mobilized to develop its strategy.

This resource-based view of the firm is rooted in a notable history (Say, 1803; Ricardo, 1817; Penrose, 1959) and has recently emerged as perhaps the dominant approach for explaining competitive dynamics in the changing environment of the 1990s. In contrast to transactional and industrial economics approaches, the resource-based perspective views the firm as an idiosyncratic portfolio of competencies, which are sources of sustainable competitive advantage (Hamel and Prahalad, 1994). Competitive acumen thus resides in the distinct capabilities of the firm and in its ability to leverage these according to strategic direction rather than, but not in lieu of, product or market positioning.

The consensus is that two main types of resources exist: tangibles and intangibles. Tangible resources can be acquired but intangibles are difficult to buy or imitate. Strategic or core competencies cannot be bought in a market and they open access to niches or contribute to customer-focused value in end products, hence differentiating a firm from its competitors (Prahalad and Hamel, 1990). They are, by definition, organization specific; useful; difficult to transfer, imitate, or substitute; as well as opaque to outside observers and seldom communicated. This latter category is therefore of greater strategic interest and a source of firm-specific competitive advantage. When a firm seeks to develop its position, it must mobilize its own competencies, develop innovations in the existing set, or acquire new ones.

Knowledge is generally counted as an intangible and both intuition and theory hold that properly deployed, it will augment the competitive position of a firm (Spender, 1996). To acquire such advantage, firms increasingly seek to combine their competencies with those of a partner. Learning-based alliances have thereby developed and are defined as opportunities to learn, share, and develop new competencies in order to increase the overall portfolio of each partner. The knowledge embedded in the competencies thus transferred may lead to competitive advantage; hence, the resource-based approach has been joined by the knowledge based theory of the firm (which is discussed in other chapters of this book, e.g., Teece, Spender, Grant, Hedberg). It is also rooted in classic works on economic rationality (Simon, 1947) and the sociology of organizations (Polanyi, 1962) that focus on the nature of human knowledge and its relationship to action. The evolutionary perspective of Nelson and Winter (1982) also contributes by introducing concepts such as organizational routines and the tacit knowledge hidden in the organization.

The firm is thus viewed as a complex system with different types and levels of knowledge in which individuals hold a very specific stock, constituting its fundamental wealth. Individual knowledge is unique or shared depending on situation-specific variables, but at the same time groups, teams, and other social entities possess and generate knowledge that is beyond the sum of any one individual. The aggregation of these different stocks of knowledge in a firm (Grant, 1996) constitutes organizational value when added, assimilated, or integrated into the existing body of knowledge.

A fundamental difficulty is the fact that knowledge is not a simple, stable quantity and, in fact, many philosophies and sociologies attempt to define the root phenomenon. One perspective in the philosophy of knowledge, for example, makes the following distinctions: *knowledge* (the subject knows that X is true), *competence* (the subject is able to do X), *acquaintance* (the subject is familiar with X), and *information* (the subject recognizes X as information). In this chapter we retain only the widely accepted distinction between explicit and tacit knowledge (Polanyi, 1958): explicit knowledge is that which can be codified or easily inscribed in artifacts and processes; tacit knowledge is held in the mind and know-how, and deeply rooted in actions and experience of each individual. From an alliance perspective, the most valuable knowledge is often tacit and embedded in organizational routines (Zack, 1999).

Despite the broad range of definitions, researchers agree that the acquisition, creation, and application of knowledge are a key to the competitive development of a firm (Grant, 1996; Kogut and Zander, 1992; Spender, 1994; Teece et al., 1987). The knowledge based approach insists on the identification and valuation of knowledge, and then its context-appropriate application. This last concern focuses on the transferability of knowledge, which is fundamental to its exploitation. Transferability is considered within the firm in terms of space, time, and mechanisms. If explicit knowledge is more obviously communicable, tacit knowledge is better transferred through practices (action) and social experiences.

This aspect of transferability is critical in the context of learning-based alliances; interaction between two firms can contribute to knowledge-related activities that enable each to better respond to changing and challenging environments. The issue becomes how an equitable and effective transfer between partners might be structured, and the operating principles for implementing it.

KNOWLEDGE, TRANSFER, AND ALLIANCES

If knowledge transfer and what can be loosely construed as organizational learning are significant trends in alliance formation, what are the key elements? How should managers think about the dynamics involved? Our research has attempted to answer these and related questions by employing a simple model of the critical phenomena, composed of four initial conditions, two dependent variables, and their interactions. Structurally, it assembles (a) strategic intent, (b) culture, (c) trust, (d) form, (e) transparency or learning capacity, and (f) the linkages, as illustrated in Figure 11.1.

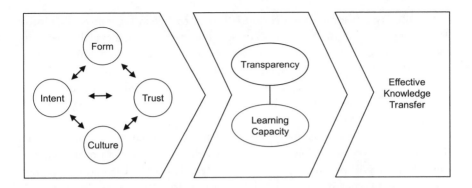

Figure 11.1   *The Factors of Knowledge Transfer in Alliances*

This six-factor model thus articulates the major elements that will determine the effectiveness of knowledge transfer and organizational learning in a strategic alliance. Four of the factors are conditions for effectiveness (intent, culture, trust, and form), and transparency and learning capacity are considered strategic process outcomes. The definition of these elements, which is rooted in both theory and application, follows.

Strategic Intent

The way a firm conceives its strategy will affect the level and type of learning that occurs in an alliance. We draw a distinction between *proactive* and *adaptive* strategy. A firm that implements a proactive strategy intentionally modifies its environment by putting the drivers of its competitive advantage into action; one that opts for an adaptive strategy tends to accommodate changes in the environment by reacting to events. The literature on this subject reveals that the choice to be proactive or adaptive is often framed in terms of competition versus collaboration. From an alliance perspective, this defines three types of strategic intent (Doz and Hamel, 1995):

- *Access*: The firm collaborates for the temporary use of competencies held by the partner. The intent is time limited and restricted to the initial collaborative agreement.
- *Internalization*: The firm wishes to transfer specific knowledge from the partner. The intent is to acquire or capture competencies in defined boundaries.
- *Integration*: Complementary competencies are combined to leverage a new common strategic competence, activity, or product. The intent is to integrate specialized competencies or resources between the partners who each want to learn the partner's knowledge and know-how with constructive intent.

In alliances in which integration is the intent, each firm must formalize its routines and organizational knowledge in order to achieve the requisite coordination, and knowledge transfer is generally enhanced where a new common competence is developed. By working to develop a common competence, firms will necessarily access some of the knowledge and intellectual capital that is embedded (e.g., tacit) in the partner (Mowery, Oxley, and Silverman, 1996; Doz and Hamel, 1998; Dussauge and Garrette, 1999); the main restriction is consistency and balance between partners' intent. When the intent is internalization, sharing is restricted to acquisition and knowledge transfer will be limited. When the intent is access, the acquisition and use of a competence is time limited and specific to constrained objectives.

Culture

Organizational culture can be defined as a set of beliefs and values shared by the members of a firm. Because culture situates, defines, and prescribes the routines and habits that influence how members learn and communicate, and the extent to which they do, cultural differences can lead to difficulties and, in fact, adjustments aimed at reducing cultural distance are often perceived to be necessary. Hofstede (1980), for example, greatly popularized the notion of cultural difference by defining a series of basic dimensions on which different cultures align themselves: certainty versus uncertainty, individualism versus collectivism, low versus high power distance, and so on. Macro schemes such as this have been employed to understand the difficulties experienced when forming an alliance. The failure of the Volvo-Renault venture, for example, has been partially attributed to significant cultural differences per the Hofstede framework. Other examples include difficulties experienced in alliances between Japanese and American firms, with reports indicating that Japanese firms found it difficult to transfer knowledge outside the framework of common activity or colocation (Inkpen, 1996; 1998).

Schein (1990) has analyzed corporate cultures according to the dialectics of external adaptation or internal integration, and the firm's capacity to change or its inclination to remain stable. These distinctions are adopted for present purposes, resulting in the assumptions that (a) cultures more inclined to external adaptation (open cultures) and (b) cultures more inclined to change (flexible cultures) will transfer knowledge and learn more effectively. Firms with open cultures tend to seek resources from outside their boundaries but those with closed cultures tend to rely on resources that exist within.

A firm with an open culture will be more prone to communicating on competencies and engaging in "learning by doing" experiments than one that is not. Cameron and Quinn (1998) have argued that firm efficiency is directly related to such characteristics. Flexible cultures, on the other hand, have an ability to modify their routines, processes, or value chains to better adapt strategic direction to a given context. Learning is seen as a lever of change in this regard (Pettigrew, 1987). Firms in a learning-based alliance are faced with the necessity of adaptation in order to benefit from a partner's intellectual capital, and this frequently implies adaptation in terms of routines, core values, and basic business processes (Newman and Nollen, 1996). Obstacles to such adaptation are more visible in firms with a heavy hierarchical culture as contrasted with those that are relatively flat and autonomous. The 1983 General Motors-Toyota NUMMI[1] collaboration, for example, adopted a management style based on the Toyota philosophy and GM's employees were required to revise and modify their mental schemes in order to benefit from Toyota's competencies.

Trust

Openness and flexibility as defined previously imply trust and, conversely, cultural characteristics influence trust in learning-based alliances. Trust has been defined as a presumption of correct behavior of each party in an unforeseen situation, a way of coping with uncertainty (Bidault, 1997). This implies an informal control mechanism that governs partners in a relationship. In an alliance context, trust is seen as an important foundation for effective knowledge transfer and, in particular, tacit knowledge dissemination (Gulati, 1995). Trust is dynamic, capable of evolving in positive or negative fashion, and can be optimized in a learning situation. It can counteract opportunistic behavior, become an important factor in the selection of a partner, and assume the role of a principal coordination mechanism in the daily functioning of an alliance, thereby reducing transactional costs (traditionally defined) and uncertainty (Arrow, 1985; Killing, 1987).

The proposition is that higher levels of trust between partners will lead to more effective knowledge transfer and organizational learning. Research around this issue (Killing, 1987; Bidault, 1997) has identified various determinants of trust but most authorities agree that three are particularly telling from a knowledge transfer perspective: (a) *interdependency*, (b) the partner's *reputation*, and (c) prior experience.

1. A form of contract based on *interdependency* favors trust in the sense that mutual needs, well expressed, have a stabilizing effect. If Party A realizes that Party B is dependent on him or her, and the same is true for Party B, the likelihood is that both will expect the other to respect commitments due to the reciprocity of needs (Sako, 1998).
2. *Reputation* has been dubbed the most important resource a firm has (Grant, 1996). Perceptions of a firm and its expertise or experience, and its reputation for fair dealing, constitute important foundations on which partners in an alliance build trust (Sako, 1998).
3. *Prior experience* is perhaps the best indicator of future behavior in a relationship. Familiarity with how a potential partner has behaved in previous relationships, or strong indicators of how that partner might behave, have been shown to be important variables (Africa and de la Torre, 1998).

Organizational Design

The form of an alliance determines the nature of its control, which, in turn, governs the nature of knowledge exchange and learning therein. A distinction is commonly made between three primary types of alliance architecture (Kogut, 1988):

1. The *non-equity* form, which is summarized by contractual relationships. Non-equity forms partially ignore hierarchical control due to a lack of structural dependence. Control is contractual and based on formalized obligations. There is limited and defined knowledge transfer in such arrangements as typically defined in a contract.
2. The *joint venture* form, in which partners are directly involved in the creation of a joint entity. Joint ventures regroup separated entities and thus require their own hierarchical control mechanisms and ownership structure. Knowledge transfer is necessary and vital for the novel entity, which has to benefit from the learning through both parents.
3. The *equity* form, which does not imply a joint entity but a serious commitment from both parties. This type includes multipoint alliances. The strong commitment of both partners and mutual interest in partners' resources lead to opportunities of real transfer, beyond the simple acquisition of defined competencies.

It is commonly accepted that the joint venture is the form that favors knowledge transfer (Kogut, 1988; Mowery et al., 1996).

These four factors—strategic intent, culture, trust, and form—constitute the essential foundations of learning-based alliances. The next sections will consider two strategic processes, *transparency* and *learning capacity*, which are rooted in the above four factors.

Transparency

Transparency has been related to the "openness" of a firm (Hamel, 1991) and here we will define it as the extent of communication and knowledge transfer that occurs between partners. In a learning-based alliance, this is obviously the goal, but one's level of success will hinge on two factors:

1. The nature of the knowledge in play and the way it is articulated
2. The willingness to distribute and integrate this knowledge

It is clear to managers and academics alike that explicit knowledge (codified, digitized, materialized knowledge) is more easily transferred than the "tacitness" of a firm's know-how, experience, mental models, organizational routines and so on. Barney (1991), for example, has observed that in spite of desires to the contrary, it is impossible to cut the experience from one top management team and paste it in another. Technical competencies may be more amenable to transfer, however, because a portion can frequently be made accessible in explicated form. Ways and means are being explored (have been explored for some time, actually, in other frameworks) for the effective transmission of both in an alliance.

There are two broad sets of options for knowledge transfer, one involving that which can be explicated and another that which is too difficult, costly, or simply impossible to explicate. Where a body of knowledge, know-how, or experience can be codified and articulated (i.e., manuals, processes, infrastructure systems), the task is to do so and ensure that communication occurs. Where a body of knowledge cannot, the task is to engage social processes (environments, ecologies) that will permit the actors to transfer the knowledge. Examples of the former embrace the information technologies we are all familiar with (intranets, groupware) as well as the manuals, training systems, and more traditional methods. Examples of the second issue include face-to-face exchanges, apprenticeship and mentoring systems, community creation, and colocation, that is, interactive learning.

Learning-based alliances are typically more interested in tacit knowledge than in explicit knowledge for the obvious reason that explicit knowledge is most probably a public good. Tacit knowledge is therefore the issue in alliance-based knowledge transfer and the soft techniques that are indicated include communities of practice, staff rotation, colocation of project teams, regular and frequent meetings between members of both entities, allocation of space and time for informal exchanges, and other ways of allowing key people to interact. The insight is that rather than managing the knowledge itself, as in putting the contents of a manual on the company's intranet, the alliance must manage the social environment in which motivated people are allowed to think and work together.

Transparency is inevitably tied to the willingness of a firm to disclose its knowledge. Strategic alliances do not avoid the schism of competition and collaboration; even if a firm is willing to cooperate, to learn and acquire new competencies, it will also strive to protect its assets. To the extent a partner perceives threat in this regard, transparency will diminish.

Learning Capacity

If *transparency* is the capacity to transfer knowledge, *learning capacity* is the ability to learn. Formally, this refers to the acquisition of new knowledge, the value the firm places on it, and the way this knowledge is exploited and embedded in existing stocks and flows. Research has linked this ability to competitive advantage (Penrose, 1959; Cohen and Levinthal, 1990; Hamel, 1991). The presumption, therefore, is that firms with greater learning capacities will benefit more from a learning-based alliance so that companies with enhanced abilities in this regard will benefit.

Internalizing new knowledge is also facilitated by shared cognitive bases (assumptions and frameworks) and communication structures (Shenkar and

Li, 1999). The assumption here is that prior experience will generally have erected both such that knowledge transfer is facilitated. Implicated are the way a partner codifies its knowledge, the way it communicates that codified knowledge to a partner, and its willingness and ability to change existing organizational routines.

Training and education can be important factors in this regard. The proposition is that firms that condition events prior to alliance formation through education programs that operationalize (for example) the factors noted in this chapter will tend to be more successful. The direct involvement of executives in knowledge sharing and routine changing has been shown to increase the learning capacity of a firm (Rolland, 1999), an approach that is generally termed "action learning." Such a process appears to favor the development of learning capacity as it encourages individuals to reflect on and become genuinely involved in alliance issues. Previous research has shown that action learning can introduce change in decision-making processes, change in the way people work together, and change in the way they share beliefs (Weinstein, 1995).

IMPLICATIONS

This review of research that lies at the intersection of learning-based alliances and knowledge management shows the red thread to be an orientation toward organizational learning coupled to a specific focus on knowledge and its transfer. Our proposition is that systems and structures can be established that enhance knowledge transfer in learning-based alliances, and we have suggested a set of four factors (strategic intent, organizational culture, trust, organizational form) that research and experience point to as the essential foundations. These appear to be the primary structural elements that, once established, lead to transparency and learning capacity.

If the motivation to establish an alliance is based on learning and knowledge transfer, consider this idealized scenario. First, the partners clearly intend to learn from one another. Second, both have open cultures, which are disposed to external interactions, and the flexibility that allows them to integrate new knowledge internally. Third, both are working with a partner whose reputation or experience was known beforehand, or who specifically fits expectations in terms of complementarity. Fourth, trust between partners is high as a result, and the form of the alliance will be oriented toward a separated entity, or joint venture, in order to capitalize the dynamics and synergies of both parents while permitting sufficient autonomy to develop specialized expertise.

In this scenario two factors are determinant and must become conscious goals in order to maximize knowledge transfer. Transparency—an essential factor as well as a motor of effective communication—will be fostered through processes that ensure the fluidity and exchange of knowledge through soft or hard technologies. Second, leaning capacity will be valorized in order to act on the knowledge transferred, allowing the partners to stock new organizational knowledge or processes, as well as transfer expertise to their individuals.

A review of public announcements reveals that the basic intent of an alliance is seldom expressed as a desire to acquire knowledge, but rather as the development of new competencies or the acquisition of new market niches. It is clear, however, that goals framed in business terms are frequently accomplished through learning and knowledge transfer. It is also the case that goals are emergent depending on the new knowledge acquired by organizations. The issue is therefore somewhat circular. One press release in the pharmaceutical industry, for example, announced a joint venture between Photogen Technologies[2] and Elan as the intent to develop a treatment of cancer in the lymph nodes. This goal was quickly followed by text that outlined the expected contributions of both partners in terms of knowledge, know-how, and intellectual property.

Cultural issues are significant. Ciborra (1991) has analyzed Olivetti's experience with regard to the unsuccessful Olivetti–AT&T attempt to develop an alliance in 1989. His conclusion is that the failure was largely a result of cultural differences. The success of NUMMI illustrates the importance of initial conditions in this regard. GM wanted to learn how to build cars more efficiently, using the Toyota "lean" production system, and Toyota wanted to expand sales in the American market and test its production methods in an American setting. NUMMI's success on both counts is generally attributed to cultural openness and flexibility from both parties, allowing them to transfer and integrate know-how and expertise.

Reputation and trust are important. Electrolux[3] and Ericsson announced a joint venture in October 1999, which intends to market products and services to the "Networked Home." This joint venture was established to develop a new business infrastructure that would make housing appliances networked and connected to external providers of information and services via the Internet. The intent for Electrolux is to learn how to develop Web technology-based household appliances, and Ericsson wants to learn about the household market and how to create new added value. This alliance leverages the market culture, brands, deep understanding of consumer behavior and retail channels, and technological expertise of two partners who trust and respect one another.

Finally, we would point out that the review provided here forms the basis for a research project that intends to test the propositions in the field. The goal is to specify the conditions and processes that lead to effective planning for, and management of, learning-based alliances. As with much research of this nature, understanding lags practice because it is clear that firms are actively pursuing alliances as ways to learn, develop, and adapt. We trust that this chapter has provided some help in sorting out the complexity of the subject and will assist firms in developing the foundations of an effective alliance-based knowledge transfer strategy.

NOTES

1. http://www.nummi.com.
2. PR Newswire 02/11/1999.
3. http://www.e2-home.com; http://www.electrolux.com; http://www.ericsson.com.

CHAPTER 12

The Social Ecology of Knowledge Management

David Snowden

**CYNEFIN:
A SENSE OF
TIME AND PLACE**

*C*ynefin (pronounced cun-ev-in) is a Welsh word with no direct equivalent in English. As a noun it is translated as *habitat*, as an adjective *acquainted* or *familiar*, but dictionary definitions fail to do it justice. A better, and more poetic, definition comes from the introduction to a collection of paintings by Kyffin Williams, an artist whose use of oils creates a new awareness of the mountains of his native land and their relationship to the spirituality of its people: "It describes that relationship: the place of your birth and of your upbringing, the environment in which you live and to which you are naturally acclimatized" (Sinclair, 1998). It differs from the Japanese concept of *Ba*, which is a "shared space for emerging relationships" (Nonaka and Konno, 1998) in that it links a community into its shared history—or histories—in a way that paradoxically both limits the perception of that community and enables an instinctive and intuitive ability to adapt to conditions of profound uncertainty. In general, if a community is not physically, temporally, and spiritually rooted, then it is alienated from its environment and will focus on survival rather than creativity and collaboration. In such conditions, knowledge hoarding will predominate and the community will close itself to the external world. If the alienation becomes extreme, the community may even turn in on itself, atomizing into an incoherent babble of competing self-interests.

This is of major importance for the emerging disciplines of knowledge management. Organizations are increasingly aware of the need to create appropriate virtual and physical space in which knowledge can be organized and distributed. They are gradually becoming aware that knowledge cannot

be treated as an organizational asset without the active and voluntary participation of the communities that are its true owners. A shift to thinking of employees as volunteers requires a radical rethink of reward structures, organizational forms, and management attitudes. It requires us to think of the
organization as a complex ecology in which the number of causal factors renders pseudo-rational prescriptive models redundant at best and poisonous at
worst. Managing a complex ecology requires a focus on interventions designed to trigger desired behavior in the members of that ecology rather than
attempts to mandate activity; it requires an understanding of the underlying
values around which the various communities that comprise that ecology
self-organize their knowledge.

An organization that has been reengineered has particular difficulties in
making this shift. Although that reengineering may well have been critical to
its survival, the mechanical metaphor that underlay process reengineering
focused on knowledge as a definable "thing" that could be subjected to rational management. Individuals and communities soon learned that if the value
of their knowledge was not immediately self-evident, then they would be
prime candidates for ritual sacrifice in the next downsizing exercise. Equally,
they started to understand that if their knowledge was perceived as valuable,
then it was safer to lease it on an as-needed—or more frequently as-
requested—basis to the highest bidder. The focus of identity moved from organizational loyalty based on mutual obligation or interdependency (lifetime
employment in exchange for loyal service) to a more fragmented and uncertain space.

TOWARD A NETWORK OF COMMUNITIES

There was, of course, no golden age of lifetime employment in the West nor,
but for a favored few, in Japan; even a cursory reading of economic history is
enough to dispel that myth. However, we have seen early signs of a shift
from hierarchical forms to one in which the organization is seen as a network
of communities, hopefully united in a common purpose. In the knowledge
management arena this has meant an increasing focus on communities of
competence or practice. Here the place, or *Ba,* of knowledge exchange and creation is groups of individuals logically organized by common expertise or interest. These logically constructed groups are often supported by sophisticated systems designed to enable collaboration and exchange when the group
members are dispersed in space, but not in time. Such logically constructed
groups are not necessarily communities—common interests and educational
background are not enough in their own right to forge a community, and
most organizations will use meetings and social space, both physical and virtual, to induce a sense of belonging and social obligation.

Camouflage Behavior

However, although a logical group may appear to have become a community there is also a danger that camouflage behavior has set in. It may display some of the superficial aspects of a community, such as the admission of (nondamaging) mistakes from which the group can learn, generation of success stories regarding the reuse of intellectual capital, and innovative associations of ideas, to name but a few. If the organization has spent its resources in creating the group, then it would be churlish, or political suicide, to fail to exhibit the behaviors that the organization has mandated. This is an age-old management dilemma; are people saying that they agree with me because they do, or because they feel they have to? We have learned to live with the dilemma in hierarchical or matrix organizations, as the effects of either option are similar. However, in the emerging knowledge economy, the divergence between the true belief of the volunteer and the compliance of the conscript can be the difference between success and failure. We need a new model for a new age, based on a greater degree of self-awareness and honesty than has been necessary in the past. Trust is, after all, the single most important precondition for knowledge exchange.

CULTURALLY BASED SENSE MAKING

Any such model has to recognize the need for diversity, ambiguity, and paradox. Too many of the modern-day practitioners of scientific management have overused its Newtonian base and abused the thinking of its founder, Taylor, by the attempted creation of universal and overly simplistic models. We need to recognize that human society is diverse and multidimensional. Volunteers can and do resist mandated behavior. Ambiguity provides scope for individual interpretation and more rapid adaptation to change; the neat and tidy structures required by traditional IT systems design oversimplify complexity in order to achieve deliverables and consequently fail to reflect the richness of human space. Paradox allows humans (but not computers) to work with apparent contradiction, and in consequence create new meaning. One of the paradoxes that will be explored later, for example, is that of maintaining rigid boundaries between formal and informal communities; the more rigid the boundary, the greater the knowledge flows across it.

The Cynefin model in Figure 12.1 uses contrasting views of culture based on the disciplines of anthropology on one dimension and a community-based sense-making view of knowledge and language on the other. An early form of the model using different labels for the dimension extremes and quadrant spaces was developed as a means of understanding the reality of intellectual capital management within IBM Global Services (Snowden, 1999a). It has been used subsequently to assist a range of other organizations to understand the ecology of knowledge, and the representation in Figure 12.1 reflects that experience and thinking. It is designed to create a holistic understanding of the different types of community and community interactions within an organization, rooted in the historic, cultural, and situational context of that organization, its changing environment, and the network of formal and informal communities that make it a living entity. As such, it is designed to acclimatize the informal communities to their responsibilities within the wider ecology of the organization, and to acclimatize the organization to the reality of its identity that is in part, if not principally, formed by those communities. It provides an easily remembered model designed to allow an organization to permit diversity of community type, within a common ecology of compatible purpose.

THE DIMENSION OF CULTURE

In seeking to understand culture we will draw on a distinction from anthropology. Keesing and Strathern (1998) assert two very different ways in which the term *culture* is used:

1. The sociocultural system or the pattern of residence and resource exploitation that can be observed directly, documented, and measured in a fairly straightforward manner. The tools and other artifacts that we use to create communities, the virtual environment we create, and the way we create, distribute, and utilize assets within the community. These are teaching cultures that are aware of the knowledge that needs to be transferred to the next generation and that create *training* programs. They are characterized by their certainty or explicit knowability.

2. Culture as an ". . . ideational system. Cultures in this sense comprise systems of shared ideas, systems of concepts, and rules and meanings that underlie and are expressed in the ways that humans live. Culture, so defined, refers to what humans *learn*, not what they do and make" (Keesing and Strathern, 1998; emphasis added). This is also the way in which humans provide "standards for deciding what is, . . . for deciding what can be, . . . for deciding how one feels about it, . . . for deciding what to do about it, and . . . for deciding how to go about doing it" (Goodenough, 1961, p. 522). Such cultures are tacit in nature: networked, tribal, and fluid. They are learning cultures because they deal with ambiguity and uncertainty originating in the environment, or self-generated for innovative purposes.

The cultural dimension encompasses technology and implicitly rejects the dualism of much current knowledge management. This dualism often manifests itself in phrases such as, "a KM solution is x% technology and y% culture." Like all dualism, this tends to a demonization and deification of the ex-

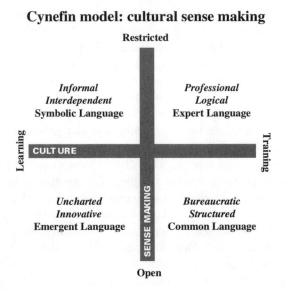

Figure 12.1 *Cynefin Model: Cultural Sense Making*

tremes of the duality, neither of which is helpful. For technologists the culture question is one that they will solve with the *next* release and for the technophobes it becomes another excuse to revert to all that is nonscalable, warm, fuzzy, and simply human. The distinction was useful for a period to drag people away from thinking that knowledge management could be achieved solely through the procurement of technology. However, it now disguises a vital aspect of any human culture; we are first and foremost a tool-making and tool-using animal. Our culture makes little sense without taking information technology, the latest manifestation of our tool-making ability into account. The issue is to see the technology of knowledge management—search engines, document management systems, yellow pages, and so on—as such a tool. The dualistic proposition has arisen as a result of the tendency of technologists to require the bio-reengineering of human hands to fit their tools rather than designing tools that naturally fit those hands.

THE DIMENSION OF SENSE MAKING

The function of knowledge in any organization is to make sense of things, both to oneself and to the communities with which one is connected. Knowledge is our sense-making capability. The developing practice of knowledge management has seen two different approaches to definition. One arises from information management and sees knowledge as some higher-level order of information, often expressed as a triangle progressing from data, through information and knowledge, to the apex of wisdom. Knowledge here is seen as a thing or entity that can be managed and distributed through advanced use of technology. Much of the thinking in this group is really not very new; the issues and problems of human interaction with information systems have been articulated for many years (Dervin, 1998). The second approach sees the problem from a sociological basis. These definitions see knowledge as a human capability to act. Like the first group, knowledge is still seen in a linear continuum with data, information, and wisdom, although the sequence is sometimes reversed with wisdom as the base (Saint-Onge, 1996).

In effect, both groups are correct, knowledge is both a *thing* and a *capability* at the same time. A parallel situation exists in physics where an electron is simultaneously both a particle and wave; if we seek particles then we see particles, if we seek waves then we see waves. The same is true of knowledge. One of the problems is that *things* are superficially easier to manage, and as a result early knowledge management has focused on knowledge as a *thing* that can be captured and codified in databases. More recent thinking is less directive and more holistic, seeing knowledge as "a fluid mix of framed experience, values, contextual information, and expert insight that provides a *framework* for evaluation and incorporating new experiences and information" (Davenport and Prusak, 1998, emphasis added).

The pragmatic issue is not one of definition, but to create a workable model that makes an intuitive common-sense impact on all levels of the organization. Attempting to resolve 2,400 years of debate since Plato first essayed *justified true belief* as a definition of knowledge in *Theatetus*, is unlikely to achieve this. What is important is to create an understanding of what it would mean to use knowledge while embracing its ambiguity. Sense making requires a knowledge user to create meaningful messages that inform other community members and that allow the community to comprehend complex and ambiguous situations without either drowning in data, or accepting the restraints of a pseudo-rational simplification. Language is key.

The use of language to include or exclude gives us the extremes of our sense-making dimension. We see communities sharing a common expert language that effectively excludes those who do not share that expertise: this is *restricted* sense making. The restriction generally results from the need to have invested time to acquire a skill set and the associated expert language within training cultures, or it can be the private symbolic language of common experience referenced through stories of learning cultures. At the other extreme, expertise is either not necessary or is inappropriate: this is *open* sense making. In teaching cultures it is open to anyone who speaks the language of the dominant culture of the organization, in learning cultures it is open in the sense that no expert language has yet developed because the situation is new.

THE CYNEFIN QUADRANTS

It is important to remember that models such as this are designed to assist in developing self-awareness and the capacity to describe the ecology in which one works. The borders between each quadrant are ambiguous in most organizations, although it will be argued later that there is considerable advantage to be gained by creating and building strong borders between the quadrants and increasing the ritual elements of transfer between them. Paradoxically, the more formal the boundary, the stronger the knowledge flows across it. Weakening borders tends to alienate the learning dimension and not only fails to improve flow, but actively inhibits it. Each quadrant represents a particular coalescence in time and space of a form of community with varying degrees of temporal continuity.

Bureaucratic/Structured

Common Language

This is the formal organization; the realm of company policy, recruitment procedures, financial controls, internal marketing; the entire panoply of corporate life that has emerged over the last century. It is a training environment. Its language is known, explicit, and open, it is the commonplace day-to-day language of the dominant linguistic group. On induction we need to communicate the basics of organizational life: how to claim expenses, reporting requirements, health and safety procedures, to name but a few. The language we use is the language of the culture, in which the organization resides, and in a multinational will generally be the language of the country in which the head office is situated, although international English is emerging as a distinct language in its own right, which often presents more problems for native English speakers used to dialect and cultural references than it does for people who have learned it as a foreign language.

While the bulk of the language is explicit, there are also organizational stories that are universal and form part of the language of the organization. These may be founder stories, or they may be stories of key transforming events in that organizations' history: near bankruptcy, key projects, major breakthroughs. There will also be a subtext beneath the formal language and stated company values. For example, in five separate assignments in different large international organizations during 1999 carried out by the author, the use of story as a disclosure mechanism for cultural values identified "Don't buck the process" as a key organizing principle underlying behavior and working practice. None of the organizations studied portrayed such a rule as part of their induction process, nor would they have accepted it as reality in a formal setting. However, such rules are learned through private association and experience, and they are unlikely to be propagated by the organization, even though their acquisition is a survival necessity for new members.

The organization has high volumes of information and embedded knowledge to communicate on a regular basis to a diverse population. Some of this needs to be done within the context of skills training, some via company publications, or increasingly via the intranet and other forms of virtual collaboration. Increasingly, the volume of information communicated by organizations results in data glut and a failure to create meaningful messages; messages that do not inform the recipient remain as data. In many organizations corporate communications are de facto ignored by field staff who have too many other demands on their time. Filtering and the shift from *push* to *pull* information provision is one solution. Organizations are also starting to rediscover the value of human filters and human channels through the reemployment of librarians and the use of story, video, and other communication forms that convey higher levels of complexity in less time-consuming forms.

A large organization is de facto a networked conglomeration of different communities both formal and informal, linked to the center in varying degrees of effectiveness. Some commentators are even forecasting a future of increasing home working, looser employment contracts, and higher levels of uncertainty. Although this may be true, and the jury is still out on that one, there will always be a requirement for a formal organization in which communication is explicit and structured. If nothing else, a significant number of individuals want to know where they stand. They want to belong to something and see a career path. Increasingly, they will recognize that such paths do not exist within one organization, but they will exist across a series of organizations, predominantly in serial but in some cases in parallel. The danger is that the formal organization with its linguistic and training norms intrudes into other domains where that structure will inhibit progress. In looking at the other quadrants of the Cynefin model, we always need to remember that the formal organization will always attempt to creep into other spaces through measurement and control, and this partially laudable endeavor needs to be controlled and channeled so that it does not inhibit the capacity of the organization as a whole to develop to meet the demands of its environment. In many ways the domain of the bureaucratic quadrant should only consist of activities that are not better or more appropriately managed in the other three.

Professional/Logical

Restricted Expert Language

The most commonly understood form of expert language is that of the professional: an individual who, through a defined training program and associated job function, acquires an ability to use explicit specialist terminology, generally codified in textbooks and via references to key concepts or thinkers. The expert language and the time and basic skill it takes to acquire that expert language form the barriers to entry and define the nature of the restriction. Although the opportunity to acquire the skill is known and available to all, in practice it is further limited by opportunity. Opportunity may be the most important and the most often forgotten factor because it frequently depends on patronage or access to decision makers rather than need. Lack of opportunity may also result from social deprivation prior to commencement of a career or during that career.

In the context of the organization such expertise may be externally and internally validated. Engineers, lawyers, and accountants have external professional bodies that largely regulate and control entry to the profession, linking tightly with academic institutions. A looser framework covers disciplines such as management, sales, and marketing, where success in practice can easily overcome lack of formal qualification. There is logic to the creation of communities around these visible common affinities. Little or no ambiguity exists over their nature or the barriers for entry.

Such communities are working at a high level of abstraction. Abstraction is the process by which we focus on the underlying constructs of data. As Boisot (1998) admirably demonstrates, the process of abstraction is focused on concepts, not percepts. Percepts, ". . . achieve their economies by maintaining a certain clarity and distinction between categories, concepts do so by revealing which categories are likely to be relevant to the data-processing task" or information creation. "Abstraction, in effect, is a form of *reductionism*; it works by letting the few stand for the many." In practice it is easier to create a construct for knowledge as a *thing*; the atomistic nature of things lends itself to codification. Knowledge as a *capability* presents different problems, mostly attributable to the constant mutation of such knowledge as it accommodates itself to different contexts.

Expert communities are able to convey complex messages more economically than nonexpert communities within their domain. Figure 12.2 illustrates the way the cost of codification decreases with the operational level of abstraction of that community. Attempts to share expert knowledge at too low a level of abstraction mean that the cost of effective codification increases exponentially and the act of codification becomes a negative act; the real experts dismiss the material as not worthy of their attention—it's back where they were in high school. Codify at too high a level and, although costs are reduced, the level of restricted access can increase to the point of elitism. In working with expert communities it is vital to understand the appropriate level of operational abstraction, and to understand the speed of decay in the uniqueness of the knowledge being shared. Highly complex knowledge with a high decay factor will rarely justify the cost of codification. As can be seen from Figure 12.2, the tolerance for ambiguity is broader for complex knowledge. This is because the populations able to use complex knowledge are generally smaller and will tend to have more homogeneity of value/belief systems.

Operating levels of abstraction

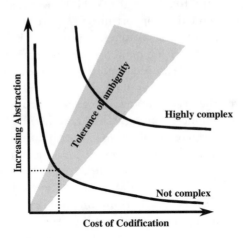

Figure 12.2 *Operating Levels of Abstraction*

Identity and Status in Professional Communities

The expertise and the process of its acquisition form a key part of the identity and status of individuals within the community. The symbols of that status may well be ritually displayed: degree certificates, 100 percent club plaques for sales staff, scrolls indicating membership in an external professional association, pictures of formative experiences associating the individual with other respected members of the community. Status in the early days is linked to clearly identified stages in the process of expertise acquisition: passing examinations and acquisition of relevant work experience. All members will expect to progress through these stages within certain acceptable time limits. Failure to do so means some loss of status; accelerated progression means increased status. After the early period the position becomes more ambiguous. Status may be linked to the capacity to find work or funding for fellow experts. It may be the consistent creation of highly valuable and original work, or it may be the ability to train and mentor new entrants. In a sales community, status is clearly linked to the achievement of readily measurable explicit targets. Although application of these qualitative criteria is often unfair, the communities in question accept it. In contrast, for a group of scientists in an R&D function, we might expect greater concern over qualitative measures with a need for clearly demonstrated fairness.

Power and Ritual in Professional Communities

There is an obvious overlap between status and power in a professional community; however, power does not necessarily correlate with status. In R&D

communities, for example, power may reside in those individuals best able to handle the interface between their fellow scientists and the senior management and finance staff of the organization. This ability may be resented, in which case there is a form of alienation between status and power that can compromise the identity and effectiveness of individuals. The ability to gain and sustain funding provides power that can be used or abused; in a bureaucratic organization (and most large organizations are bureaucratic) *budget* substitutes for *land* in a new form of feudalism. Feudalism was often despotic, and occasionally used patronage to encourage creativity, but was never democratic. Ritual is interesting. There are rituals in the gaining of profession qualifications and the giving of sales awards, to take two examples. However, they are rarely thought out. In medieval craft halls the transition from apprentice to journeyman was a highly formalized ritual that took place in front of the entire community. The purpose of this ritual was not self-aggrandizement, but establishing the new place and responsibility of the individual within the community. More work needs to be done in this area, but there is a case to be made that we have lost the capacity to use formal ritual to enable transformation and learning. This is partly caused by an understandable reaction to the pomp and circumstance often associated with it. Although informal rituals abound as they satisfy a human need, formality has advantages at key turning points, and its reintroduction may be worth considering.

Informal/Interdependent

Restricted Symbolic Language

Informal communities are more rigidly restricted than professional ones. The community, or individuals within it, use criteria for the inclusion or exclusion of members that are unspecified and rarely articulated, but are intuitively understood. Members in the gray zone between acceptance and rejection may be unaware of the process itself. Membership is always ambiguous and if lost can result in bad feeling arising from a sense of personal betrayal that goes beyond the normal cut and thrust of organizational politics in the formal organization. Some cases groups are absolutely restricted; they are linked to past unique experiences and in consequence are not open to new membership. Such groups are also more readily identifiable. At the other extreme, membership criteria may be clear, and the group open in consequence. An example from one organization is a group that meets virtually on a Monday morning to celebrate or mourn depending on the results of a weekend football match. Support of the football club transcends other loyalties and organizational boundaries. In general, such groups coalesce as a result of some form of stimulus: common experience, common values or beliefs, common goals, or common enemies or threats. In addition, there is a question of the degree of emotional intensity, which also has a significant impact on the duration of the community created, and its restriction on access for new members. Informal communities are by their nature ambiguous.

Symbolic Language: The Role of Story

An examination of primitive symbolic or pictorial languages reveals some interesting features. Primary among these is the ability of symbolic languages to convey a large amount of knowledge or information in a very succinct way. Each symbol has a different meaning according to the combination of symbols that preceded it. The problem is that such languages are difficult to comprehend and nearly impossible to use unless you grow up in the community of symbol users. In some primitive societies the symbols are stories, often unique to a particular family who train their children to act as human repositories of complex stories that contain the wisdom of the tribe. The ability to convey high levels of complexity through story lies in the highly abstract nature of the symbol associations in the observer's mind when she or he hears the story. It triggers ideas, concepts, values, and beliefs at an emotional and intellectual level simultaneously.

We observe the same use of symbolic language in modern organizations—primitive forms are remarkably persistent despite the superficial appearance of rationalism! Any community has its repository of stories that are used to suggest appropriate behaviors or teach in a variety of ways. Some of these are fairly pervasive and visible. A rewarding exercise is to ask staff who have been with the organization for just under a year what stories they have been told that summarize what it is to work for that organization. Another such exercise is to ask staff who are known for their ability to mentor what stories of their own experience they tell their proteges following a serious mistake on their part. These are often inspirational stories from the organization's history of failure being turned into success through human ingenuity. Both types of story, once they reach a critical mass, can be used to identify and codify simple rules and values that underlie the reality of that organization's culture (Snowden, 1999b).

Strong stories become part of the private symbolic language of informal and to a lesser extent professional and bureaucratic communities. The induction course may take only a few weeks, but it can take months or years to be told all the corporate stories to the point where one understands the oblique references to past events, or the appropriation of common words and phrases to reference *goodness* or *badness*. An experienced member of staff will use such words to associate a current proposal with past success or failure to support or destroy that proposal. The proposer may not even be aware of the associations that innocent common-sense language has triggered.

These stories convey complex meaning and can often be captured by a new breed of corporate historian (Kransdorff, 1998), with consequential reductions in induction time and improved staff retention and leadership:

"Nothing serves a leader better than a knack for narrative. Stories anoint role models, impart values, and show how to execute indescribably complex tasks" (Stewart, 1998). Story is a developing discipline in knowledge management, which has a major impact on strategy models (Snowden, 1999b), communication, and cultural change programs.

Organizational stories exist in professional and bureaucratic space as well as voluntary space, and story has a major impact in all communities both as a knowledge disclosure technique and as a knowledge trigger (Snowden, 2000) there are also private stories linked to informal, interdependent groups of individuals. These private, trusted networks are at the heart of any large organization. Their members have worked together on projects in the past or all belong to a social club, to take two different examples. They form a community whose identity exists within and without their organizational identity. In some such interdependent groups bonding is very tight due to some shared success achieved in the face of overwhelming odds, or through protective behavior: rescue of group members from redundancy, covering up a fireable offence, assisting in a promotion—the list is endless. Such groups are able to communicate far more effectively than others. Coded reference to past experience or shared values, highly specialized language utilizing a reference base outside of the organizational context, deceptive use of commonplace language to maintain camouflage, derision of an unaware third party—all of these and many more are the reality of the informal networks that for good or ill are a critical element of corporate life. Membership in such groups is always voluntary and uncertain. Failure to conform to the unwritten values and norms of the group can result in social exclusion.

Organizations need to realize the degree of their dependence on such informal networks. The danger is of chronic self-deception in the formal organization, partly reinforced by the camouflage behavior of individuals in conforming to the pseudo-rational models. A mature organization will recognize that such informal networks are a major competitive advantage and will ensure scalability through automated processes and formal constructions while leaving room for the informal communities to operate.

Status, Power, and Ritual

Status is very closely tied to leadership. Such communities often form as disciples around a powerful leader whose values and beliefs are assumed by the community as a whole. In these groups proximity to and influence over the leader are key to the status of individuals. In cases where the leader is highly dominant, individual identity in the followers may start to blur to the point where the outside world sees them as clones. Such communities can be both positive and negative in outcome. Often the dominant personality of the leader will allow new meaning to be created as the community's single, purposeful drive breaks through old assumptions and work practices. Equally, the subverting of individual identity may inhibit or prevent innovation. In contrast, the goal-seeking behavior of some communities may subvert the attempts of any one individual to gain a dominant position.

Power in informal communities is difficult to isolate, as they are totally voluntary. Where individuals become dependent on a dominant leader, they may lose touch with this fact, but it is always there. Strongly held beliefs or goals may lead to martyrdom, but this extreme is rare in business communities. What are very common are initiation rites and rituals. Initiation may involve hazing ceremonies designed to test good humor, or more serious tests of trustworthiness. Often such tests are not set up deliberately but occur in day-to-day discourse. They may require totemistic behavior such as a ritual condemnation of a common enemy. Rituals in informal communities serve to remind members of the original coalescence point. An annual reunion of a group originating in a course or other program may involve ritual retelling of stories from the original experience, often with participants almost reciting responses to reinforce their role or position within the group. Communities formed around common beliefs or common threats will typically tell myth form stories that reinforce the belief or deride the enemy. Rituals may also test continued commitment; the Friday night drink and monthly bowling evening are events that one may miss once, but continued absence will lead to partial exclusion at best.

These rituals can extend to granting of membership. Often any individual within a group, particularly dominant individuals, can grant membership almost at whim. The new member will be introduced to the group with some form or phrase that has specific meaning for the group: "Hi guys, this is Paul, he's a *good guy*," effectively says that Paul is not one of the bad guys but is aware of who the bad guys are and is opposed to them. Equally, the phrase, "Hi guys, this is Peter. Peter comes from the London office," may say to this particular group, "You don't know Peter but he's one of the bad guys so watch what you say"; commonplace language has assumed a specialized symbolic meaning.

A Negative Aspect of Voluntary Communities

Informal communities exist for good or evil, but they do exist. Attempts to abolish them are foolish; it just isn't possible, although you may make them invisible. Foolishness is also a natural component of corporate life when it comes to people, but in this case it is more than that: it is a missed opportunity. Informal communities are the repositories for knowledge both of *things*, but more particularly of *capabilities*. The scale and scope of that knowledge dwarfs what is possible in the formal organization. Creating an environment in which such communities can organize their knowledge in private, and then managing interventions on the border between formal and informal knowledge exchange, means that the informal knowledge can be *volunteered* when it is needed on a just-in-time basis.

It is also the case that some informal communities become "old boys" groups inhibiting progress of innovative talent, securing promotions for the in crowd, and protecting bonus payments, all through the manipulation of bureaucracy. Attempts to regulate this type of behavior just provide a richer framework of rules to be manipulated. Paradoxically, reducing the rules reduces the capability of such negative groups to act because it provides greater common-sense checks on the behavior by the wider community. The point being made here is that the Cynefin model does not require toleration of informal communities that actively damage organizational values. However, rule-based and directive management intervention is rarely successful. Interventions will be unique to each situation: using natural predators to balance the ecology.

Uncharted/Innovative

Emergent Language

So far we have dealt with the two forms of restricted communities in which a specialized language, explicit or symbolic, is developed to make sense of incoming stimuli. We now reach a domain in which such language does not exist because the situation is new. It may be that a completely new market has emerged, or that new competitors have appeared from nowhere or by lateral movements of brand: for example, the entry of Mars into ice cream. The newness may be technology induced, creating new possibilities; the growth of the Internet is an obvious example, and we will see increasing levels of uncertainty as the impact of pervasive commuting starts to bite. This is the ultimate learning environment. We have no idea of what it is that we need to train, and the language of our previous expertise may be inappropriate at best, or appear to be appropriate (even though it is not) at worst.

Faced with something new, the organization has a problem; it will tend to look at the problem through the filters of the old. The history of business is littered with companies who failed to realize that the world had changed and who continued to keep the old models and old language in place. In hindsight such foolishness is easy to identify, but at the time the dominant language and belief systems of the organization concerned make it far from obvious. This is particularly true where the cost of acquiring knowledge within the organization is high, as this tends to lead to knowledge hoarding and secrecy that in turn can blind the organization to new and changed circumstances. Other organizations deliberately share knowledge, depending on speed of exploitation as the means of maintaining competitive advantage (Boisot, 1998).

The requirement in uncharted space is to make sure that the past does not blind us to the possibilities of the present and to the opportunities of the future. There are three internal models that are used by organizations when faced with a new situation, aside from prayer:

1. *Bureaucratic Quadrant*: The organization sets up a task force or allocates responsibility to individuals trusted within the organizational hierarchy and established within its command and control structure, including candidate members for such groups: management trainees, proteges, and the like. If we use a community of trusted or trainee executives, we are choosing individuals who are good at exploiting new circumstances for career progression and who represent particular interest groups within the organization. The short- or medium-term goals of those interest groups may not coincide with the change associated with accommodating new ideas. The tendency of such formally constituted groups is to ensure that all interests are represented, and functional conflict may result in a failure to understand the nature of the change. The formal language and stories of the organization will create blindness to the new situation.

2. *Professional Quadrant*: Individual competence groups may have a responsibility to monitor changes and produce an organizational response, or the task may be assigned to such a group by senior management. The danger of sectional interests is more extreme than for bureaucracy. The restricted nature of this language, a strength in ensuring rapid and effective knowledge sharing, becomes a handicap when a significantly new situation is encountered. If it is radically different there may not be a problem; the danger is where the difference isn't slight, but significant. Also, professional communities may be more radically threatened by new circumstances than are bureaucratic ones. Individuals in bureaucratic communities are concerned with power through the manipulation of resources and can adapt and change to new circumstances: they don't mind what they manage, as long as they are the managers. In professional communities the individuals will have invested years in developing a particular skill or expertise and if they have made the wrong bet on the longevity of that skill set, they will be more defensive.

3. *Informal Quadrant*: Solutions emerge without organizational intervention and are either used or, more frequently, ignored until it is too late. This can happen when individuals or groups within the organization see or perceive that something has changed, and attempt to make the organization aware of the issue or keep it private until they feel safe to expose the idea to corporate scrutiny, by which time it may be too late. A more recent phenomenon is that the individuals concerned take the idea out of the organization in a business startup, often in competition. Using professional or bureaucratic communities at least has the benefit of visibility: the decision makers are aware that something is going on and will often have been involved in its formation. With visibility comes responsibility. Making new sense in an informal community is a fundamentally flawed behavior. Intellectual property in informal communities is private and may be subsequently volunteered in the right circumstances. This privacy is the only sensible and sustainable way in which the bulk of an organizations' knowledge can be organized. However, in new sense making the process of moving knowledge from informal to formal

is too haphazard, and attempts to force the flow to meet the time require-ments of innovation will only damage future flows, even if they are effective in the first place. Facing a new situation requires awareness at all relevant levels of an organization—it cannot be left to chance.

The organization needs to recognize that in new sense making we "see as through a glass darkly," to quote St. Paul (1 Cor. 13:12). New sense making takes place at a high level of abstraction with extensive use of metaphor and paradox. Most corporate decision makers are unhappy with both metaphor and paradox, and it may be necessary to create mediating communities be-tween the new sense-making group and the decision makers, or the sense makers will be listened to, but not heard.

How can we avoid these dangers? None of our current communities, for-mal or informal, will make sense of the new without problems, some of which may be fatal. Based on a series of engagements, we can identify four elements that should be present for new sense making.

1. *Team Selection*: Most organizations do not really know what they know, and in many cases the solutions are already known somewhere in the rich-ness of the informal community space. In new sense making what matters is to find the individuals who have access to the knowledge of the organization together with a natural networking capability to access external knowledge assets. Psychometric tools such as Belbin analysis are useful to check that the necessary skills are present. However, direct access to knowledge networkers can be obtained by use of network analysis (Foster and Falkowski, 1999). This approach requires a series of "who would you ask if you wanted to know about X" questions, asked, re-asked and developed across appropriate segments of the organization. The results of the answers are fed into a soft-ware tool borrowed from the telecom industry and designed to reveal traffic density and nodal points. The graphical result of this work reveals the key in-dividuals across a community and the key communities within an organiza-tion who, even if they do not know the answer themselves, know someone who does. These key individuals are often sidelined middle managers, secre-taries, and administrators. They are often more motivated by connecting people than by progression within the organization. These individuals or communities have access to the knowledge assets of the organization, and their selection by this indirect disclosure method prevents the competing self-interests that are likely in the event that the individuals are formally selected by virtue of their status in the professional or bureaucratic quadrants.

2. *Language Disruption*: The team selection process may bring together dif-ferent expertise and may be enough to disrupt the language norms of the or-ganization. However, it will normally be necessary to include other knowl-edge assets. This may include key customers, particularly those who are troublesome! Breakthrough developments can also usefully involve lead us-

ers (von Hippel, Thomke, and Sonnack, 1999) or competitors' customers. It is also effective to use knowledge assets from parallel environments. To take an example from the author's own direct experience: confronting experts from the marketing department of a major retailer with experts from missile defense systems. The two groups realized that they faced similar problems. When they looked at these problems, without the constraints of previous assumptions, there was very little difference between an incoming ballistic missile and an outgoing disloyal customer. Disruption may also need to be continuous or directed at key points in the program.

3. *Humor and Ritual*: The disruption of language can be reinforced by a degree of ritual around specific negative acts or behavior. Another direct experience with a team in a crisis on a systems delivery issue will illustrate this. The group concerned was over-reliant on process and assumed that key checks were taking place because the process said that they would be. Increasing pressure of time, client dissatisfaction, and the threat of legal action were increasing this particular fault. A simple ritual involving the use of a comical hat with elephant ears and an elephant trunk achieved the behavioral change. Following agreement by the team that assumptions must not be made, the first person caught making an assumption had to wear the hat until someone else was caught in a similar mistake. Judicious advance planning meant that the most senior member of the group made the first assumption, which prevented victimization of junior members until the ritual was properly established. Over the course of the next three days the hat rotated on a regular basis until it was no longer necessary; a significant behavior shift had been achieved. Humor was critical as it diffused tension and enabled learning.

4. *Time, Space, and Resources*: Innovation and lateral thinking are not always achieved through resource provision. There is some evidence that starvation of resources, provided it is not excessive, increases creativity and with it innovation; there are overlaps between creativity and innovation but they are not the same thing, although often confused in organizations. Starvation may also force groups into changing the rules of the game with consequent benefit to changing customer requirements and innovation. In one experiment, two groups of children were asked to compete in building a hut. One group was given inferior materials and was unable to build as good a hut as their competitors. The disadvantaged group then attempted to introduce new criteria into the competition by, among other things, building a garden around the hut (Kastersztein and Personnaz, 1978). There are no simple formulas to apply here, and the environment or direct threat for which the intervention is planned may constrain the ideal allocation of resources. There are some principles that can be applied: (1) the time allocated should always be less than is estimated—this increases pressure and forces the team to use resources other than their own; (2) conventional tools and approaches that lead to conventional or forecastable solutions should generally be avoided and consciously removed; (3) part-time or full-time is always a question—

part-time will naturally create more networking into the organization, but full-time ensures focus; and (4) a unique physical as well as virtual environment is important—a social space where things can be pinned on walls, non-team members can visit, and conversations can take place.

The uncharted space is one of the most interesting in the Cynefin model. We have explored some of its aspects and some techniques for intervention. However, there are many other models and interventions that have been and could be devised.

ASPECTS OF COMMUNITY INTERACTION

The value of a concept-based model such as Cynefin is in its ability to assist in descriptive self-awareness within an organization and to understand the flow of knowledge. The nature of the flows can indicate the sort of organization we are dealing with and to some extent its likely future direction. Maintaining boundaries between communities can be vital in ensuring knowledge exchange. There is a wonderful poem by Robert Frost entitled "Mending Wall" that makes this point. It tells the story of two farmers who go out in spring to "set the wall between us once again." One farmer challenges the other as to the point of the task and receives a response that summarizes the importance of boundaries:

> He is all pine and I am apple orchard.
> My apple trees will never get across
> And eat the cones under his pines, I tell him.
> He only says, "Good fences make good neighbors."

The point is a profound one. The current circumstances may not require a wall, but the presence of the wall means that we are secure in our boundaries. Individuals need to know that the private learning they share with trusted confidants in informal space will remain private. If they *believe* it may become public, then the degree of disclosure will be inhibited. In a virtual community there are a broad range of interventions that can encourage this. In IBM Global Services the best part of 50,000 private collaborative workrooms exist de facto in informal space, while professional space is organized into just over 50 competences. The self-organizing capabilities of informal space allow a vast quantity of knowledge to self-organize, allowing investment to be concentrated into professional space. What then matters is the creation of flags and search techniques that allow the informal communities to volunteer their knowledge into the professional and bureaucratic communities when it is needed (Snowden, 1999a).

Given that a large part of exchange takes place within a virtual space, it is also critical to look at issues of social responsibility. In a physical environment, participation in a community is self-evident at both a conscious and unconscious level to all members of the community. In a virtual space this is more difficult. Recent work within IBM's Labs (Erickson et al., 1999) has experimented with the use of social proxies in virtual space. All members of a virtual collaborative community are represented by different colored dots within a circle or *Babble*. The dots of active members cluster in the center, but those of members who fail to participate gradually drift to the edge of the circle. The social proxy was combined with persistent chat line—both synchronous and more recently asynchronous. Babble had some remarkable effects. It blurred "the distinction between work and play, encouraging a freedom that is often more productive and more enjoyable than the more formal exchange of other forums. . . . You're free to relax and joke and exchange half-finished theories, building freely on each other's ideas until something new is born." Babble also became a distinctive place with multiple Babbles opening up to handle different topics. The visibility to the individual, and to the virtual community of which the individual is a member, induces responsibility by providing a virtual equivalent of the social clues that we get in day-to-day interaction in conventional space. The application of the principle of social translucence that underlies Babble offers a fertile source of future work on the dynamics of community interaction within the Cynefin model. Erickson et al. (1999) state, "Socially translucent systems provide perceptually-based social clues which afford awareness and accountability." They illustrate the concept with the case of a door that opens into a hallway at their office. People opening the door can hurt people on the other side of the door, a problem not really resolved by a "Please Open Slowly" notice that soon goes unnoticed by regular users. A glass window in the door would be more effective because it allows the door opener to perceive movement on the other side of the glass; it also brings into play the social rules of a "culture which frowns upon slamming into other people." However, there is a third reason for the window. "Suppose that I don't care whether I harm others: I am still likely to open the door slowly because *I know that you know that I know* you're there, and therefore I will be held *accountable* for my actions. This distinction is useful because, while accountability and awareness are generally entwined in the physical world, they are not necessarily coupled in the digital realm."

Trust, responsibility, and accountability are key requirements for human interaction. They operate at different levels in different circumstances. I may trust the organization to pay me every month, but it does not follow that I will trust the organization with a new, half-formed idea—but I will trust people who share my value/belief system. Different issues and problems will have different requirements for community interaction and we need some form of decision model to determine which space (or spaces) we are operating in, which recognizes the fluid uncertainties of social interaction.

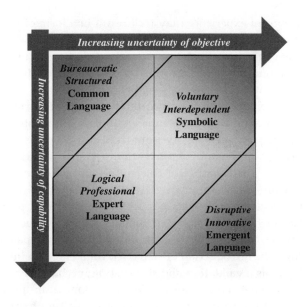

Figure 12.3   *Uncertainty Model*

The Uncertainty Matrix

Uncertainty is the new reality. The horizon for planning has been radically reduced over the past few years. Strategy thinking is shifting from thinking about products and marketplaces to focusing on resources and capabilities (Zack, 1999). This increasing uncertainty requires a focus on the effective and immediate deployment of appropriate intellectual capital. Given that the most valuable intellectual capital resides in the network of communities that make up the organization, understanding which type of community is most appropriate in different circumstances is important. The Cynefin model allows us to map different communities, and provides an understanding of the nature of their usefulness.

The uncertainty model in Figure 12.3 has been used before (Snowden, 1999b) to understand different models of strategy and will now be used to create a framework for the partial determination of the applicability of the different communities in the Cynefin model. The matrix contrasts two types of uncertainty. In the horizontal dimension, the further we go to the right, the higher our uncertainty about what it is that we are trying to achieve. In the vertical dimension, the further down we go, the more uncertain we become about our capabilities to achieve the objective. Where we are dealing with known objectives and capabilities, the bureaucratic communities of the formal organization are able to respond on the basis of their previous experience, strategic plans, and formal process. However, when uncertainty creeps in, the limitations of experience may well result in a form of corporate myopia. At the other extreme, when both objectives and capabilities are uncertain, we require the disruptive capability of uncharted space in which the expert and symbolic languages of our restricted communities are disrupted in a creative and innovative new sense-making process.

Between the extremes we face greater ambiguity. Informal and professional communities are always in some form of dynamic interaction and solutions in this space will also involve some mix of the two, as indicated in Figure 12.3. However, the balance of interaction will differ. Where we are certain of our capabilities, the expertise of the competence-based professional communities is ideally placed to resolve issues, and the organization should be prepared to delegate responsibility for action to or at least promptly accept recommendations from the formal custodians of their competences. We may qualify this by testing that our assumptions of known capabilities are still correct through the introduction of maverick thinkers from inside or outside the organization as a validation and stimulating mechanism for our experts. The free right of challenge to conventional wisdom is an age-old tradition that goes back to the court jester and beyond. Institutionalization of such challenge is an opportunity for organizations, and in the last decade several international companies have experimented with jester-type roles; in one case the title of Jester was even used on the individual's business cards.

Uncertainty of capability, coupled with certainty of objective, is a difficult thing for an organization to admit. It means that we have failed to manage our intellectual assets to make the right skills and talent available when we need it. This may be through an overenthusiastic adoption of process improvement, which has optimized the company for a specific context that no longer exists. Evidence of this can be seen in the significant number of organizations who have had to re-employ redundant staff as consultants. It may also be that the market is changing too quickly. In such circumstances the normal reaction is either to attempt to headhunt in the skills from a competitor, or to seek external partnerships. Of these, the latter is often more effective than the former, because headhunting takes time, and the individuals hunted may not be of use without the team that surrounded them in their former employment. However, too few organizations make use of their informal space, which is often a richer and more reactive source of intellectual capital than external sources. It may include mavericks excluded by rapidly ossifying experts in professional space or private interests. Discovery of private interest, one of the easiest ways of enabling intellectual asset disclosure in informal space, is often a fertile source of new resources. Equally, appeals for volunteers through bulletin boards, or use of "node holders" identified through network analysis or similar methods are all means by which the organization can first look to itself, before it looks outside. One highly effective method is to ask the leadership of the professional communities who *would not be suitable*, and then find and test those individuals; often they will be people who have challenged conventional wisdom or have a degree of self-belief or conviction that does not permit the compromises necessary for comfortable existence in expert communities. A note of caution: in this space the political interests and possibly the survival interests of professional communities in the professional space may be threatened. Reaction from such communities in these circumstances is often immediate, unplanned, and unconscious, in the same way as the body's white blood cells respond immediately to invasion. Preparing for and disrupting such reaction, particularly when it takes the form of bureaucratic inertia, needs to be deliberate, planned, and above all, ruthless.

ALIENATED AND INTEGRATED ORGANIZATIONS

The Cynefin model has been applied to self-diagnosis and mapping within different organizations. It can also be used to understand the nature of intra-community knowledge flows. There are many examples of this, but to illustrate its use we will look briefly at three forms of alienation of an organization from its intellectual capital, and one integrated or holistic form. Illustrative solutions to the various forms of alienation are suggested, but it should be emphasized that interventions to overcome the alienation of communities are nearly always incrementally progressive and context specific. No recipe is being proposed.

Expert Alienation from Strategy

In Figure 12.4, the main flows between communities take place in the horizontal dimension. The organization has turned in on itself, focused on formal processes, hierarchy, and status. It recognizes its expert communities and may even invest in their development and support. However, when the chips are down, politics take over. New situations and strategy are directly managed by the formal organization, often using external expertise in the form of expensive consultants to define future strategy, or even operational practice. Expert communities are informed of the strategy, once it is determined, and they are expected to implement it. In extreme cases, a group of executives motivated by a desire to exploit the latest fad may even go off site to define their organization's approach to a new subject such as knowledge management and ignore their own experts who are inconveniently motivated by their belief in the subject. The organization has become alienated from its intellectual capital.

This may be because of unnecessary (as opposed to necessary) barriers created between, say, a research and development community and marketing: poor communication and lack of responsiveness from the expert researchers, compounded by failure to invest time in understanding by the marketing function. The normal dynamics for formal and informal interaction between restricted communities takes place and may even be strength-

Cynefin: alienation from strategy

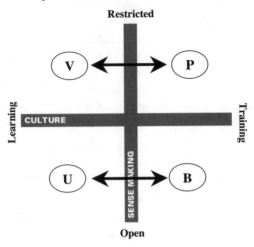

Figure 12.4 *Alienation from Strategy*

ened by a common enemy who not only doesn't understand, but also controls the purse strings. In such cases, the underlying value/belief systems may be so disconnected from each other that the only sensible solution is the introduction of mediating communities formed internally or externally.

Alienation from the Creative Unknown

Where the main flows are vertical, we have a different problem. Here the bureaucracy and its professional groups of experts happily work within the reality of known space, ignoring the innovative capacities of their own staff in informal space, and changing markets and competitive activity in uncharted space. This form is characteristic of organizations that feel themselves to be in a dominant position within their industry. Revenue and profit may well be at acceptable or higher levels, but the organization is assuming that change will be linear. Unfortunately, a step change in the environment may lead to such organizations floundering.

In these cases, individuals and communities in the informal space are often aware of the change, and may be dynamically interacting with new thinkers external to the organization. They may even be attempting to be heard, but are ignored by the formal organization. In such cases alienation is created not just between the formal and informal communities within an organization, but also between the organization and its current and future customers. The market usually forces dramatic change in this situation, but the organization may not recover. The organization is now blind to change and difference. Only some form of catastrophic intervention will result in change.

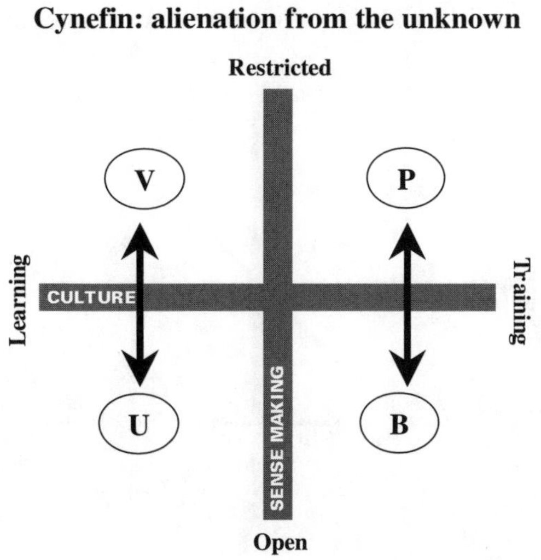

Cynefin: alienation from the unknown

Restricted

Open

Figure 12.5   *Alienation from the Unknown*

Alienation of Formal from Informal

Figure 12.6 shows a more complex situation, which could be characterized as a pseudo-rational organization. The formal organization is open to and received stimulation from its environment, and passes new situations and problems to its known experts.

The various professional communities in turn receive stimuli from the environment and interact with bureaucratic space to develop informed strategy that is then executed by the organization to respond to change, or create new opportunities. Such a model is sustainable in situations where the expertise of the professional space is constantly renewed and the environmental change is not too drastic. The alienation in this case is the disconnection of the formal from the informal.

In practice, many such organizations may deny the independent existence of the informal. They will have invested in knowledge systems to support their communities of practice, and will be aware of the need to support dialogue between individuals through the use of knowledge cafés and the like. Having done this, they may now believe that knowledge exchange will take place within the designed structures and may attempt to enforce the use of those structures through the use of knowledge targets in assessment schemes or the use of financial reward for knowledge contribution. Herein lies danger. The most common reason for knowledge retention is not power, for which financial reward and status-based punishment systems may be appropriate: the most important reason is fear of abuse. Valuable knowledge, particularly new or innovative knowledge, is precious to the knowledge creator, individ-

Cynefin: Alienation of formal from informal

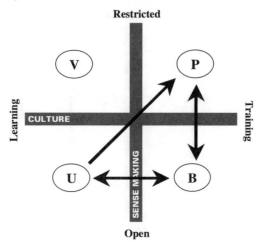

Figure 12.6 *Alienation of Formal from Informal*

ual, or community. Equally, failure in a project is a valuable resource to the organization, but the reasons for failure may be withheld because abuse of the confidence is anticipated.

Another issue with this model, common in knowledge-aware organizations, is that the expert communities are informed by activity in uncharted space, but do not interact with it to influence it to create new forms and requirements. It is a lot better to create a market for Post-it Notes than to attempt to create a competing product after the event. Expert communities are often not risk takers, and innovation and new sense making both reward and punish risk. One alternative to this approach is to change the dynamics of the flow, one model for which is suggested next.

Holistic Professional Model

This model has been developed on the basis of the author's experience in professional service organizations. It also has proven applicability outside that domain in organizations with a strong need to interface marketing and research and may have wider application. Here the formal bureaucratic space assumes a new role as a framework and control mechanism for dynamic networks of interacting sense-making communities. In this model the organization disrupts its expert communities by regularly moving them into uncharted space by the creative use of time, space, and alternative expert languages outlined in the discussion of uncharted space earlier.

Expert communities probably remain in existence for a period following the disruption, but the emphasis is on renewal through the judicious and in-

Cynefin: holistic services

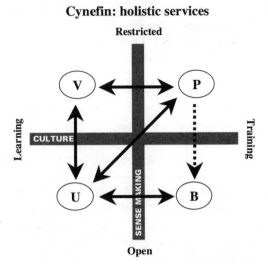

Figure 12.7   *Holistic Services*

formed creation of teams to make sense of new situations, stimulated by environmental change or by the organization's own desire to initiate change. This means that new informal communities are formed in informal space, based on the common experience and initiating event of the sense-making task. The organization is then mature enough to allow that new understanding to coalesce in the ambiguous interactions of informal space, from which new forms of expert knowledge and, in consequence, new formal expert communities in professional space will emerge and be recognized. The role of the bureaucratic space is to initiate the disruption by a constant interaction with anticipated and potential futures. In practice, the forms and structures of the organization will be retained, and are necessary to provide security to the various members that comprise it. Knowledge flow, however, would not take place to a significant level in bureaucratic space, which receives the conventional or stable information and knowledge flows from professional space.

REFLECTIONS

An underpinning argument in all that has gone before is that the organization needs to perceive itself as an ecology of communities, which will have different value/belief systems from the organization as a formal entity. There are no single solutions or models that will satisfy the needs of corporate governance. A portfolio of models, methods, and interventions is necessary to support the complexity of the modern organization. Too many organizations fail to realize that one can have a common purpose or goal, without common value/belief systems, provided those goals are not incompatible (the double negative is deliberate) with the value/belief systems of relevant communities.

Compatibility of such value/belief systems may be desirable, but a limited degree of creative dissonance is necessary for growth. Organizational values will follow and conform to the values of dominant communities within the ecology. It is also necessary to recognize that the identity of individuals and communities is closely linked to these value/belief systems, and the potential exists for abuse of power through organizational forms that alienate individuals from these evolved and historically rooted systems.

Current knowledge management is split between the mechanical, technology-based practice of the modern Newtonians, and the new thinking of organic knowledge management. Properly understood, *organic knowledge management* is the developing body of methods, tools, techniques, and values through which organizations can acquire, develop, measure, distribute, and provide a return on their intellectual assets. It is fundamentally about creating self-sustaining ecologies in which communities and their artifacts can organically respond to, and confidently proact with, an increasingly uncertain environment (Snowden, 1999a).

For organic knowledge management, a fundamental starting point is to recognize the current state of the ecology and its roots into the shared history of its communities and individuals. Once this is understood, then interventions can be devised to move forward. The concept that a desired future space can be designed and logical steps determined to achieve that design is specifically rejected. An organic approach recognizes that in evolution there are many dead ends and many new opportunities that emerge during the journey. These new opportunities may be more desirable than the original goal; they are certainly more achievable. Such evolution requires a degree of redundancy of function that is best managed within the informal spaces that a mature organization will permit and encourage. Goal-based programs too often attempt to mandate desired behavior and common values or, even worse, they may just assume them. The reality of the values and behavior of constituent communities rarely coincides with the declared values of the organization, although camouflage behavior may deceive senior managers into thinking that it does. A willingness to live with diversity itself permits a diverse and more innovative response to uncertainty.

The Cynefin model was not designed to mandate behavior but to allow an organization to understand, within a holistic framework, the diverse portfolio of communities that constitute it. It focuses on developing a self-aware descriptive capability from which action can be determined through collective understanding. Such self-awareness has to be rooted in the multiple birthplaces of the different communities and their developing history to which their members are naturally acclimatized.

Cynefin is different from *Ba* in that it is less concerned about tacit-explicit conversions: partly because it rejects the mind-body dualism implicit in Nonaka's SECI model, but in the main because of its focus on descriptive self-awareness rather than prescriptive organization models. Cynefin provides a different and more holistic space for the "cyclical cultivation of resources" (Nonaka and Konno, 1998) than that offered by scientific management.

The models of Newtonian science, adopted by the founders of scientific management, continue to apply, but we now know the boundaries of their applicability. In an increasingly uncertain world we need new organic models that embrace paradox, utilize the ambiguity of metaphor, and recognize the dynamic interdependence and interactivity of human agents and their tools, technology based or otherwise. We too often forget that Newton himself was simultaneously both an alchemist and a scientist.

PART IV

Toward
the Future

CHAPTER 13

The New Organizations: Managing Multiple Arenas for Knowledge Creation

Bo Hedberg

INTRODUCTION

Modern organizations often trade hierarchies for markets and replace tightly coupled structures with more loosely coupled networks. The perspective of imaginary, or virtual, organizations is useful in helping us understand these new enterprises. Such organizations form metasystems that tie various partner companies and individual actors together in order to share resources, pool competencies, and gain flexibility to produce good value for and with customers. Imaginary systems learn from customers, they learn from partners within the system, and they typically rely on individuals who need to learn daily and who every so often have to unlearn and relearn in changing environments. But do imaginary organizations differ in this sense from conventional organizations with respect to how they learn? This chapter presents a knowledge-intensive and knowledge-creating imaginary organization, Skandia AFS, as empirical background, and then proceeds to discuss organizational learning in this context. The chapter concludes that imaginary organizations have a potential for organizational learning that goes beyond that of conventional, integrated organizations. Learning with customers and learning with partners are two important engines that, in addition to intra-organizational processes, drive this learning. And it takes place within a renewed business logic where shared knowledge is multiplied knowledge and where trust in others, and respect for others, set the stage for interaction.

ORGANIZATIONAL LEARNING IN PRACTICE: POISONED BY SUCCESS AND UNABLE TO UNLEARN

The reader of contemporary management books might conclude that organizational learning is the normal state of affairs. Students of *The Fifth Discipline* (Senge, 1990) learn to handle tools to implement learning procedures in their companies, and Japanese companies excel in continuous learning, Kaizen. Consultants sell learning packaged as TQM or BPR (Hammer and Champy, 1993), promising daily improvements or radical restructuring of strategic business processes.

Still, the inability to learn characterizes many organizations. Successful organizations find it difficult to unlearn and relearn when times change and failures occur. Organizational inertia stabilizes organizational development both when stability is functional and when it is dysfunctional. To unlearn previously successful strategies and to learn new ways to direct behavior is often very difficult. What Argyris (1992) termed "double-loop learning" is often referred to, but rarely demonstrated, at least not as it concerns unlearning and new learning at the strategic level in organizations (cf. Hedberg, 1981; Starbuck and Hedberg, 1999; Hedberg and Wolff, 1999).

Most theories of organizational learning developed out of cognitive psychology and were built on the current understanding of how individuals learn through their cognitive systems. These cognitive models were mostly based on stimulus-response (S-R) mechanisms in which individuals, interacting with their environment, learned to discriminate within repertoires of stimuli and to connect these stimuli to repertoires of behavior. Successful couplings were reinforced by feedback, strengthened and maybe refined, and then turned into action programs (i.e., standard operating procedures, SOPs). When organizations learn, they learn through individuals and these individuals may form groups, departments, subsidiaries, or other organizational arrangements (Kim, 1993). They may be employed now or they may have been employed in the past. Thus, even if individuals learn on behalf of organizations, *organizations* may well memorize, and such memories form sediments for the future. "This is the way we do things in this bank," says the experienced banker. The "IKEA spirit" tells new employees a lot about behavior and attitudes and forwards previous learning to coming generations of employees in the worldwide IKEA empire (Salzer, 1994).

Most theories of organizational learning model the interaction between an organization and its environment. Organizations react to organizational conditions but they also attempt to enact favorable outside conditions. Repeated cycles of interaction form the basis for learning, programming, and reinforcement. *Observing, reflecting,* and *acting* are the three basic processes of the genuine learning cycle. One should note, however, that learning in organizations often also takes place through *imitation* (Bierly and Hämäläinen, 1995; Sahlin-Andersson, 1995).

The S–R cycle implies that learning requires both change and stability in the relationship between organizations and their environments. If there is too much turbulence, the learning system will have difficulties in mapping anything. And by the time observations are translated into actions, these actions might well be obsolete. Too much stability, on the other hand, is also dysfunctional. If established and functional behaviors almost never grow obsolete, there is marginal interest to learn and to improve. Situations with much stability offer little information and few opportunities for learning, and situations with much turbulence may produce a lot of data, but poor grounds for learning (Nystrom et al., 1976). So those who are responsible for the viability and efficiency of organizations should be especially concerned about these balances to the extent that they can be designed and determined (Hedberg et al., 1976).

One result of these mechanisms is that successful organizations easily develop inertia. Hedberg and Ericsson (1979) made a distinction between *insight inertia* (time delays in discovering problems) and *action inertia* (time delays in implementing change), and Miller (1990) demonstrated how successful companies often carry their strategies to the extremes so that downfall follows excellent performance. Spender (1989) showed that populations of companies (industries) tend to copy each other's successful recipes, so that pluralism and variety are lost. Weick (1991) discussed these various couplings between stimuli and responses within a learning framework, and Hedberg and Wolff (1999) used Weick's framework as shown in Figure 13.1.

	Focus on Seeing (Perceiving)	**Focus on Acting**			
Type	*Stimulus*	*Response*	*Initiators of change*	*Organization learning mode*	*Strategy formation*
I	Same	Same	Kaizen, BPR, TQM	Refinement	Planning as reproduction
II	Same	Different	Strategic planning	Single loop	Planning as technology
III	Different	Same	Failure, crisis	Deadlock	Planning as defense
IV	Different	Different	Learning strategy	Double loop	Planning as discovery
	Insight Inertia	**Action Inertia**			

Figure 13.1   *Four Modes of Learning (Based on Weick, 1991)*

Modern organizations face new challenges. One is that environments are becoming increasingly turbulent and unpredictable, so the need for flexibility and speed-to-market grows. The other is that innovation and early problem detection require that organizations invite more variety into their decision systems. Both these challenges counteract organizations' inclination to reduce uncertainty, and they call for new systems for governance and new forms or organizing, that is, they raise the need for improved knowledge management. Thus we witness the development of very successful enterprises that organize rather differently.

Weick (1991) analyzed the combinations of S-R couplings in Figure 13.1 and concluded that most studies of learning focus on the "same-different" coupling, but the "different-different" coupling poses the greatest challenge and the "different-same" coupling—the inability to learn in situations that call for radical reorientation—is far too common. Starbuck and Hedberg (1999) reviewed a number of studies of learning processes in organizations that experienced success or failure and concluded that organizations' ability to deal with negative feedback (noxity) often is very low, especially when failure follows a sequence of successes or when the magnitude of change signals evolve in small steps. The deadlock situation in Figure 13.1 is far too frequent in contemporary organizations, although changes in the market lead to shorter economic time zones (Williams, 1999) and an almost continuous need for renewal.

KNOWLEDGE MANAGEMENT AND THE NEW ORGANIZATIONS

Organizational learning has hitherto been studied mainly in traditional, integrated organizations and is thus typically described as an intraorganizational activity. The growing complexity of products and intense global competition have, however, made organizations increasingly dependent on partnerships and networks (Hagedoorn, 1993; Inkpen and Crossan, 1995; Larsson et al., 1998; Helleloid and Simonin, 1994). Powell et al. (1996) thus noticed: "Sources of innovation do not reside exclusively inside firms; instead, they are commonly found in the interstices between firms, universities, research laboratories, suppliers, and customers."

Partnerships represent one response to growing insights among organizations that competence or learning-based alliances can be formed in order to boost strategic learning possibilities (Sanchez and Heene, 1997). Though still rather modest, there is an increasing body of theoretical research and empirical studies that focus on organizational learning as a major purpose for collaboration. Such endeavors are typically referred to as *interpartner learning* (Hamel, 1991), *interorganizational learning* (Larsson et al., 1998), or *grafting* (Huber, 1991).

Research on interorganizational learning has focused on how single organizations learn in partnerships and strategic alliances. Because the unit of analysis has typically been two or a few collaborators, this work has not been extended to a collective of partners in a truly interorganizational perspective. A collective perspective on interorganizational learning is important because borders between partners in contemporary partnerships tend to become increasingly blurred, resulting in the emergence of new, networked forms of organizations. These are the virtual organizations of modern terms.

Although early definitions of the concept of organization envisaged organizations as tightly integrated units, a second reading does not exclude networks from this definition of organizations. Consider for example Pfiffner and Sherwood (1960): "Organization is the pattern of ways in which large numbers of people, too many to have intimate face-to-face contact with all others, and engaged in a complexity of tasks, relate themselves to each other in the conscious, systematic establishment and accomplishment of mutually agreed purposes."

These phrases might well describe a modern and virtual organization: "pattern of ways," keeping together, "mutually agreed purposes." But the concept of organization has typically been restricted to denote integrated systems where production takes place inside the organizational boundaries and the market and the competition is outside in the environment. The need for new concepts and other perspectives arises from a changing business world where an increasing number of new enterprises are characterized by partnerships, networks, shared resources, and common visions and objectives that unite many actors. And many old companies transform themselves to become more focused, cooperative, and outsourced. We find ourselves in an increasingly interconnected business world.

Concepts such as virtual organizations (e.g., Hale & Whitlam, 1997; Grenier & Metes, 1995), imaginary organizations (Hedberg et al., 1997), strategic alliances (e.g., Hamel, 1991; Harrigan, 1988), and temporary organizations (Lundin, 1996) are typically used to describe these new patterns of organizing. The common denominator is that these systems *behave* as organizations although they consist of more or less permanent and more or less loosely coupled partnerships. That is, the organizational and the interorganizational perspectives merge, and the boundaries between organization and environment are blurred. Some of these new patterns of organizing rest on rather solid legal structures, although most of them mainly rely on trust and on explicit and clear-cut gain–gain situations.

We will focus the discussion in this chapter on learning in "imaginary organizations," which is the empirical focus in our own research program that has been going on for almost a decade at the School of Business, Stockholm University.

Our definition of imaginary organizations reads as follows:

Imaginary organizations are organizations where important processes, actors, and resources appear both inside and outside of the legal unit of enterprise, both outside and inside of the accounting system and of the organization charts. Markets and hierarchies are interconnected through networks of cooperating people and coordinating information technology. Imaginary organizations are greatly facilitated through advanced IT, although IT in itself does not create imaginary organizations.

We have studied and documented a number of imaginary organizations since the early 1990s. Skandia AFS is one of them, and I will use that rapidly growing and successful company as an illustration throughout the second half of this chapter.

SKANDIA AFS: MEDIATOR IN A BOOMING FINANCIAL SAVINGS INDUSTRY

Skandia AFS (Assurance and Financial Services) is a group of companies within the leading Swedish insurance company, Skandia AB. Although the parent company was a fairly conventional insurance company until the early nineties, AFS is a highly successful, rapidly growing, and very interesting imagi-

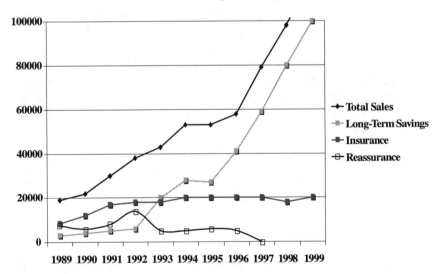

Figure 13.2 *Skandia's Transformation from Insurance Company to a Booming LTS Business*

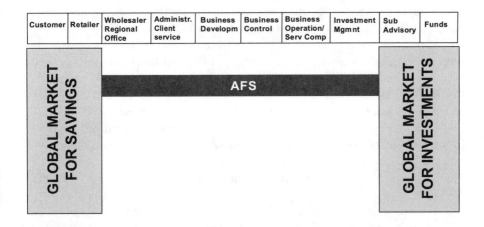

Customer	Retailer	Wholesaler Regional Office	Administr. Client service	Business Developm	Business Control	Business Operation/ Serv Comp	Investment Mgmnt	Sub Advisory	Funds

Figure 13.3   *Skandia AFS: A Mediator between Two Global Markets*

nary organization that in less than ten years totally has redefined the Skandia Group. Consider the rough diagram in Figure 13.2.

Although the insurance business together with reassurance dominated the company in 1989, long-term savings (the AFS branch) equaled insurance in 1993. The reassurance business was sold in 1997. As of June 1999 the traditional insurance business has been transferred to a partly owned (33% of voting power) joint venture called "if" with Norvegian Storebrand and Finnish Pohola. The Skandia Group has divested in its traditional platform, unlearned, and moved into a new industry where long-term savings, Internet banking, IT infrastructure, investments in NFCs, and development of new imaginary organizations (such as Skandia Life Line—networked health care) form the basis for current profits and future growth.

Skandia AFS prospers from the growing concern of people in many countries that retirement systems and other welfare arrangements are endangered and may not deliver on their promises. Therefore, families and individuals are increasing their savings. Skandia is able to collect a portion of these savings and places them with fund managers who promise to beat inflation. In short, Skandia AFS is a global savings organization with unit-link arrangements to tie those private savings to growth investments (Figure 13.3).

AFS pictures itself as a provider of focal processes (product development, packaging, and administration) that interface with those of the fund managers and that support the activities of the financial advisers. AFS's leadership uses the term *process edge* to describe a dynamic system of labor divisioning where each actor focuses on its core competencies and where repeated outsourcing takes place. When excellent and unique processes have become common knowledge in the industry, Skandia focuses on the development and packaging of financial products and provides the infrastructure and the administrative backbone. Partners sell and distribute the products, and other partners invest the money and manage the resulting funds.

Skandia AFS now operates in twenty-seven countries on four continents outside Scandinavia. Some seventy people make up the headquarters, and they are mainly located in Sweden and in Shelton, Conn., U.S.A. An additional 2,600 Skandia employees run the national companies. And these people engage some 91,000 partners in the various countries where AFS has established markets. The partners are money managers and financial advisers in the United States. In Spain, a major savings bank collects household savings for placement through Skandia. Finally, some 1.4 million customers, or "contracts," form the outer circle of the imaginary organization, Skandia AFS.

The leadership of Skandia AFS describes their company as a federation. The company operates in between a global market for savings and a global market for investments. The core company acts as an exchange system between these two markets, as shown in Figure 13.3. Partners interact directly with clients (households) and investment opportunities. AFS, like the Skandia group in general, is simultaneously a publicly quoted company with shareholders, boards of directors, and direction from the top down. Thus, the financial capital works downward through a hierarchy, and so does the structural capital—the knowledge, procedures, and manuals AFS has managed to formalize and store in its structure and processes. However, the market capital (customers and local networks) and the knowledge capital possessed by the financial advisers and fund specialists in the partner network, work from the bottom up. In the latter sense one could perhaps claim that Skandia AFS is a federative organization in which the power and dynamics come from the markets and are delegated upwards according to the principle of subsidiarity.

Imaginary organizations need one or several attracting forces, or purposes, in order to glue together their networks. Examples are:

1. Sharing infrastructure
2. Pooling financial resources, or resources that require capital
3. Pooling competencies
4. Building mutual trust between partners and also inside each participating unit
5. Building trust and relationships to and from the marketplace

Information technology is a very important coordinator within both the inner system and the outer system of the AFS network. The national companies in twenty-seven countries are connected through a global area network (GAN) and intranets that facilitate both remote management and remote administration. A global management information system is another way to keep the worldwide organization together. The IT infrastructure also allows existing national companies to provide back-office support for newly estab-

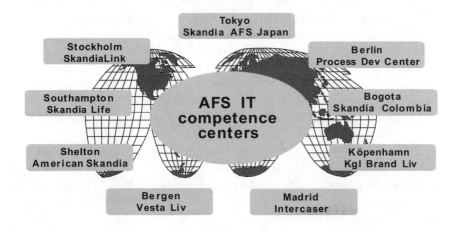

Figure 13.4   *The Global Area Network (GAN) and Its AFS Nodes*

lished subsidiaries. Thus, the back-office work for the pioneer companies in Mexico and in Japan is managed from American Skandia in Connecticut. In general, when new national companies are formed, AFS subsidiaries in other countries, together with headquarters, provide the financial products, the organization, market communication systems, and administrative programs. Years of experience in establishing green-field enterprises in national markets have resulted in a prototype that is installed and then customized to fit a new country and new markets. As a consequence of its ability to move rapidly and to be very flexible, Skandia AFS has been the first invader to establish itself on foreign national markets in many countries following deregulation. The IT resource is carried by a number of computing centers around the world (Figure 13.4).

Another important "glue" for the AFS organization has been to provide agents and financial advisers on the market with powerful IT support. Thus, 18,000 CD-ROM copies of a system called ASSESS were first distributed in the United States before Christmas 1995. The system has since been upgraded several times and extended to new users. The ASSESS system contains a multimedia presentation of American Skandia (the U.S. branch of AFS), but its real value lies in the sales-support system. AFS experts and other national expertise help the salesperson to explain various savings programs and tax consequences to the client. Also, the fund managers appear on the laptop screen to describe their business, their track record, and their investment policies. The ASSESS system does an excellent job in helping the salespeople to make the financial products understandable and to make the investment experts human and trustworthy. A new release of ASSESS with more storage capacity on CD–ROM will also contain a "virtual university" with short courses for the continuing education that money managers are required to take, pass, and have recorded in order to remain authorized. The ASSESS system illustrates several of the attracting forces that we listed previously. It is shared infrastructure in that it provides IT support and connections to AFS computing centers. It represents sharing of competence as will be further discussed in the following paragraphs. It also provides an interesting way to build trust, credibility, and recognition from the marketplace, as will also be discussed later on.

The AFS case illustrates how IT nowadays often will be an indispensable tool in managing an imaginary organization. It provides access for the organization's members to shared information resources. The structural capital just mentioned largely resides in data warehouses, application tools, and corporate intranets and extranets.

With around 2,700 on the payroll, another 91,000 partners, and more than 1.3 million customers, AFS's CEO, Jan Carendi, says that in order to lead the company he has to realize that he is managing a "voluntary organization." If these people around the world do not give their best by their own free will, he has no power to command them. In order to keep the AFS network together, he attempts to create a challenging vision, fast feedback on performance, and a "high-trust culture." Everyone in this voluntary organization has to be a "trustee" who deserves the trust of others and who trusts his or her collaborators.

The concept of trust has moved into the focus of organization research in recent years and there are strong indications that trust is especially important between actors in imaginary organizations. Voluntary performance cannot be commanded through legal frameworks. Contracts are perhaps useful when people are about to come apart, but less useful when people are about to come together. Trust is what keeps good marriages alive. Trust has little room when people divorce.

Trust is present when there is no mistrust, and mistrust is a major reason relationships are formalized in legal frameworks. But this is a negative definition and also partly misleading. Trust may well coexist with law and contracts. The legal institution of marriage or a publicly owned corporation sets the rules and this does not preclude the development of trust.

The leadership at Skandia AFS sets out to build a *high-trust culture* (HTC). This is manifested through strong emphasis on affective trust in dyadic relations and in team building in the interpersonal networks. It is also present in the emphasis on expertise (cognitive trust) and even more so in the continuous feedback from market performance. CEO Jan Carendi spends a lot of time at the head offices or touring the world to visit national companies and build interpersonal relationships. This process of establishing affective trust begins in the very elaborate recruiting procedures in which Carendi often takes part. In a series of white papers, normally published in the company magazine

New Horizons, Carendi attempts to build a boundary-spanning business culture, create internal heroes, and underpin cognitive and performative trust. Several of these trust-building processes address both the inside and the outside world of AFS.

IMAGINARY ORGANIZATIONS: NETWORKED, TRUST BASED, AND CLIENT DRIVEN

With the description of Skandia AFS as a background, let us now discuss the general structure and business logic of an imaginary organization (Figure 13.5). The great majority of imaginary organizations we have studied in our research program thus far take their starting point in the market. That is where the greatest uncertainty lies, along with the scarcity of customers that characterizes most industries today. Uncertainty in the market calls for flexibility in the production system. Thus, considerable parts of the production system are arranged as partner networks. Also, delivery systems and market communication are often handled through partners. The leader organization (IO leader) takes on the role of the *director of a businessplay*, manages the extended company, and typically faces the customers. In order to maintain leadership and power, the IO leader has to possess some strategically important core competence (Prahalad and Hamel, 1990) that provides competitive edge.

The customer base rarely consists of passive customers as "target groups," but rather of various communities of interest with which the imaginary organization seeks to establish dialogues and engage in mutual value creation. This

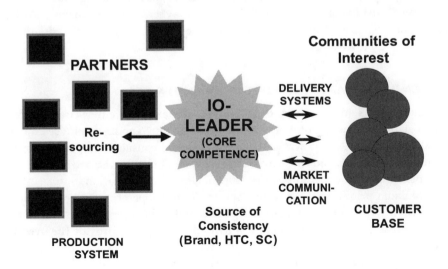

Figure 13.5 *The Structure of an Imaginary Organization*

is a way to co-opt important sources of uncertainty in the market, but also to tap into valuable mechanisms for knowledge creation to assist the enterprise in product development and customization. Since all systems, and particularly this kind of loosely coupled network, run the risk of disintegration and entropy, the IO leader has to provide some source of consistency, a force that maintains and develops the extended organization. A shared vision, a strong brand, a high-trust culture, and shared structural capital (SC) are some examples.

The business idea is expressed in the system that links the IO leader with its core competence to the customer base, and the realization of the business idea comes through resourcing of this core system by partners with other core competencies who together make the business idea viable. The *virtual enterprise* is often described as a temporary organization and sometimes as a very opportunistic and short-lived arrangement. Our empirical data suggest that imaginary organizations might well be more long-lived than traditional business organizations and that the market-sensitive network organization is designed to provide robustness and longevity in a world where economic time zones (Williams, 1999) are getting shorter.

Trust is the basis for building relationships in the network. There are, naturally, some legal contracts between partners, but trust-based relationships dominate in imaginary organizations. Legal structures might prove useful when partners divorce, but contracts are of little help in boosting peak performance in the interplay between partners who represent various core competencies. Also, superior knowledge-creating systems rely on cultures of sharing where the time to learn and the time to disseminate knowledge are crucial parameters. Such systems build on principles of sharing and mechanisms of trust in contrast to strategic alliances where the relationship mostly is legally elaborated and ownership of emerging knowledge, patents, and processes is clearly regulated.

KNOWLEDGE MANAGEMENT IN SKANDIA AFS

Skandia AFS is an imaginary organization. The extended enterprise involves almost 100,000 people of whom less than 3,000 are Skandia employees. Sales and investments, most service delivery systems, considerable parts of systems development, and the provision of legal and tax expertise are handled by cooperating partners who resource the imaginary organization.

Skandia prides itself on being "specialists in cooperation." They develop new savings products. They prototype national sales organizations that they then spread to two or three new countries per year. They provide the overall leadership and couple or uncouple links within the network.

A major part of Skandia's role concerns knowledge management. The ASSESS system is the most obvious example on an operative level. ASSESS provides tens of thousands of financial advisors in the field with supportive expertise on tax legislation, investment opportunities, and historic performance of various wealth-creating strategies. ASSESS serves as a trust builder to the client also by actually showing and presenting the investors who are going to handle the money and by putting names and faces to a networking organization that otherwise easily could be said to be abstract and evasive.

GAN, the Global Area Network, is another important instrument for knowledge creation and knowledge distribution, especially inside Skandia's core organization. GAN makes it possible to provide back-office support from sister organizations when newly established national companies go out to find customers. The systems development center in Berlin makes extensive use of the GAN infrastructure to distribute new systems and more efficient procedures.

On a strategic level, the AFS magazine *New Horizons* serves as a platform for AFS leaders and especially for the CEO Jan Carendi, from which they can formulate visions and challenges, set priorities, and name internal heroes. A series of white papers from the CEO has succeeded in "writing the organization" (Maravelias, 1999) and "editing trust" through the nine years during which AFS has grown from a minor business within the company to actually defining and being the company.

AFS makes deliberate attempts to exploit and explore variety in background, skills, expertise, sex, and age throughout the organization. Intra-organizational learning and also learning between partners is encouraged through platforms for face-to-face interaction (Skandia Future Centers) and by attempts to establish knowledge markets where knowledge can be traded as freeware or as commercial products.

KNOWLEDGE MANAGEMENT IN IMAGINARY ORGANIZATIONS

Imaginary organizations offer several interesting arenas for knowledge creation and these arenas offer rich sources of variation. The leader organization finds itself as knowledge manager in the midst of four arenas for knowledge creation (Figure 13.6). One is the CRM system where interaction with customers and between customers takes place. Building relationships with numerous clients provides rich opportunities to tap into sources of knowledge and variation, especially if market communication truly follows the one-to-one concept. The other arena invites partners in the extended organization to share and develop useful knowledge. Again, variation could make this source for knowledge creation very powerful.

A third arena consists of intra-organizational communication systems where the LO's own staff could create knowledge and produce value added. This arena is greatly improved when intranets begin to spread and be used. Intranets, combined with intelligent matching agents, have the potential to boost intra-organizational learning, especially in the sense that existing

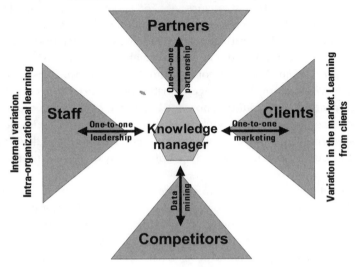

Figure 13.6 *Arenas for Knowledge Creation in Imaginary Organizations*

knowledge can be widely disseminated throughout the organization. The phrase "imagine if we knew what we know" could be taken from hopes to reality. Of course, a combination of routines that secure proper documentation, incentives to declare knowledge profiles among "publishers" and "subscribers" in the organization, and a culture of curiosity and sharing are necessary in order to release the potential that new technologies can provide. These possibilities are not only open to imaginary organizations, of course, but can be extended to include other parts of the extended network (such as partners) in ways that traditional organizations rarely can offer.

Information technologies can also augment these many dialogues between partners, clients, staff, and the IO leaders so that individual dialogues are possible, and so that the resulting knowledge is stored for further use. If one-to-one marketing is a reality, there is no reason why one-to-one partnership and one-to-one leadership could not be practiced. In addition to knowledge creation on and between these three arenas, imaginary organizations have the same opportunities to explore their outer environments (competitors, economic developments, technologies, etc.) as all other business organizations have. Data warehousing and applied data mining are then the conventional solutions.

The modes for organizational learning are closer to the models suggested by Nonaka (1991), Nonaka and Takeuchi (1995), and Baumard (1995; 1996) than to traditional interactive models based on S-R couplings. Individual knowledge is explicated and then socialized into the organizational arena. However, networks of partners or individual actors rather than formal organizations constitute the arenas for knowledge creation.

IMAGINARY ORGANIZATIONS AS CONSTELLATIONS OF NETWORKED BUSINESSES

"Unbundling the Corporation" was the message in a Spring of 1999 article by Hagel and Singer. The authors suggested that the modern enterprise often should be seen and managed as consisting of three enterprises with different business logics. The first had to do with CRM—customer relationship management. The second was about product innovation management, and the third concerned infrastructure management. Hagel and Singer claimed that these different systems should have different foci and concern themselves with different types of economic issues, such as different scarce resources that are subject to management and stewardship (recall that "economics" is the discipline of the stewardship of the "house").

Hagel and Singer identified three distinct foci of the enterprise. I would add another that deserves equal attention, namely knowledge management. From the perspective of imaginary organizations one could add a fifth, that of leadership, but this system could also be included in the knowledge management enterprise (Figure 13.7).

Hagel and Singer argued that these enterprises within the enterprise have radically different characteristics and often should be managed as separate entities. Customer relationship management must focus on the customer, while the product innovation unit should concern itself with the innovators, engineers, and lab people. Infrastructure management should focus on tangible assets. These three enterprises are guided by radically different economies.

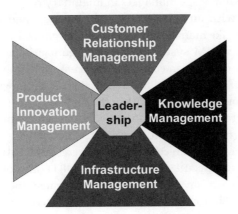

Figure 13.7   *The Unbundled Organization (Inspired by Hagel and Singer, 1999)*

Customer Relationship Management	Focus on Customers	Economy of Reach & Range
Product Innovation Management	Focus on Employees (R&D, scientists, engineers)	Economy of Speed
Infrastructure Management	Focus on Tangible Assets	Economy of Scale
Knowledge Management (and Leadership)	Focus on Staff & Partners in Networks	Economy of Trust

Figure 13.8 *The Four Enterprises of the Enterprise*

CRM attempts to maximize customer reach and delivery range. Product innovation seeks to minimize time to develop and then time to market. And infrastructure management runs under the regime of economies of scale.

Experiences from recent major mergers in the pharmaceutical industry suggest that mergers founded on the logic of infrastructure management (e.g., economies of scale in production and in the organization of sales representatives) have caused major damage to product innovation, which rarely improves linearly with scale. Arguments have thus been raised that product innovation should be spun off from the big pharmaceuticals in order to create a separate industry of pharmaceutical innovators.

In addition to the three enterprises that Hagel and Singer identified, I would add knowledge management (and leadership). Knowledge management focuses on interaction and information exchange between all humans in the networks. Knowledge managers in imaginary organizations are particularly concerned with interchange between partners and learning with the customer but also, like managers in traditional organizations, with the establishment of effective KM systems for intraorganizational learning. Knowledge management operates in economies of trust, especially in the context of imaginary organizing (Maravelias, 1999). We end up with the following identification of four enterprises within the enterprise (Figure 13.8).

There are several possible explanations why the new organizations often take the form of networks. Information technology has certainly enabled structures that were desirable before, but were rarely attainable. Transaction-cost theories (Coase, 1937; Williamson, 1981) offer other explanations; lower transaction costs have made it possible to replace hierarchies with markets. The model in Figure 13.8 offers a slightly different line of explanation: the modern complex organization consists of several enterprises that operate under rather different conditions. In times of increasing competition, shorter economic time zones (Williams, 1999), and focus on world-class core competencies, it is simply very difficult and inefficient to maintain the integrated enterprise. The imaginary organization, with loose couplings, varied outsourcing and resourcing, and people in networks of partnerships emerges as a viable opportunity, especially in terms of competing in the management of knowledge.

Let us return to Skandia AFS and apply the model to get a new perspective on the way AFS organizes and runs its imaginary organization (Figure 13.9). Skandia keeps the design and development of financial products and the creation and distribution of knowledge close to its organizational center. Thus, product innovation and knowledge management are core activities where the AFS leadership tries to maintain process edge and to build and maintain trust (high-trust culture). Customer relationship management is mainly outsourced to partners such as financial advisers (self-employed agents), banks, and so on, and so is the major part of the infrastructure that reaches customers and handles investments and funds. Skandia, however, attempts to influence large parts of the system through white papers, visionary statements, and sales support systems (such as the ASSESS system).

In summary, many new organizations will be networked organizations, which manage and coordinate a business that relies on the constructive cooperation between a number of partners who perform distinct functions. Each partner has its core competence and the pattern of resourcing varies over time, reflecting changing demands from the value-creating process in the dialogue with and between communities of clients. Although dynamic, these

Figure 13.9 *Coordinating the Four Enterprises through AFS's Leadership*

networked organizations are set up to last and accommodate changes in the market, changes in technologies and short economic time zones. Knowledge creation and knowledge management are crucial to the success and viability of these new organizations.

Thus, while managers of traditional organizations managed money, machinery, and measurements, their new colleagues will focus on meaning, respect, and trust. Trust me!

NOTE

Figures from Skandia's presentation material used with written permission of Jan Carendi (Skandia AFS's CEO).

CHAPTER 14

Managing Knowledge in Adaptive Enterprises

Stephan H. Haeckel

T he need to be adaptive creates special knowledge management requirements for large organizations. Whereas the historic emphasis on business efficiency led to a focus on the codification of *existing* knowledge (creating methods, procedures, knowledge bases, databases, and so forth), adaptiveness in the face of unprecedented change places the emphasis on managing the creation of *new* knowledge. In the sense-and-respond model for large-scale adaptiveness, three knowledge management requirements are preeminent:

- Placing people skilled at discerning patterns in apparent noise in organizational roles that are subject to high degrees of environmental uncertainty
- Providing those individuals with role-specific information support that augments their ability to make sense out of apparent noise and to invent appropriate responses
- Representing, in a systematic way, how the organization does and could create value

Organizational system designs and ad hoc processes are the two major types of knowledge that must be continually created within an enterprise to sustain adaptive behavior. This discussion on knowledge management in adaptive enterprises will be based on the sense-and-respond model, a prescription for creating and leading large organizations that can systematically deal with unpredicted change.

Parts of this chapter are extracted from *Adaptive Enterprise: Creating and Leading Sense-and-Respond Organizations*, published by the Harvard Business School Press in June, 1999.

WHY ADAPTIVENESS HAS BECOME AN IMPERATIVE

Increasingly unpredictable and rapid change is an unavoidable consequence of doing business in an Information Age, and the only strategy that makes sense in the face of unpredictable change is a strategy to become adaptive. Speed to market, customer intimacy, operational excellence, and organizational agility, however important, are not adequate strategic objectives in and of themselves. They are attributes of the real objective: successful and systematic adaptation. Adaptation implies more than agility. It requires *appropriate* organizational response to change. And when change becomes unpredictable, it follows that the appropriate response will be equally so.

In this environment, therefore, *planned* responses do not work. If the underlying reality is an inherent unpredictability in what customers will actually need, having sufficient organizational agility to get to market first with quality offerings based on customers' predictions of what they will want is a fool's errand. Adapting to the unprecedented places a premium on ad hoc processes, not on codifications of current "best practices."

Complexity theory makes an enormous contribution to our understanding of the information management requirements in unpredicted circumstances. But it is insufficient as a business model, because it does not address the unique properties of social systems—which are precisely what human organizations are. Individuals can and do make decisions *within* the system *about* the system. These decisions include if and how to change their own behaviors inside the system, the structure, the rules, and even the purpose or function of the system. For this reason, the sense-and-respond model adds *intentionality* and *purposefulness* to "complex" and "system" as essential organizational properties of adaptive enterprises.

Unpredictability stems from a fundamental and lasting change affecting more and more businesses. Harvard sociologist Daniel Bell characterized this change as a shift in the basis of wealth creation. Once based on tangible and scarce resources such as land, labor, energy, and capital, wealth is today predominantly based on information and knowledge—intangibles that are not consumed, don't wear out, and don't depreciate.[1] The software industry demonstrates the new economic importance of intangibles: the value of software resides in intellectual content captured as symbols in computer code, not in the disks on which those symbols are recorded. Software represents what economist Brian Arthur calls "congealed knowledge," as opposed to the "congealed resources" of traditional manufactured goods.[2] Increasingly, global wealth derives from codified knowledge and the ability to manipulate it at electronic speed. Because these intangibles can be transformed and transmitted so quickly, rapid and discontinuous change has become the hallmark of information-intensive industries. Uncertainty is not a passing symptom but a fact of economic life in the information era.

THE SENSE-AND-RESPOND MODEL FOR LARGE-SCALE ADAPTIVENESS

The sense-and-respond model provides large organizations with the means for meeting the challenges of discontinuity. A sense-and-respond organization does not attempt to predict future demand for its offerings. Instead, it identifies changing customer needs and new business challenges *as they happen*, responding to them quickly and appropriately, before these new opportunities disappear or metamorphose into something else. Adaptability has come to be increasingly valued in recent years, but most people have yet to come to grips with its deeper implications. To be truly adaptive, an organization must have a fundamentally new structure: it must manage information in particular ways, it must be managed as a system, and its leaders and employees must commit themselves to new behaviors and responsibilities. Traditional organizations cannot simply add adaptiveness to their current set of capabilities. They must *become* adaptive organizations. In other words, no acquired tips, habits, or techniques will transform a traditional organization into an adaptive one. Instead, large organizations must challenge long-established concepts of leadership, strategy, and responsibility.

Make-and-Sell Versus Sense-and-Respond

Successful large corporations of the twentieth-century Industrial Age have been make-and-sell organizations. Automobile manufacturers, appliance manufacturers, and even the computer makers of past decades were superbly organized to produce large quantities of products efficiently and then sell them to customers whose needs they could assume, predict, and even, to some degree, control. Human workers in Henry Ford's world functioned as parts of the machine, each carrying out a specified, unvarying sequence of tasks. In fact, the efficient offer-making machine is an appropriate metaphor for make-and-sell companies. Like most machines, such firms are designed to consistently carry out particular purposes in predefined ways. They are characterized by replaceable parts, economies of scale, and replaceable people executing repeatable procedures in accordance with prescribed business plans.

Where change occurs gradually and predictably, the concept of business-as-efficient-system depicted in Figure 14.1 is appropriate and effective. Beginning with the premise that what customers want is sufficiently predictable, leaders plan to make and sell as efficiently as possible what they predict the market will need. They create a mission statement and a strategy, expressed as a plan of action to achieve the mission.

Structure follows strategy—that is, the organization's form is designed to carry out the strategic plan in the most efficient way. A central staff manages the process by which the strategy is developed, ensures that operating executives make the commitments required to carry out the plan, and follows up

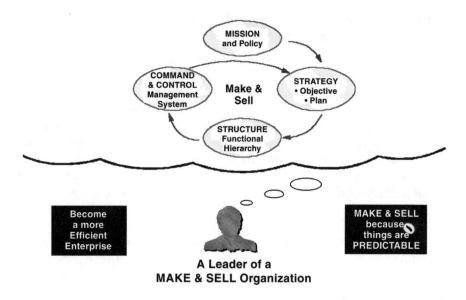

Figure 14.1   *Business as a Closed System*

to ensure that the commitments are kept—escalating exceptions to the leadership.[3] In spite of rhetoric suggesting that a new and daring strategy is developed each year, the fact is that the annual process is really an update of existing strategy because making more than midcourse corrections to a strategy is disruptive, and disruption is the enemy of efficiency.

Most disruptive of all, of course, is a change in the mission itself, because a change in mission requires a significant change in both strategy and structure. It means reorganizing the tightly integrated efficient machine that was built to carry out the old mission, which creates "breakage," implies new learning curves, and takes a lot of time. As a result, signals that a change is required tend to be ignored for as long as possible, because change breeds inefficiency. When dramatic changes in strategy are espoused, they will be resisted in the interest of avoiding the substantial cost in time and money required to "turn the ship around."

The structure-follows-strategy maxim emphasizes efficient execution of a specific strategy. Managers issue directives from the bridge on what to do and make sure that employees learn how to execute the repeatable procedures that were designed to enhance the efficiency of operations. Because they believe they can predict what products and services customers will want, their prudent assumption is that competitors can, too. Business strategy is therefore conceived as a game against competitors—a game of creating differentiated offers and barriers to entry in a quest for competitive advantage. This way of thinking continues to dominate the strategic literature, even in the

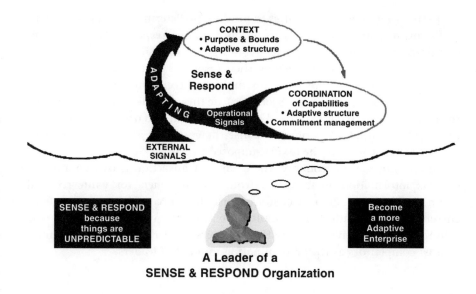

Figure 14.2 *Business as an Open System*

face of an increasing chorus of prescriptions for becoming market driven and customer-centric.

But in unpredictable markets, where customers themselves become unreliable predictors of their future needs, the efficiency model breaks down and adaptiveness must take precedence. Premiums now flow to those who excel at playing *games with customers*—to firms that can sense early and accurately what their customers currently want and who can respond in real time to those needs—individual customer by individual customer. The sense-and-respond organization is a network of modular internal and external capabilities. An organizational context provides the purpose and bounds of the enterprise, and establishes a high-level system design that structures these capabilities into dynamic responses to the current requests of individual customers. Adaptation occurs at two levels: people in the organization, adapting to changing circumstances, produce results within the current organizational context while leadership adapts the context itself.

The relationships between strategic capabilities in a sense-and-respond enterprise are defined in terms of outcomes rather than activities. Its capabilities are coordinated by using technology to keep track of commitments made between the people in roles accountable for using the capabilities to produce outcomes. Because it captures more information about individual customers, the business can differentiate its value proposition from customer to customer. Its strategy is no longer expressed as a plan, but as a design in which strategies are dynamic and reorganization is continuous.

Rather than schedule *activities* to produce predetermined offerings, adaptive firms dispatch capabilities to produce unique responses to one-off requests from customers. Customer requests, not a business plan, determine what they do and how they deploy their resources. The difference is analogous to that between a bus company and a taxi company. Bus drivers don't need customers to perform their job, because the schedule and procedures tell them where to go, what to do, and how to do it. But taxi drivers cannot begin their work without a customer, because the customer is the only one with knowledge about where the taxi is supposed to go.

In an information economy, the primary transaction is this kind of exchange: information about value (from the customer) for value received (from the producer). Because customers are the source of information about current value attributes, and the ultimate arbiter of whether the value was delivered, collaborative games with customers must replace win-lose games against competitors as the predominating mindset of leaders.

Thinking "Customer Back" Rather Than "Firm Forward"

Sense-and-respond firms operate from the customer back, not from the firm forward. Individual customer wants or needs constitute the engine driving the company's operations; they set the firm in motion. The customer occupies the center of the sense-and-respond universe. In make-and-sell companies, however, the plan comes first, driving operations from the firm forward. Most make-and-sell companies invest in market research aimed at fine-tuning their products and gathering requirements for new offerings. But such research relies heavily on predictions, focusing on current estimates of the common future needs of many customers, rather than on knowledge about the specific current needs of individual customers. In firm-forward companies, individual needs become homogenized into market segments, and new products are targeted at the most attractive segments. The firm, its plans, and the efficiency of its processes remain at the center of the make-and-sell universe.

When customer needs are stable, predictable, or controllable, businesses can afford to look inward, focusing on how to do most efficiently what they know they need to do. As long as their targets move slowly enough, these companies can refine a precision mechanism that will hit bulls-eyes over and over again.

But when customer needs become unpredictable, firms, to survive, must move their center of attention to understanding those changing needs. Adaptive organizations require, first of all, a systematic ability to search out, capture, and interpret clues about as yet emerging and unarticulated customer preferences. They must employ equal vigilance in both sensing developments that might enable new capabilities and in making sense out of environmental dynamics, such as regulatory or political changes. Like athletes in the ready position, sense-and-respond firms must excel at sensing subtle change earlier, and adapting to it faster than their competitors. Such firms can establish reinforcing cycles of success that provide profit and drive change at a pace that rivals can't match.

Sense-and-respond is not necessarily reactive. That is, it does not always mean "listen and comply." Sense-and-respond can also mean "anticipate and pre-empt," to use Adrian Slywotzky's term for its proactive form.[4] In this case the firm invests in gathering and interpreting contextual data about changes in current customer preferences. The term "anticipate" does not mean "predict," at least not in this context. It means interpreting earlier than the customer can what the customer's current needs are. This is the value that a physician adds by interpreting symptoms and test results to conclude that a patient has a specific condition, say appendicitis. The physician is not *predicting* appendicitis, but learning about it earlier and anticipating the patient's need for an appendectomy. Businesses that are very good at doing this, as the online grocery company Peapod or the bookseller amazon.com seek to be, will eventually come to know more about their customers' preferences than do the customers themselves. (If amazon.com is successful in achieving this position over a sufficiently broad scope of individual needs, its present market capitalization may actually turn out to be a realistic anticipation of its future value.)

In summary, a business has only two options: to make offers to customers or to respond to their requests. This essential difference separates make-and-sell from sense-and-respond organizations. All businesses do some degree of both, of course; and some try to institutionalize a hybrid form. Nevertheless, at the enterprise level, the two functions call for fundamentally different organizing principles. The make-and-sell company is conceived as an efficient machine for making and selling offers; the sense-and-respond company as an adaptive system for responding to unpredicted requests. The make-and-sell company concentrates on mass production, making and selling as much of the same thing as possible to achieve economies of scale. The sense-and-respond company focuses instead on modular customization, allowing it to economically produce what its customers ask for. Such companies realize economies of scope by reusing modular assets to reduce the cost of customization. The make-and-sell company excels at planning and control: orders cascade down a chain of command to be carried out by those "below." The sense-and-respond company consists of dynamic networks of capabilities making decentralized decisions based on a shared understanding of organizational purpose. The make-and-sell company schedules activities; the sense-and-respond company dispatches capabilities. Make-and-sell stresses efficiency and predictability; sense-and-respond prioritizes flexibility and responsiveness. Table 14.1 summarizes these distinctions.

Table 14.1
Comparing Make-and-Sell to Sense-and-Respond

Characteristic	Make and Sell	Sense and Respond
Mindset behind Strategic Intent	Business as an *efficient mechanism* for making and selling **offers** to well-defined market segments with predictable needs.	Business as an *adaptive system* for responding to unanticipated **requests** in unpredictable environments.
Know-How	*Embedded in products.* The expertise of designers, engineers, or actuaries is captured as a new braking system, style innovation, or insurance policy that is incorporated in an offer.	*Embedded in people and processes.* Expertise is codified in processes or identified by individual. It is applied on demand to respond to a customer request.
Process	*Mass production.* Emphasis on repeatable procedures, replaceable parts, and standard job definitions to efficiently make a high volume of the offers *defined by the company.*	*Modular customization.* Modular products and services, produced by modular capabilities that are linked to create customized responses to requests *defined by customers.*
Organizational Priority	*Efficiency and predictability.* Control company's destiny by accurately forecasting changes in market demand, and *scheduling* the production of offers at low cost.	*Flexibility and responsiveness.* Manage change, rather than try to predict it. Invest in capabilities and a system for rapidly and dynamically *dispatching* them into the processes required to respond to an individual customer request.
Profit Focus	*Profit margins on products, and economies of scale.* Make and sell as much of the same thing as possible to reduce the fixed cost per unit of production.	*Returns on investments, and economies of scope.* Reduce cost of customized responses by reusing modular assets over a wide range of product components and customers.
Operational Concept and Governance Mechanism	*Functional and sequential activity.* Centralized planning and follow-up by a specialized planning staff. Cascade orders down the chain of command in accordance with a predefined value chain.	*Networked and parallel activity.* Dynamically formed teams making decentralized decisions within a shared enterprise context. Use of a common commitment management protocol to coordinate the production of customized value chains in accordance with the business design.

Table 14.1 *(continued)*

Characteristic	Make and Sell	Sense and Respond
Information Architecture	*Functionally managed,* and optimized. Each function creates its own view of "what's going on out there" and has its own processes for "how we do things around here." Focus on providing the information needed to execute the business plan.	*Enterprise management* of essential information to create a unified view of environment and key processes. Support decentralized decision making. Focus on providing the information needed to determine what the business plan should be for a specific request.
IT Architecture	*Host-centric.* Shadowing the hierarchical top-down command-and-control management system.	*Network-centric.* Shadowing the dynamic network of people and teams.
Articulation of Strategy	*Strategy as plan* to aim defined products and services at defined markets.	*Strategy as adaptive business design* to sense earlier and respond faster to unpredictable change.

I am grateful to Vince Barabba for his contribution to the more extended versions of this table that appear in Barabba (1998) and Haeckel (1999).

A SIMPLE TYPOLOGY OF KNOWLEDGE

The term *knowledge management* covers a very broad spectrum—too broad to make valid any but the most general of statements about it. At a minimum, we should distinguish between the knowledge of knowers, and the codifications of that knowledge—the latter being the focus of much of the current literature (and investment) on the subject.

The issues associated with managing codified knowledge are essentially those of managing information: classification, establishment of attributes and relationships, access, transmission, security, relevance, accuracy, and so on. The issues related to managing knowledge itself include these, but in addition pertain directly to the management of knowers: identifying talented knowers, what they know, and how good they are at putting what they know to use. Because knowers are, either directly or indirectly, the source of all knowledge, techniques for "extracting" and codifying what knowers know are required.[5] Finally, there is the question of systems-level knowledge: knowledge that is generated as the result of exchanges between individual knowers.

To facilitate the discussion of knowledge management in adaptive organizations, we will use the following simple typology to operationalize definitions of three kinds of knowledge.

- *Know what* is manifested as cognitive knowledge about something. Its associated knowledge management tools and methods are those used to manage entity/attribute/relationship information about the knowledge, and those used to provide people with access, where relevant, to its codification through the use of such tools as data models, data, information and text retrieval software, search engines and browsers, and the like.
- *Know-how* is manifested as skill or competence. The relevant knowledge management tools are training methods. These include classroom lecture, on-the-job learning, apprenticeship, distance learning, and so forth. The codifications of know-how are called such things as recipes, methods, procedures (including software and micro code procedures), guidelines, and methodologies.
- *Know why* is manifested as systems knowledge. It incorporates context and an understanding of how the parts relate to the whole. Its codifications are typically in the form of system design representations and philosophy books.[6]

Naturally, every person in every role in a business has and requires all three types of knowledge. But the importance of each knowledge type varies by role. The leaders of sense-and-respond organizations, for example, must have, and must codify, systems knowledge (know why). Their primary responsibility is to establish and then continuously adapt the context within which people responsible for operations work. Know what and know-how knowledge are of primary importance to individuals responsible for producing results by adapting within the current organizational context—that is, important to the people responsible for operations.

We will discuss systems knowledge later. First, let's look at the adaptive process by which all humans—in fact all adaptive systems whether biological, mechanical, or ecological—sense and respond to changes in their environment.

THE ADAPTIVE LOOP: MANAGING "KNOW WHAT" AND "KNOW-HOW"

Success in iterating through a four-phase adaptive loop constitutes the crucial competence of sense-and-respond organizations. This competence depends on a particular way of managing knowers, and of managing codified information and codified knowledge to support adaptiveness by the knowers.

Both adaptive individuals and adaptive organizations must first sense the signals that augur changes in their environments and internal states. They then impose patterns on these signals to interpret the changes in the context of their experience, aims, and capabilities, separating threats from opportunities and discarding irrelevant information. Having made sense of the changes, they then decide how to respond and act on their decision. The progression from sensing to interpretation to decision to action becomes an iterative loop as the adaptive system monitors the results of its previous actions and picks up environmental changes that have occurred since the previous cycle.

Organizations of all kinds, including make-and-sell firms, follow these basic steps to adapt their behavior. Even make-and-sell firms change over time. But they try to stay in the act phase as long as possible, relying on learning curve effects to increase their profits by improving efficiency as they do the same things over and over again. They behave like closed systems, responding to environmental change only when it becomes too great to ignore. Sense-and-respond organizations, on the other hand, are aggressively open systems. Rather than ignore environmental change, they probe for advance signals, cycling through the adaptive loop as quickly as possible to leverage the changes they sense into new and profitable responses.

No organization, of course, can interpret, let alone respond to, more than a fraction of the flood of signals that pour in from the environment. Where organizations choose to place their sensory probes, and how they distinguish meaningful signals from random noise determines whether they will be sufficiently aware of "what is happening out there." Once aware, they must dispatch capabilities from their repertoire to produce an effective response. Although information technology plays an essential role in this process, human skill in recognizing patterns and thinking creatively about unanticipated challenges will continue to mark the difference between successful firms and unsuccessful ones. Knowledge management at the individual level in adaptive enterprises, therefore, must satisfy two requirements. First is the implementation of role-specific information support systems that capture the relevant signals, help interpret them with the appropriate models, feed decision processes, and link decisions to the transaction system. Second is the population of roles in highly unpredictable environments with people skilled at using metaphors and experience to impose pattern on signals that make no sense in the current context. These are the kinds of people who excel in high-performance teams, not on continuous improvement projects. They are people like Bob Hippe.

Bob Hippe was already a legendary figure in IBM in the 1960s. He was the sales rep who covered the Boeing Wichita account, and he closed an order for IBM's largest scientific computer in a way never envisioned by the authors of the company's fabled and famous (at that time) "sales cycle" process—a process that was drilled into all IBM sales trainees during their first eighteen months with the company.

Having tried for several weeks to schedule a 20-minute meeting with the chief engineer at Boeing, Hippe arrived at the appointed time to find his customer's office in turmoil. Engineers and scientists were scurrying in and out of the chief engineer's office, shouting and waving designs and carrying yellow pads with reams of equations on them. The secretary told Hippe that the chief engineer would not be able to see him that day because a major crisis had arisen: the mechanism for weighing airplanes had broken down, which meant that none of the B-52's at Wichita could take off, because federal regulations required that they be weighed prior to every flight.

Now, this is the talent that made Bob Hippe special: no sooner had the secretary finished describing the crisis, than Hippe, without hesitation, asked her whether the chief engineer would give him 30 minutes of his time in exchange for Hippe showing him how to weigh a B-52. He was immediately ushered into the office and asked what equipment he would need. Hippe's response: some string, a ruler, and a tire gauge.

When these had been found, Hippe took them out to the first B-52 on the tarmac. He wrapped the string around one of the tire pods; used the tire gauge to determine the pressure in each of the tires; calculated the average pressure of the tires in that pod; multiplied the pressure times the width and length of the rectangle formed by the string; repeated this procedure for all the pods, and totaled the results to arrive at the weight of the bomber.

What made Hippe special was not his knowledge that weight is a force, and that force equals pressure times area. Everyone involved in the crisis team had learned that in high school physics. But only Hippe, among them, was able to invoke the knowledge he had gained in an earlier and different context and apply it in this one. He was able to identify a similar pattern in an abstraction he had learned years earlier in school and in Boeing's problem of weighing an airplane—and to come up with that pattern match in the context of a sales call. In doing so, he was exhibiting exceptional skill in carrying out the primary information management function of any complex adaptive system: it must convert apparent noise into meaning at a faster rate than apparent noise comes at it.[7] Because of this, roles subject to high degrees of uncertainty must be populated by people like Bob Hippe. The United States Air Force, and other armed services, use extensive screening processes to identify individuals with this kind of aptitude. Fighter pilots and people in high-performance teams are qualified, in part, on the basis of their ability to turn apparent noise into meaning consistently better than others.

This is a very different knowledge management skill than that required of workers in Frederick Taylor's efficient organization. In that model, speed in learning and accuracy in carrying out prescribed procedures was more in demand than ad hoc creativity. Because of this priority, the use of technology to automate those well-defined procedures was the primary justification for selling computers well into the 1980s.

But in sense-and-respond organizations, the priority changes. Technology's primary contribution is to augment adaptiveness by providing role-specific support of people's adaptive loops.

ADAPTIVE ENTERPRISE DESIGN: MANAGING "KNOW WHY"

Ant colonies know how to build anthills, but individual ants do not. NASA knows how to put a man on the moon, but no human does. Both organizations demonstrate system-level behavior that is complex, coherent, and totally different than the behavior of any of its constituent parts. Their behaviors emerge from the way the parts sense and respond to their local environment and the way they relate to each other *in the context of the system to which they belong.* This system context—comprised of purpose, rules, and essential structure—*emerges* in the case of ant colonies but it is intentionally *imposed* in the case of NASA. The conscious imposition of intention is a hallmark of human organizations.

For firms operating in stable markets, a highly integrated business model—one that connects the procedures of the business in a high-level process model—may be an effective way of expressing context. Because such a model predetermines, or "hardwires," the interactions between procedures, isolated decision making is possible only within the limited scope allowed by a precisely defined plan or schedule. These tightly integrated business models correspond to Frederick Taylor's ideal and are very much suited to command-and-control management: standard operating procedures, detailed commands, and a mechanism for tight control.

As markets become less stable and assumptions about them more unreliable, this inflexible, hierarchical model no longer works well: it is no longer possible to react in time to unpredicted events "from the top down." Increased delegation of authority to the front lines is necessary. This erodes the integrity of the business model, because lower-level decisions made in splendid isolation become a recipe for incoherent enterprise behavior.

A coordinated business design may exist as a shared model in the heads of people running a small business. At some point, though, a growing business reaches a complexity threshold that makes it impossible to work from a purely mental model. The usual response to complexity is to break the system into smaller, manageable units. This leads to fragmented and locally optimized behavior by units that no longer link to each other in a consistent way. Synergies are lost. Managers develop functional perspectives of the business, thinking in terms of financial models, production models, or marketing models. They may also fragment their thinking horizontally, by cross-functional process. Some add yet another dimension of anti-systemic disaggregation: a set of independently managed company-wide projects. They divide and delegate responsibilities in the interest of clarifying responsibility and speeding up decision making. But they cannot possibly "keep in mind" all that is necessary to ensure coordinated, coherent behavior that cuts across lines of designated responsibility.

Leaders of large enterprises must design an enterprise that exhibits coordination and coherence. To do so in an unpredictable environment requires the will and competence to design and manage the organization as a complex, adaptive *social system*. Such systems are intrinsically dynamic, unstable, and dependent on an ability to adapt rapidly to chance events. For this reason, their specific behaviors cannot be predicted, and therefore cannot be prespecified. In this situation, coherent, system-level behavior is possible only by *governing* rather than dictating subsystem behaviors. The sense-and-respond approach to enterprise leadership and governance is called "context and coordination." It requires leaders to create, promulgate, and enforce an unambiguous organizational *context*. Then they must develop a system of *coordination* to govern, but not dictate, individual behaviors.

THE LEADER'S ROLE: PROVIDING CONTEXT AND COORDINATION

The word *context*, popularly taken to mean information providing an explanatory background, has a much more specific meaning in the sense-and-respond model. Organizational context encompasses three basic parts: the organization's reason for being, its governing principles, and its high-level business design. Unlike typical mission and vision statements, which propose a (sometimes inconsistent) mix of goals and principles, a reason for being statement unequivocally defines the organization's primary purpose—the one outcome that justifies its existence. It also identifies the primary beneficiary of that outcome and any absolute constraints on how it is to be achieved. For example, the Employee Benefits division of Old Mutual, the largest South African insurance company, recently converted its mission statement into a reason for being. In place of a mission to provide quality benefits packages (something they must do in order to exist), they identified what they exist to do: "Enhance the financial security of individuals through group arrangements."

Governing principles set forth the organization's unreachable limits on action, establishing boundaries that its members must always observe in their pursuit of the firm's purpose. One of the Employee Benefits division's governing principles, for example, is "We will never outsource, and will always invest in, those competencies and resources designated as distinctive: relationship management, our brand, our capability to construct profitable responses to clients, and our intellectual capital." Governing principles also establish the outcomes that the enterprise must deliver to its other important constituents. If the reason for being has identified customers as the primary constituent, and defined the bundle of value attributes, or value proposition, that the firm will deliver to customers, then the governing principles will establish the firm's other constituents (shareholders, employees, and the community, for example) and specify what the firm must deliver to these parties before it begins making all trade-offs in favor of the primary constituent. Governing principles (which are different from *guiding* principles, which identify behaviors that will help the organization succeed) define the things the organization must do to exist. The reason for being defines what the enterprise exists to do. It is the "why" that gives, or should give, meaning to all organizational activities, tasks, and plans.

The third element of context is the high-level business design. This is a systems design, which implies that creating and managing it successfully will require an understanding of what it means to manage an organization as a system.

Managing Organizations as Systems

The high-level business design imposes a structure on a network of strategic capabilities that transforms them into a value-producing system. A system is a collection of components that interact with each other to produce a function that cannot be produced by any subset of the components. By definition, a system produces synergy—not in the sense of producing more than the sum of its parts, but in the sense of producing something *different* than the parts can produce individually or in groups. The system design shows how the parts relate to one another, thereby providing the "know why" systems context for each of the parts.

Capabilities should be thought of as subsystems that have the potential of producing one or more specified outcomes. The potential is made real when a human being is assigned to an organizational role and made accountable for delivering the outcomes specified. The relationships of those capabilities, both inside and outside the organization, are defined in terms of the outcomes they owe one another—the subsystem outcomes essential to achieving the enterprise reason for being. As technology drives down the cost of doing business on the Internet, the proportion of a firm's value proposition that is created outside its internal structure will increase rapidly and the quality of the high-level business design, more than proprietary ownership of capabilities, will determine an organization's success.

An adaptive social system must be managed by focusing on the interactions between roles, not the activities of the roles. In the sense-and-respond model, this is accomplished by managing the commitments between roles. A universal, general, rigorous, and scalable commitment management protocol is used for this purpose, making it possible for technology to replace the large central staff in keeping track of the dynamics of inter-role commitments—of who owes what to whom.

Together, the three components of context tell accountable, empowered people where the organization is headed, the boundaries on their actions, and how what they do relates to what others do and to organizational purpose. A well-articulated context provides an unambiguous framework for individual activity, aligning and bounding organizational actions without dictating what those actions should be. It leaves empowered individuals free to choose the best responses to unanticipated requests within a unifying framework of unambiguous purpose, principles, and structure.

Developing and adapting organizational context establishing the "know why," and populating organizational roles with people who have the adaptive skills required (the know what and know-how), is the sole responsibility of leadership in sense-and-respond organizations. The competence required to do this well differs considerably from the problem-solving skills that many senior managers still consider their principal work, and that got many of them where they are.

Coordinating Commitments Rather Than Controlling Activities

Leaders' responsibility does not end with creating context. They must ensure that organizational behavior accords with it. This requires tracking the important commitments negotiated among accountable, empowered people. Defining organizational roles in terms of commitments made to deliver particular outcomes to particular internal or external customers puts appropriate emphasis on the *interaction* of system elements, not on their actions. It also emphasizes the system-defined outcomes required of these roles—that is, their contribution to organizational purpose—as opposed to the procedures required to produce that contribution. People in roles defined this way come to understand that they are not accountable for their actions but for the *consequences* of their actions.

Coordinating commitments, rather than supervising activities undertaken to meet them, is a crucial distinction. Supervising activities is the focus of make-and-sell management, the function of which is to keep the organizational machine running smoothly by making sure that people perform specified tasks at or above specified levels of productivity and quality. In a sense-and-respond organization, roles are not defined in terms of activities because responding effectively to unanticipated customer requests requires the continual invention of new ways of doing things. Sense-and-respond leaders must manage the dynamically interlocking sets of commitments required to marshal a one-off response consistent with the enterprise context. Deciding *how* those commitments are met—the processes used to produce the outcomes—falls to those making the commitments within the limits established by governing principles.

MANAGING THE SENSE-AND-RESPOND TRANSFORMATION

Some executives have already begun to adopt the sense-and-respond model. Reg Munro, who retired recently as Executive General Manager at Old Mutual Insurance in South Africa, has led an executive team of the Employee Benefits division through the intensive process of creating a reason for being, governing principles, and a customer-back high-level business design. He acknowledges the difficulties of "trying to introduce a radically different idea in a time of major industry and environmental change." He goes on to say, "Of course, that's the very reason it has become necessary. Despite the very real problems experienced to date, I am convinced that the sense-and-respond transformation is a nonnegotiable requirement for managing businesses in the future." Vince Barabba, the executive general manager responsible for developing and implementing the strategy development process at General Motors, looked for places where the company could benefit from specific applications of the sense-and-respond model both in the short and the long term. He developed a multistage strategic framework to guide GM's transition from a "mainly make-and-sell to a mainly sense-and-respond" hybrid. The recent introduction of the On Star mobile communications service is one early example of a customer-back, sense-and-respond extension of GM's value proposition. And Ann Drake, CEO of DSC Logistics, has made the transformation to sense-and-respond a strategic imperative. These pioneers have discovered that changing from the make-and-sell to the sense-and-respond model requires transformation, not merely reformation.

Transforming a system involves changing both its purpose and its structure.[8] Leaders must take into account the effects on the whole system of each change they make to any part of it. A system cannot be improved, much less transformed, by making isolated adjustments to individual capabilities. The transformation from make-and-sell, however, should not, and probably could not, happen all at once. Transformation, by its very nature, is not incremental change. But the process that achieves it can be gradual. There is nothing incremental, for example, about the change from water to ice, yet it is possible to cause this transformation by gradually lowering the temperature of water.

Small units of large companies can make themselves islands of sense-and-respond in an ocean of make-and-sell. Entire companies have developed certain sense-and-respond capabilities, but not others. In general, leaders should focus first on the particular business areas experiencing the most unpredictable change. These will benefit most from sense-and-respond capabilities. Most make-and-sell organizations will, like GM, evolve into hybrids of make-and-sell and sense-and-respond, developing sense-and-respond capabilities only as these create value for their customers. The competencies required to create and manage large, adaptive organizations are rare and will have to be developed. Many firms will nevertheless undertake the transformation because, in the long run, they have no alternative—survival in our age of discontinuity depends on it.

The premise of the sense-and-respond model is increasing marketplace unpredictability. For large enterprises, the promise of this model is systematic and successful adaptation without sacrificing the benefits of scale and scope.

In between acceptance of the premise and realization of the promise lies a new way of thinking about strategy, structure, and governance.

Sense-and-respond is not a universal prescription. Even in an information economy, some firms will find and exploit important niches for predictable products and services. Furthermore, the rate at which individual organizations become information intensive will vary, allowing some more time than others to manage the transition. Because the transformation to sense-and-respond will require such fundamental change in the way people lead and work, it is very important that leaders accept and internalize the premise as a first priority. For this reason, the first step for a prudent leader is to launch an investigation of whether they should expect an increasingly discontinuous future, and, if so, what this implies for their business.

How will a business know when it has completed the transformation to sense-and-respond? In one sense, of course, it never gets there if "there" means finding another oasis of stability. The challenges of *becoming* a sense-and-respond organization give way to the challenges of *being* a sense-and-respond organization. Further transformations are likely to become necessary—not *to* the sense-and-respond model, but *within* it. Systematic adaptiveness requires that context be continually reviewed and adapted. Normally, the business design will adapt most rapidly, the principles more slowly, and the reason for being rarely. Because a new reason for being establishes a different purpose, which may imply a different structure, changing the reason for being is likely to require yet another transformation. But, because of their modularity and type of governance, transformations are much less traumatic for sense-and-respond organizations. Like other living systems, sense-and-respond organizations must continue to adapt, even if that means continuous transformation, or they will perish. Those that succeed will be proficient in managing know why, as well as know what and know-how. And the knowers in these adaptive enterprises will no longer view change as a series of problems to be solved, but as an indispensable source of energy and growth.

NOTES

1. Bell (1973).
2. Arthur (1990).
3. The demise of the central staff, which occurred in virtually every large company in the 1970s and 80s as these staffs proved unable to cope with the pace of change, created a governance vacuum. These staffs, which provided the "control" of command and control, have not been replaced to this day, except by pseudo management systems involving a financial model and carefully crafted statements of mission, vision, and values. But "communicate and hope" is not a viable replacement for command and control. The sense-and-response governance system outlined in this chapter and described in detail in Haeckel (1999) is called "context and coordination." It uses technology to carry out the commitment management function of the defunct large central staff, and can be used to govern make-and-sell functional hierarchies as well as sense-and-respond capability networks.

4. Adrian Slywotzky coined this description of proactive sense-and-respond in the Foreword of Haeckel (1999).
5. The techniques available today are rudimentary. They include the transcription of what people know and can articulate and interviewing strategies to elicit from subject matter experts some of what they know they know but have difficulty articulating. Recent research in neuroscience suggests that a substantial amount— perhaps an overwhelming percentage—of what we know remains at the subconscious level. In short, we may not know most of what we know, and must await those unpredictable moments of inspiration, insight, and intuition to become aware of what is in our cognitive repertoire. Efforts to understand how to gain access to this cache are in their infancy. See Gerald Zaltman (1995) for an interesting and promising example.
6. This typology is adapted from a similar one shown by James Brian Quinn in a talk given to the trustees of the Marketing Science Institute on April 27, 1999.
7. Lloyd (1995).
8. Ackoff (1994).

CHAPTER 15

New Metrics:
Does It All Add Up?

David J. Skyrme

INTRODUCTION
T
he knowledge economy has entirely different characteristics than those economies that came before it. It needs new rules, new forms of governance, and new ways of gauging success. Old ways of managing and measuring need updating. This chapter considers the kinds of measures that are needed to guide managers and policy makers alike. It starts by considering the context in which any new metrics will apply. The limitations of widely used industrial-era measures are then discussed. Four types of measurement focus are reviewed: asset- or value-based systems, benchmarking and assessment tools, action-oriented performance systems, and benefit chains. A strong theme that emerges in all four strands is the need for metrics of intellectual capital. Several pioneering examples of intellectual capital measurement systems are compared, and some practical guidance given. The chapter concludes with some of the challenges and implications of these new approaches, which defy the precision we generally seek for metrics.

NEW ERA, NEW RULES

Although forward-looking writers like Peter Drucker and Karl Erik Sveiby wrote about the emerging knowledge economy and knowledge based companies over a decade ago (for example, see Drucker, 1988a and Sveiby, 1987), it is only during the last few years that these topics have achieved widespread attention in management and policy circles. Initially there was some skepticism that knowledge management was a fad, but as examples emerge of good practice and significant bottom-line benefits (e.g., Skyrme and Amidon,

1997), most informed people now realize that knowledge is fundamental to future prosperity and wealth.

As has been indicated earlier in this book, the majority of large organizations have some form of knowledge initiative, and a growing number of public agencies and governments have also taken on board the need to address knowledge within their policies. Recent examples of the latter are The World Bank's latest development report, entitled *Knowledge for Development* (World Bank, 1998) and the U.K. government's latest white paper on competitiveness, entitled *Building the Knowledge Driven Economy* (DTI, 1998). At both firm and national level, knowledge is becoming a primary, and perhaps even the most important, economic factor.

A consequence of this growing interest in knowledge is a changing economic landscape and new ways of working. The environment that will dominate our work lives in the future will be characterized by:

- *Growth in knowledge workers*: Already it has been estimated that some 70 percent of workers in the developed world are primarily working with information and knowledge. Even in factories, much formerly physical work has been automated with workers now handling information.
- *Knowledge-intensive businesses and industries*: Businesses like pharmaceutical companies and management consultancies depend almost exclusively on the knowledge base of their professionals and managers—scientists, engineers, financial analysts, marketers, and so on. Two of the world's largest and fastest growing industries are financial services and education—both knowledge intensive. The biotechnology industry barely existed a decade ago.
- *Networked and virtual structures*: The dynamic nature of work means that enterprises have to continually restructure to adjust to changing demands, using structures such as the virtual organization described in earlier chapters. More attention needs to be given to ensure that knowledge is not lost in any restructuring.
- *Information and knowledge products*: An increasing number of products that are almost 100 percent information or knowledge are now on the market. These range from online information services, consultancy, and sales of intellectual property. For example, U.S. license revenues from patents are now estimated to be worth more than $100 billion annually, compared with just $3 billion in 1980.
- *Reusable information and knowledge*: One characteristic of information and knowledge that defies the normal economic rules of scarcity is that of reuse. You can sell the same piece of information or knowledge many times over. Even after it has been transferred from seller to buyer, unlike a physical product, the seller still retains it for future use or resale.
- *New technologies*: The Internet is revolutionizing almost every business. The constraints of time and geography are sharply diminished and the

cost of conducting many business activities significantly reduced. Other technologies, such as intelligent agents, are making it easy to bring to a user's desktop relevant information from wherever it might reside in the world. Technology is making it easy to access and widely distribute knowledge.

- *New markets*: New electronic markets are emerging as places to trade. Fast information flows, for example, on pricing, remove many of the inefficiencies in existing markets. As well as conventional goods, such as those traded at online auction site eBay (http://www.ebay.com), knowledge in the form of publications, online advice sessions or master-classes is being sold by organizations such as Bright (http://www.bright-future.com) using a specially designed knowledge trading platform named IQPORT (http://www.iqport.com).
- *New perspectives*: The free flow of information and knowledge across global networks is creating a greater sense of awareness of ethical and governance issues by many individuals and organizations. We are likely to see a growing interest in knowledge ethics, addressing issues such as ownership and use of knowledge for the public good (such as genetic knowledge).

These developments mean that the way we view, regulate, and report on economic performance, company results, and a whole host of economic and environmental variables will need to change significantly. There are several obvious consequences of these developments if the knowledge economy is to evolve smoothly. Clearly there is a need for more international harmonization. At the legal and regulatory levels, this requires agreed standards for electronic commerce. It also requires common approaches to data gathering and statistics. At the commercial and technical level, rules are needed for taming "wild" intelligent agents that trade with each other, because left to their own devices they could create high volatility in knowledge markets. Another consequence is the need for forums and structures in which to develop regulatory frameworks for trading and governance. These could be extensions of existing frameworks such as the World Trade Organization, but the pace of development in the knowledge economy, as exemplified by the Internet and the resultant many gray areas in legislation, means that existing bodies are usually too slow to react. Each of these issues, and more, warrants intensive ongoing discussion and the implementation of new methods and frameworks appropriate to the knowledge economy. The field of metrics is a typical one in which significant changes to the status quo are needed.

ANOMALIES AND ANACHRONISMS

How can it be that an apparently healthy advertising company (Saatchi and Saatchi in 1987), at least according to its published financial accounts, is actually in terminal decline? How can it be that a biotechnology company (British Biotechnology in 1997) that has never sold a product is worth over $2 billion? How can it be that the market value of amazon.com, which has not yet made a profit, is five times that of profitable bookseller Barnes and Noble, whose revenues are ten times larger? The principal reason, apart from stock market sentiment, is that traditional financial accounting focuses primarily on tangible assets. Yet the examples cited are where knowledge assets are primarily involved. Charles Kaufman, in a letter written to *Business Week* in 1997, noted that $148.5 billion would buy Microsoft or five large companies combined—Boeing, McDonalds, Texaco, Time Warner, and Anheuser-Busch, or all 40 companies ranked 961–1,000 in the "Global 1000." He wrote (Kaufman, 1997): "Either the former is overpriced or the others are underpriced."

In fact, Microsoft is one of a large number of companies whose market value is ten times or more their book value. Another example from the list, McDonald's, according to financial accounts is worth a fraction of Burger King. The reason is that the latter is part of Diageo and its asset base reflects goodwill when it was taken over, yet McDonald's, whose growth is all internally generated and not the result of mergers, can show no similar asset on its balance sheet. In short, today's financial accounting is becoming increasingly irrelevant for the knowledge economy. Baruch Lev, a typical critic of current methods writes (Lev, 1997): "Conventional accounting performs poorly with internally generated intangibles such as R&D, brands and employee talent—the very items considered the engine of modern economic growth."

These are only some of the reasons why financial accounts are losing relevance. In a study of how external financial reporting might help firms, Burns and colleagues found only three areas, other than reporting demanded by law, where they had any usefulness: influencing external judgment, comparisons where uniform financial procedures were used, and feeding data into management reporting systems. They concluded (Burns, Scapens, and Turley, 1996): "The procedures of external reporting are quite remote from the day-to-day operations of the business, and have no direct influence on management decisions."

In summary, financial metrics look backwards and focus on physical assets. What they do not report are the "hidden" intangible assets that are on average several times those of the tangible assets. In June 1997, the ratio of market to book value for all the Dow Jones Industrial companies was 5.3, a figure that was closer to 1 when Nobel Prize winner for economics James Tobin analyzed these differences in 1961. This growing discrepancy between market and book value is largely attributable to intellectual capital, the intangibles of the business that underpin future growth. Intellectual capital includes assets such as brands, customer relationships, patents, trademarks, and of course, knowledge.

Financial accounting is therefore something of an anachronism in today's knowledge economy. It is a legacy of the industrial era and of the accounting methods developed by Paccioli in the fifteenth century. The argument for intellectual capital accounting is therefore growing strongly. Proponents cite several reasons why it is an appropriate form of measurement for the new economy:

- It more truly reflects the actual worth of a company.
- Demands are growing for effective governance of intangibles, of which social and environmental reporting is already evident.
- What gets measured, gets managed—it therefore focuses management attention on protecting and growing those assets that reflect value.
- It supports a corporate goal of enhancing shareholder value.
- It provides more useful information to existing and potential investors.
- It makes for more efficient stock markets, in that investors are better informed of the underlying business fundamentals, and thus price fluctuations are minimized and the long-term cost of capital reduced.

As you look around you will see many other anomalies. Value, for example, is very context dependent. The same information at a different time and place has different value. There is information free on the Internet that only hours before was handsomely paid for by market analysts or news subscribers. A further example illustrates another characteristic of the knowledge economy: combinatorial value. MCI, the subject of a merger in 1997, was valued by BT at around $16 billion, yet by Worldcom at $24 billion. Combining different assets in different ways gives rise to different sets of values. Thus the particular combination of BT's portfolio with Worldcom's was seen as more valuable than another combination (at least by Worldcom!).

NEW MEASURES OF SUCCESS

In the knowledge economy success is not just measured by financial metrics. In fact, for many citizens, it has never been so. I recall the days in the 1970s when Italy was deemed the "poor" country in Europe, at least in financial terms. Yet any traveler could find a populace with verve for life and full of enjoyment. It is no accident that bellwether countries, like Sweden, put the quality of life of its citizens as an important measure of success. In its *Tomorrow's Company Inquiry*, the RSA identified that a company should also manage and be judged by the quality of the relationships a company has with its stakeholders—customers, employees, local community, and so on. Its final report comments (RSA, 1996): "The companies which will sustain competitive success in the future are those which focus less exclusively on financial measures of success—and instead include all their stakeholder relationships, and a broader range of measurements, in the way they think and talk about their purpose and performance."

In seeking what range of factors to measure, the reports on the competitiveness of different countries from two competitors—The World Economic

Table 15.1
The Massachusetts Innovation Index

Inputs (16) (Resources or Ingredients)	Processes (9) (Recipes)	Results for People and Business (8)
Human resources	Business innovation	Job growth
population growth	industry value added	Average wages
education level	value of intangible assets	Income distribution
assessment scores	Commercialization	Export sales
Technology	licence royalties	Business climate
per capita R&D	FDA drug approval rates	New industry clusters
corporate R&D	Entrepreneurship	
Investment	no. of "gazelle" companies	
venture capital	innovation awards	
research tax credit use	initial public offerings (IPOs)	
Infrastructure	Idea generation	
ISDN availability	patents files	
Internet connectivity		
classroom Internet access		
international airline routes		

Forum, Geneva (WEF, 1999) and IMD, Lausanne (IMD, 1999)—have some instructive indicators. The categories of metric that they evaluate include a county's technological infrastructure, its education system, quality of government and management, openness to trade, and overall infrastructure. Another instructive approach is that of the Massachusetts Innovation Index. A consortium of academics, business leaders, and state government developed a set of metrics that, "more clearly identify and better explain the essential ingredients, dynamics and comparative values of the innovation economy" (Massachusetts Technology Collaborative, 1997). An interesting feature of this is the grouping of its 33 indicators into three categories that can be considered resources (inputs), recipes (processes), and results (Table 15.1).

Too frequently national indicators consider only inputs. For example, a regular publication by U.K. authorities is the R&D scorecard. This ranks companies according to the proportion of revenues they invest in R&D. OECD has also spent much effort in detailing methods of measuring and normalizing R&D statistics, through its "Oslo" and "Frascati" manuals, so that international comparisons can be made. However, the methods are strongly geared toward traditional models of innovation such as converting science inputs into material products, rather than more suitable metrics for the knowledge economy. To be fair, the OECD has addressed the problem and identified five categories of indicators relevant to the knowledge economy: inputs, stocks and flows of knowledge, knowledge outputs, knowledge networks, and levels of education and learning (OECD, 1996). It gives four reasons why knowledge metrics will never be as comprehensive and rigorous as those of traditional indicators:

1. The lack of standard recipes for converting inputs to outputs
2. No reliable way of pricing knowledge
3. Difficulty in assessing the stock of knowledge, because knowledge creation is not necessarily an addition to this stock, nor is its depletion recorded
4. No standard accounting definition analogous to traditional national accounts

The very intangible nature of much knowledge, particularly tacit knowledge in people's heads, will mean that many of these issues will remain for a long time. The last point is more readily addressable but governments have been slow to do so. Even as economic output has evidently shifted from industrial production to services, standard industrial classifications (SIC codes), against which many statistics are collected, have not kept pace. For example, the whole of the software and services has typically been collapsed into a single code while different kinds of metal products have their own distinctive codes. Belatedly, a new North American Industry Classification System (NAICS) recognizes over 300 distinct new industries and has introduced a new information sector that embraces publishing, software, motion pictures, broadcasting, and telecommunications. However, it will not be until 2002 that data collection and analyses fully come into line. Nevertheless, there are distinct trends toward new metrics.

This macroeconomic perspective highlights a couple of points that are essential if we are to develop any sensible effective metrics for the new economy. First, there must be a common and relevant classification of goods and services in the new economy. Second, there must be distinction between inputs, outputs, and outcomes.

METRICS FOR MANAGERS

Analysis of which metrics are relevant for managers in knowledge intensive businesses suggests that there are four areas of focus, abbreviated here to the acronym ABBA:

- Asset—focus on important, often intangible, assets; this focus also includes valuation of a company or parts of a company for mergers and acquisition, management buy-outs, and so on

- Baseline—benchmarking core activities against those of "best in class," not necessary in the same industry
- Benefits—understanding the causal relationships between activities and their outcomes
- Action—performance measurement with a view to prioritizing activities and driving management behavior

VALUE-BASED SYSTEMS

The asset focus is represented in value-based systems such as EVA™ (Economic Value Added). Developed by New York consultancy Stern Stewart & Co, this provides a measure of return on capital employed. To develop this measure, many anomalies of current accounting systems are removed through adjustments—over 150 in all. A typical adjustment is to capitalize R&D, thus recognizing it as an investment rather than an expense. It is possible to capitalize R&D under certain circumstances in formal accounts, but the standards are rigorous and many companies do not feel it worth the effort. EVA and most similar systems focus attention on the growth in asset value, making future cash flow projections feature prominently. Therefore, knowledge of investment in intellectual capital and developments in the pipeline are important tools to assess this accurately. But there are no formal requirements or standards for doing this. Many companies, particularly pharmaceutical companies with long product lead times, selectively disclose relevant information, such as details of their drug development pipeline, to analysts. Companies seeking equity funding similarly disclose much more relevant and detailed information in their prospectuses than is the case later.

EVA is also used as a management tool, fairly widely in the United States though less so in Europe. It is claimed that it forces managers to act in a way that focuses on good asset management and development. One of its critics as a management tool, Professor Keith Bradley, likens its use to having an "elevator mentality": "You know it is going up or down, but you don't know how you got there. There is little understanding of cause and effect" (Bradley, 1997). Nevertheless, value-based approaches are widely used by analysts. There is also a whole range of other measurement systems that come into this category, such as brand valuation methodologies like that of Interbrand.

BASELINE ASSESSMENTS

The baseline focus is exemplified by benchmarking, in which an organization evaluates the level and quality of its practices against other organizations, ei-

---

EVA is a trademark of Stern Stewart & Company.

ther individually through peer visits and meetings, or collectively through an independent clearinghouse. If knowledge is a fundamental plank of the new economy, then an organization needs a good set of practices to manage and exploit it. Therefore, knowledge management should also be one of the activities that organizations benchmark. One of the most widely known knowledge management assessment tools and benchmarking programs is KMAT™ (Knowledge Management Assessment Tool) jointly developed by Arthur Andersen and APQC (American Productivity and Quality Center). Organizations complete a set of questions about their knowledge management practices. These are then aggregated and participants can compare their ratings with those of various industry, geographic, and other clusters. They fall into four categories: leadership (including linking knowledge management to business strategy), technology (including the development of computer-based organizational memory), culture (including the existence of a climate where learning and innovation is encouraged), and measurement and process (linking knowledge management to financial results). Needless to say, factors in the last group concerning measurement showed the greatest gap between organizations' aspirations and their current performance. A comprehensive 50-question checklist divided into ten categories can be found in Skyrme (1999). As well as factors covered by KMAT, they also include knowledge products and services and external marketing. Such tools have been found to be good diagnostics in directing attention to areas where better knowledge management practice will make a difference (Figure 15.1).

The benefits focus is closely linked to the action focus but forces people to articulate clearly how various benefits are achieved. We have to get away from managers claiming credit when things go well and finding all kinds of external factors as excuses when they do not! Useful tools are business modeling and benefit chains that demonstrate the interdependencies. In knowledge management, for instance, there is now a good repertoire of cases in which knowledge management has been clearly demonstrated to save costs, improve customer service, shorten time to market for new products, and a whole host of other visible benefits. The principal difficulty is that, as with other infrastructure investments such as information technology, the costs are generally clearly identifiable but the benefits are often diffused and not as predicted. An example is the installation of an intranet—the hardware and software costs are well known, but a key benefit may be the saving of small amounts of time of many professionals throughout the organization. Figure 15.2 shows a typical benefits chain for a knowledge management project.

The final focus is an action-based one. It is based on the adage that "what gets measured, gets managed." Many companies now use performance measurement systems that add nonfinancial metrics to guide management ac-

KMAT is a trademark of Arthur Andersen.

Key Dimensions

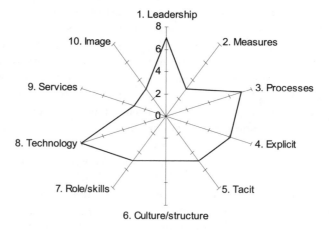

Figure 15.1 *Example of the Result of a Knowledge Management Assessment (Skyrme, 1999)*

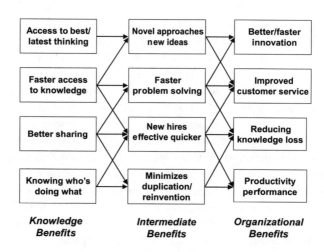

Figure 15.2 *A Knowledge Management Benefits Chain (Adapted from Wiig, 1994)*

tion. One of the most common is the Balanced Business Scorecard. It balances financial measures with measures related to customers, internal processes, and innovation. Another is the EFQM (European Foundation for Quality Management) excellence model that has five categories of enablers (including people and processes) and five results categories (including customer satisfaction and impact on society). Critics of these models argue that they do not explicitly focus on intangible assets such as knowledge, and in practice tend to drive short-term behaviors. The next version of the EFQM model meets part of this criticism by adding metrics for innovation, knowledge, and management of partnerships. However, there are already in existence several measurement and management systems that do explicitly address intellectual capital (Skyrme, 1999).

INTELLECTUAL CAPITAL MEASUREMENT SYSTEMS

The first stage of any measurement system is the classification of things to measure. For intellectual capital, an increasingly popular classification divides intellectual assets into three categories:

1. *Human capital*: what is in the minds of individuals—knowledge, competencies, experience, know-how, and so on
2. *Structural capital*: "that which is left after employees go home for the night"—processes, information systems, databases, and so on
3. *Customer capital*: customer relationships, brands, and trademarks

There are variants on such a classification. One is to separate out those assets protected by law—intellectual property. This includes trademarks, patents, copyrights, and licenses. The point of classifying is to develop a set of measures that can be used to assess progress. Edvinsson and Malone (1997), for example, report 90 measures in five groups developed by insurance company Skandia:

1. *Financial (20)*: income per employee, market value per employee, and so on
2. *Customer (22)*: number of customer visits, satisfied customer index, lost customers
3. *Process (16)*: administrative error rate, IT expense per employee
4. *Renewal and Development (19)*: training per employee, R&D expense/administrative expense, satisfied employee index
5. *Human (13)*: leadership index, employee turnover, IT literacy

These five categories are the key groups found in the Skandia Navigator, one of the most publicized intellectual capital models. Although it has similarities to the balanced scorecard, there are a couple of significant differences. First, the elements are drawn from an intellectual capital hierarchy. Second, Skandia makes much use of representing the model as a visual metaphor alongside a rich language to aid management communication. The Navigator is now widely used in Skandia as a management tool, and since 1994 the company has published IC indicators for some of its businesses in twice yearly Intellectual Capital Supplements to its financial reports. There is also a

Competencies	External Structure	Internal Structure
G r o w	t h / R e n	e w a l
E f	f i c i e n	c y
S t	a b i l i	t y

Figure 15.3 *Outline of Intangible Assets Monitor (Adapted from Sveiby, 1997)*

PC-based system, Dolphin, which allows managers to get real-time updates on their key indicators.

Another system is Karl Erik Sveiby's Intangible Assets Monitor (Sveiby, 1997). This divides intangible assets into external structure, internal structure, and competence of people. A particularly interesting feature of Sveiby's model is a subcategorization of indicators into those associated with efficiency, stability, and renewal/development (Figure 15.3). Thus stability in competencies may be an indicator of staff turnover, and renewal/development in the external structure may be the number of "competence enhancing customers"—those that stretch the organization's capabilities and draw it into new products and services.

A more mathematically rigorous and sophisticated system is the Inclusive Value Methodology (IVM™) of Professor Philip M'Pherson. This combines financial and nonfinancial factors into hierarchies of value. Values are assigned to each factor on a scale of 0 to 1, where 0 represents the worst possible and 1 represents perfection. Teams developing a model determine what factors to include and can assign weightings to each of them. A computer model works up through the hierarchy and calculates weighted metrics for each group of factors. It also allows sensitivity analysis, which identifies where management effort is best spent in improving the overall result.

A similar approach has been developed by Göran Roos and colleagues in their IC Index™. This also uses factors weighted in a hierarchy, in this case called a distinction tree. Like other IC systems, the branches of the tree include human capital, structural capital, renewal and development capital, and business process capital. Unlike other methods, the IC Index introduces metrics for flows, for example, between human capital and business process capi-

IVM is a trademark of M'Pherson Associates.
IC Index is a trademark of Intellectual Capital Services.

tal. It also computes a single index, allowing relative comparisons over time or different business units.

Each of these methods has some interesting and sometimes unique characteristics. Unlike raw balanced scorecards, taken together they help managers focus, not just on specific metrics, but on the drivers of value, trends and momentum, interactions, dependencies, sensitivity to risk, and so on.

PRACTICAL CONSIDERATIONS

Ask any manager where the organization's most vital knowledge is and invariably the answer will be that it is in people's heads and not in the organization's databases. Many commentators reckon that 70 percent or more of an organization's knowledge is in the form of human capital. It is tacit knowledge, not immediately visible, that surfaces from the deep recesses of the brain when needed in a particular situation. Metrics in the human capital category are the most difficult to quantify. Certainly some input metrics, such as level of education, are relatively easy to measure. But some of the most successful entrepreneurs in the knowledge economy have become successful after dropping out of formal education. Many organizations put significant effort into competency profiling systems, but will they ever be able to say how that competency will be applied in practice? What more forward-looking companies are paying attention to are the flows between human and structural capital. They are considering how well they are converting at least some of the tacit knowledge into explicit form, for example, in best practice databases, and how well they are recording the existence of tacit knowledge, for example, in expertise directories. The marketplace knows only too well the dependency of an organization on its people. Often, when a particular individual or a whole team leaves, such as a team of investment managers in a merchant bank, then the stock price follows. Therefore, perhaps some of the best measures in this category are actual job performance data and motivation levels. Measuring human capital remains very problematic.

The very difficulty of capturing precise analytical data should not deter organizations from thinking about their sources of knowledge and how they convert them into valuable products and services. In my opinion, a focus on knowledge flows and conversion will generate some of the more useful metrics. Here, links need to be made between IC systems and the assessment systems mentioned earlier. Typical metrics might relate to the quality of knowledge absorption and capture from the external environment, the quality of databases measured by the speed and accuracy of finding relevant information, and the matching capabilities of idea data banks with those of customers' needs and problems.

Because of the difficulties of measuring intangibles, few companies have followed Skandia's lead in developing specific IC metrics, though this number has grown considerably in the last year or so. If you do embark on such an approach, there are several practical considerations that can improve its effectiveness:

- The organization's strategic objectives, business priorities, and critical success factors should be the starting point for determining the categories of measure and high-level company-wide indicators.
- The indicators chosen should reflect a mix of different types, such as inputs, processes and outputs, absolute numbers, ratios, percentages, and subjective ratings.
- Develop indicators with a future orientation, that is, lead indicators of financial performance.
- Have enough, but not too many, indicators in each category (typically two to four, giving around 12–15 key indicators in total).
- Develop causal loop models that help you understand the interdependencies.
- Develop indicators as a team process, so that people are sharing knowledge and coming to a common understanding of the business.
- Allow a degree of customization across business units, but have some common ones to aid comparisons.
- Align individual goals and metrics with those of the organization's measurement system.

Companies that are applying such measures have found that it gives them better understanding of the drivers of value and is improving management and growth of these vital assets. For example, Skandia has used both their Navigator and tools such as the Intellectual Capital Index to set management goals and drive business growth that has far exceeded the industry average over the last five years. Similarly, Dow Chemical has focused on active management of one component of its intellectual capital—its patent portfolio. Using the Technical Factor method, developed with Arthur D. Little, alongside their own management model, they have generated over \$125 million new revenues from their patents.

CHALLENGES AND IMPLICATIONS

We are at an early phase in the development of the knowledge economy. The innovators are breaking the rules and the tried and tested methods of the past. For example, who would have thought even a year ago that providing free Internet access was a good commercial proposition? Yet the U.K. retailer, Dixons, introduced Freeserve and gained over 1 million U.K. subscribers (a number that took CompuServe over a decade to achieve), and is poised for a successful spin-off company. They gain revenues from advertising and a proportion of the telephone usage fees. Other Internet companies have shown that mass-appeal free products and services can be the launch pad for more successful ventures. Netscape distributed 6 million free copies of its browser to become established as a major player, though the pace of change in the knowledge economy meant that three years later its success had evaporated. As noted earlier, the stratospheric value of many Internet stocks defies all conventional financial analysis, yet proponents see them as having huge future potential because current usage levels are a fraction of what is possible. But like other earlier wonder stocks, their prices will be volatile and some of today's stars will be among tomorrow's casualties. The price of biotechnology company stocks has similarly waxed and waned.

In such an environment, aided by technology like the Internet, knowledge diffuses rapidly and is emulated more easily. The recipes of converting knowledge into sustainable value are not fully understood. Does it even make sense to develop and apply knowledge based metrics? The tendency of many people is to measure that which is easiest to measure, rather than that which might be more important to measure.

The measurement of intellectual capital is still relatively new, with only a handful of pioneering companies widely using these newer metrics. One major hurdle is that external bodies, such as accounting standards bodies, have been slow to get to grips with the knowledge economy. Their discipline is one of precision and additive arithmetic, not the fuzziness of intangibles and combinatorial arithmetic of knowledge. Many senior managers and policy makers are also reluctant to introduce new metrics and measurement systems when the new ones have not yet been fully developed. Despite this measurement myopia, there are some good pioneering efforts. The Society of Management Accountants of Canada has been active in research and education, and the Danish Ministry of Business is currently instigating IC reporting into a pilot group of some 20 companies. The U.S. accounting standards body FASB is considering how companies should report their intellectual capital. It could well be that companies will be obliged to report indicators in a standard format, along the lines that Skandia does now. But is this enough?

What are the implications in an era of paradoxes, when much information is free but knowledge is the foundation of wealth, the things you can measure easily are irrelevant but that which seems important to measure is fuzzy, and performance comparisons need a degree of stability yet the rate of change in the business environment is rapid? Some of the implications are shown in Table 15.2.

Metrics are a tool for a growing number of users, including policy makers, market analysts, economists, and managers. Each wants different metrics for different purposes. The challenge will be to satisfy the wide range of demands. Metrics themselves are codified knowledge and will need to be managed like knowledge. Analysts and customers might therefore expect explicit metrics to be constantly updated and accessible, when and where they need them. Policy makers will expect some standard categorizations to enable comparisons. As well as the codified metrics beloved by economists and ac-

Table 15.2
Comparisons of Industrial Era vs. Knowledge Era Metrics

Industrial Era	→	Knowledge Era
Tangible	→	Intangible
Finance Focus	→	Balanced Set
Event-Driven	→	Process-Driven
Cost	→	Value
Periodic Reporting	→	Instant Access
Past Orientation	→	Future Orientation
Value in Things	→	Value in Flows
Production Statistics	→	Innovation Statistics
Metrics for Reporting	→	Metrics for Managing
Standards and Standard	→	Common yet Customized

countants, other metrics, like management competency, that are difficult to codify will be tacit. They will be shared through dialogue and discourse. That's why face-to-face meetings with analysts and financial backers are important to knowledge-intensive companies.

As with organizational knowledge, the biggest debate is likely to be over disclosure. What metrics represent proprietary knowledge not to be divulged to anyone outside the organization? At the moment, many companies do not openly offer what is considered sensitive information, but competitive analysts or pressure groups can, with assiduous work, find this information, either from public sources or even from detailed statutory disclosures not widely publicized. It is a paradox of the present situation that many financial analysts within companies expend tremendous effort in aggregating information for reporting purposes, which market analysts then spend comparable effort in disaggregating! As with organizational knowledge, there is often too much paranoia over protection when the free flow of information would benefit all concerned. After all, when most of an organization's vital knowledge is tacit, it will take others time to emulate the organization even if all of their explicit knowledge was more widely available. That does not mean that a price should not be put on this information.

What is clear about the current state of confusion and disarray is that the different interested stakeholders in measurement of knowledge and intangibles will need to work together to discuss their varied needs. No longer should there be a sharp divide between how macroeconomists look at regional or national economies and how companies look at their intellectual capital. The process and outcomes of the Massachusetts Innovation Index mentioned earlier have important lessons for how organizations should process and categorize their metrics. Wider sharing of knowledge across organizational boundaries and between the different groups of stakeholders will help to increase everybody's knowledge about the new economy and what might be appropriate metrics. What is also clear is that organizations and policy makers are probably spending too much effort in collecting metrics that have little relevance to today's economy. Much of this effort could be usefully diverted into sharing and building models of the new economy rather than collecting and analyzing detailed and irrelevant statistics. What is not so clear is whether the very fuzziness and intangibility of many of the metrics means that we should ever spend as much effort on knowledge era metrics as we do now on industrial era metrics. It could be that the age of precision metrics is over, and that of more open tacit sharing emerging.

FROM MEASUREMENT MYOPIA TO KNOWLEDGE LEADERSHIP

My conclusion from this analysis is that perhaps by focusing too much on metrics we will suffer from measurement myopia and lose sight of new opportunities. Interviews I have conducted with individuals and managers in organizations that are clearly successful with innovation and with knowledge initiatives show that they demonstrate vision and leadership. Innovators and knowledge leaders do not try to justify a priori investment in new products and services or in knowledge and intellectual capital programs. They understand the dynamics of their business environment and the strategic role of knowledge and act accordingly. They encourage the innovators in their organizations. They stimulate experimentation and learning. In other words, they don't rush into detailed metrics before exploring in person the way the knowledge economy is unfolding. Action, experimentation, and learning take priority over fretting about return on investment. Their ultimate metric is how successful they feel they have been in retrospect, not necessarily financially but in terms that reflect their personal values and aspirations.

In this field, because we are all at the beginning of a steep learning curve, it is better to be roughly right rather than precisely wrong. The time is now ripe for organizations and policy bodies to develop their understanding of the knowledge economy, to experiment with new metrics, but above all to enter into constructive dialogue that will guide them more clearly to a prosperous future, however that is gauged. If that means doing and succeeding, but not measuring, then who is to say that it doesn't add up?

Bibliography

Ackoff, Russell A.,1994, *The Democratic Corporation*. Oxford: Oxford University Press.

Africa, A., and J. de la Torre, 1998. "Learning from Failure: Towards an Evolutionary Model of Collaborative Ventures," *Organization Science*, 9(3) (May-June): 306–323.

Alvesson, M., 1993, "Organizations as Rhetoric: Knowledge-Intensive Firms and the Struggle with Ambiguity," *Journal of Management Studies*, 30(6): 997–1015.

Amabile, T.M., and R. Conti, 1999. "Changes in the Work Environment for Creativity during Downsizing," *Academy of Management Journal*, 42(6) (December): 630–640.

Argyris, Chris, 1992, *On Organizational Learning*, Cambridge, MA: Blackwell Publishers.

Arrow, K., 1985, "Informational Structure of the Firm," *American Economic Review*, 75(2) (May): 303–307.

Arrow, K., 1974, *The Limits of Organization*. New York: W.W. Norton.

Arrow, K.J.,1962, *Economic Welfare and the Allocation of Resources for Invention*. In National Bureau of Economic Research, *The Rate and Direction of Inventive Activity*. Princeton: Princeton University Press, pp. 609–625.

Arthur, Brian, 1990, "Positive Feedbacks in the Economy," *Scientific American*, February: 92–99

Austin, Robert D., 1996, *Measuring and Managing Performance in Organizations*. New York: Dorset House.

Barabas, C., 1990, *Technical Writing in a Corporate Culture*, Norwood, NJ: Ablex.

Barabba, Vincent P., 1998, *Revisiting Plato's Cave: Business Design in an Age of Uncertainty*. In *Blueprint for the Digital Economy*, edited by D. Tapscott. New York: McGraw Hill.

Barnard, C., 1938, *The Functions of the Executive*. Cambridge, MA: Harvard University Press.

Barney, J., 1991, "Firm resources and sustained competitive advantage," *Journal of Management*, 11(2): 153–169.

Barrett, F.J., 1998, "Creativity and Improvisation in Jazz and Organizations: Implications for Organizational Learning," *Organization Science*, 9 (5): 605–622.

Baumard, Philippe, 1996, *From Infowar to Knowledge Warfare: Preparing for the Paradigm Shift*. Taken from the Internet site http://www.indigonet.com/annexes/289/baumard.htm.

Baumard, Philippe, 1995, *Organisations Déconcertées La Gestion Stratégique de la Connaissance*. Paris: Masson.

Baumard, Philippe, 1996, *Organizations in the Fog: An Investigation into the Dynamics of Knowledge*. In Moingeon, Bertrand, and Amy Admondson (Eds.), *Organizational Learning and Competitive Advantage*. London: Sage, pp. 74–91.

Bayliss, C.Y., and K.B. Clark, 1997, "Managing in an age of modularity," *Harvard Business Review*, September–October: 84.

Bechara, Antoine, Hanna Damasio, Daniel Tranel, and Antonio R. Damasio, 1997, "Deciding Advantageously Before Knowing the Advantageous Strategy," *Science*, 275: 1293–1295.

Beer, Stafford, 1972, *Brain of the Firm*. New York: Herder and Herder.

Bell, Daniel, 1973, *The Coming of Post-industrial Society*. New York: Basic Books.

Bell, Daniel, 1978, *The Cultural Contradictions of Capitalism*. London: Heinemann.

Bell, Daniel, 1979, *The Social Framework of the Information Society*. In *The Computer Age —The Next Twenty Years*, Dertouzous, M. and J. Moses (Eds.). Boston: MIT Press.

Berger, P.L., and T. Luckmann, 1966, *The Social Construction of Reality*. Garden City, N.Y.: Doubleday.

Besser, T., 1996, *Team Toyota: Transplanting the Toyota Culture to the Camry Plant in Kentucky*. Albany: State University of New York Press.

Bidault, Francis, Gomez Pierre-Yves, and Marion Gilles, 1997, *Trust: Firm and Society*. London: MacMillan Business.

Bierly, P., and T. Hämäläinen, 1995, "Organizational Learning and Strategy," *Scandinavian Journal of Management*, 11(3): 209–224.

Blackler, Frank, M. Reed, and A. Whitaker, 1993, "Editorial: Knowledge Workers and Contemporary Organizations," *Journal of Management Studies*, 30(6): 851–862.

Boisot, M., 1988, *Knowledge Assets*. Oxford: Oxford University Press.

Boulding, Kenneth E., 1966, "The Economics of Knowledge and the Knowledge of Economics," *American Economic Review*: May, 1–13.

Bradley, Keith, 1997, *The Case for Valuation and Disclosure of Intangibles*, Conference presentation at *Turning Knowledge into a Corporate Asset*. Business Intelligence, London (October).

Brand, A., 1998, "Knowledge Management and Innovation at 3M," *Journal of Knowledge Management*, 2(1) (September): 17–22.

Brown, John Seely, and Paul Duguid, 1991, "Organizational Learning and Communities of Practice: Toward a Unified View of Working, Learning, and Innovation," *Organization Science*, 2(1): 40–57.

Brown, John Seely, and Paul Duguid, 1998, "Organizing Knowledge," *California Management Review*, 40(3): 90–111.

Brown, S.L., and K.M. Eisenhart, 1998, *Competing on the Edge: Strategy as Structured Chaos*. Boston: Harvard Business School Press.

Burns, John, Bob Scapens, and Stuart Turley, 1996, *The Influence of External Reporting on Management Decisions*. CIMA Research Update (September).

Burton-Jones, A., 2000, *Knowledge Capitalism*. Oxford: Oxford University Press.

Cameron, K., and R. E. Quinn, 1998, *Diagnosing and Changing Organizational Cultures*, Reading, MA: Addison-Wesley.

Cannon-Bowers, Janis A., and Eduardo Salas, 1998, "Team Performance and Training in Complex Environments: Recent Findings from Applied Research," *Current Directions in Psychological Research*, March 1999: 83–87.

Castells, M., 1999, *The Information Age: Economy, Society, and Culture*. Oxford: Blackwell.

Chandrasekaran, B., John R. Josephson, and V. Richard Benjamins, 1999, "What Are Ontologies, and Why Do We Need Them?" *IEEE Intelligent Systems*, 14(1): 20–26.

Chesbrough, H., and D.J. Teece, 1996, "When is Virtual Virtuous? Organizing for Innovation," *Harvard Business Review*, January–February: 65.

Choo, C.W., 1998, *The Knowing Organization*. New York: Oxford University Press.

Churchill, E.F., and D. Snowdon, 1998, "Collaborative Virtual Environments: An Introductory Review of Issues and Systems," *Virtual Reality*, 3(1): 3–15.

Ciborra, Claudio, 1991, *Alliances as Learning Experiments: Cooperation, competition and change in the high tech industries*. In Lynn K. Mytelka (Ed.), *Strategic Partnerships and the World Economy*. London: Pinter Publishers.

Ciborra, C., 1993, *Teams, Markets and Systems: Business innovation and information technology*. Cambridge: Cambridge University Press.

Clancey, W.J., 1997, *Situated Cognition—On Human Knowledge and Computer Representations*. Cambridge: Cambridge University Press.

Clark, K., and T. Fujimoto, 1991, *Product Development Performance*. Harvard Business School Press: Boston.

Cleveland, Harlan, 1985, *The Knowledge Executive: Leadership in an information society*. New York: Truman Tally Books, E.P. Dutton.

Clippinger, J.H., 1999, *The Biology of Business: Decoding the Natural Laws of Enterprise*. San Francisco: Jossey-Bass.

Coase, R., 1937, "The nature of the firm," *Economica*, 4: 386–405.

Cohen, D., 1998, "Toward a Knowledge Context: Report on the First Annual U.C. Berkeley Forum on Knowledge and the Firm," *California Management Review*, 40(3): 22–39.

Cohen, W.M., and D.A. Levinthal, 1990, "Absorptive Capacity: A new perspective on learning and innovation," *Administrative Science Quarterly*, 35: 128–152.

Conner, K.R., and C.K. Prahalad, 1996, "A Resource-Based Theory of the Firm: Knowledge Versus Opportunism," *Organization Science* 7(5) (September-October): 477–501.

Cranfield and Information Strategy Knowledge Survey, 2000, "Europe's State of the Art in KM." Available at http://www.cranfield.ac.uk/som/home4.htm.

Cranfield and Information Strategy Knowledge Survey, 1998, "Europe's State of the Art in KM," London: Information Strategy: The Economist Group.

Crossan, M.M., 1998, "Improvisation in Action," *Organization Science*, 9(5): 593–599.

Crossan, M.M., H.W. Lane, L. Klus, and R.E. White, 1996, "The improvising organization: where planning meets opportunity," *Organizational Dynamics*, 4 (Spring): 20–34.

Cusumano, M.A., 1997, "How Microsoft makes large teams work like small teams," *Sloan Management Review*, Fall: 9–20.

Cusumano, M.A., 1985, *The Japanese Automobile Industry—Technology and Management at Nissan and Toyota*. Boston: Harvard University Press.

Das, T.K., 1987, "Strategic Planning and Individual Temporal Orientation," *Strategic Management Journal*, 8(2) (March–April): 203–209.

Davenport, Thomas H., 1997, *Information Ecology*. New York: Oxford University Press.

Davenport, Thomas, D. Delong, and M. Beers, 1998, "Successful Knowledge Management Projects," *Sloan Management Review*, Winter: 43–57.

Davenport, T.H., and L. Prusak, 1998, *Working Knowledge*. Boston: Harvard University Press.

Davenport, T.H., and K. Pearlson, 1998, "Two Cheers for the Virtual Office," *Sloan Management Review*, 39(4) (Summer): 51–65.

Davidow, William H., and Michael S. Malone, 1992, *The Virtual Corporation*. New York: Harper Collins Publishers.

Davis, Stan, and Chris Meyer, 1998, *Blur*. Reading, MA: Addison-Wesley.

De Gues, A., 1988, "Planning as Learning," *Harvard Business Review*, 66(2): 70.

Demsetz, H., 1988, "The Theory of the Firm Revisited," *Journal of Law, Economics and Organization*, 4(1) (Spring): 141–161.

Denison, A., 1968, *Economic Growth*. In R.E. Caves (Ed.), *Britain's Economic Prospects*. London: Brookings Institute/Macmillan.

Department of Trade and Industry (DTI), 1998, *Our Competitive Future: Building the Knowledge Driven Economy.*

Dervin, B., 1998, "Sense Making Theory and Practice: An Overview of User Interests in Knowledge Seeking and Use," *Journal of Knowledge Management—MCB*, 2(2) (December): 36–48.

Despres, C., 1996, "Work, Management and the Dynamics of Knowledge," *Sasin Journal of Management*, 2(1): 24–36.

Doz Yves, 1996, "The Evolution of Cooperation in Strategic Alliances: Initial Conditions or Learning Processes?" *Strategic Management Journal*, 17: 55–83.

Doz Yves, and Gary Hamel, 1998, *Alliance Advantage.* Harvard Business School Press: Boston.

Doz Yves, and Gary Hamel, 1995, *The Use of Alliances in Implementing Technology Strategies.* Working Papers, INSEAD 95/22.

Doz Yves, and A. Shuen, 1995, *From Intent to Outcome: The Evolution and Gouvernance of Interfirm Partnerships.* Working Papers, INSEAD 95/19.

Downes, L., and C. Mui, 1998, *Unleashing the Killer App.* Boston: HBS Press.

Drucker, Peter F., 1988a, "The Coming of the New Organization," *Harvard Business Review*, 66(1) (January–February): 45.

Drucker, Peter F., 1988b, "Management and the World's Work," *Harvard Business Review*, 66 (September–October): 65.

Drucker, Peter F., 1993, *Post-Capitalist Society.* New York: HarperBusiness.

Durkheim, Emile, 1974, *Sociology and philosophy*; translated by D.F. Pocock; with an introd. by J.G. Peristiany. New York: Free Press.

Dussauge, P., and B. Garrette, 1999, *Cooperative Strategy.* New York: Wiley.

Dyer, J.H., and H. Singh, 1998, "The relational view: cooperative strategy and sources of interorganizational competitive advantage," *Academy of Management Review*, 23(4): 660–679.

Earl, M.J., 1996, *Information Management: The Organizational Dimension.* New York: Oxford University Press.

Earl, Michael J., and David F. Feeny, 1994, "Is Your CIO Adding Value?" *Sloan Management Review*, 35(3) (Spring): 11–20.

Earl, Michael J., and Ian A. Scott, 1998, *What on Earth is a CKO?* London: London Business School and IBM Inc.

Earl, Michael J., and I.A. Scott, 1999, "What is a Chief Knowledge Officer?" *Sloan Management Review*, 40(2) (Winter): 29–38.

Earl, M.J., and P. Vivian, 1993, *The Chief Information Officer: A Study of Survival.* London: Egon Zehnder International and London Business School.

Earl, Michael J., with P.D. Vivian, 1999, *The New CIO: A Study of the Changing Role of the CIO.* London: London Business School and Egon Zehnder International.

Edvinsson, Leif, and Michael S. Malone, 1997, *Intellectual Capital: Realizing Your Company's True Value by Finding Its Hidden Brainpower.* New York: HarperBusiness.

Eisenstein, S.M., 1953, *The Rhetorics of Movies.* Tokyo: Bunko.

Erickson, T., D.N. Smith, W.A. Kellogg, M.R. Laff, J.T. Richards, and E. Bradner, 1999, "Socially Translucent Systems: Social Proxies, Persistent Conversation, and the Design of 'Babble.'" In *Human Factors in Computing Systems: The Proceedings of CHI '99.* Pittsburgh, PA: ACM Press.

Financial Times, 1999, "Inside Track: A Mission to Complain," June 28:12.

Fine, H., 1998, *Clockspeed.* Boston: Harvard Business School Press.

Foster, F., and G. Falkowski, 1999, "Organization Network Analysis: A Tool for Building a Learning Organization." Unpublished IBM paper available from the author.

Fujimoto, T., 1999, *The Evolution of a Manufacturing System at Toyota.* New York: Oxford University Press.

Gardner, Howard, 1983, *Frames of Mind: The theory of multiple intelligences*. New York: Basic Books.

Gardner, Howard, 1985, *The Mind's New Science: A History of the Cognitive Revolution*. New York: Basic Books.

Giddens, A., 1993, *New Rules of Sociological Method*. Oxford: Polity Press.

Giddens, A., 1984, *The Constitution of Society: Outline of the Theory of Structuration*. Oxford: Polity Press.

Goodenough, W.H., 1961, "Comment on Cultural Evolution," *Daedalus* 90: 521–528. Quoted in Keesing and Strathern (op cit).

Granovetter, M.E., 1985, "Economic Action and Social Structure: The Problem of Embeddedness," *American Journal of Sociology*, 1991: 481–510.

Grant, Robert M., 1996, "Toward a knowledge-based theory of the firm," *Strategic Management Journal*, 17: 109–122.

Grenier, R., and G. Metes, 1995, *Going Virtual. Moving your Organization into the 21st Century*. New Jersey: Prentice Hall.

Grindley, P., and D.J. Teece, 1997, "Managing intellectual capital: licensing and cross-licensing in semiconductors and electronics," *California Management Review*, 39 (Winter): 8–41.

Gulati, R., 1995, "Social Structure and Alliance Formation Patterns: A Longitudinal Study," *Administrative Science Quarterly*, 40: 619–652.

Gummesson, Evert, 1995, *Relationsmarknadsföring: Från 4P till 30R*. Malmö Hagel: Liber-Hermods.

Haeckel, Stephan H., 1999, *Adaptive Enterprise: Creating and Leading Sense-and-Respond Organizations*. Boston: Harvard Business School Press.

Hagedoorn, John, 1993, "Understanding the Rationale of Strategic Technology Partnering: Interorganizational Modes of Cooperation and Sectoral Differences," *Strategic Management Journal*, 14: 371–385.

Hagel, J., and M. Singer, 1999, "Unbundling the Corporation," *Harvard Business Review*, 77 (March–April): 133–141.

Håkansson, Håkan, and Ivan Snehota, 1959, *Developing Relationships in Business Networks*. London: Routledge.

Hale, R., and P. Whitlam, 1997, *Towards the Virtual Organization*. London: McGraw Hill.

Hamel, Gary, 1991, "Competition for Competence and Interpartner Learning within International Strategic Alliances," *Strategic Management Journal*, 12: 83–103.

Hamel, Gary, Doz Yves, and C.K. Prahalad, 1989, "Collaborate with your Competitor and Win," *Harvard Business Review* 67(1): 133–139.

Hamel, Gary, and C.K. Prahalad, 1994, *Competing for the Future*. Boston: Harvard Business School Press.

Hamel, Gary, and C.K. Prahalad, 1990, "The Core Competence of the Corporation," *Harvard Business Review* 68(3) (May-June): 79–91.

Hammer, Michael, and James Champy, 1993, *Reengineering the Corporation. A Manifesto for Business Revolution*. New York: Harper Business.

Hansen, M.T., N. Nohria, and T. Tierney, 1999, "What's your strategy for managing knowledge?" *Harvard Business Review*, 77 (March–April): 106–129.

Hardin, G., 1968, "The Tragedy of the Commons," *Science*, December: 1243–1248.

Harrari, O., 1994, "The Brain-Based Organization," *Management Review*, 83(6): 57–60.

Harrigan, K.R., 1988, "Strategic Alliances in Partner Asymetries." In F.J. Contractor and P. Lorange (Eds.), *Cooperative Strategies in International Business*. Lexington, MA: Lexington Books.

Harrigan, K.R., 1986, *Managing for Joint Venture Success*. Lexington, Mass: Lexington Books.

Hayek, F.A., 1945, "The uses of knowledge in society," *American Economic Review*, 35: 1–18.

Hedberg, Bo, 1981, "How Organizations Learn and Unlearn," *Handbook of Organizational Design*, 1: 3–27.

Hedberg, Bo, and Anders Ericsson, 1979, "Insiktströghet och manövertröghet i organisationers omorientering." In Hedberg, Bo, and Sven-Erik Sjöstrand (Eds.), *Från företagskriser till industripolitik.* Malmö: Liber, pp. 54–66.

Hedberg, Bo, Göran Dahlgren, Jörgen Hansson, and Nils-Göran Olve, 1997, *Virtual Organizations and Beyond. Discover Imaginary Systems.* London: John Wiley & Sons.

Hedberg, Bo, and Rolf Wolff, 1999, "Organizing, Learning and Strategizing," In M. Dierkes, A. Berthoin Antal, J. Child, and I. Nonaka (Eds.), *The Handbook of Organizational Learning.* Oxford: Oxford University Press (forthcoming).

Hedberg, Bo, Paul C. Nystrom, and William H. Starbuck, 1976, "Camping on Seesaws. Prescriptions for a Self-Designing Organization," *Administrative Science Quarterly*, 21: 41–65.

Heilbruner, R., 1976, *Business Civilization in Decline.* New York: Norton.

Helleloid, D., and B. Simonin, 1994, "Organizational Learning and a Firm Core Competence." In Gary Hamel and Aime Henne (Eds.), *Competence-Based Competition.* New York: John Wiley & Sons, pp. 213–239.

Hilmer, Frederick G., and Lex Donaldson, 1996, *Management Redeemed: Debunking the Fads that Undermine our Corporations.* New York: Free Press.

Hofstede, Geert, *Culture's Consequences: International Differences in Work-Related Values*, Beverly Hills, CA: Sage.

Huber, G.P., 1991, "Organizational Learning: The Contributing Processes and the Literatures," *Organization Science*, 2(1): 88–115.

Iemura, H., 1999, *Prius to iu yume—Toyota ga hiraketa 21 seiki no tobira [The dream called Prius—Toyota opened the door towards the 21 century].* Tokyo: Sanko Insatsu, 1999.

IMD, 1999, *Word Competitiveness Yearbook.* Lausanne: IMD.

Inkpen, A., 1996, "Creating Knowledge through Collaboration," *California Management Review*, 39(1): 123–140.

Inkpen, A., 1998, "Learning, Knowledge, Acquisition and Strategic Alliances," *European Management Journal*, 16(2).

Inkpen, A., and M.M. Crossan, 1995, "Believing Is Seeing: Joint Ventures and Organizational Learning," *Journal of Management Studies*, 32: 595–618.

Inkpen, A., and K.Q. Li, 1999, "Joint Venture Formation: Planning and Knowledge-Gathering for Success," *Organizational Dynamics*, 27(4): 33–47.

Ishida, T. (Ed.), 1998, *Community Computing—Collaboration over Global Information Networks.* New York: John Wiley & Sons.

Itazaki, H., 1999, *Kakushin Toyota Jidosha—Sekai wo shinkan saseta Prius no shogeki.* Tokyo: Nikan Kogyo Shinbunsha.

Ito, M., 1989, "Kigy-kan kankei to keizoku-teki torihiki." In K. Imai and R. Komiya (Eds.), *Nihon no kigyo.* Tokyo: Tokyo University Press, pp. 109–130.

Jantsch, E., 1980, *The Self-Organizing Universe.* Oxford: Pergamon Press.

Jaworski, J., 1996, *Synchronicity: The Inner Path to Leadership.* San Francisco: Berett-Koehler.

Jensen, M.C., and W.H. Meckling, 1998, "Specific and general knowledge and organizational structure." In M.C. Jensen (Ed.), *Foundations of Organizational Strategy.* Cambridge, MA: Harvard University Press, pp. 103–125.

Johansen, Robert, and Rob Swigart, 1994, *Upsizing the Individual in the Downsized Organization.* Reading, MA: Addison-Wesley.

Kao, John, 1996, *JAMMING: The Art and Discipline of Business Creativity*. New York: Harper Business.

Kaufman, Charles, 1997, "Letters," *Business Week*, 28 July: 5.

Keesing, R., and A. Strathern, 1998, 3rd Ed., *Cultural Anthropology: A Contemporary Perspective*. Orlando: Harcourt Brace & Co.

Kelly, Kevin, 1996, "The Economics of Ideas," *Wired*, 4 (6): 149.

Kelly, S., and M. A. Allison, 1999, *The Complexity Advantage: How the science of complexity can help your business achieve peak performance*. New York: McGraw Hill.

Kidder, T., 1982, *The soul of a new machine*. New York: Avon Books,

Killing, J.P., 1988, "Understanding Alliances: the role of task and organizational complexity." In F.J. Contractor and P. Lorange (Eds.), *Cooperative Strategies in International Business*. Lexington, MA: Lexington Books, pp. 55–67

Kim, Daniel H., 1993, "The Link between Individual and Organizational Learning," *Sloan Management Review*, Fall: 1–24.

Klein, Gary, 1998, *Sources of Power: How people make decisions*. Cambridge: MIT Press.

Kogut, B., 1988, "Joint Venture: Theoretical and empirical perspectives," *Strategic Management Journal*, 9(4): 319–332.

Kogut, B., 1988, *A study of the life cycle of joint venture*. Lexington, MA: Lexington Books.

Kogut, B., and U. Zander, 1996, "What Do Firms Do? Coordination, Identity, and Learning," *Organization Science*, 7(5) (September-October): 502–518.

Kogut, B., and U. Zander, 1992, "Knowledge of the firm, combinative capabilities, and the replication of technology," *Organization Science*, 3: 383–397.

Kransdorff, A., *Corporate Amnesia*. Woburn, MA: Butterworth–Heinemann, 1998.

Kuhn, Thomas, 1970, *The Structure of Scientific Revolutions*, 2d Enlarged Ed. Chicago: University of Chicago Press.

Kunitomo, R., 1998, *Seven-Eleven no Joho Shisutem [The Information System of Seven Eleven]*. Tokyo: Paru Shuppan.

Kurtzman, Joel, 1999, "An Interview with Howard Gardner," *Strategy & Business*, 14 First Quarter 1999: 90–99.

Kuznets, Simon, 1966, *Modern Economic Growth*. New Haven, Conn.: Yale University Press.

Lakoff, George, 1987, *Women, Fire, and Dangerous Things: What categories reveal about the mind*. Chicago: University of Chicago Press.

Lambert, R., and A. Bytheway, 1998, *Organisational competencies for harnessing IS/IT—Good Practice Guide*. ISRC-COMP-98009.

Larsson, R., L. Bengtsson, K. Henriksson, and J. Sparks, 1998, "The Interorganizational Learning Dilemma: Collective Knowledge Development in Strategic Alliances," *Organization Science*, 9(3): 285–305.

Lave, Jean, and Etienne Wenger, 1991, *Situated learning: Legitimate peripheral participation*. New York: Cambridge University Press.

Leonard, D., and W. Swap, 1999, *When Sparks Fly: Igniting Creativity in Groups*. Boston: Harvard Business School Press.

Lev, Baruch, 1997, "The Old Rules no Longer Apply," *Forbes ASAP* (7 April).

Lloyd, Seth, 1995, "Learning How to Control Complex Systems," *Bulletin of the Santa Fe Institute*, Spring.

Lucier, Charles E., and Janet D. Torsilieri, 1997, "Why Knowledge Programs Fail: A CEO's Guide to Managing Learning," *Strategy & Business*, Fourth Quarter 1997, (9): 14–28.

Lundin, Anders, and Bob Johanson, 1996, "Sweden," *International Financial Law Review Mergers and Acquisitions Supplement*, April: 51–56.

Mahoney J.T., and J.R. Padian, 1992, "Resource based view within the conservation of strategic management," *Strategic Management Journal*, 13(5): 363–380.

Mowery, D.C., J.E. Oxley, and B.S. Silvermann, 1996, "Strategic alliances and interfirm knowledge transfer," *Strategic Management Journal*, 17: 77–91.

Maravelias, Christian, 1999, "The Networked Organization. Trust and Leadership in Skandia AFS," Ph.D. dissertation, School of Business, Stockholm University.

March, A., and D.A. Garvin, 1997, *A note on knowledge management*. Boston: Harvard Business School note 9-398-031.

March, J., and H. Simon, 1958, *Organizations*. New York: Wiley.

March, J.G., 1996, "Continuity and Change in Theories of Organizational Action," *Administrative Science Quarterly*, 41: 278–287.

Marchand, D., and J. Roos, 1996, *Skandia AFS: measuring and visualizing intellectual capital*. Case GM 624, Lausanne: IMD.

Markus L.M., and R.I. Benjamin, 1996, "Change Agentry—The Next IS Frontier," *MIS Quarterly*, December 1996.

Martiny, M., 1998, "Knowledge Management at HP Consulting," *Organizational Dynamics*, Autumn: 71–77.

Massachusetts Technology Collaborative, 1997, *New Index of the Massachusetts Innovation Economy*, http://www.mtpc.org.

Mayo, A., and E. Lank, 1994, *The Power of Learning: A Guide to Gaining Competitive Advantage*. London: St. Mut.

McDermott, Richard, 1999, "How to Encourage Learning Across Teams," *Knowledge Management Review*, 8 (May–June): 32–35.

McKenna, R., 1997, *Real Time Marketing*. Boston: Harvard University Press.

Miller, Danny, 1990, *The Icharus Paradox. How Exceptional Companies Bring About Their Own Downfall*. New York: Harper Business.

Mills, D., and B. Friesen, 1992, "The Learning Organization," *European Management Journal*, 10(2): 146–156.

Mintzberg, H., 1973, *The Nature of Managerial Work*. New York: Harper and Row.

Mintzberg, H., 1988, "Opening up the definitions of strategy." In H. Mintzberg, J.B. Quinn, and R.M. James (Eds.), *The Strategy Process: Concepts, Contexts, and Cases*. Englewood Cliffs, NJ: Prentice Hall, pp. 13–20.

Mirvis, P.H., 1998, "Practice Improvisation," *Organization Science*, 9(5): 586–591.

Mitsugi, Y., T. Takimoto, and M. Yamazaki, 1998, "Waga Kuni Kourigyo no Shinryutsu Senryaku to Johogijutsu" [New Retail Strategy and Information Technology in Our Country's Retail Business]. *Chiteki Shisan Sozo*, 6(2): 18–29.

Morgan, Gareth, 1986, *Images of Organizations*. London: Sage.

Mowery, D.C., J.E. Oxley, and B.S. Silverman, 1996, "Strategic Alliance and Interfirm Knowledge Transfer," *Strategic Management Journal*, 17: 77–91.

Nelson, R.R., and S.G. Winter, 1982, *An Evolutionary Theory of Economic Change*. Boston: Harvard University Press.

Newman, K., and S.D. Nollen, 1996, "Culture and Congruence: The Fit Between Management Practices and National Culture," *Journal of International Business Studies*, 27(4) (Fourth Quarter): 753–779.

Nohria, N., and R. Eccles, 1992, *Networks and Organizations*. Boston: Harvard Business School Press

Nonaka, I., 1990, *Chishiki Sozo Keiei: Nihon Kigyo no Epistemoroji" [Knowledge Creation Management: Epistemology in Japanese Companies]*. Tokyo: Nihon Keizai Shinbunsha.

Nonaka, Ikujiro, 1991, "The Knowledge-Creating Company," *Harvard Business Review*, November–December: 96–104.

Nonaka, I., and H. Takeuchi, 1995, *The Knowledge Creating Company: How Japanese Companies Create the Dynamics of Innovation*. New York: Oxford University Press.

Nonaka, I., and N. Konno, 1998, "The Concept of 'Ba': Building a Foundation for Knowledge Creation," *California Management Review*, 40(3): 40–54.

Nonaka, I., and N. Konno, 1999, *Chishiki Keiei no susume: Narejimanejimento to sono jidai [Recommending Knowledge Creation: The age of knowledge management]*. Tokyo: Chikuma Shinsho.

Nonaka, I., and P. Reinmoeller, 1999, *Knowledge Creation Architecture: Constructing the Places for Knowledge Assets and Competitive Advantage*. Internationales Management, Wiesbaden: Gabler, pp. 22–46.

Nonaka, I., P. Reinmoeller, and D. Senoo, 1998, "The ART of Knowledge," *European Management Journal*, 16 (6 Dec.): 673–684.

Nonaka, I., P. Reinmoeller, and R. Toyama, 2000, "Integrated IT Systems for Knowledge Creation." In M. Dierkes, A. Berthoin Antal, J. Child, and I. Nonaka (Eds.), *The Handbook of Organizational Learning*. Oxford: Oxford University Press (forthcoming).

Nonaka, I., and R. Toyama, 1999, "Leading Knowledge Creating Process: Innovation of Toyota Prius," Paper presented at the "Strategic Innovation," INSEAD, France.

Nonaka, I., and R. Toyama, 1999, "Why Do You Create Knowledge?: A Shared Epistemological Manner of a Firm," Paper presented at the Knowledge Forum 1999, Haas School of Business, UC Berkeley, CA.

Nonaka, I., R. Toyama, and N. Konno, 2000, "SECI, Ba, and Leadership: A Unifying Model of Dynamic Knowledge Creation." In Teece, D.J., and I. Nonaka (Eds.), *New Perspectives on Knowledge-Based Firm and Organization*. New York: Oxford University Press (forthcoming).

Normann, Richard, and Rafael Ramírez, 1994, *Designing Interactive Strategy: From Value Chain to Value Constellation.* Chichester: John Wiley & Sons.

Northey, P., and N. Southway, 1994, *Cycle Time Management: The Fast Track to Time-Based Productivity Improvement*. Portland, OR: Productivity Press.

Nystrom, Paul C., Bo L.T. Hedberg, and William H. Starbuck, 1976, "Interacting Processes as Organization Designs." In Kihlmann, Ralph H., Louis R. Pondy, and Dennis P. Slevin (Eds.), *The Management of Organization Designs*. New York/Amsterdam: North-Holland, pp. 209–230.

O'Dell, C., and C. Jackson, 1998, *If Only We Knew What We Know: The Transfer of Intenal Knowledge and Best Practice*. New York: Free Press.

OECD, 1996, *The Knowledge-Based Economy*. OCDE/GD(96)102, Paris: OECD.

Ogawa, S., 2000, "Nihon ni okeru ryuzukigyokiten no seihin kaihatsu," *Nihongata Maketing*, Tokyo: Chikura Shobo, pp. 77–96.

Okamoto, H., 1998, *Yokado Group: Koshueki he no Shisutemu Kakushin [Yokado Group: The System Revolution towards High Profits]*. Tokyo: Paru Shuppan.

Penrose, Edith T., 1959, *The Theory of the Growth of the Firm*. New York: Wiley.

Perrow, C., 1973, "The Short and Glorious History of Organization Theory," *Organization Dynamics*, Summer.

Petrash, G., 1996, "Dow's journey to a knowledge value management culture," *European Management Journal*, 14 (August): 365–373.

Pettigrew, M., 1987, "Context and Action in the Transformation of the Firm," *Journal of Management Studies*, November: 649–670.

Pfiffner, J.M., and F. Sherwood, 1960, *Administrative Organization*, Piscataway, NJ: Prentice-Hall.

Pierce, Charles S., 1963, "What Pragmatism Is." *Collected Papers of Charles Sanders Pierce. Vol. V*, C. Hartshorne and P. Weiss, eds. Bristol, U.K.: Theommes Press.

Polanyi, M., 1958, *Personal Knowledge: Towards a Post-Critical Philosophy* (Gifford Lectures, University of Aberdeen, 1951–52), London: Routledge & Kegan Paul.

Polanyi, M., 1962, *Personal Knowledge: Towards a Post-Critical Philosophy.* Chicago: University of Chicago Press.

Polanyi, Michael, 1966, *The Tacit Dimension.* New York: Garden City.

Porter, M.E., 1980, *Competitive Strategy.* New York: Free Press.

Postman, Neil, 1993, *Technopoly: The Surrender of Culture to Technology.* New York: Vintage/Random House.

Powell, V.W., K.W. Koput, and L. Smith-Doerr, "Interorganizational Collaboration and the Locus of Innovation: Networks of Learning in Biotechnology," *Administrative Science Quarterly*, 41: 116–145.

Prahalad, C.K., and Gary Hamel, 1990, "The Core Competence of the Corporation," *Harvard Business Review*, 68(3) (May–June): 79–91.

Quinn, J., P. Anderson, and S. Finkelstein, 1996, "Leveraging intellect," *Academy of Management Executive*, 10(3): 7–27.

Quinn, J.B., 1988, *Beyond Rational Management.* San Francisco: Jossey-Bass.

Quinn, J.B., 1992, *Intelligent Enterprise.* New York: Free Press.

Reinmoeller, P., 1999a, "Knowledge and Time: A Forgotten Factor in Knowledge Management." Presented at European Group for Organization Studies Colloquium, July 4–6 1999, Warwick, U.K.

Reinmoeller, P., 1999b, "Organizational 'Being' and Strategic Dialectics: Thriving on Discrepancies Between Potential Knowledge and Contexts." Presented at Strategic Management Society Annual Conference, October 3–6, 1999, Berlin, Germany.

Ricardo, David, 1817, *On the Principles of Political Economy and Taxation.* London: John Murray.

Rolland, N., 1999, *Business Driven Action Learning in French Multinationals.* Business Driven Action Learning: Best practices, Boshyk Yury.

Romer, P., 1999, "The new economy." Presentation to the Strategic Leadership Forum Annual Conference, Chicago, April 19.

Romer, Paul, 1989, *What Determines the Rate of Growth and Technological Change?* World Bank Working Papers, WPS 279.

Roos, Johan, Göran Roos, Leif Edvinsson, and Nicola Dragonetti, 1998, *Intellectual Capital: Navigating in the New Business Landscape.* New York: New York University Press.

Rorty, Richard, 1979, *Philosophy and the Mirror of Nature.* Princeton, NJ: Princeton University Press.

RSA, 1996, *Tomorrow's Company Inquiry: Final Report.* London: RSA.

Ruggles, Rudy, 1997, *Knowledge Tools: Using Technology to Manage Knowledge Better,* website at http://www.businessinnovation.ey.com/mko/html/toolsrr.html.

Ruggles, R., 1998, "The State of the Notion: Knowledge Management in Practice," *California Management Review*, Special Issue, 40(3): 80–89.

Sahlin-Andersson, Kerstin, 1995, "Imitating by Editing Success. The Construction of Organizational Fields." In Czarniawska, Barbara, and Guje Sévon (Eds.), *Translating Organizational Change.* Berlin: de Gruyter.

Saint-Onge, H., 1996, "Tacit Knowledge: The Key to the Strategic Alignment of Intellectual Capital," *Strategy and Leadership*, 24(2) (March/April): 10–14.

Sako, Mari, and Susan Helper, 1998, "Determinants of Trust in Supplier Relations: Evidence from the Automotive Industry in Japan and the United States," *Journal of Economic Behavior & Organization*, 34(3): 387–417.

Salzer, Miriam, 1994, "Identity Across Borders. A Study in the 'IKEA-World.'" Published Ph.D. Thesis, Department of Management & Economics, Linköping University, Sweden.

Samuelson, P.A., 1995, "Diagrammatic Exposition of a Theory of Public Expenditure," *Review of Economics and Statisitics*, 37: 350–356.

Sanchez, R., and T. Mahoney, 1996, "Modularity, flexibility and knowledge management in product and organization design," *Strategic Management Journal*, 17 (winter special issue): 63–76.

Say, Jean-Baptiste, 1803 [1971], *A Treatise on Political Economy.* New York: Augustus M. Kelley,

Schank, R., 1997, *Virtual Learning—A Revolutionary Approach to Building a Highly Skilled Workforce.* New York: McGraw-Hill.

Schank, Roger C., and Robert Abelson, 1977, *Scripts, Plans, Goals, and Understanding: An Inquiry into Human Knowledge Structures.* Hillsdale, NJ: Lawrence Erlbaum.

Schein, E., 1990, *Organizational Culture and Leadership.* San Francisco: Jossey-Bass.

Schumpeter, Joseph, 1942 [1962], *Capitalism, Socialism and Democracy.* New York: Harper and Row.

Schumpeter, J.A., 1951, *The Theory of Economic Development*, Cambridge, MA: Harvard University Press.

Scott, R., 1987, *Organizations: Rational, Natural, and Open Systems*, Englewood Cliffs, NJ: Prentice Hall.

Seely Brown, John, and Paul Duguid, 1998, "Organizing Knowledge," *California Management Review*, 40(1): 90–111.

Senge, Peter M., 1990, *The Fifth Discipline: The Art & Practice of the Learning Organization.* New York: Doubleday Currency.

Shapiro, C., and H. Varian, 1999, "The Art of Standards Wars," *California Management Review*, 41/2 (Winter): 8–32.

Shapiro, C., and H. Varian, 1999, *Information Rules*, Boston: Harvard Business School Press.

Shaw, G., R. Brown, and P. Bromiley, 1998, "Strategic Stories: How 3M is Rewriting Business Planning," *Harvard Business Review*, May–June 1998: 41–50.

Shenkar O., and J. Li, 1999, "Knowledge Search in International Cooperative Ventures," *Organization Science*, 10(2): 134–143.

Shout, P., 1999, "Towards the realization of one-to-one with 30 milion profiles," *Nikkei Multimedia.* February: 104–105.

Simon, H.A., 1947, *Administrative Behavior.* New York: Macmillan.

Simon, Herbert A., 1976, *Administrative Behavior: A Study of Decision-Making Processes in Administrative Organizations* (3rd Edition). New York: The Free Press.

Simonin B.L., 1999, "Ambiguity and the process of knowledge transfer in strategic alliances," *Strategic Management Journal*, 20: 595–623.

Sinclair, N., 2000, in his preface to Kyffin Williams, *The Land & the Sea.* Llandyand, Wales: Gomer Press.

Skyrme, David J., and Debra M. Amidon, 1997, *Creating the Knowledge-Based Business.* London: Business Intelligence, Ltd.

Skyrme, David J., 1999, *Knowledge Networking: Creating the Collaborative Enterprise.* Woburn, MA: Butterworth–Heinemann.

Skyrme, David J., 1998, *Measuring the Value of Knowledge.* London: Business Intelligence, Ltd.

Snowden, David, 1998a, "I only know what I know when I need to know it—embracing the active management of tacit knowledge," *Knowledge Management*, 1(3) (March): 1.

Snowden, David, 1998b, "Thresholds of Acceptable Uncertainty—achieving symbiosis between Intellectual Assets through mapping and simple models," *Knowledge Management*, 1(5) (May): 1–9.

Snowden, David, 1999a, "Liberating Knowledge." Introductory chapter to *Liberating Knowledge*. CBI Business Guide, London: Caspian Publishing.

Snowden, David, 1999b, "The Paradox of Story," *Scenario and Strategy Planning*, 1(5).

Snowden, David, 2000, "Organic Knowledge Management pt 1: The ASHEN Model as Enabler of Action," *Knowledge Management* 3(7) (April).

Sobek, D.K., A.C. Ward, and J.K. Liker, 1999, "Toyota's Principles of Set-Based Concurrent Engineering," *Sloan Management Review*, Winter: 67–83.

Spear, S., and H. Kent Bowen, 1999, "Decoding the DNA of the Toyota Production system," *Harvard Business Review*, September–October: 97–106.

Spender, J.-C., 1996, "Competitive Advantage from Tacit Knowledge? Unpacking the Concept and its Strategic Implications." In Moingeon, B. and A. Edmondson (Eds.), *Organizational Learning and Competitive Advantage*. London: Sage, pp. 56–73.

Spender, J.-C., 1994, "Organizational Knowledge, Collective Practice, and Penrose Rents," *International Business Review*, 3: 353–367.

Spender, J.-C., 1989, *Industry Recipes—The Nature and Sources of Managerial Judgement*. Oxford: Basil Blackwell.

Spender, J.-C., 1992, "Limits to learning from the West," *The International Executive*, 34 (September/October): 389–410.

Spender, J.-C., 1998, "Pluralist Epistemology and the Knowledge based theory of the firm," *Organization*, 5(2): 233–256.

Stalk, T.M., and G. Hout, 1990, *Competing against Time: How Time-Based Competition is Reshaping Global Markets*. New York: Free Press.

Starbuck, William H., and Hedberg, Bo, 1999, *Organizational Learning from Feedback*. In Dierkes, Meinholf, John Child, and Ikujiro Nonaka (Eds.), *Handbook of Organizational Learning and Knowledge*. New York: Oxford University Press (forthcoming).

Steensma, H.K., 1996, "Acquiring technological competencies through interorganizational collaboration: An organizational learning perspective." *Journal of Engineering and Technology Management*, 12: 267–286.

Stewart, Tom A., 1991, "Brainpower," *Fortune*, 123 (11) (June 3): 44–60.

Stewart, Tom, 1998, "The Cunning Plots of Leadership," *Fortune*, September 7: 165–166.

Stewart, Tom, 1997, *Intellectual Capital: The New Wealth of Organizations*. New York: Doubleday.

Suchman, Lucy, 1995, "Making Work Visible," *Communications of the ACM*, 38(9): 56–65.

Suchmann, L., 1987, *Plan and Situated Actions: The Problems of Human Machine Communication*. New York: Cambridge University Press.

Suzuki, K., 1998, "Tsuyoi 'Ishi' to 'Tetteiryoku' koso ga subete" [Strong "Intention" and "Determination" are Everything], *2020AIM*, 156(5): 40–45.

Sveiby, Karl E., and Tom Lloyd, 1987, *Managing Know-How*. London: Bloomsbury.

Sveiby, Karl Erik, 1997, *The New Organizational Wealth: Managing and Measuring Intangible Assets*. San Francisco: Berrett Koehler.

Szulanski, Gabriel, 1997, "Intra-firm Transfer of Best Practices." In A. Campbell and K. Sommers Luchs (Eds.), *Core Competency-Based Strategy*. London: International Thomson Business Press.

Tagami, K., 1998, "Humanoid Robot Development," Presentation, Kanazawa Institute of Technology, October 31.

Tapscott, Don, 1995, *The Digital Economy*. New York: McGraw-Hill.

Tapscott, Don, 1997, "Strategy in the new economy," *Strategy & Leadership*, 25: 8–14.

Taylor, F.W., 1916, *The principles of scientific management*, Bulletin of the Taylor Society, December. Reprinted in J.M. Shafritz and J.S. Ott, *Classics of Organization Theory*. Chicago: Dorsey Press, 1987, pp. 66–81.

Taylor, Jim, and Watts Wacker, 1998, *The 500 Year Delta: What Happens after What Comes Next*. New York: HarperBusiness.

Teece, D.J., 1998, "Capturing Value from Knowledge Assets: The New Economy, Markets for Know-How, and Intangible Assets," *California Management Review*, 40(3) (Spring): 55–79.

Teece, D.J., ed., 1987, *The Competitive Challenge: Strategies for Industrial Innovation and Renewal*. New York: Harper & Row.

Teece, D.J., 1980, "Economies of Scale and Scope of the Enterprise," *Journal of Economic Behavior and Organization*, 1(3): 223–247.

Teece, D.J., 1996, "Firm Organization, Industrial Structure, and Technological Innovation," *Journal of Economic Behavior and Organization*, 31: 193–224.

Teece, D.J., 1976, *The Multinational Corporation and the Resource Cost of International Technology Transfer*. Cambridge, MA: Ballinger.

Teece, D.J., 1986, "Profiting From Technological Innovation," *Research Policy*, 15:6.

Teece, D.J., 1982, "Towards an Economic Theory of the Multiproduct Firm," *Journal of Economic Behavior and Organization*, 3: 153–177.

Teece, D.J., and G. Pisano, 1994, "The Dynamic Capabilities of Firms: An Introduction," *Industrial and Corporate Change*, 3:3.

Teece, D., G. Pisano, and A. Shuen, 1997, "Dynamic Capabilities and Strategic Management," *Strategic Management Journal*, 18(7): 509–533.

Thompson, J.D., 1967, *Organizations in Action*. New York: McGraw Hill.

Toennies, Ferdinand, 1971, *Ferdinand Toennies on Sociology: Pure, Applied, and Empirical*. Selected writings edited by Werner J. Cahnman and Rudolf Heberle. Chicago: University of Chicago Press.

Turban, E., E. McLean, and J. Wetherbe, 1999, *Information Technology for Management: Making Connections for Strategic Advantage*. New York: John Wiley & Sons.

Ueno, N., 1999, *Shigoto no naka de no gakushu: jokyoronteki apurochi* [Learning at work: situation theoretical approach]. Tokyo: Tokyo University Press.

Usui, M., 1998, "Kigyo wo kaeru Web Kompyutingu—Henka Taiou to Atarashii Shisutemu Moderu" [Web Computing changes the firm—adaptation to change and new system models]. Seven-Eleven Japan, Information System Division (presentation material).

von Hippel, E., 1994, "Sticky Information and the Locus of Problem Solving: Implication for Innovation," *Management Science*, 40: 429–439.

von Hippel, E., T. Thomke, M. Sonnack, 1999, "Ideas at Work: Creating Breakthroughs at 3M," *Harvard Business Review*, (Sept/Oct): 47.

Wacker, Watts, Jim Taylor, and Howard Means, 2000, *The Visionary's Handbook: Nine Paradoxes That Will Shape the Future of Your Business*. New York: HarperBusiness.

Ward, A., 1999, "Making knowledge work in the real world." Presentation to Strategic Leadership Forum, Chicago, April 20, 1999.

Weick, K.E., 1979, "Cognitive processes in organization." In B.M. Staw (Ed.), *Research in organizational behavior* (Vol. I). Greenwich, CT: JAI Press.

Weick, Karl, 1993, "The Collapse of Sensemaking in Organizations: The Mann Gulch Disaster," *Administrative Science Quarterly*, 39(4): 628–652.

Weick, Karl E., 1991, "The Nontraditional Quality of Organizational Learning," *Organization Science*, 2(1) (February): 116–123.

Weick, Karl E., 1995, *Sense-Making in Organizations*. Thousand Oaks, CA: Sage.

Weick, K.E., and K.H. Roberts, 1993, "Collective Minds in Organizations," *Administrative Science Quaterly*, 38: 357 –381.

Weinstein, Krystyna, 1995, *Action Learning: A Journey in Discovery and Development*. Glasgow: HarperCollins.

Wellman, Barry, and Keith Hampton, 1999, "Living Networked On and Offline," *Contemporary Sociology*, 28(6) (November): 648–654.

Wenger, Etienne, 1998, *Communities of practice: learning, meaning, and identity*. New York: Cambridge University Press.

Wenger, Etienne, 1999, "Communities of practice: the key to a knowledge strategy," *Knowledge Directions*, 1(2).

Wenger, Etienne, 2000, "Communities of practice and social learning systems." To appear in *Organizations*.

Wenger, Etienne, and William Snyder, 2000, "Communities of Practice: The Organizational Frontier," *Harvard Business Review*, 78(1) (January–February): 139–146.

Wernerfelt, B. (1984). "A resource-based view of the firm," *Strategic Management Journal*, 5: 171–190.

Wiig, Elisabeth H., and Karl M. Wiig, 1999, *On Conceptual Learning*. KRI Working Paper 1999–1. Arlington, TX: Knowledge Research Institute, Inc.

Wiig, Karl M., 1993, *Knowledge Management Foundations: Thinking about Thinking — How People and Organizations Create, Represent, and Use Knowledge*. Arlington, TX: Schema Press.

Wiig, Karl, 1994, *Knowledge Management: The Central Management Focus for Intelligent-Acting Organizations*. Arlington, TX: Schema Press, p. 157.

Wiig, Karl M., 1995, *Knowledge Management Methods: Practical Approaches to Managing Knowledge*. Arlington, TX: Schema Press.

Wiig, Karl M., 1997, "Knowledge Management: Where did it come from and where will it go?" *Expert Systems with Applications*, 13(1): 1–14.

Williams, Jeffrey R., 1999, *Renewable Advantage: Crafting Strategy Through Economic Time*. New York: Free Press.

Williamson, O.E., 1985, *Economic Institutions of Capitalism*. New York: Free Press Publishers.

Williamson, Oliver E., 1975, *Markets and Hierarchies: Analysis and Antitrust Implications*. New York: Free Press.

Williamson, O.E., 1981, "The Modern Corporation: Origins, Evolution, Attributes," *Journal of Economic Literature*, 19(4) (December): 1537–1568.

Williamson, Oliver, and Sidney Winter, eds., 1991, *The Nature of the Firm*, New York: Oxford University Press.

Winograd, Terry, 1988, *Byte*, 13(11) (December): 256.

Wittgenstein, L., and David Bloor, 1983, *A Social Theory of Knowledge*. New York, NY: Columbia University Press.

World Bank, 1999, *The World Development Report 1998/99: Knowledge for Development*. New York: Oxford University Press.

World Economic Forum, 1999, *The Global Competitiveness Report 1999*. Geneva: World Economic Forum.

Zack, Michael H., 1999, "Developing a Knowledge Strategy," *California Management Review*, 41(3) (Spring): 125–145.

Zack, M., 1999, *Knowledge and Strategy*. Newton, MA: Butterworth–Heinemann.

Zaltman, Gerald, and Robin Hige Coulter, 1985, "Seeing the Voice of the Customer: Metaphor-Based Advertising Research," *Journal of Advertising Research*, 35(4) (July–August): 35–51.

Index

Butterworth-Heinemann Business Books . . . for Transforming Business

5th Generation Management: Co-creating Through Virtual Enterprising, Dynamic Teaming, and Knowledge Networking, Revised Edition,
Charles M. Savage, 0-7506-9701-6

After Atlantis: Working, Managing, and Leading in Turbulent Times,
Ned Hamson, 0-7506-9884-5

The Alchemy of Fear: How to Break the Corporate Trance and Create Your Company's Successful Future,
Kay Gilley, 0-7506-9909-4

Beyond Business as Usual: Practical Lessons in Accessing New Dimensions,
Michael W. Munn, 0-7506-9926-4

Beyond Strategic Vision: Effective Corporate Action with Hoshin Planning,
Michael Cowley and Ellen Domb, 0-7506-9843-8

Beyond Time Management: Business with Purpose,
Robert A. Wright, 0-7506-9799-7

The Breakdown of Hierarchy: Communicating in the Evolving Workplace,
Eugene Marlow and Patricia O'Connor Wilson, 0-7056-9746-6

Business Climate Shifts: Profiles of Change Makers,
Warner Burke and William Trahant, 0-7506-7186-6

Business and the Feminine Principle: The Untapped Resource,
Carol R. Frenier, 0-7506-9829-2

Choosing the Future: The Power of Strategic Thinking,
Stuart Wells, 0-7506-9876-4

Conscious Capitalism: Principles for Prosperity,
David A. Schwerin, 0-7506-7021-5

Corporate DNA: Learning from Life,
Ken Baskin, 0-7506-9844-6

Cultivating Common Ground: Releasing the Power of Relationships at Work,
Daniel S. Hanson, 0-7506-9832-2

Flight of the Phoenix: Soaring to Success in the 21st Century,
John Whiteside and Sandra Egli, 0-7506-9798-9

Getting Attention: Leading-Edge Lessons for Publicity and Marketing,
Susan Kohl, 0-7506-7259-5

*Getting a Grip on Tomorrow: Your Guide to Survival and Success in the
Changed World of Work,*
Mike Johnson, 0-7506-9758-X

Innovation Strategy for the Knowledge Economy: The Ken *Awakening,*
Debra M. Amidon, 0-7506-9841-1

Innovation Through Intuition: The Hidden Intelligence,
Sandra Weintraub, 0-7506-9937-X

The Intelligence Advantage: Organizing for Complexity,
Michael D. McMaster, 0-7506-9792-X

Intuitive Imagery: A Resource at Work,
John B. Pehrson and Susan E. Mehrtens, 0-7506-9805-5

The Knowledge Evolution: Expanding Organizational Intelligence,
Verna Allee, 0-7506-9842-X

Large Scale Organizational Change: An Executive's Guide,
Christopher Laszlo and Jean-Francois Laugel, 0-7506-7230-7

Leadership in a Challenging World: A Sacred Journey,
Barbara Shipka, 0-7506-9750-4

Leading for a Change: How to Master the 5 Challenges Faced by Every Leader
Ralph Jacobson, 0-7506-7279-X

Leading Consciously: A Pilgrimage Toward Self-Mastery,
Debashis Chatterjee, 0-7506-9864-0

Leading from the Heart: Choosing Courage over Fear in the Workplace,
Kay Gilley, 0-7506-9835-7

Learning to Read the Signs: Reclaiming Pragmatism in Business,
F. Byron Nahser, 0-7506-9901-9

Leveraging People and Profit: The Hard Work of Soft Management,
Bernard A. Nagle and Perry Pascarella, 0-7506-9961-2

Marketing Plans That Work: Targeting Growth and Profitability,
Malcolm H.B. McDonald and Warren J. Keegan, 0-7506-9828-4

A Place to Shine: Emerging from the Shadows at Work,
Daniel S. Hanson, 0-7506-9738-5

The Power of Collaborative Leadership: Lessons for the Learning Organization,
Bert Frydman, Iva Wilson, and JoAnne Wyer, 0-7506-7268-4

Power Partnering: A Strategy for Business Excellence in the 21st Century,
Sean Gadman, 0-7506-9809-8

Putting Emotional Intelligence to Work: Successful Leadership Is More Than IQ,
David Ryback, 0-7506-9956-6

Resources for the Knowledge-Based Economy Series
The Knowledge Economy,
Dale Neef, 0-7506-9936-1

Knowledge Management and Organizational Design,
Paul S. Myers, 0-7506-9749-0

Knowledge Management Tools,
Rudy L. Ruggles, III, 0-7506-9849-7

Knowledge in Organizations,
Laurence Prusak, 0-7506-9718-0

The Strategic Management of Intellectual Capital,
David A. Klein, 0-7506-9850-0

Knowledge and Communities,
Eric L. Lesser, Michael A. Fontaine, and Jason A. Slusher,
0-7506-7293-5

Knowledge, Groupware and the Internet,
David Smith, 0-7506-7111-4

Knowledge and Social Capital,
Eric L. Lesser, 0-7506-7222-6

Strategic Learning in a Knowledge Economy
Robert Cross and Sam Israelit, 0-7506-7223-4

The Rhythm of Business: The Key to Building and Running Successful Companies,
Jeffrey C. Shuman, 0-7506-9991-4

Setting the PACE® in Product Development: A Guide to Product And Cycle-time Excellence,
Michael E. McGrath, 0-7506-9789-X

Time to Take Control: The Impact of Change on Corporate Computer Systems,
Tony Johnson, 0-7506-9863-2

The Transformation of Management,
   Mike Davidson, 0-7506-9814-4

Unleashing Intellectual Capital,
   Charles Ehin, 0-7506-7246-3

What Is the Emperor Wearing? Truth-Telling in Business Relationships,
   Laurie Weiss, 0-7506-9872-1

Who We Could Be at Work, Revised Edition,
   Margaret A. Lulic, 0-7506-9739-3

*Working from Your Core: Personal and Corporate Wisdom in a
      World of Change,*
   Sharon Seivert, 0-7506-9931-0

To purchase any Butterworth-Heinemann title,
please visit your local bookstore or call 1-800-366-2665.